Male Beauty

MALE BEAUTY

Postwar Masculinity in Theater, Film,
and Physique Magazines

KENNETH KRAUSS

SUNY
PRESS

Published by
STATE UNIVERSITY OF NEW YORK PRESS
Albany

© 2014 State University of New York

For information, contact
State University of New York Press
www.sunypress.edu

Production, Laurie Searl
Marketing, Kate McDonnell

Library of Congress Cataloging-in-Publication Data

Krauss, Kenneth, 1948–
    Male beauty : postwar masculinity in theater, film, and physique magazines /
Kenneth Krauss.
        pages cm.
    Includes bibliographical references and index.
    ISBN 978-1-4384-5001-8 (hc : alk. paper) 978-1-4384-5000-1 (pb : alk. paper)
    1. Masculinity in mass media.   2. Masculine beauty (Aesthetics)
I. Title.
    P96.M385K83 2013
    306.4'613—dc23   2013012466

10 9 8 7 6 5 4 3 2 1

Contents

Acknowledgments

Many people have helped me throughout the long process of researching and writing this book. Preeminent among them was Richard Harrison, who was kind enough to meet with me and discuss his career as a physique model in California. His kindness, intelligence, and wit launched my protracted exploration of the physique magazines of the 1950s and 1960s. At the same time, I was able to look at actual copies of these publications, some of which had been collected at the University of Southern California's One Archives, where the staff allowed me access to its holdings, which were at that time in storage.

Eventually, my need to look for a more comprehensive collection of these physique publications sent me to a website organized by Tim Wilbur, a bodybuilder who lives in Vermont; timinvermont.com, which was the name of his website, offered hundreds and hundreds of digital copies of virtually every physique magazine published. Without this online archive, I would not have been able to follow the careers of each of the three models about whom I had chosen to write. My dependence on this collection, which is probably more comprehensive than any other on- or offline archive of such materials, is responsible for any of the appearances by the models whose careers I follow that I have missed.

Just as Tim Wilbur's online resources made possible the final section of the book, the New York Public Library's Theatre Research Library made possible the first section of the book. Its holdings of promptbooks, programs, photographs, ephemera, and reviews proved to be the definitive research collection for my exploration of the three plays that I examine early in the book. Toward this end, a grant from The College of Saint Rose, where I have taught theater and literature for more than two decades, allowed me the time that I devoted to the necessary archival research and made possible my stay in Midtown Manhattan. The college also gave me a semester off as sabbatical during which I completed much of the writing of the manuscript.

Two important sources of the illustrations contained in the three chapters devoted to physique models allowed me to use their material: Dennis Bell, president of the Athletic Models Guild and director of the Bob Mizer Foundation and Rick Storer, executive director of Chicago's Leather Archives and Museum, which controls the rights for photos and publications originally created by Chuck Renslow. Without their cooperation, I would not have been able to illustrate Chapters 7, 8, and 9. All photos taken by Bob Mizer and/or featured in *Physique Pictorial* are reproduced through special arrangement with AMG and the Mizer Foundation; all photos taken by Chuck Renslow and Kris Studios and/or featured in Renslow's and Kris's publications are reproduced through special arrangement with Leather Archives and Museum.

Several friends provided early criticism and approval for my initial drafts. David Burke, with whom I attended the University of Sussex as an undergraduate, offered much appreciated praise. Rik Devitt supplied several critiques of my first completed draft; his bar, Bongo Johnny's, on Arenas Road in Palm Springs, supplied some much needed wine as I was working through my revisions. My best friend, Gary Palmer, commented on the final draft and offered much needed support. Last and certainly not at all least, my colleague and dear friend Barbara Ungar was there from the beginning of the research through the book's acceptance by the publisher and repeatedly went through my drafts, providing lively and engaging criticism, as did my friend Stuart Bartow.

This book began when I reached back in my memory to show students in my Gay and Lesbian Literature class what homosexual men used to look at during the 1950s. The proliferation on the Internet of images from physique magazine era reawakened my own memory of what these publications meant and allowed me to present them to my students, who found them interesting and amusing if not exactly evocative. I found that these images unlocked an era that my students never knew, one with which I (who had been a child during the period) had been only somewhat acquainted. To some degree, they deserve my thanks for sending me back to the years when physique models in posing straps represented forbidden desires.

Introduction

This study examines various cultural artifacts from a specific period and geographical situation in order to understand changes within a particular gender construct. The time is the postwar era and the place, the United States; the gender construct is masculinity. Although time and place are easily understood, the gender construct is far more complicated.

Masculinity is difficult to discuss. In their everyday comprehension of the world, most people tend to believe, as Uta Brandes puts it, that "[a] human being must be either male or female and . . . each gender is given characteristics and attributes" (139). This notion of two complementary genders—a binary—is pervasive. So is the idea that gender is innate, essential, something with which men and women are naturally born. Thus, the figure of what many would call a "masculine man" may be construed, according to Giannino Malossi, as "radiating the confidence that comes from an unexamined relationship with one's own gender" (24). Despite common belief, over the past hundred years, the binary opposition of two sexes and two genders and the notion that gender is purely instinctive, have been subjected to intense scrutiny.

A host of academic writers have explored the nature of gender and of masculinity in particular. In reviewing their work, Todd W. Reeser, in *Masculinities in Theory: An Introduction*, points out how masculinity, in its primary position in binary opposition to femininity, "tends to function as 'unmarked,'" just as in the binary that opposes heterosexuality to homosexuality, the former becomes the most known and the least different (8). Because of this, modern investigations of gender began not with masculinity (which has functioned as the norm) but with femininity and with gender constructs that differed (due to race, class, or sexuality or other factors) from what was conventionally thought to be masculine.

Reeser suggests that masculinity is in some ways like an ideology or rather a series of ideologies (20). Masculinity, in this view, exists as a set of beliefs that people accept unquestioningly and experience as ordinary and

1

genuine; just as Americans consider capitalism as "a normal part of everyday life, . . . a large percentage of people take masculinity for granted as part of real life" (21). However, because "[a] series of ideologies are at play" (28), the discourse of masculinity, subject to shifts in individual component ideologies, is by necessity contradictory (32–33). Resistance to masculinity, in forms that in some way spotlight these contradictions, may come most noticeably from individuals or groups excluded from the construct, but resistance also comes from those included in the construct (34); women, for example, may launch a critique of masculinity, as happened during the late 1960s, but at the same time, so-called "men" may rebel against and defy the gender construct supposedly created by and for them. As sets of ideologies, masculinity and femininity are open to inquiry.

Reeser proposes, in the terminology of Jacques Derida, that femininity exists as supplementary to masculinity (37) and that even though masculinity may appear to "function alone and on its own terms, it inevitably functions in implicit or explicit relation to a series of others" (41). In other words, masculinity cannot exist without the existence of everything that is supposedly contrary to masculinity. Thus, to some degree, it is logical that someone operating within the gender construct would have to learn (rather than know instinctively) at least some of what is and what is not proper to masculinity. For example, are we born to recognize that certain colors denote specific genders or sexualities, or are we taught these color codes? Perhaps then it is understandable that a male "experiences a nearly consistent move or oscillation between . . . two poles," that is, between the belief that masculinity is instinctive to males and the recognition that certain aspects of masculinity are obviously learned and acquired (50). A male will also experience in himself and others missteps—momentary lapses or lapses of a longer duration—that appear not to be masculine in nature.

Even so, Reeser indicates, gender fluidity is usually taken as exceptional when in reality it is omnipresent (73). Still, people tend to see masculinity as "coherent" and thus immune to such fluidity because so many aspects of it are repeated "in ways that are perceived as coherent. Once that coherence is imagined, people may . . . ignore or not perceive elements that do not fit in the image that they already have. . . ." As Reeser concludes, "[I]t is the necessity of repetition that reveals the hollowness of masculinity underneath" (82). Nonetheless, if the elements that "do not fit" are so outrageous as to be unavoidably noticeable, people cannot avoid noticing and in some way adjusting their views of the construct.

These are some of the ideas surrounding and governing this study. As I admit in the course of the work, I am largely a proponent of nonessentialist thought—I tend to believe that gender is not born but bred. In any case, what I have chosen to examine are materials that I think not only carry evidence of a significant change in postwar masculinity but that also contain instructions for the postwar reader or viewer on how to be a man.

On some levels, this book and its contents make sense. I can defend with some logic my selection of specific cultural artifacts and the appropriateness of these choices. Yet, to be perfectly honest, my own connection to this book's overall subject matter and the specific material I examine resonate with personal significance. In the name of academic honesty, I feel obliged to disclose my connections with the material.

I was born into a culture that was emerging from World War II, a culture in which money and morals were tight. There were still strict codes governing how one should behave; one's identity was forged from a variety of details, many of which were expected to conform to what the culture itself apparently demanded. Failure to conform often proved highly problematic, even (in certain cases) fatal.

My personal circumstances, of course, played a large role in how I saw the world: I was the youngest of three children; my brother was 17 years old when I was born and my sister, 12. My mother suffered some kind of breakdown after giving birth to me, so much of my time was spent with my sister. My father worked every day but Sunday, from eight in the morning, when he would open the men's wear shop that he managed, until six in the evening, but on Mondays and Fridays until nine o'clock. When he was home, he did very little although he and my mother often argued. By the time I comprehended that I had a memory, around the age of 3, my brother was gone, off to college and then, because of a serious illness, in the hospital for several years. So the people who raised me were female.

This perhaps may explain, at least in part, my early identification with girls and women, whom I saw as capable and kind. My brother, when I did spend any time with him, was not terribly warm, and my father often lost his temper around me. When I pretended to be a girl, my brother would mock me, and my father became noticeably revolted to the extent that by the time I was 4, I had learned what was and was not appropriate for a boy to do and had begun, somewhat half-heartedly, to create a persona that to some degree appeared to conform to how I thought I, as a male, was expected to act. I write "to some degree" because I never felt fully compelled to take on what turned out to be called masculinity

One thing that separated males and females was that it was widely known that females could be beautiful, elegant, charming. Males could be handsome, but I had already been warned that handsomeness was not in itself deserving of trust. What a man did determined his worth; indeed, handsomeness in men often was a sign that the man, because of his attractiveness—by this point I knew I was attracted to it—was usually less than he appeared to be.

I had been shielded as a child from all kinds of information, including the facts that my brother had been conceived before my parents had married and that my own conception had been an accident. However, as I grew older, I began to discover all sorts of things. In spite of my efforts to pass as male, I was still thought of as sufficiently unmasculine to become an object of ridicule and contempt at school and on the streets. Even as a late adolescent, I often resisted the kind of behavior masculinity required; as Robert Jensen so eloquently puts it, "somewhere in my gut I knew there was something wrong, not only with my ongoing failure to be man enough but with the whole concept of being a man" (5).

I had been molested by a bellboy at a summer resort when I was 7 but did not really understand what had been going on. Then, while I was 10 and stumbling through puberty, I realized that although I had always felt attracted to females, I was far more attracted sexually to males. The little I knew about my feelings for my own sex told me I could neither speak of nor act on them. In fact, the language of ridicule and contempt to which I continued to be subjected was riddled with words signifying the sort of person who did speak of and act on such feelings. I attempted to deny I had any such feelings. I was made particularly uncomfortable by males whom I sensed might have had similar feelings, much as my father had become infuriated by my performances as a girl. Yet as much as I attempted to contradict my feelings, I could not resist the temptation to satisfy my desires.

This all changed sometime in 1960 when I found in one of the steamer trunks piled into a corner of the attic a large manila envelope that contained a cache of what were then called "physique magazines" and many copies of a questionnaire seemingly intended to be answered by men who engaged in weight lifting—social science surveys perhaps. As I looked through the magazines, I could hardly believe what I had uncovered: Their pages were filled with photographs of young men in swimsuits or posing straps, revealing their bodies and faces to the camera. This of course suggested that I certainly wasn't the only male in the world (somehow I knew the magazines were intended for males) who had come to appreciate the beauty of males and that there were obviously a sufficient number of such males that magazines were published for them.

However, these were not easy conclusions to maintain. Everything else and everyone around me told me that they could not be true. The world was composed of men and women who married and had children. Of course, I had several aunts who worked in offices every day who had never married, but they always were regarded as exceptions. In fact, my mother would always refer to them as "poor Anne" and "poor Flora." They were not normal. Normal people lived their lives with their families and created new families. I had known from the time I was 6, when the lady downstairs became pregnant, that only women had children. So what kind of life could two men have?

Nonetheless, the evidence from the magazines was difficult to dismiss. The black-and-white photos and drawings clearly depicted what I found particularly interesting, and I would come back to them frequently for stimulation. At some point I did recognize that the men in the magazines, many of whom were said to be married, would probably have had the same disgust for me that the boys at school and on the block did. And so, even while I returned again and again to their images, I was not entirely comfortable with where all this could possibly lead me, and I longed to be normal.

Many years later, after I had come out and had several lovers and boyfriends, after I had figured out that what I actually wanted to do was to get a PhD and become a college professor, I found myself teaching a class on gay and lesbian literature—the first of its kind—at the recovering-Catholic institution where I had ended up.

Because a large part of my background was in theater, I had always included in my teaching of literature much visual imagery. It was only when I got to the part of the class that dealt with a homosexual novel written in the 1950s that I remembered the photographs I had studied so many decades before. Most of them had floated onto the Internet, from which they were easily circulated and downloaded. As I re-examined them, this time from the point of view of someone trying to describe mid-twentieth–century gay culture to students who had been born in the 1970s, I began to understand them better: These were artifacts of a time through which I, who was barely cognizant of what these pictures really signified, had lived.

What I came to understand then, as an adult looking back on photos that had been prominent features in the lives of many of the men who had gazed on them, was that these images constituted an aesthetic that was in many ways antithetical to the aesthetic prevalent among males who identified themselves as men—that is, as normative heterosexual males whose sexuality and gender conformed to the strictures that American society had ordained. The physique magazines carried images that were not merely sensual and/or sexual—they were images of males that the gazers found beautiful. Like many other languages, English plays fast and loose with gender when it comes to certain adjectives: A woman may be judged to be beautiful, but a man must be said to be handsome; nonetheless, the images in physique magazines, whether of handsome, sensual, or merely available males, represented what was received as male beauty.

In that same class I taught three plays by Tennessee Williams, whom I regarded not merely as a playwright who happened to be gay but also as one who actually wrote about sexuality and gender from the perspective of a gay man. It occurred to me that what I had witnessed in the beefcake magazines printed for homosexuals was apparent, although less blatantly so, on the stage at the same time, and after watching the film made by Elia Kazan based on Williams's A Streetcar Named Desire, I saw it in this and also in other movies.

Yet the crucial event that had released this profusion of art works became clear to me only when I went back a decade earlier: It was clearly the war. The shift in masculinity from the traumatized 1930s to the burgeoning 1950s was prompted by the vast and brutal event known as World War II. The great irony was that this conflagration, which had tragically taken the lives of millions of people, had necessitated changes in social attitudes and conventions that had previously seemed so unalterable. As a child, I had no way of knowing that what I was experiencing was actually in part a reaction to the social upheaval that the war had initiated. The women's movement would see in the domestication of women in the 1950s an attempt to make them forget that, as they had proven throughout the war, they could work as well as men might. Similarly, the intense pressure to go back to the notions of home and family as they had been understood two decades before made my mother call Auntie Anne "poor."

The war required soldiers and sailors, pilots and marines, who were young men, some of them still teenagers. They were so young that they were referred to, affectionately, as "the boys." Traditionally, young men had been considered boys, but the sacrifices they were obliged to make required society to see them as fully developed examples of the male gender construct—in short, as men. Thus masculinity became younger, and thus a plethora of traits that had previously excluded these boys from manhood had to be construed anew and in a very different way.

Many felt, once the war was over, that the servicemen who had functioned as men should go back to being boys. One way to do that was to send them to college, which the government did in great numbers. Recasting them as college boys set them into an educational context in which they could be trained to find their places in the hierarchy that they had left behind in order to fight overseas. They would emerge from universities ready to fit into the social order, assume a career, begin a family, and preserve life as it had been lived, or rather as some wished to remember it had been lived, before the war.

Of course, that never happened. As hideously repressive as the 1950s were, there was no way to go back to a mythologized past. The town of Bedford Falls in Frank Capra's It's a Wonderful Life looks as if it has reverted to the values and ideals that its residents had previously cherished, but the film, made in 1946, actually forecasts a world in which the changes from the war would be instated to create a more egalitarian world. Even with the reactionary leadership of a Republican administration, the witch-hunting of the FBI and congress, the insistence on conformity, the anti-communist resurgence of religion, and the power of racist and sexist institutions, there remained meaningful acts of resistance that occasionally manifested themselves before being eradicated. I already knew that one of the prime causes of the explosive 1960s was the repressive 1950s.

In retrospect, I realize that my choices of the material I examine in this book were hardly random. With regard to dramatic literature, each of the plays that I discuss had some meaning in my life. I first watched a scene from Tennessee Williams's *The Glass Menagerie* as a junior in high school and immediately identified with the son in the play, who was struggling to leave home and family behind. Although I had never seen or read Robert Anderson's *Tea and Sympathy* until I was an adult, I knew about it because the movie version had been shown at the camp I attended a few weeks before I arrived there; I am sure on some level, someone in charge had thought it a good way to teach the boys to differentiate between homosocial and homosexual emotions they might be feeling, but repeated references to the film made me paranoid. Edward Albee's *The Zoo Story* seemed to me, when I first read it at the age of 25, a rather cryptic piece, and yet it always remained a fascinating work that I continued to teach. Little had I realized that the one-act's depiction of masculinity (or rather, masculinities) was what made me keep coming back to it.

The choice of Montgomery Clift, Marlon Brando, and James Dean for the section on men on screen in some ways seemed obvious. As a child, I was kept away from most of Brando's movies—I remember my mother refusing to let me attend a matinee of *A Streetcar Named Desire* because I was "too young" to understand it—but eventually my parents took me to see *Sayonara*, and I wondered what all the fuss had been about. I later saw Brando in *The Young Lions*. I was impressed with his portrayal of a German soldier, but I identified with the character played by Montgomery Clift who was, like myself, Jewish and sensitive. I first encountered James Dean a year or two after he had died. My sister took me to a screening of *Giant*, which I found so huge and long that I couldn't understand what it was about. I remember that as I watched the film, I recalled the news stories on television about Dean's car crash, and I was confused as to how I could be watching someone who seemed so alive but who was in fact dead. I think I was 7 years old.

In the final section of the book, in which I look at three men who were models in physique magazines, my selection process had begun very early. As a 12-year-old, my first glimpse of John Tristram, who was featured on the back cover of *Tomorrow's Man*, was startling: He was photographed standing on a beach in a tight black swimsuit that laced up the sides. He looked so tough and so sexy I was immediately drawn to his image. Many

years later I would learn that he was one of the few homosexual bodybuilders who appeared in these magazines. Glenn Bishop also figured among the
young men whom I discovered within the cache, but at the time I didn't
find him all that attractive; many years later, when I discovered through
various websites an abundance of nude shots of him, I began to appreciate
his looks and his grace.

The one man whom I didn't know from these magazines was Richard
Harrison, who after playing a few small parts in Hollywood, went on to
become, like Steve Reeves and many other musclemen, a star in Italian
and other foreign B movies, including gladiator films, spaghetti westerns,
spy intrigues, and ninja adventures. I discovered an early photo of him in
a book about beefcake magazines published in the 1990s. But eventually I
recalled that in the late 1950s I was taken to see the movie version of *South
Pacific* and that early in the picture a good-looking blond pilot with blue eyes
was flying John Kerr to an island. I remember being terribly disappointed
to find out that John Kerr (who ironically had made his name in the play
and film versions of *Tea and Sympathy*), and not the handsome aviator, was
one of the leads and that I would never see the pilot again; the flier was
played by Richard Harrison.

These are some of the personal circumstances that led me to write
this book. Although I do not regard this work as a personal history, I do
believe my motivations for writing it were as much personal as scholarly. If
I do, from time to time, revert to my own memories related to the subject
matter, it is merely to reiterate my firsthand knowledge and understanding
of what I am writing about, not to tell my own story.

My own story is not as significant as the larger story I am trying to tell,
which concerns how the imagery of masculinity began to change with the
end of the war. To do so, I look at different phenomena drawn from different
cultural contexts in postwar America, high culture (the theater), popular
culture (the cinema), and the gay subculture (the physique magazines). Each
of these phenomena illustrates how American manhood became younger and
more aesthetically attractive and sexually ambiguous after the war. Despite
the repressive world in which I remembered growing up, the artifacts of the
time reveal mixed, often confusingly contradictory messages. I did not start
receiving any of these diverse transmissions until I was a teenager in the
1960s—or perhaps it would be fairer to say that I received them from the
time I was born but could not make sense of them until later. Even then I
was never sure on how to construe them.

My lack of surety was a result not merely of the strength of the training of the postwar culture but a product of the pronouncements of the new
culture that was coming into being in the late 1960s and early 1970s. In
various identity wars waged by women, African Americans and Hispanics,

and also gays and lesbians, the new culture called for an eradication of previous ideas and the installation of new precepts. Thus, women who raised children at home were seen as reactionaries, Louis Armstrong was dubbed an "uncle Tom," and gay history was said to have begun with the Stonewall Riot (or to put that event in the later language of correctness, the Stonewall Rebellion or Uprising). Previous experiences did not count; any experience that did not completely challenge the culture at large was always suspect.

In the 1980s, a reevaluation of the past slowly took shape. Initially, the very criteria that had dismissed all that had come before remained in play, even as they were applied (perhaps more gently now) than they had been a decade earlier. Thus, some of the works that I examine were offered a more complex analysis before being dismissed almost entirely. Yet other studies followed that illuminated the connections between the near and distant past and that showed how the events at the Stonewall Inn were less motivated by the death of Judy Garland than by a decade and a half of gay culture and politics.

This study strives to examine that period between the war and the early 1960s when American culture, perhaps largely unwittingly, underwent a significant revision in its view of males and masculinity. Such a revision helped in itself to allow additional cultural factors to change. And the iconography of masculinity after the war led to further transformations, which in turn led to a prolonged period of social revolt through which our understanding of identity seriously altered.

At the same time, as the book's title indicates, one of the important aspects of the study is to document that in the wake of the war, there came a tacit, often wary, realization that men were and could be beautiful. Manhood's admirable qualities in the past included strength, loyalty, and wisdom, but beauty was always regarded, especially from a male point of view, as dubious. The postwar shift in masculinity changed that.

CHAPTER 1

Seeing Through
The Glass Menagerie

The Emerging Specter of Male Beauty

Re-readings

In Tennessee Williams's *The Glass Menagerie*, written and first produced before World War II had ended, the figure of the defiant, nonconformist young male, which would haunt American culture during the late 1940s and through the 1950s, first appears on stage; presciently, Williams creates a character who will dominate much of the literature of the postwar period. The young man who escapes the traditional, approved social and sexual norms and attempts, through his alienation, to thwart the middle-class rules that impose themselves on the individual, remains a romantic emblem of youthful defiance in an oppressive and repressive era. Tom, the narrator of the play and a character in it, and his father, in whose footsteps he follows and whose likeness he bears, anticipate a long line of angry young men that would give meaning to a generation struggling through the age of conformity.

In the midst of this drama, is the image of the handsome, grinning man, the attractive but dangerous icon around whose memory Tom and his family live their lives. The handsome face of the escapee, of the absent yet present father, whose image hangs on the wall in an enlarged photograph, becomes central to the play. Thus, the notion of male beauty is introduced as not merely attractive but dangerous as well.

Tom's gender and sexuality in the context of the culture surrounding him are especially radical in this wartime work. In *The Glass Menagerie*, connections and disconnections between gender and sexuality play out in a complex and sometimes ambiguous way. Although his later works would more overtly portray the interplay between these two separate but related constructs, Williams's first Broadway success quietly but seriously questions how men and women become who and what they are. If the writing seems more implicit and less controversial in *The Glass Menagerie* than in those later, often sensational plays, it is nonetheless highly revealing here: Our inner desires and our performances of them for the outer world combine in an uneasy alliance, the latter striving to hide and shield the former, the former seeking fulfillment in spite of the latter.

The Glass Menagerie may at first glance seem a strange place to look for evidence of a questioning of gender and sexuality, for the traditions of watching and reading that have surrounded this text have helped shape generations of responses to it that rarely lead to such a question. As Michael Paller puts it in *Gentlemen Callers: Tennessee Williams, Homosexuality, and Mid-Twentieth Century Broadway*, the "perception of *The Glass Menagerie* as a pleasant, non-threatening affair stems from the reactions of the newspaper and magazine critics who witnessed the first production. . . ." At the same time, readers of what Paller calls Williams's "nice play" (33) seem to miss the references that would lead them to an understanding of how the play comments on what at the time were considered not-so-nice subjects. The apparent understatement in both the play's dialogue and visual elements is, in fact, a careful encoding of issues that Williams wished to explore. These wary inquiries, about sex and the objects and practices of sexuality and about the nature of masculine and feminine behavior, were intended to communicate to audiences—perhaps specifically to important subgroups within those audiences—in a time when any serious interrogation of gender and sexuality was, at least on stage, usually taboo.

The same may be said for readers: Mark Lilly, for example, suggests that "gay readers can see the various meanings . . . in a way unperceived by heterosexuals . . ." (153). In any case, initial reactions to the play and subsequent reception of additional stagings, along with readings of the scripts, helped create the myth that this script was, despite the playwright's subsequent career, somehow innocent of the rather adult themes that characterized his subsequent oeuvre.

Indeed, according to one late twentieth-century literary critic's reckoning, "Williams's first Broadway success, *The Glass Menagerie* (1944),[1] is rare among his works in that the sexuality of his characters is not a significant factor" (Fisher 15). Such a statement conforms to the long-time practice of how this script is interpreted. In reality, however, not only are the sexuality and the gender of the characters in *The Glass Menagerie* a significant factor, but also as in all Williams's work, they probably constitute *the* significant factor. That they and their importance are not immediately obvious to many make them perhaps even more significant.

Any discussion of the play's dramatic, as well as theatrical, text is complicated by the fact that there are two "official" versions, both printed within a year of the play's Broadway premiere, a "reading" text prepared by Williams in 1945, in which he attempted to restore many of the cuts and changes made by the first production, and a "performance" text from the same year, which reflects the changes made to and also the original direction of the premiere production.[2] Choosing between the two is difficult, for the reading text includes many of the innovative stage techniques Williams had first envisioned in composing the work; the performance text incorporates many of the alterations made by Williams and others before the play first opened in New York. Most who have read the play know it from the reading version; most who have seen the play know it from the performance edition.

Because my intention is to discuss *The Glass Menagerie* not merely as a text assigned to students but rather as the basis of stage performances, I rely on the performance text. This version of the script is very close to the reading version. Where the two coincide, I first note the page number for the performance version, then for the reading version. Where the two diverge, I will indicate any significant inconsistencies parenthetically.

In examining the written text(s) of this play, I attempt to locate (as most critics try to do) certain signs, some linguistic, some visual, some nonverbal, to support my thesis. Nonetheless, there remains one sign that is conspicuous not because of its presence but because of its absence. This forbidden topic, the great unmentionable, is appropriately signaled by an apparent lack of signs, and this lack has been traditionally read to point to something left indeterminate. This absence, still, is telling. Indeed, in an earlier work, Lillian Hellman's *The Children's Hour*, a prolonged lack of sound that is dramatized in the form of a whispered conversation between two characters whom the audience cannot hear, serves to name the particular perversity from which two other characters allegedly suffer. Similarly, in *The Glass Menagerie*, "the love that dare not speak its name" echoes through the artifice of euphemism and the profound silence that inevitably and unavoidably name it. For Hellman, such silence was a matter of taste and tact—she was able to "name" the characters' supposed "crime against nature" without offending anyone; for Williams, however, this silence is part of an ongoing defensive strategy in an era when homosexuality was almost universally despised.

For more than half a century, then, the prevailing method of interpreting *The Glass Menagerie* was to preclude that which is unspoken and unseen. "If Williams had wanted us to know what Tom does when he goes out at night, he would have told us or showed us," goes the self-fulfilling explanation. Yet much of the play is clearly devoted to the meaning of absence and to the presence of that which is not there. Even if we would like to stand by Lear's assertion that "nothing will come of nothing," we cannot avoid the fact that "nothing" is certainly capable of signifying "something."

If Tom's rebelliousness is due, at least in large part, to the conflict between his feelings about his sexuality and his attempt to "perform" a "masculine" role, much the same may be said of Williams himself, whose ambivalence and marginalization as a homosexually identified male cast him, certainly in his own eyes, as an outsider. Nonetheless, neither he nor the character is the gay liberator who would emerge in the late 1960s. Williams firmly believed, in contrast to the identity politics that would later gain currency, that one should not be identified by one's sexuality because sexuality was highly private, even idiosyncratic, and peculiar to oneself.

Chez Wingfield

The first act or part (act in the performance version, part in the reading text) of *The Glass Menagerie* follows life inside the apartment of the Wingfield family in Saint Louis. Amanda, a former Southern belle who has been abandoned by her alcoholic husband some years earlier, is striving to take care of her two grown children, Tom, who fancies himself a poet but currently clerks in a shoe warehouse, and Laura, a sickly, desperately shy girl with a limp. As scene follows scene into the intermission—in the performance version, Scenes 1 to 6, in the reading version Scenes 1 to 5—the principal action builds from Amanda's realization that Laura is incapable of earning her own living to Amanda's plan to try to marry her off; Amanda hints to Tom, whose unhappiness at home and work becomes increasingly observable, that once Laura has secured a husband, he may leave.

In the second act or part of the play, Tom brings home to dinner a work acquaintance, who turns out to be the very young man with whom Laura was once infatuated in high school. The meeting ultimately turns disastrous when Jim, Laura's would-be gentleman caller, reveals that he is already engaged.

This summation necessarily excludes the better part of the play, which is dramatized in a somewhat fragmented way and with the device of Tom, at a later age, telling the story. George W. Crandell asserts that "[t]he success of . . . [this narration] depends upon willing subjects, viewers who will permit the fictional character, Tom Wingfield, to define the spectators' point of view" (6). Yet others, such as Brian Richardson (683) and Nancy Anne Cluck (84), remind us that, as Williams himself cautions, "The narrator is an undisguised convention of the play. He takes whatever license with dramatic convention is convenient to his purposes."[3] The self-conscious monologue that sets up the opening scene is addressed directly to the audience:

> I have tricks in my pocket—I have things up my sleeve—but I
> am the opposite of a stage magician. He gives you illusion that

has the appearance of truth. I give you truth in the pleasant disguise of illusion. (Performance 11; Reading 144, with slight variations)

This comparison of a magician's routine with a dramatic performance, which implies that traditional stage realism is nothing more than a set of illusions that give the impression of reality and that reality itself is highly illusory, is continued later in the play, when Tom speaks to Laura about a stage magician, Malvolio, whom he has just come from seeing; however, coming as they do at the beginning of the play, of course, these lines seem enigmatic, and the succeeding information does little to clarify them: Tom speaks of the play being set in "that quaint period," the Great Depression, "when the large middle class of America was matriculating from a school for the blind" (11; 145, with "huge" instead of "large" and the period described as "the thirties"). Tom makes references to the Spanish Civil War and to American labor conflicts, and declares, "This is the social background of the play" (11; 145). "The play is memory," he announces, and relates the dim lighting, the sentimentality, the lack of realism, and the music, which has just begun to be heard, as stage conventions consistent with memory. He then introduces himself and the three other characters, Amanda, Laura, and Jim, calling the audience's attention to "a fifth character who doesn't appear other than in a photograph hanging on the wall" (11; 145).

The picture, an oversized portrait of Tom's father, "is the face of a very handsome young man in a doughboy's First World War cap" (10; 144), the stage directions tell us. The father, who "left us a long time ago" (11; 145), will reemerge metaphorically in the context of the stage magician. Mr. Wingfield's "vanishing act" will become the one trick that Tom wishes Malvolio would teach him—that is, how to disappear without harming anyone or anything. Such a feat is, in real life, impossible, Tom suggests, and his "very handsome" father[4] has come to symbolize just how hurtful escape can be to those left behind.

As rambling as the opening monologue may sound, a central trope does emerge as the speech unwinds. The whole idea of hiding tricks in one's pocket and things up one's sleeve refers to the illusion of sudden "magical" manifestation, pretending to conjure what is absent into something that is present. The middle class had "matriculated from a school for the blind," but its sightless members were "having their fingers pressed forcibly down on the fiery Braille alphabet of a dissolving economy" (11; 145); in other words, the experience of trying to read the invisible but decipherable signs of the truth is painful and difficult. The violent visual image of "revolution" in Spain (11; 145, the name *Guernica* is also invoked) and of the less horrific but analogous "shouting and confusion" in Midwestern cities, amplifies the "fire" of the "Braille alphabet." The summation of characters, both those who are present and the one who is absent, and the ironic description of the vanishing father—"He was a telephone man who fell in love with long distance" (11; 145, distances)—set the tone for the father's non-presence: His last communication was "a picture-postcard from the Pacific Coast of Mexico, containing a message of two words: 'Hello—Good-bye!' and no address" (11; 145, adds "from *Mazatlan*, on the Pacific Coast . . ."). Thus, from the play's first moments, the spectators are asked to consider what they can and cannot see, to question the reality of what is and is not present, and to separate themselves from the conventions of stage realism that attempt to reconstruct an empirical reality that is less true than the one depicted by this play.

In the original production, the photograph of the father was of Eddie Dowling, the actor who played Tom. This use of Dowling is evident from stills from the original production and from the promptbook, which specifies,

THIS IS VERY
IMPORTANT
| The actor who |
plays Tom, poses for
the father's photograph,
with his <u>widest grin</u>.
The photo should be
very large, for
when it lights up,
the play gets some
of it's [sic] laughs

(Promptbook, *The Glass Menagerie*, 1–2)[5]

From the beginning, then, the audience is asked to see Tom as his "handsome" father and vice versa. This coincidence of imagery serves as a sign during the play to suggest that Tom and the absent man are one and the same, and that with their first glimpse of Tom on stage, "dressed as a merchant sailor" (10; 144), he has already become a man who has disappeared. So Tom is twice present on stage and, eventually, twice absent.

In the short scene that follows the monologue, Amanda harangues Tom over dinner, suggesting that his eating habits verge on the bestial: "Animals have secretions in their stomachs which enable them to digest their food without mastication, but human beings must chew their food before they swallow it down" (12; 146). References to animals abound throughout the play—the very title *The Glass Menagerie* assures that such imagery is germane—but Amanda's differentiation of human from animal behavior is especially meaningful. Later in this act (Scene 4 in Performance; Scene 5 in Reading), she proclaims, "Instinct is something that people have got away from! It belongs to animals! . . . Only animals have to satisfy instincts!" (30; 174) In the role of mother, Amanda repeatedly instructs her now-grown children on how to sublimate their "animalistic" feelings so they can construct what she would call "human" personas. In the first segment of the play, she attempts to correct, along with Tom's eating habits, his posture (22; cut), his reading material (23; 161), and his tendency to spend his nights elsewhere (23–24; 163–164).

But the real object of Amanda's pedagogy becomes Laura rather than Tom. Even in this early scene, before she finds out that Laura has dropped out of the business school in which Amanda had enrolled her, she instructs her daughter on how to "be the lady" (13; 147) and to await her "gentlemen callers" (13–15; 147–150). In reminiscing about her own beaux from decades past, Amanda reveals her Southern, middle-class background, describing what a young woman was expected to be: "It wasn't enough for a girl to be possessed of a pretty face and a graceful figure—although I wasn't slighted in either respect. She also needed to have a nimble wit and a tongue to meet all occasions" (13; 148). This gender construct, which Amanda, despite the decades that have followed her career as a belle, still plays out, is precisely modeled by the mother for the daughter through role-playing; in the next scene, the pressure to fit Laura into this gender role becomes more intense and less play-like. In fact, as Amanda rattles on about her gentlemen callers, contrasting them at one point with the man whom she actually married (14, "looks at picture on L. wall"; 149), Laura confides to Tom, "Mother's afraid that I'm going to be an old maid"[6] (15; 150). She is evidently all too aware of the gender construct that represents the female who is not sufficiently attractive to males. This gender role, of the "old maid," the unmarriageable female, is the opposite of the one Amanda wishes Laura to play.

It may be worth pausing for a moment over the term *role*, especially in light of its above coupling with *gender*. In recent years, gender has been discussed as performance, primarily but not exclusively by Judith Butler, who asks us to "[c]onsider gender, for instance, as a corporeal style, an 'act,' as it were, which is both intentional and performative, where '*performative*' suggests a dramatic and contingent construction of meaning" (177). Given just the short first scene, we may notice just how much *The Glass Menagerie* is already about role-playing and performance. Tom performs as the narrator and a character; the other characters are described in his monologue according to their roles ("my mother, Amanda, my sister, Laura, and a gentleman caller" 11; 145). When Tom reacts to Amanda's images of animals salivating by leaving the table, Amanda responds by calling him a prima donna: "Temperament like a Metropolitan star!" (12; 147) During the scene, Amanda slips in and out of playing the mother; when she asks Laura to act the part of "the lady," she proposes that she will "be the colored boy" (13; 147, "darky"). She also recites a long list of men she could have married, men who were attractive and successful and who left their widows well provided for. "But what did I do?" she asks with a stare at the photograph on the wall, "I went out of my way and picked your father!" (14; 148, with variation) This list, along with Amanda's reminiscences, has, incidentally, clearly been recited before; "She loves to tell it" (13; 147), Laura notes to Tom. In the end, Amanda insists that Laura, who reluctantly remains seated as the "lady," continue playing the attractive, marriageable woman: "Stay fresh and pretty! It's almost time for our gentlemen callers to start arriving. How many do you suppose we're going to entertain this afternoon?" Laura is being tutored on how to reconstruct her gender. It is after this that Laura makes her sad admission, "Mother's afraid that I'm going to be an old maid," as the lights fade into the next scene, in which Amanda plunges into her performance of the injured mother. In the medium of theater, which relies on actors performing roles, Williams offers the audience actors playing characters who seem to be performing their lives.

That Amanda's response to Laura's disappearance from typing classes is nothing less than a role to be performed becomes obvious when Amanda enters, pronounces her repeated condemnation, "Deception, deception, deception!" (16; 151, "Deception? Deception?"), and then allows Laura to feign innocence so that Amanda can play out to full effect her discovery of the deception. Laura recognizes her mother's role distinctly: "you get that awful suffering look on your face, like the picture of Jesus' mother in the Museum!" (18; 155, "museum"). Once identified as the wounded Madonna, Amanda invokes the frightening, cautionary sign of the old maid:

> I know so well what happens to unmarried women who aren't prepared to occupy a position in life. (. . .) I've seen such pitiful cases in the South—barely tolerated spinsters living on some brother's wife or a sister's husband—tucked away in some mousetrap of a room—encouraged by one in-law to go visit the next in-law—little birdlike women—without any nest—eating the crust of humility all their lives! (18; 156, "living on the grudging patronage of sister's husband or brother's wife . . .")

The implication, of course, through Amanda's use of imagery is that the "old maid" is less than a person, a small, inhuman creature who is to be pitied and loathed. Just as Amanda, the abandoned wife, is the pitiful counterpart to the well-provided-for widow, the old maid is set into a binary pairing with the happy wife. Having produced this dreaded symbol, Amanda ends her monologue with a question pertaining not to Laura's gender but to her sexuality, "[H]aven't you ever liked some boy?" (18; 156)

Once Laura has confirmed that she has "liked" a boy, Amanda proceeds with added vehemence to align her daughter's gender with her sexuality. The problem, as Amanda perceives it, is that Laura's attraction to males must be more clearly incorporated into her everyday gender performance, which in turn must result in males being attracted to her. When Laura protests that she is unable to play this role—"I'm—crippled!" (19; 157) she objects—Amanda outlaws the culprit word and tries to reduce the handicap to "a slight defect" (19; 157, "a little defect"). Yet like the marriage shoe offered to Cinderella's stepsister, the construct of attractive, marriageable woman simply does not fit Laura.

Scene 2 is the only scene in the first part of the play from which Tom is entirely absent. The audience may wonder how it can be included in the play, if the play is Tom's memory, or maybe they may conclude that this scene has been formed by what Tom has been told; perhaps, however, they have been drawn into the narrative and have stopped questioning how the narrator can and does relate to the narrative by this point. In any case, Tom, at least as Tom, never appears during the scene nor is he even mentioned. Yet Tom's double, the portrait of the missing father, is referred to twice and watches over the scene. When Laura talks about the boy in high school whom she liked, she shows Amanda his photos in the yearbook. "See his grin?" (19; 157) she asks. In the performance version, Amanda actually looks at her husband's photo on the wall and mutters, "So he had a grin too!" (19), but the mere mention of "grin" links the two pictures and the two (or rather three) male subjects. At the end of the scene, while encouraging Laura to "cultivate" something else, in order to make up for her "defect," Amanda remarks that the only thing Laura's father possessed a lot of was "charm" (20; 58); the photo on the wall is once again made prominent.[7] The implication, then, is that even as Amanda tries to adjust Laura's gender role, the role of the male remains fixed, deceptive, attractive but dangerous, and sardonically grinning.

Just as the image of the old maid presided over the previous scene, Scene 3 begins with the symbol of the gentleman caller. Tom tells the audience that

the image of the gentleman caller haunted our small apartment. An evening at home rarely passed without some allusion to this image, this specter, this hope. . . . [H]is presence hung in my mother's preoccupied look and my sister's frightened, apologetic manner. (20, 159)

Yet, although the scene begins with this image, the monologue takes a sharp turn. Rather than the image of the ideal male, Tom goes on to describe the ideal (marriageable) female, whose image haunts the pages of the women's magazine Amanda is trying to sell over the phone. Ladies in the stories in *The Homemaker's Companion*, as Tom describes them, have "cuplike breasts, slim tapering waists, rich, creamy thighs, eyes like wood-smoke in autumn, fingers that soothe and caress like soft, soft strains of music. Bodies as powerful as Etruscan sculpture" (20; 159). Tom's sarcastic description of ladies' fiction is especially pointed because he, after the monologue, is discovered trying to write (21–22; 162). A fight ensues in which Amanda confronts Tom about where he goes at night. Her skepticism about his explanation that he goes to the movies becomes insistent: "I think that you're doing things you're ashamed of. . . . Nobody goes to the movies night after night. . . . People don't go to the movies at midnight, and movies don't let out at two A.M." (23; 163). As the fight drags on, Tom offers a false confession, a revelation cobbled from scraps of Depression-era popular culture that is so melodramatic that it is humorous:

> I'm not going to the movies. I'm going to opium dens. Yes, opium dens, dens of vice and criminals' hangouts, Mother. I've joined the Hogan gang. I'm a hired assassin, I carry a tommy-gun in a violin case! I run a string of cat houses in the valley! They call me killer, killer Wingfield; I'm really leading a double life. By day I'm a simple, honest warehouse worker, but at night I'm a dynamic czar of the underworld. Why I go to gambling casinos and spin away a fortune on the roulette table! I wear a patch over my eye and a false moustache, sometimes I wear green whiskers. On those occasions they call me—El Diablo! Oh, I could tell you things to make you sleepless! (24; 164)

Scene 3, then, which opens with the images of the gentleman caller and the marriageable woman, ends with the construct of the gangster, a mocking representation of the 1930s criminal protagonist celebrated in *Scarface*, *Public Enemy*, and *Little Caesar*.

Tom's comedic admission forms a counter image to the polite constructs of successful and happy male and female heterosexuals that began the scene. Despite the obvious fiction, he manages to disclose his status as an outlaw, someone beyond the paradigmatic sexual and gender roles by which society, as Amanda defines it, and family life have been secured. He has made fun of the desperately awaited gentleman caller and the gentlewomen built like "Etruscan statues." If not the flamboyant crimes Tom describes, what acts that he is "ashamed of" has he committed? What would some-one—in this case, a single, young man—possibly do at a movie theatre all night? And when the theatre has closed, where would he go—and with whom—to do what? By this point, the "indeterminate" nature of Tom's life away from the family begins to fade. There are clues even in this speech that at first glance appears to be a subterfuge.[8] Tom divulges that he has been living "a double life."

Williams, of course, is drawing on a strategy of which homosexual men then and now were and are acutely aware. In situations where heterosexual men reveal their sexuality through references to women, it is safer for a homosexual man not to say something about his own sexuality than to admit his inclinations. One does not have to lie if one says nothing, and yet the refusal to identify oneself, which on one level feels truthful, ultimately serves as an identifier for those with an awareness that in American culture the overwhelming assumption is always that all sexuality is heterosexual and that a refusal to acknowledge that is tantamount to an admission of deviant sexuality. Tom's initial irony about the idealizations of heterosexual men and women is further compounded by his ironic "confession" to his mother. In Tom's supposed "secret life," there are no women, apart from those he claims to pimp for in the "cathouse,"[9] and there is no glamour girl, no gun moll, no Bonnie to his Clyde. Once again, the fictive alibi, despite its attempt to eradicate Amanda's curiosity through ridiculous hyperbole, is in itself an admission.

Lilly might add that Tom's use of paradox (evident in his description of the ideal matron) and camp humor (palpable in his 1930s-B-movie of his secret gangster life) "reject mainstream culture, . . . in favor of a private world, an imaginative space in which gay experience can be albeit indirectly, articulated" (153). One might see in Tom's wry commentary the kind of irony deployed by gay people to point out the contradictions in the world that condemns them. The "private world," which Tom keeps hidden from his mother (and the one that Laura ultimately offers to expose to Amanda and Jim), Lilly sees as a space of resistance to the world at large: "[I]t is precisely Williams's purpose to show that one of the worst tyrannies is to allow oneself to accept the account of the world given by society, or a group within it, as uniquely 'real' " (154).[10]

In the next scene, Tom returns to the apartment. After his angry row with Amanda, which concluded the previous scene, he now comes home very early in the morning, obviously drunk. It is here, on encountering Laura, that he talks about Malvolio's stage show, pulling one of the magi-cian's tricks, a rainbow-colored scarf, from his pocket. He describes how Malvolio managed to change water into wine, then beer, and finally whiskey but is most impressed by another stage trick:

But the wonderfullest trick of all was the coffin trick. We nailed
him into a coffin and he got out of the coffin without removing one nail. (. . .) There is a trick that would come in handy
for me—get me out of this 2 by 4 situation!. . . . You know it
don't take much intelligence to get you out of a nailed-up coffin, Laura. But who in hell ever got himself out of one without
removing one nail? [As if in answer, the father's grinning photograph
lights up. . . .] (26; 167–168, slight variations)

With this in mind, Tom goes to bed but is soon awakened by his mother's
instruction to Laura to rouse him.[11] Amanda quickly sends Laura out to buy
butter, and now, alone with Amanda and her motherly agony, Tom apolo-
gizes for his insults. In an attempt to play the "man" of the family, Tom
is patient with his mother, tries not to take issue with her. In response to
her request that he not become a drinker, he answers wryly, "I won't ever
become a drunkard, Mother" (28; 171, "[turns to her grinning] I will never
be a drunkard, Mother.") This coy ploy, of course, manages to remain true
if only by its phrasing, for as Tom has demonstrated, he is already, like his
grinning father, a seasoned alcoholic.

When Amanda tries once more to pry into his nighttime activities,
Tom offers her an answer that, in recent terms, sounds like the US Armed
Services' policy of "Don't-ask, don't-tell." Pressed by his mother's demands,
he replies,

You say there's so much in your heart that you can't describe
to me. That's true of me too. There's so much in my heart that
I can't describe to you! So let's respect each other's—(30; 173)

The word cut off is probably "privacy," but its neutral tone, even unspoken,
cannot hide that what Tom does is unspeakable—or rather, is the unspeakable.[12] As for his manhood, Tom unwittingly offers his definition of masculinity to explain why his life at work is so unsatisfying: "Man is by instinct
a lover, a hunter, a fighter, and none of those instincts are given much
play at the warehouse" (30; 174). This occasions Amanda's retort quoted
earlier: "Instinct is something that people have got away from! It belongs
to animals! . . . Only animals have to satisfy instincts!" Tom, the reader of
"that insane Mr. Lawrence" (22; 161),[13] who seems to be in search of an
authentic self that he cannot describe to his mother, is thus confronted by
the argument that people (as opposed to other creatures) must reconcile
their desires with their social obligations. Amanda's unstated condemnation
of her husband is that he succumbed to his desires; his behavior, which has
come to define masculinity for her, and which she reluctantly detects in her

son, is not consonant with a middleclass heterosexual woman's image of a man; rather, the departed Mr. Wingfield's gender seems in part based on a male's image of men, often referred to as "a man's man," that ultra-masculine and quintessentially homosocial construct of manhood. His grinning portrait becomes a sign of his masculinity, for which marriage (to a woman) is death. Tom has already posed the question of how a male can escape the coffin of family life. Man may be "a lover, a hunter, a fighter . . ." declares Tom, but of whom? For all three, the answer, as the syntactical structure insinuates, is the same.

By the end of this scene, Tom, under duress, has agreed to bring home a man "for sister," a surrogate to replace himself in the family. In the next scene, which closes Act I, the prospect of the gentleman caller beams a ray of hope throughout the household. Once Tom has revealed that one of his work acquaintances will be coming to the apartment for dinner the following evening, Amanda erupts with anticipation. Nonetheless, here as in the play's opening, the dramatized action is preceded by an opening monologue that again poses Tom, at a later age, against the events of years past.[14] Tom begins his speech to the audience by describing the Paradise Dance Hall just across the alley:

> Sometimes they'd turn out all the lights except for a large glass sphere that hung from the ceiling. It would turn slowly about and filter the dusk with delicate rainbow colors. . . . The young couples would come outside, to the relative privacy of the alley. You could see them kissing behind ashpits and telephone poles. This was the compensation for lives that passed like mine, without change and adventure. (33; 179, with slight differences)

Just as in Williams's later work, in which a streetcar named Desire takes one to the Elysian Fields, the image of a dancehall named Paradise, from which lusting couples emerge to make love in the alley, is charged with erotic significance. In a way, the implied scene of Tom at the window looking down on these couples recalls the first story in Christopher Isherwood's *Goodbye to Berlin*, in which the male narrator notes with regret that the whistles of men outside are for their girlfriends, rather than for him.[15] Here, even though, Tom hints that the intoxication that these lovers share excludes him; the heterosexual "compensation" they find eludes Tom, although his working life is passed as theirs.

As in the play's opening monologue, the subject shifts from the personal to global events, suggesting that the international "[c]hanges and adventure" lacking from these young people's lives "were imminent this year" (33; 179, "Adventure and change . . ."). References to Berchtesgarden and

Chamberlain's umbrella, and to Guernica, point the World War II audience back to when "Peace in our time" and the triumph of the Spanish Republic glimmered hopefully. Yet the contrast between Europe and America is repeated:

> In Spain there was Guernica! Here there was only hot swing music and liquor, dancehalls, bars, and movies, and sex that hung in the gloom like a chandelier and flooded the world with brief, deceptive rainbows . . . (33; 179 with slight variation)

The image of the rainbow, invoked in an earlier scene to describe Malvolio's magic scarf, re-emerges twice in this monologue, first to describe the pretty colored light swirling into the dim apartment from the dancehall and then to characterize the attractive profusion of popular culture, in which "movies" is followed significantly by "sex." The "brief, deceptive" diversions from the mundane are a substitute for the "changes and adventure" of which Tom has spoken. The comforts of ordinary life, he implies, are short-lived and illusory.

The specter of the gentleman caller, which is coincident with the specter of the handsome, departed father, is of course yet another rainbow. This association is made plain when Amanda quizzes Tom about the young man whom he is bringing to dinner:

AMANDA: Irish on both sides and he doesn't drink?

TOM: Shall I call him up and ask him? . . .

. . . .

AMANDA: When I was a girl in Blue Mountain, if it was (. . .) suspected that a young man was drinking and any girl was receiving his attentions—she'd go to the minister of his church and ask about his character. . . . [T]hat's how young girls in Blue Mountain were saved from making tragic mistakes. (*Picture dims in and out.*)

TOM: How come you made such a tragic one?

AMANDA: Oh, I don't know how he did it but that face fooled everybody. All he had to do was grin and the world was his. . . . (37–38; 185–186 with much variation)

With the portrait of the grinning Mr. Wingfield shining during this conversation and his role as the runaway beau established, Amanda places Tom, if only temporarily, into the role of *pater familias*:

> AMANDA: I hope Mr. O'Connor is not too good looking.

> TOM: As a matter of fact he isn't. His face is covered with freckles and he has a very large nose.

> AMANDA: He's not right-down homely?

> TOM: No, I wouldn't say right-down—homely—medium homely, I'd say.

> AMANDA: Well, if a girl had any sense she'd look for character in a man anyhow.

> TOM: That's what I've always said, Mother.

> AMANDA: You've always said it—you've always said it! How could you've always said it when you never even thought about it?

> TOM: Aw, don't be so suspicious of me. (38; 186, with much variation)

Perhaps enchanted by his own rainbow—the fantasy of escape without consequences—Tom for once seems to play along. In this brief, carefree moment, he actually admits to having feelings about another man's looks and lets slip a remark about how someone looking for a male partner should judge men, implying that he has considered this question. Amanda even picks up on his comment, but as before she seems unwilling to comprehend its significance, turning back instead to a seemingly less threatening matter, the gentleman caller. The moon rises in the sky, and Amanda calls in Laura, who is still unaware of the expected visitor, to make a wish on it.

Enter the Man

Between the close of Act or Part I and the opening of Act or Part II, Laura has learned that a man is coming to dinner. She is apprehensive about the visitor even before she learns his name. Amanda continues to prep the nervous girl, dressing her up and placing padding in her bodice, "Gay Deceivers" (42; 192). Amanda, as we have heard earlier, used to work at a department store, "demonstrating" brassieres (16; 134, indicates the store was "Famous-Barr"). Her efforts to change the girl from an old-maid-in-the making into an attractive young woman, prompt Laura to remark, "You make it seem like we are setting a trap." Interestingly, Amanda agrees: "All pretty girls are traps and men expect them to be traps" (43; 192, with variation). For a moment, Amanda has pulled back the curtain on romantic heterosexual love and revealed its socioeconomic framework; indeed, her views on the subject seem to be strikingly similar to those of Tom, who sees normative married family life as a coffin from which he must escape. Yet, although Tom seems to rebel against the institution, Amanda wholeheartedly embraces the "trap" of love as the way things must be. That her beliefs are outmoded is perhaps made all the more emphatic when she appears, a few moments later, in a gown from three decades earlier.

The frock is not only the dress that she wore to important balls but also the dress in which she met her future husband. Now, ready to greet the gentleman caller who will save the family, she dons it once more and recollects her youthful romances: Sickened, she says, by a slight case of malaria, young Amanda feverishly plunged into a whirlwind of parties and was successfully pursued by the man she would marry. "Malaria fever, jonquils, and your father" (44; 194, "and then—this—boy" instead of "and your father"), she sighs, virtually equating her physical attraction toward her fiancé with her dizzying performance of the diseased debutante.

Shortly after, when Amanda reveals that the male caller is named Jim O'Connor, Laura too becomes unnerved and feverish, explaining that he was the one whose photo she showed her mother in the yearbook. To Amanda's question, "[W]ere you in love with that boy?" Laura can reply only, "I don't know, Mother" (45; 195). That Laura did "love" him, whatever that may have meant to Laura then and now, however, is insinuated by her tremendous panic.

Yet even before this scene has begun, Tom has delivered an introductory monologue in which he (in a later time) tells the audience about Jim, who was always a center of attention that seemed "to move in a continual spotlight." Tom describes him as a source of energy, "forever running or bounding," "always just at the point of defeating the laws of gravity." Yet after being a sports star, "captain of the debating team, president of the senior class and the glee club," and leading man in the operettas in high school, Jim has gone on to the same warehouse where Tom has ended up, in almost the same lowly capacity. Although Tom admits to the audience that Jim was the only one at work with whom he was on "friendly terms," he explains their connection rather cynically: "I was valuable to Jim as

someone who could remember his former glory . . ." (40; 190, some variation). Still, if Jim needed him, Jim also was of use to Tom. Jim's "friendship,"
Tom adds, affected Tom's relationship with the other males at work, who
viewed Tom with hostility. "And so after a time they began to smile at me
too," Tom tells us, "as people smile at some oddly fashioned dog that trots
across their path at some distance" (41–42; 190–191, with some variation).
Jim's masculine qualities—his sense of leadership and camaraderie—help
"normalize" Tom's queer behavior, such as his hiding out in a bathroom stall
to write poetry (41, 190). Nonetheless, when Tom characterizes himself as
an "oddly fashioned dog," he is stating that at least in his own eyes he does
not fit in with other males, that he is something "other."

In contrast to Tom, who deliberately struggles to prevent his gender
from revealing his sexuality, Jim O'Connor's gender more than announces
his. From his entrance, Jim is confident, even brash, with moderately hearty
jokes to the very withdrawn Laura (46, 198). While waiting for Amanda to
enter, Tom offers him a section of the newspaper:

TOM: Comics?

JIM: Sports! Ole Dizzy Dean is on his bad behavior

TOM (starts to door R. Goes out.): Really? (45; 198–199, with
variations; in Reading text, Tom's last line begins with stage
direction: [*uninterested.*])

Tom's lack of attention and sudden departure (to smoke a cigarette) distinguish him from Jim and his typically "masculine" American response.
As the play progresses, Jim's normative masculinity, his ease with playing
the young man to Amanda's belle, his ability to make social conversation,
his flirtation with Laura, and his subsequent confession that he is already
engaged, all outwardly appear to reflect, for better and for worse, a heterosexual masculine identity.

When Jim follows Tom onto the fire escape to smoke, Tom remains
skeptical as Jim tries to "sell" him "a bill of goods" (47; 199), talking up a
public speaking class he is now taking. Jim cautions that Tom should open
his eyes to his failing career in the warehouse:

JIM: You're going to be out of a job soon if you don't wake up.

TOM: I'm waking up—

JIM: Yeah, but you show no signs.

TOM: The signs are interior. (47; 200)

Interestingly, Jim sees no evidence from Tom's external behavior to convince him that Tom is at all serious. Even as Tom offers his "interior" signs, attempting to tell Jim about his theory about life and adventure, Jim cannot understand him. As in the monologue that opened the last scene in Act or Part I, he refers to the "movies":

> People go the *movies* instead of *moving*. Hollywood characters have all the adventures for everybody in America, while everybody in America sits in a dark room and watches them having it. Yes, until there's a war. That's when adventure becomes available to the masses! . . . I'm tired of the movies and I'm about to move! (48; 201, with variation)

Jim remains incredulous, so Tom reveals even more: He has spent the money that should have gone toward the electric bill on Merchant Seamen's Union membership. Yet even the card verifying this cannot convince Jim that Tom will actually run away. "You're just talking, you drip. How does your mother feel about it?" (48; 202, with variation). In Jim's construct of how a male lives his life, such an act is not possible. A man must take care of his women; a man must be superior to women and "others" because he is not dependent, as they are, but is the one on whom they must depend. To Jim, it is unthinkable that Tom could leave. Tom explains his forthcoming escape, which will inevitably hurt his mother and sister, as genetic: "I'm like my father. The bastard son of a bastard. See how he grins? And he's been absent going on sixteen years" (48; 202, with specific reference to the photo).

In short, Jim seems everything that Tom is not, all that Tom's father should have been but wasn't. Or at least this is how he presents himself. In Amanda's system of binaries, where the wealthy widow opposes the discarded wife and the happy wife is the positive counterpart to the old maid, Mr. Wingfield, "the bastard," the alcoholic, selfish runaway, is the false gentleman caller, the counterfeit to be avoided at all costs; "Old maids are better off than wives of drunkards!" Amanda asserts at the end of Part I (only in Reading text, 184). Jim, who appears to hold out the hope of a worthwhile, secure future, when confronted by Amanda's performance of Southern charm, performs as if he were a genuine gentleman caller.

However, there is a problem that Laura has already anticipated: Jim may not be single. Earlier, while showing Amanda the yearbook picture, Laura has mentioned that she read a notice in the newspaper that Jim and Emily Meisenbach, the best-dressed girl at school, were engaged (19; 157), something that Amanda has forgotten entirely. Laura's suspicions, which inevitably prove true, make her so ill that she has to be excused from sitting at the dinner table.

At the start of the final scene of *The Glass Menagerie*, Amanda, Tom, and Jim are finishing dinner and Laura is resting in the next room on the sofa. The electricity, the bill for which Tom has failed to pay, gives out just as the meal is over, but Amanda, buoyed by the social interaction and the promise of a son-in-law, makes light of the sudden plunge into darkness and has Jim light some candles. Having set the scene for romance, the overdressed matron, who seems to be ripped from the pages of *Gone With the Wind*, takes her son into the kitchen to wash the dishes, withdrawing so that romance may take its course. And so Jim enters the living room, candle in one hand, a glass of dandelion wine in the other. What follows is a brief encounter that, according to the stage directions, is an unimportant incident for him but for Laura is "the climax of her secret life" (54; 210). It is also a scene without the narrator on stage. In its own way, what is played out is nothing less than a seduction and a betrayal, albeit a rather chaste one. Nonetheless, although sex at least seems to be absent, the scene between the two characters is extremely intimate.

Jim's foray into Laura's space is a quick campaign, complete with hearty jokes. He hands her the glass of wine—"Well, drink it—but don't get drunk!" (54; 211)—and places the candelabra on the floor. He settles himself on the floor as well, asking Laura's permission to do so only after he has sat down, and then, after requesting a pillow, he has her sit on the floor too, goading her next into moving closer to him (54; 211–212). As he has already indicated to Tom, this is what Jim believes he has learned in his public speaking class, "the ability to square up to somebody and hold your own on any social level!" (47; 199, with variations). Jim literally as well as figuratively brings Laura down to his own level. Once she is there, as he takes out a stick of chewing gum, he muses over the fortune made by the man who invented it and who built the Wrigley Building in Chicago, where two years before Jim saw The Century of Progress exposition. Impressed by the Hall of Science exhibit, Jim assures Laura about "what the future will be like in America," which will be "more wonderful than the present time is" (55; 212, "even more wonderful"). The irony is that the "present time," which is the Great Depression, is not wonderful at all, even according to Jim.

Yet Jim's America remains the land of opportunity or perhaps opportunism. His peculiar views of democratic capitalism lead him to make a number of contradictory statements; in fact, his "ability to square up to somebody and hold your own on any social level," came as part of the answer to questions that he had just posed: "what's the difference between you and me and the guys in the office down front? Brains? No! Ability? No!" The

performance of "Social poise!" as Jim calls it, is the key to success in rising
above the masses of people (47; 199). Yet people, he explains to Laura,

> are not so dreadful when you know them. . . . And everybody
> has problems, not just you but practically everybody. . . . You
> think of yourself as being the only one who is disappointed. But
> just look around you and what do you see—a lot of people just
> as disappointed as you are. (57; 216, with variations)

So, Jim seems to be suggesting that, whatever her problems, Laura is pretty
much like everyone else. People are not really "so dreadful"; they are just
pretty much the same. Yet Jim seems to be saying something quite different
a little while later, when he describes

> [a] world full of common people! All of 'em born and all of 'em
> going to die! Now which of them has one-tenth of your strong
> points! Or mine! Or anybody else's for that matter? (60; 221,
> with variations)

So we are all much the same and all very different? Each one of us is
simultaneously common *and* special? His pronouncements quickly turn into
sheer Babbittry:

> . . . I believe in the future of television! . . . Oh, I've already
> made the right connections. All that remains now is for the
> industry itself to get under way—full steam! You know, *knowl-
> edge*—ZZZZppp! *Money*—Zzzzzzpp! *POWER!* Wham! That's the
> cycle democracy is built on! (Pause.) I guess you think I think
> a lot of myself! (60; 222)

Suddenly America is all about being in the right place at the right time.
What Jim has to say is in actuality less about America and more about
himself. Even when he talks to Laura about Laura—to whom he only inter-
mittently listens—he is talking about himself and justifying his own present
and future in an egocentric rhetoric that is obviously inconsistent twaddle.

Jim's question, then, "I guess you think I think a lot of myself!" is
something of an understatement. His performance of interest in Laura masks,
at least for her, that he is playing a role. She is unaware that his amateur analysis of her problems—"Inferiority complex!" (59; 221)—is merely
a demonstration for his own benefit of his social poise, his ability to talk
to anyone from any "level" about anything. The exercise also allows him
to consider how good he is at knowing how people think. Laura, however,

who has received little if any attention from anyone other than her mother and brother, delights in Jim's company, which in turn reifies his belief in his "social poise."

Laura is encouraged too by Jim's revelation that he and Emily Meisenbach were never really engaged (58–59; 219). The two end up waltzing about the room to the music of the dancehall across the alley (62–63; 224–226). This closeness, which Tom has earlier characterized as a prelude to physical embrace, ends in a kiss, Laura's first (and presumably last; 64; 228). Only when Jim realizes that he has played the socially poised gentleman caller a little too well, does he back away from his performance. Suddenly he must confess that he has a girlfriend, whom he met on a moonlit cruise and who is both Catholic and Irish (64; 229–230). And because of Betty, he tells Laura, he must never see Laura again. Thus, the consolation he has offered—"Oh, boy, I wish you were my sister" (63; 227, with variations)—is nothing more than a social nicety to cover his imminent and final departure.

The play draws its title from the collection of small glass animal figurines that Laura displays in the living room. Up until this scene, it has figured only occasionally in the play, but now it suddenly becomes the central image for what is transpiring on stage. When pressed about what she has been doing since dropping out of high school, Laura tells him, "My glass collection takes a good deal of time." Jim, who isn't really listening ("What did you say—about glass?"), abruptly proclaims that he has figured out that Laura suffers from an inferiority complex (59; 220). The next time the glass menagerie, as her mother has named it, comes up is when Jim asks Laura about her main interest; her response, ". . . my—glass collection" is met with Jim's unknowing questions (61; 222).

Laura again tries to explain what she means but then goes to the shelf on which the collection sits and takes a small glass unicorn, which she hands to Jim. At first, Jim doesn't know what to make of the object ("Say, what kind of thing is this supposed to be?" 61; 223, with variation), but once Laura points him to the animal's horn, he recognizes it as a creature "extinct in the modern world." Slowly, this conversation entwines with the one that they have already begun:

JIM: Poor little fellow must feel kind of lonesome.

LAURA: Well, if he does he doesn't complain about it. He stays on a shelf with horses that don't have horns and they all seem to get along nicely together. (61, 223)

This discussion is interrupted by Jim's perception of how large his shadow in the candlelight looms on the wall; this sense of largesse, along with the dancehall music prompts him to make Laura dance with him. Their waltz ends once Jim has clumsily knocked the glass unicorn from the table where he placed it. The piece is intact except for its distinguishing horn. Even though Laura has already mentioned that this piece was her favorite (61; 223), she is willing to deny that she has any favorites and to see the injury in a different way:

> He's lost his horn. It doesn't matter. Maybe it's a blessing in disguise. . . . I'll just imagine he had an operation. The horn was removed to make him feel less—freakish. (. . .) Now he will feel at home with the other horses, the ones who don't have horns. (63; 226, with variations)

Laura's observations, which Jim has of course inspired, inspire Jim to praise Laura:

> You know—you're—different than anybody else I know? . . . You make me feel sort of—I don't know how to say it! . . . Did anyone ever tell you you were pretty? . . . And in a different way from anyone else. And all the nicer because of the difference. . . . Being different is nothing to be ashamed of. Because other people aren't such wonderful people. They're a hundred times one thousand. You're one times one! . . . (63; 227, with stage directions)

This sudden appreciation of the "other," of someone who is "different" and of Jim's repeated wish to help Laura (if she were his sister) gain more confidence, precede the moment when they kiss.

As noted above, everything falls apart after the kiss. Immediately, all of Jim's statements up to the kiss begin to ring false. The rather specious argument about the insignificance of a signifying difference drops away, and Laura gives the stammering gentleman caller the hornless unicorn as a "souvenir." She is and remains different while he, true to his own admission, "I always take [the chewing gum] out when the flavor is gone" (60; 221), seems to dart from one flavor to the next. As if to drive home Laura's recognition of herself as different, Williams has Amanda enter with a pitcher of lemonade, singing an old ditty: "Lemonade . . . it's good enough for any old maid" (64; 231). Laura seems already to have accepted what the future holds for her.

When Amanda learns that Jim is in a hurry to pick up his impatient intended at the station, she understands immediately. "I know all about the tyranny of women," she remarks pointedly (66; 234, with variation).

Jim exits. Amanda's anger drives her to state the predicament in the very words she has previously and most carefully avoided: "Don't think about us, a mother deserted, an unmarried sister who's crippled and has no job!" Enraged, she blames Tom for not having known that Jim was engaged. "The warehouse," he tells her, "is the place where I work, not where I know things about people!" Just as he has kept his identity secret at work, so, it appears, has Jim. His mother's accusations continue; Tom starts to leave. "I'm going to the movies," he tells Amanda (67; 225), but her ridicule that he is a selfish hedonist, drives him farther.

"And so—good-bye!"

The guilt-ridden closing monologue of *The Glass Menagerie* is a compelling speech that perhaps offers clues to Tom's identity. The drifting, the gnawing memories, and the restlessness reflect what had, by the time the play was written, already become Tennessee Williams's lifestyle. The playwright's diary, at least those parts that have been extracted into Lyle Leverich's biography of Williams, records in great detail his wanderings and his escapades before and during the time he wrote the play. One word that appears conspicuously in the final speech is "companions": "Perhaps I am walking along a street at night in some strange city, before I have found companions" (68; 237). During an August 1942 sojourn to Saint Augustine, Florida, Williams jotted down the following entry:

> *Mon. Night*—This evening a stranger picked me up. A common and seedy-looking young Jew with a thick accent. I was absurdly happy. For the first time since my arrival I had a companion. (463)

Throughout his life, Williams tried to flee from and at the same time embrace the knowledge that he was regarded by most people as "the other." He craved the presence of people if only for the short-lived respite they offered him from his own isolation. In this case, his remarks about the greenhorn—perhaps an escapee from the yet-unnamed Holocaust—remind us how "otherness" was described linguistically at the time.

There are plenty of "others" in *The Glass Menagerie*. In addition to Tom, there are Laura and Amanda, who even by their own standards see themselves as "different," the former a crippled soon-to-be old maid, the latter the estranged wife of a drunkard, which (we have been told) is even worse than being an old maid. Moreover, despite Jim's cheerfulness about democracy, the speech of all the characters in the play divulges just how

American society viewed those who were "different." A black male is referred to as "colored boy" (13) or, as the Reading script would have it, "darky" (147) and "nigger" (148). Northern Episcopalians are obviously different from Southern ones (12; cut). In the cinema where Tom has spent the night, there is a fight between "a fat lady" and an usher (26; 167). The delicatessen where the family owes money is run by a Jew: "Sticks and stones may break our bones," says Amanda, "but the expression on Mr. Garfinkle's face won't hurt us" (27; 169). To get the house ready for the gentleman caller, Amanda has to work "like a Turk" (42, stage direction; 183, dialogue, 191, stage direction). "Irish" means Catholic; "Catholic" means fish on Friday (35; 183); "Irish Catholic male" means drinker (36; 185). Even Jim's disparaging remark about his high school sweetheart, Emily Meisenbach—"That kraut-head!" (58; 219)—makes us recall that the audience who first saw this play were used to calling their enemies overseas "Krauts" and "Jerries," "Nips" and "Japs"; indeed, at the time the script was written, Americans with Japanese ancestry were being sent away to internment camps.[16] The play makes clear that the only way to discuss the "other" is by his or her distinguishing characteristic; thus, contra Jim's celebration of Laura's differentness, the "other" remains forever "the other."

"Companion" may seem a rather nonspecific term, but in addition to Williams own usage of it to describe a homosexual sex partner, its vagueness supports the notion I proposed earlier, that in a culture where sexuality immediately is taken to refer to a binary world, composed of heterosexual men and women, the refusal to disclose, to be specific, and the desire to achieve some "gender" neutrality, counts as a signifier of difference. Williams's diaries, as quoted by Leverich, contain a plethora of homosexual terms that survive today in addition to "companion": "fairy" (372), "butch" (425), "gay" (430), "piss-elegant" (433), "sissy," "dished" (439), "trade" (456 and elsewhere), "cruising" (478), and "tight-assed" (523), just to cite a few. Williams, rather than choosing a word that might be recognizable by the general public as a word used by what he called "homo-society," chose the word "companions," the very impartiality and noncommitment of which serves to identify the speaker as someone who refuses to divulge his sexuality and is therefore, in contemporary terms, deviant.

Thus, The Glass Menagerie looked forward to a host of marginalized characters that would populate Williams's later works, characters for whom sex, sexuality, and gender would be problematic. This play, like all his dramas, concerns itself with difference and otherness. Nevertheless, in this play Williams carefully contrasts a male whose manly gender is enacted to communicate his sexuality with a male who carefully guards his gender while attempting to perform the task of not disclosing his sexuality. The play appeared toward the close of a war during which the armed services frequently and virulently punished homosexuals, both on the battlefield and on the home front. In the context of the world as it was then, and to an alarming extent, in the context of the world that we all know now, saying and meaning nothing are necessarily construed to indicate something.

Williams's Tom does not seek to overturn the way things are: As stated earlier, although his mother is a firm supporter of heterosexual culture and he is marginalized from it, both acknowledge its existence. Tom wishes simply to escape it, preferably without hurting his family, although ultimately he exits, as did his father, leaving a trail of destruction behind him.

One, of course, may argue that *The Glass Menagerie* is, after all, Tom's play. Or is it? Does the whole idea of Tom as narrator hold together through-out the action, or does it seem a dramatic device that breaks down as the scenes progress? I have pointed earlier to two scenes from which Tom is entirely absent and speculated, regarding the first of these, about how spec-tators might relate to his absence; with regard to the second scene, if Tom leaves his family when the play shows him leaving, he would not have any idea of what exactly transpired between Jim and Laura. Indeed, Amanda's outburst and Tom's statements that he had no inkling of Jim's fiancée, suggest they were not listening to the couple through the kitchen door. How then is the audience to make sense of all the action on stage? Is it all invented by Tom—Tom's version of events, all conveyed from Tom's point of view? Or is there a truth underneath the illusion that seems more real than the illusion we watch—a truth about people and life?

Several of the play's first New York critics had difficulty with the narra-tor device, not because it had never been used before, but because, for many, it seemed unnecessary. "The narration," complained Lewis Nichols in *The Times*, "is like that of 'Our Town' and 'I Remember Mama' and it probably is not essential in 'Glass Menagerie.'"[17] George Freedly, who happened to be head of the Theatre Research Collection at The New York Public and also the reviewer for *The Morning Telegram*, found the narration the play's major flaw: "If Mr. Williams had restrained himself more, particularly in Mr. Dowling's prologue and asides, he would have written a better play." Louis Kronenberger, in *P.M. New York* judged that "Mr. Williams isn't really master of his showy (and derived) devices. . . ." Despite such criticisms, virtually all of them wrote positively about the dramatized scenes.

It would be unfair not to mention that most of the reviews of the original New York opening focused less on the play than on the production, most notably on the acting of Laurette Taylor, who played Amanda. Long remembered as the definitive role of the postwar period, Taylor's extraor-dinary characterization especially influenced young actors at the time who saw in her performance the realization of all that they had studied of "the Method." Ironically, Taylor was more a veteran of the boards of Broadway than a devotee of any particular acting school or studio. Her powerful work on stage was occasionally interrupted by the effects of her acute dependence on alcohol, which proved problematic only in the short run. Although Eddie Dowling, who produced the show and played Tom, Julie Haydon (as Laura), and Anthony Ross (as Jim) received glowing reviews, the critics gave the play to Taylor. Thus, even Williams's play seemed to many less important than the performance it had inspired.

Yet the unwieldy use of a narrator seems, by the end of the play, less of a failed attempt at narration on stage than a construct that only makes sense until the audience begins to identify with the stage action—at which point its actual narrative function falls away, and it remains only as a device to inject Tom—a Tom who exists in a "present" where he is older than he is in the scenes in St. Louis—into scenes from which he is otherwise absent. We may recall that Williams tells us, "The narrator is an undisguised convention of the play. He takes whatever license with dramatic convention is convenient to his purposes." Perhaps the lack of coherence in the narrative strategy is Williams's way of questioning the nature of coherence in any construct. In a piece written for *The Times* in 1947, entitled "The Catastrophe of Success," which later served as in an introduction to the 1945 Reading text, Williams observes, "Somebody you are when you 'have a name' is a fiction created with mirrors . . ." (140). Constructs when one is "somebody" are no less constructs than when one is oneself or even no one.[18] Certainly, he deliberately shows us how Jim's and Amanda's gender identities are flawed by inconsistencies, and how Tom's and Laura's fragmentary gender identities seem inconclusive. Is it possible, he may be asking, for anyone's sexual identity to make complete rational sense?

Certainly, in the world in which the play is set, structured as it is by rigid middle-class values, very little makes "rational sense." Tom may be aware of this because of the estrangement he feels due to his sexuality, but he exits not because he is a homosexual but because he refuses to look for happiness in this world. Many years later, a writer would speak of "the male rebel who actually walks away from responsibility in any form": "The possibility of walking out, without money or guilt, and without ambition other than to see and do everything, was not even immanent in the middle-class culture of the fifties" notes Barbara Ehrenreich, speaking not of Tom but of the Beats. She goes on to define this generation:

> Dropping out of their own mostly lower-middle-class backgrounds, they worked, when they worked at all, as manual laborers, seamen or railway workers, and hung out in a demimonde inhabited by drifters, junkies, male prostitutes, thieves, would-be poets and actual musicians. (56)

Although Ehrenreich is describing Jack Kerouac and his associates, these words may be easily applied to Williams and Tom alike.

Of course, the Beats were attractive, some of them very handsome, young men. Like the escapee father, whose good-looking physiognomy is all we see of him, their images would haunt the conforming middle-class home, perilously luring the young male to break with the image of the respectable, responsible husband-father. Popularized on the screen by Montgomery Clift, Marlon Brando, and the cause-less rebel, James Dean, such men seemed to transcend the usual male–female and gay–straight binaries. Just two or three years after the play's debut, masculinity would appear to polarize between the two projected faces, the handsome, young rebel and the tough, loyal patriarch as Clift confronted John Wayne in *Red River*. Yet that would happen gradually over the next two decades.

In *The Glass Menagerie*, "one of the worst tyrannies," as Lilly calls it, is "to allow oneself to accept the account of the world given by society, or a group within it, as uniquely 'real,'" is not perpetrated: Tom removes himself from his home and family, releasing himself into a world in which he may live by his own account of the world; however, the terrible cost of separation and the accompanying sadness almost create a cautionary moment as the final curtain falls.

The ghostly figure of the handsome smiling male, worshipped and reviled by Amanda, is renovated by Tom Jr., who is never described as handsome. Yet if he is the double of the senior Tom, who fell in love with long distance, he must carry and to some degree purify the image of male beauty that Amanda so regretfully recalls.

CHAPTER 2

Dangerous Male Beauty and the Masculine Style

Regular and Irregular Guys in *Tea and Sympathy*

More Tea than Sympathy?

Although hailed in its day as an insightful and serious work, Robert Anderson's first hit on Broadway, *Tea and Sympathy*, seems today a terribly confused and contradictory drama. Ultimately, the play only makes sense in narrative terms; once the audience starts to think about the implications of the actions they have witnessed, what the play means (or appears to be intended to mean) seems to deflate like a well-made soufflé taken from the oven too soon and too roughly. Six decades later, we may be able to separate what the play thinks it is saying from what the play in fact says; such a distinction was far more difficult for spectators in 1953, when gender conformity was generally accepted as something positive and homosexuality was clearly aberrant.

Although the ostensible subject of the play appears to be sexuality, specifically homosexuality, the actual issue here is gender: Postwar masculinity is presented as an unstable construct that relies on close bonds between males and yet is fraught with homophobia. One major component of the glue that cements the homosocial bond is style; it isn't so much what a male does as how he does it that marks him as either masculine or nonmasculine and thus effeminate. A crucial problem in the play is that the playwright appears to accept without question many of the binaries that governed popular and professional discourse at the time, such as one is either a male or a female, a man or woman, a "regular" guy or a queer, manly or girlish, and so on. These simplifications, which at the time supported the already wobbly framework of masculinity, inevitably keep the play from going very far in exploring how sexuality and gender relate to each other. The script never asks audiences to consider homosexuality as anything other than negative and offers heterosexuality as the genuine indicator of genuine masculinity. True, *Tea and Sympathy* does suggest that gender may be far less revealing about a person's sexuality than people generally acknowledge, but Anderson portrays the gender roles of his characters very broadly, virtually as types, including the "effeminate" male, the "man's man," the "average" or "regular guy" who strives to fit in, the girl who is a tart, the female who enjoys playing the tease, and—perhaps most disturbingly—the adult woman who is drawn to underage or boyish males.

At the same time, *Tea and Sympathy* loads the dice; despite "outing" the highly arbitrary and relative nature of gender roles, it refrains from offering any sympathetic representation of homosexuals. In fact, the play seems to reject homosexuals and says nothing about their mistreatment. Anderson's script, which was inevitably compared to Lillian Hellman's *The Children's Hour*, not only because Hellman's work had been revived the season before but also because both were set in New England private schools and depicted smear campaigns about the alleged homosexual behavior of certain parties, fails to dramatize that an individual's homosexual orientation is nothing to fear. On the contrary, Anderson's "provocative" play appears to view homosexuality (as opposed to effeminacy) in the same way that its characters do—as an abnormality. While *The Children's Hour*, which in its 1952 run seemed to resonate with McCarthyism's use of rumors, uses lesbianism as a plot device rather than a social theme, Hellman does allow the irony that one of the two women accused of being a lesbian may actually be one (she conveniently commits suicide near the end of the final scene). Thus, despite the often melodramatic storyline, Hellman at least implies and in a way demonstrates that homosexual women (as well as women who are heterosexual and accused of being lesbians) may well be the innocent victims of persecution. In Anderson's rendition, however, the playwright seems to reify the idea, which is strongly dramatized, that although the person who is falsely accused of being "queer" is worthy of our sympathy, the person who is correctly accused of homosexuality gets what he deserves.

This aspect of the play—its ultimate intolerance of homosexuality—is no doubt the reason that *Tea and Sympathy* is most ridiculed (and perhaps justly) by gay critics, who view it as a terribly archaic and nonsensical work. Michael Bronski, in *Culture Clash: The Making of Gay Sensibility*, says of it, "Now hopelessly dated and silly, the play managed simultaneously to bring up and ignore the subject of male homosexuality" (122). David Savran, in *Communists, Cowboys, and Queers: The Politics of Masculinity in the Work of Arthur Miller and Tennessee Williams*, describes how it

> dramatizes the extraordinary level of anxiety—and the emotional
> disarray that coalesces around the constitution of the male social
> bond, which Anderson characterizes as both a shield against
> homosexuality and a symptom of homosexual desire. [Yet] the
> ending . . . does not attempt to resolve this contradiction, but
> buries it in a flurry of heterosexual passion and sentiment. (88)

John M. Clum calls *Tea and Sympathy* "the classic version of mainstream American treatment of homosexuality" in which "accusations of homosexuality taint a male society, and the threat of homosexuality is eliminated by the final curtain" (120). Likewise, gay theater critics of the first major New York revival of the play in 2007 had similar qualms. Hilton Als, in *The New Yorker*, asks, "Do we have to keep dragging out polite works from the past that are, to say the least, dated?" (91) Michael Feingold, in *The Village Voice* asserts, "[T]here's no point in giving away what Anderson makes so hilariously obvious. The very crudity of the play, which gives it a crude, iconic potency, also makes it seem touchingly ancient. . . ." Certainly, the early success of *Tea and Sympathy*, first on stage, then transliterated (with much revision) onto the screen, lent to the ideas carried by the drama a certain credibility. Inevitably Anderson's hit reified the heterosexist belief that it was fine for a male to act in a manner that could be construed as unmanly (or even effeminate) as long as his sexual orientation was exclusively toward women. Accordingly, *Tea and Sympathy* attracted accolades and great interest from a homophobic press and public. The work has probably earned much of the ridicule it now carries.

Nonetheless, others have argued, and probably quite justifiably, that for many Americans the play remains an intriguing and challenging work. Indeed, Gina Bellafonte, critiquing the 2007 production mentioned above for the all-important *New York Times* review, insists that it "rings with a relevance that makes the revival every bit worth the wait" (7). In *The Daily News* notice, Joe Dziemianowicz states early on, "Some might think Robert Anderson's 54-year-old play 'Tea and Sympathy,' . . . is such a relic that audiences can't relate to it," and then asks—and answers—the necessary question: "Is the play dated? Yes. And no. . . . [T]he notion that the confused Tom needs to be saved, even if he is gay, lives on" (52). Even Mark Blankenship, in *Variety*, while recognizing the "dated" play's limitations, argues that in this production many of the script's shortcomings are somehow ameliorated by the direction and the acting (34). Obviously, from a heterosexual perspective, the play (which was, after all, written by someone with that perspective) may still make a lot of sense.

Such comments, both the positive and the negative, seem at odds with the original production's New York notices. Many critics in 1953 raved

about the play itself. Richard Watts, in *The Post*, added to his description
of the plot that the script "handles it with taste, delicacy, and considerable
emotional skill" and actually blamed director Elia Kazan for any of the
apparent shortcomings. *The Journal American* headline read, "Excellent Play,
Brilliantly Done." John Chapman, in *The Daily News*, began his critique,
"'Tea and Sympathy' has been beautifully written by Robert Anderson . . ."
and in *The World-Telegram and The Sun*, William Hawkins called the play "a
triumph." The dean of critics, Brooks Atkinson, in *The Times*, declared that
the play, under Kazan's direction, "restores our theatre to an art again with
a fine play put on the stage with great skill and beauty." There were those
who found the play very flawed who, unlike Watts, blamed the playwright,
most notably Robert Coleman in *The Daily Mirror*, but overall the play was
a bona fide success.[1]

If today *Tea and Sympathy* succeeds on any level, however, it may be
in opening a dialogue, which it too quickly closes, on what it means to be
a gendered individual in postwar society. The play accepts that gender is
performed and that the way it is performed in some sense serves as a communication between people; at the same time, it emphasizes that gender
is not a reliable sign of an individual's sexuality. In the long run, *Tea and
Sympathy* maintains that the only true indicator of a man's identity as a man
is his attraction to women: Heterosexual orientation is the only indisputable
trait of masculinity. In keeping with this, Anderson's heroine announces that
only a woman can distinguish a "real" man from a "queer."

Yet, if it is possible to separate the play from the homophobia and
misogyny of the time, which the script tends at times to embrace and trans-
mit, we may be able to glimpse another possibility—Anderson is clumsily
attempting to address an apparent crisis in gender performance in the years
following World War II. Although the answer(s) to the question: "What
makes a man a man and a woman a woman?" can never be satisfactorily
explained by the playwright, except in highly relative, cultural terms, the
need to explain has become increasingly urgent. The specter of male beauty,
as much as it is allowed in the play, is brief but remains central: The
handsome man more than any other threatens the construct of masculinity
and brings males who are attempting to perform that construct into crisis.
And the male whose style of performance does not conform to the style
of normative masculinity challenges the validity of masculinity altogether.

An Evolving Story

If *The Glass Menagerie* grew out of its playwright's efforts to come to terms
with his own guilt over his sister's 1943 lobotomy, the origin of *Tea and*

Sympathy seems to have originated, similarly, in its author's recognition of how a young woman at a private school that he attended managed to make his life bearable. Just as Williams' first play on Broadway grew from a short story, then continued through dramatic treatments of the plot and characters, so did Anderson's: A note in his own hand, on an early onionskin typescript of the play in The New York Public Library's Theatre Research Collection, reads,

> This was a version of Tea and [S]ympathy written in 1948, but not produced. I later "crossed" it with a short story I wrote in 1946, called "Katherine and pity and love and I"[2] and that together with some new material became the 1952 version of Tea and [S]ympathy, as produced in 1953. [signed] Robert Anderson.

In this "Ur text" of *Tea and Sympathy*, Katherine Morrison, the daughter of a now-deceased teacher, has stayed on as a dormitory mother at the boy's school where her father once taught. One of her charges, Tom Lawson, has been picked on and isolated, in part because of his physical disability: a club foot. Into this dorm comes Paul Bennett, a former star athlete and student at the school, whom Katherine knew through her father. Paul is now a no-nonsense teacher and the new dorm master. The two former friends differ on how boys should be raised, Katherine offering understanding and sympathy for their problems, Paul maintaining that they will only become men if they are taught to be tough.

Although Tom is drawn romantically toward Katherine's kindness and is repelled by Paul's harshness, Katherine senses that Paul is unable to talk about what is truly bothering him. Rumors of his annulled marriage have followed him to the school. When Katherine confronts him about them, he confesses that the reason for his break up was because he didn't want children; "love," he tells Katherine, "is something more than a biological urge" (2-2-29). Katherine, who was briefly married to a young man who died in the war, a man who is now symbolized by the boys whom she takes care of, can see that Paul is suffering. He finally admits, knowing that he and Katherine are falling in love, that he is sterile. Katherine accepts his proposal of marriage anyway; Tom manages to learn from Paul, as well as Katherine, how to live his life. Everyone ends happily.

If this 1948 version seems less sexually charged than the *Tea and Sympathy* that was produced five years later, it also is far less problematic. In the script that followed, Katherine becomes Laura, a former actress who, like Katherine, was married to a young man who died in the war. Paul becomes Bill, a 40-year-old bachelor teacher and house master, whom Laura met and wed in Italy. Laura comes to the school a stranger, who because of her husband is supposed to lend an ear to the problems of the boys in his house. One of the faculty wives, a Mrs. Marley, whose bitchiness sharply contrasts with Katherine's sweetness, becomes Lilly, a faculty wife who is acutely aware that every boy in the school views her as sexually desirable, which she finds amusing and somewhat gratifying; Lilly's earthiness now contrasts with Laura's idealization of youth and her reticence about reducing everything to sex.

Tom Lawson becomes Tom Lee, a young man whose behavior isolates him as "different" from the other boys. Tom, in a time when every male sports a crew cut, has long hair; he enjoys playing the guitar and likes to sing old folk songs; and rather than engaging in manly sports, such as football, basketball, or baseball, Tom excels at tennis. Instead of the club foot,[3] Tom Lee has a different disability: He has successfully performed in female roles in the all-boys productions and is an unrepentant fan of Grace Moore in the film, *One Night of Love*, which has earned him the nickname, Grace (13); he even hides in a drawer photographs of scantily clad muscle men. Most shockingly, however, classmates have seen Tom Lee sunbathe in the nude with the teacher who encouraged his music; Tom is suspected of being homosexually involved with the teacher.

This teacher is worth mentioning if only because in a play ostensibly about homosexuality, he is produced as the only ostensibly self-aware homosexual. David Harris, who appears only in this later version and only at the beginning of Act I, is described quite simply as "a good-looking young master" (17). That Harris is a homosexual is never questioned or proven; the rumors that he may have seduced Tom are sufficient for his immediate dismissal. Bill tells Laura about the incident, and although she is reluctant to assume that either Tom or Harris is a homosexual, Bill is especially adamant about the boy: "Tom's always been an off-horse. . . . Look at the way he walks, the way he sometimes stands" (26). When Laura dismisses this evidence, Bill plays the gender card: "a man knows a queer when he sees one" (27). As for the "good-looking young master," when Tom's flustered father arrives to ask, "[W]hat was a guy like Harris doing at the school?" Bill retorts, "I tried to tell them" (31). By this point, Bill has demonstrated his own homophobia, and as the play builds, a bit of "common sense" will emerge as irony—namely, it takes one to know one. Bill, the macho man, the rugged nature trekker who spends much of his time with young men in the wilderness, is ultimately unmasked as a man with problems—perhaps as a male in homosexual panic, perhaps even as a repressed homosexual.

What makes the handsome Mr. Harris suspect? Because the script tells us so very little about him, we must assume it is his beauty. The handsome man had, decades before, been viewed by many other males as effeminate, unmanly, even perverse: The great example is, of course, Rudolf Valentino, whose looks had captivated women and, upon his death, created what was described as mass hysteria. The idea of male beauty was viewed traditionally as something about which females might talk but about which males must feign total ignorance. For a male to acknowledge the beauty of a male was for him to acknowledge the possibility of his being attracted to that male and thus to males in general, and in a world in which homosexuality had been officially classed as nonmasculine, males who wished to be seen as masculine could not positively evaluate another man aesthetically and at the same time remain manly.

Bill, Laura's macho, mountaineering husband, assists the school in vilifying both Mr. Harris and Tom. Tom's roommate, Al, a captain of the baseball team, decides (as a result of fear of association) to move out. Al and the other boys in the dorm mock and then persuade Tom into going to see the local floozy to prove his manhood; the floozy, named Ellie Martin, over whom few tears are shed, eagerly tells anyone who will listen that Tom was unable to perform and attempted suicide. At this point, Bill is happy to let Tom leave the school, and Tom is somewhat happy to go, even as his alumnus father is deeply ashamed of what Tom has brought upon them. Tom's carefree and negligent mother does not factor into the equation, for after she and Tom's father were divorced, Tom was eventually turned over to his father's custody and never saw her again (15). Yet his father seems negligent too: Tom has little to do with him, spending his vacations in the company of an aunt with whom he attends plays and concerts (16) while the rest of the year he is sent away to school and summer camps. Tom's father recounts how he once forced himself to have a man-to-man talk with the boy, who even before the talk could begin "got sick to his stomach" (34).

All this is well and good, but there is nothing to account for Tom's profound ignorance of his own flawed performance of masculinity. Having played Lady Macbeth in the school production and now cast in the role of Lady Teazle in *The School for Scandal* (14–15), Tom must have some cognizance that males and females are expected to behave differently. Certainly he is aware that the nickname he has been given, "Grace" (15), is not an endearment and that he has already been branded a sissy. Yet Laura maintains that Tom is quite innocent, not only of any homosexual act but also of any knowledge of homosexuality (33–34), which is not entirely accurate. Thus, when Tom's father, with the delightfully prosaic name of Herb, actually speaks with his son about the accusations, he feels obliged to spell out why Mr. Harris was fired, which Tom has apparently been too oblivious to understand: ". . . I'll say it plain, Tom. He's a fairy. A homosexual" (36).

Bill, as noted earlier, has already uttered the word "queer," and Herb manages both another slang term and also the clinical one. Again, the audience never knows definitively what Harris's sexuality really is, but spectators are asked to accept what the characters believe; the play offers no sympathy (and no tea) for the good-looking young master, who whether he is a homosexual or not, is fired from his job. If *Tea and Sympathy* is to be construed as a play about the unfairness of smearing someone—as were *The Crucible* and the revived *Children's Hour*—then the message is perhaps complicated by McCarthyism and Anderson's liberal response to it: To be a homosexual, like being a Communist, was in itself culpable, whether one practiced one's sexuality, like practicing one's Communism, or not; sympathy was reserved for those who were *falsely* accused and then branded as reds and pinks, fellow travelers and premature anti-fascists. The Communist who actually was a Communist, whatever he or she did (and/or did not do), was a criminal, just as the celibate homosexual was nonetheless a homosexual and therefore justly persecuted. So Tom, who becomes the innocent victim in the play, can never be regarded as actually being attracted to men, for that would suddenly change his status from innocent to deserving. This was made much of when the play was first staged. The press repeatedly described the plot as involving "a misunderstood youth" who "is wrongly suspected of homosexual tendencies."[4] Harris, whose homosexuality is presumed because of his good looks, and Bill, whose homosexuality is ultimately suspected, necessarily become objects of pity and scorn.

The most understanding character in the play is supposed to be Laura, who at first seems—as someone who had worked in the theater—extremely tolerant and accepting. Yet however much time she spent on stage, Laura seems to have acquired some dislike for homosexuals. After Tom has been associated with the suspect master, Laura talks about asking the girl next door to accompany Tom to the dance the following night.[5] Tom, who has planned on accompanying Laura, with whom he is obviously infatuated, takes this to mean that she wants nothing to do with him and that she believes, like his father and the others, that he is queer. Laura asserts, "Tom, I asked her over so we could lick this thing." Tom pointedly asks, "What thing? What thing?" (42) before retreating to his room. In spite of my desire to read double meaning into this dialogue, which I cannot defend, I infer that Laura means that she wants to "spin" Tom's unjustly smeared reputation, which of course means that being *wrongly* suspected of homosexual tendencies is a terrible slander.

And Laura's attempt to persuade Tom's roommate, Al, not to abandon Tom, seems to indicate that she is well aware how easily sexuality and gender can be "spun":

LAURA: Al, what if I were to start the rumor tomorrow that you were—well, queer, as you put it?

AL: No one would believe it.

LAURA: Why not?

AL: Well, because—

LAURA: Because you're big and brawny and an athlete. What they call a top guy and a hard hitter?

AL: Well, yes.

LAURA: You've got something to learn, Al. I've been around a little, and I've met men, just like you—same setup—who weren't men, some of them married and with children. (47)

What Al gets from this conversation is not that anyone can be easily smeared but that he, like any other male, is always vulnerable to the accusation of homosexuality, an accusation he has determined to avoid by moving out and foregoing his friendship with Tom. He even asks Laura if she is threatening to malign him, which she denies.

Laura, in confronting her sadistic husband about his mistreatment of Tom, declares that, contra Bill, men are not capable of determining who is truly manly: "You men think you can decide on who is a man, when only a woman can really know" (83). When Bill counters, quite correctly, that Laura is attracted to boys rather than men, she proceeds to point out that what he persecutes in Tom is what he fears about himself (83–84). By suggesting that Bill is afraid that he has homosexual tendencies (which he has projected onto Tom), Laura reduces him to something less than a man—for she has met men "who weren't men." After Bill leaves, she offers herself physically to Tom as the curtain falls (88).

Yet Laura's supposed deep sympathy is hardly as pure as Anderson might wish it to be. She has a history that suggests that what makes boys different from men is what she finds attractive. Although Bill is all of 40 and she is in her 20s (7), what drew her to him was his own neediness and his willingness to allow himself to be seen by her as vulnerable (29). This has worn off by now, and Laura eventually deduces that he needed her as a cover for his own self-doubts or perhaps for his homosexuality. Bill becomes uncomfortable when Laura refers to John, her first husband, whom she compares to Tom: "He was just this age, eighteen or so, when I married him—We both were. And I know how this age can suffer. It's a heartbreaking time—no longer a boy—not yet a man" (28). Bill does not

wish to be identified with the troubled and gender-compromised young man
Laura married. She tells Tom of John:

> He was killed being conspicuously brave. He had to be con-
> spicuously brave, you see, because something had happened in
> training camp—I don't know what—and he was afraid the others
> thought him a coward. He showed them he wasn't. . . . In trying
> to prove he was a man, he died a boy. (66)

Her first husband was uneasy about his own manliness; she becomes skeptical of her second husband's manliness. She may claim not to know what
happened in training camp, but her clear identification of John with Tom
may tell the audience more than the playwright would wish us to know:
Laura is attracted to males who are sexually ambiguous, who differ from
the model of masculinity that Bill attempts to perform. She prefers to turn
boys into men, men who, from time to time, can act boyish. She is guilty
of what Bill alleges: "You were more interested in mothering that fairy up
there than in being my wife" (84). Sexual ambiguity, as Bill is well aware,
is not in the repertory of masculine performance, at least for men. Among
boys it is thought of as a phase, something "we all go through," so Laura,
perhaps not out of choice entirely, tends to seek out younger men.

L'école des hommes

Anderson's selection for Tom's upcoming role in a play is Lady Teazle in
The School for Scandal. The eighteenth-century comedy by Sheridan depicts
a London social scene ruled by gossip, most of it invented to embarrass
and shame others; Lady Teazle, a young country girl, who has recently wed
a much older gentleman, is a newcomer in the London drawing-rooms.
Here she learns the value of spreading scandal but ultimately abandons the
beau monde when she herself becomes the major topic of gossips. Anderson
probably had in mind the theme of smear-by-tale-telling as it related to
the play he was writing. Yet *Tea and Sympathy* might best be summed up
not by Sheridan's title but by one that Molière might have coined: "The
School for Men."

Of course, Molière had no need for such a title or play because in
his time, manliness was brilliantly and definitively performed by his patron,
Louis XIV. Yet in the postwar world of the early 1950s, who was there to
play the perfect prototype of masculinity? Harry Truman, Joseph McCarthy,
and Dwight Eisenhower were all somewhat troubling figures. Many of the
manly movie stars were getting older. It was almost as if those who came

of age after the war and who did not share in its experience had to be taught to be men. Or at least this is what the play implies. How then are boys to become men?

One obvious answer, endorsed by *Tea and Sympathy*, is that boys must be taught to be men. The play is of course set in a boy's school and features a variety of characters who expect Tom Lee to learn how to act like a man. Tom's father, Herb, brings up Tom's "problem" pointedly: "Why isn't my boy a regular fellow?" Herb feels Tom has been given "every chance" to be "regular": "boys' camps every summer, boarding schools. . . . He's always been with men and boys. Why doesn't some of it rub off?" (31). Herb's belief is that such homosocial institutions will teach his son how to act in a recognizably manly way.

Prior to Tom's arrival at this school, Herb advised him "to make friends slowly" and "to make sure they were the right kind of friends" (35). To meet these "right kind of friends," Herb did not demand that Tom "go out for sports like football, hockey" although that was where he would meet the "pretty good guys" (35–36). Tom, instead, played tennis, in which he did excel but not, according to Herb, in a manly way. "[H]e doesn't even play tennis like a regular fellow," Herb tells Laura. "No hard drives and cannon ball serves" (31). He adds to this evaluation an anecdote: After he watched Tom win a tennis championship, Herb overheard two men in the locker room decrying Tom's victory by saying of his opponent that he was "such a regular guy" (32).

What Tom lacks is not the ability to perform manly tasks but the style that would mark these actions as masculine. As Todd Reeser indicates, Judith Butler has described masculinity as a style (83), in spite of the fact that styles vary widely across cultures (84) and are thus obviously arbitrary markers of gender. Nonetheless, the practice is pervasive in our society: Just as one might characterize a piece of clothing, a room's décor, or an automobile as "masculine" or "feminine," one supposedly can recognize through a collection of stylistic elements the apparent gender of nongendered articles. Style of course constitutes an important part of any performance—even engendering what ought to be genderless.

Herb expects his old school chum, Bill, to coach Tom into manliness. Bill even says that Herb "put the boy in my house hoping I could do something with him" (25). Even Tom, who tells Laura about it, is aware of his father's expectations: "My father put me into this house two years ago, and when he left, he told your husband, 'Make a man of him.' He's failed, and he's mad" (69–70). Perhaps Herb has chosen the wrong mentor. Although in front of Herb, Bill seems willing enough to induct Tom into masculinity, as when he states that Tom has always been welcome to join his mountaineering expeditions (40), in reality Bill has always viewed Tom with suspicion. While getting the details from Tom regarding his failed attempt with the local tart, Ellie Martin, Bill is confronted by his own dislike for the boy: "You couldn't have stood it, could you if I'd proved you wrong?" Tom asks. "You'd made up your mind long ago, and it would have killed you, if I'd proved you wrong" (75). What Tom has been referring to is that Bill had decided Tom was "queer" long before the accusations were made, a fact that is made clear early in the play, when Bill argues with Laura about the validity of the claim that Tom and Harris were having sex. "Look at the way he walks, the way he sometimes stands," says Bill, as if offering clear evidence. (Having learned that these are what "give Tom away," Laura later asks Al to consider his own stance [47]; poised with his hands at his hips, he immediately changes pose.)

Most significantly, Bill's use of words, which in part probably derives from the school, betrays his prejudice. Even before the audience learns about the accusations against Harris and Tom, Bill refers to a boy in one of the other houses as a "regular" guy (23), the same adjective used repeatedly by Herb to describe what his son is not. In addition, Bill introduces Herb to another phrase, one that Bill first uses in describing Tom to Laura (26): "He's certainly an off-horse, Herb." Rather than feeling insulted by the phrase, Herb replies that it is "a good way of putting it" and that Tom will "have to learn to run with the other horses" (33).

Such a metaphor may bring to mind the glass unicorn from *The Glass Menagerie*, whose horn is broken off accidentally when Jim stumbles into a table. Laura Wingfield's hopeful interpretation is that this accident will make the creature's life better: "I'll just imagine he had an operation. The horn was removed to make him feel less—freakish. (. . .) Now he will feel at home with the other horses, the ones who don't have horns" (63; 226). Laura's allusion to the "operation" and a loss of "freakishness" come in the wake of Jim's attempt to make Laura's differences into positive instead of negative attributes, almost as if she herself, at least at the moment this remark is made, feels that she might be better off in a more traditional role (as Jim's wife). In *Tea and Sympathy*, however, Tom as a horse is not different—he is "off" and therefore inferior. In the world of manhood, at least as Bill understands it, conformity is everything.

The great irony, of course, is that the institutionalization of the homo-social does not exist independent of the homosexual but is rather one of several possibilities of male bonding of which the homosexual is yet another. Thus, Herb's expectation that being with other males will make his son less "queer" and more manly because Tom will learn to imitate them, is on one level quite absurd. As Reeser pointedly asks, "If gender itself is unstable, how can the sex reserved for identification and the sex reserved for desire remain separate?" (57). If Tom is to long to be like other males, what will keep his longing from becoming erotic? Certainly Bill, the paragon of active masculinity, is so infatuated with imparting what makes him manly to other males that his feelings for them become sexual. Because of this, Tom's "style" serves (as Laura has suggested) as both a blatant sign of a sexuality Bill must disown and as a contrasting mode of behavior that, through contrast, makes Bill seem "masculine."

If Bill refuses to teach Tom to be a man, Tom's peers at the school attempt to through mocking and ridicule. The name-calling, shunning, and physical violence may be construed, even by Bill and Herb, as a means to correct the boy's "negative" tendencies and to lead him into performing normative masculine behavior. Al, having been reproached and challenged by Laura for abandoning Tom, later suggests to Tom that he have his long hair cut (50) and change the way he walks; Al even demonstrates how to walk, but Tom is not capable of imitating him.[6] Aware finally that his physical deportment has made him an object of scorn, Tom complains, "Everything I've been doing all my life makes me look like a fairy" (51), thus exposing one of the central points in the play, that reading someone's gender as an absolute sign of his or her sexuality is wrong. Anderson even seems to acknowledge a few lines earlier the arbitrary nature of gender constructs, as Al explains, "I don't know the reasons for these things [what makes a crew cut manlier than long hair]. It's just the way they are" (50); in other words, what makes a male a man cannot be discussed rationally. Here, as elsewhere, the attribution of gender to a style of walking and a style of hair—which Al concedes seem to be illogical—nevertheless indelibly marks an individual's gender and by extension, his sexuality.

Thus comes Al's final suggestion to Tom, that he go visit the town slut. In this instance, Al is sure that the act itself, no matter what the style, will be sufficient to mark Tom as a man, and the visit will definitively demonstrate Tom's masculinity by defining him as heterosexual, which Tom supposedly is. Nevertheless, the ultimate teacher in *Tea and Sympathy* is the former actress, Laura. She fits Tom for the costume of Lady Teazle and tries to teach him to dance. She also overhears Tom's phone call to Ellie Martin (58). By attempting to prevent his visiting the notorious Ellie, Laura tries to teach Tom that an actual relationship with a female—in this case with her—is preferable to the mere physical sex act. Yet Tom's infatuation with Laura leads him to interpret her offering as sexual. When he actually embraces and kisses her—which her behavior has in effect prompted him to do—he is mortified by her apparent rejection (70).

Laura's motives are not entirely pure. She has gone beyond the tea and sympathy that she, as house mother, is supposed to dispense. Her involvement with Tom has been particularly complicated by her own dissatisfaction with her husband, who has ceased to behave in an affectionate manner, and with their sex life together, which she feels has lost any emotional intimacy (55). Laura is attracted to what makes males more than the traditional role of masculinity allows—a softness, a vulnerability, a neediness. These so-called boyish qualities drew Laura to Bill, and, as noted above, to her first husband. But what, according to Laura, did these two men and Tom need? A woman to verify their manhood? Just as Bill has seen Laura's influence on Tom as emasculating (25), Laura blames Bill and the homosocial network of boys and men at the school for Tom's final shame (81); from there, it is a short distance to accusing Bill of hiding homosexual tendencies. Yet this cruel remark, which brands Bill as much as he has branded Tom, is preceded by a statement that suddenly seems out of place in their conversation. In recounting for Bill her attempt to keep Tom from seeing Ellie, she tells her husband,

> I tried to stop him by being nice to him, by being affectionate. By showing him that he was liked—yes, even loved. I knew what he was going to do—and why he was going to do it. He had to prove to you bullies that he was a man, and he was going to prove it with Ellie Martin. Well—Well, last night—last night, I wished he had proved it with me. . . . I know what I should have done. I knew it then. My heart cried out for this boy in his misery—a misery imposed by my husband. And I wanted to help him as one human being to another—and I failed. At the last moment I sent him away. (82)

What would Tom have proven with Laura? As Laura puts it, "only a woman can really know" a man's true sexuality. She even declares to Bill, "This boy is more of a man than you are" (83). At this point, of course, Laura is talking speculatively.

Anderson stages the last, short piece of the play in Tom's tiny bedroom. Here, in this closet of a space into which he has withdrawn, Tom laments his realization that he must be a homosexual, a fate worse than, or perhaps merely tantamount to, death. Determined to prove him wrong, Laura tries to talk him out of this conclusion and out of his suicidal feelings. Unable to convince him, she leaves (86–87). In the end, however, she returns, opens her blouse to him, instructing him, "Years from now—when you talk about this—and you will—be kind." As the lights slowly dim out, she brings his hands toward her breasts (88).

This ending was, in 1953, considered sensational, and if we keep in mind the kind of media coverage and notoriety that has publicized affairs between adult female teachers and adolescent students more recently, we can derive a sense of why it was so powerful. Yet for the original audience, the age difference was perhaps less shocking than Laura's matrimonial state: She is married. In keeping with patriarchal beliefs, the very same beliefs that lead Herb at first to greet the news about his son's visit to the tart with happiness, which Anderson makes fun of (76–78), a young man was "lucky" to "get lucky" with an older woman, from whom he could "learn." Laura's position in the school and her pathology as it has been exposited and dramatized in the play, are never really a concern. Indeed, if we take into account what Laura tries to say in explanation, we find that the words do not express what she thinks they do: "I wanted to help him as one human being to another—and I failed." Yet Laura never really approaches Tom as one human being to another. She is an attractive woman with whom, she realizes, young Tom is desperately infatuated. Her attempts to control him are every bit as calculated as Lilly's control of the boys who ogle her—and much more serious. She sees Tom not as another "person" but as a gendered male, a boy-man who has yet to conform to the rigid construct of masculinity. She takes advantage of a situation that, as the play itself hints early on, could have ended with the polite rejection at the end of Candida by George Bernard Shaw (14). Yet intent on proving, in spite of his critique on gender roles, that heterosexuality is the only sexual game in town, Anderson must resist what makes Shaw's comedy so splendid—the notion that perhaps men and women really can be friends.

The Unspeakable and the Unmentionable

In its out-of-town, pre-Broadway tour, Tea and Sympathy played in New Haven, Connecticut, then Washington, D.C.[7] Before the production opened on the road, there was much publicity about the play, much on Deborah Kerr's debut on the New York (and American) stage. She had appeared in several films that had already been shown in the United States, and during the run of Anderson's hit, her film, From Here to Eternity, in which she also played an attractive, faithless wife, would open to great acclaim. As a female film star, Kerr's photographic image usually accompanied the publicity. Often she was pictured in a swimsuit, and under the photo an appreciative note from the masculine point of view would be appended. The West Coast gossip columnists and the New York theater writers mentioned her soon-to-be Broadway debut often. An adoring painting (tasteful but admiring) of her graced the pages of Esquire, in which she was "Lady Faire" of the month.

One of the early rumors about the play, in addition to Deborah Kerr being signed for it, concerned the legendary movie idol, Tyrone Power, who was said to be considering the role of Laura's husband. When these rumors subsided, it was announced that Leif Erickson, who had appeared in secondary film roles since the mid-1930s, would play Bill Reynolds. Certainly Erickson appeared to have the gruff, masculine looks that the part demanded, and yet one can only guess what Power might have brought to the production. In his prime, during the 1930s and 1940s, Power was a startlingly handsome leading man. By the time he would have played the role on Broadway, he had aged some, but he would have made Bill seem at least the equal of Mr. Harris. If Power had played Bill, the alienated, repressed homosexual might have seemed more attractive; the threat of male beauty to masculinity might have been more powerfully depicted. Yet playing a homosexual on stage was in 1953 a big risk, especially for a star like Power, who was always suspect because of his looks and his own sexual ambiguity (Power was later rumored to have had an affair with Errol Flynn). As it was, Erickson played Bill both on stage and in the film version, along with Deborah Kerr and, in the role of Tom, John Kerr.[8]

The studio that produced the film of *Tea and Sympathy*, which was released in 1956, struggled to convince the various organizations that monitored the movies that, as David Gerstner puts it, "the film would clearly punish the sexual transgression of the married woman, and that it would not overtly or covertly make any reference to homosexuality" (13). As incredible as that may sound, the project moved forward; by framing the story with a later plot, in which Tom Lee, now happily married and successful, returns to a school reunion and finds an apologetic letter from Laura awaiting him, the producers were able to persuade the censoring groups that the woman's "misdeed" would be seen as just that; and by excluding any direct references to homosexuality, the screenplay appeared to the Motion Picture Association of America, the Production Code Administration, and the Catholic Legion of Decency to have fulfilled their second requirement. Yet as Gerstner argues, the "film's structured silence" (14) on all things homosexual served in itself to imply just what these groups wanted to eradicate. As with the script of *The Glass Menagerie*, what was left unspoken spoke quite loudly. Also, asserts Gerstner, the film's director, Vincente Minnelli, himself a sometimes closeted, sometimes "out" homosexual, also used color to encode the theme of sexuality (16–17).

Gay historian Christopher Capozzola marked the fiftieth anniversary of the film's release with an essay, in which he speculates that "the very evasiveness" of *Tea and Sympathy* "may have been what gave its gay viewers a shield of generality behind which they could come to their own conclusions. The film's acts of denial made it possible to go see the movie without owning up to its obviously central theme—all the while knowing full well what it was about." Yet Capozzola sides with "gay critics [who] have been right to assault the use of homosexuality in 1950's theatre as mere metaphor, suited only for making a point about something else" (35). Nonetheless, the discrediting of pre-gay culture by post-Stonewall writers has for the last few decades ignored the actual affect of proto- or pre-gay plays from the 1950s. It may be important to admit that the play now seems dated, but at the same time *Tea and Sympathy* fascinatingly demonstrates what American culture was like at the time and to an extent shows how people who thought of themselves as gay fit and did not fit into it.

Indeed, while Noel Coward complained that the film version was "a mixture of naïveté and dishonesty . . . treated untruly and lasciviously" (qtd. Capozzola 35), the out-of-town theatre reviews of the original stage production generally hailed the play as an important new work. The Connecticut reviews refrained from referring directly to homosexuality: *The Journal Courier Register* avoided the subject entirely while *The Meriden Record* noted a "sexual aberration" and compared the play to *The Children's Hour* (and also to Terrence Rattigan's *The Winslow Boy*). In the nation's capital, only *The Sunday Star* revealed that Tom Lee was "accused of homosexual tendencies" although the Sunday *Washington Post* confirmed that Tom "is shown to be a heterosexual youth"; the same review indicated that play was about "a 'shocking subject," and *The Post*'s review in its daily edition made references to *The Children's Hour* and John van Druten's *Young Woodley*.[9] *The Times-Herald* went on about Deborah Kerr's wardrobe. *The Catholic Standard* mentioned "illicit relations." Only after *Tea and Sympathy* opened in New York did the Broadway critics use the "H" word more freely, and only then did the out-of-town reviews of the Broadway production follow suit. Still, some reviews from the provinces refrained from being too descriptive: *The Springfield Sunday Republican* said Tom "was accused of queer conduct"; *The Boston Sunday Globe* put out that Tom was rumored "not a real male." *The Columbus Citizen* indicated the accusation was about "unnatural sex tendencies." Many national magazines, such as *Newsweek*, which stated, "Tom isn't a sissy" and *Life*, which noted that he was "falsely accused of lacking masculinity," treaded carefully over what they obviously considered a societal land mine, and yet *The Saturday Review* and other weeklies brought themselves to use the dreaded term. If nothing more, these responses do illustrate not only that in 1953 homosexuality was considered in much of the United States as something one did not talk about but that the very word itself was forbidden. Once the New York City papers had included the word in reviews of the play, it was more easily used across the country.

Perhaps part of the play's influence on its original audiences is best explained by Giannino Malossi, whose main interest is in the style of male apparel and fashions but whose comments on clothing may be extended to masculine style as manifested throughout a culture:

There is a fragment of powerful truth in every male image that
does not correspond to the canons of male style, because each
of these images allows us to glimpse another possibility, more
or less improbable in reality but already visible in the world of
spectacle. (31)

To some degree, spectators who had never before seriously considered the
problems of gender conformity and the normative significance of heterosexuality might glimpse in Tom and the handsome young master possibilities that
were far beyond their range of experience; certainly this would explain why
gay audience members found the play reductive if not offensive.

In the spirit of the commercial theater, one might conclude that
indeed there is no bad publicity. Better to be spoken of negatively than
not to be spoken of at all. Thus when the love that dared not speak its
name was associated with a well-received hit on Broadway, the American
public's awareness of the topic and ability to discuss it, regardless of what
people said, was a substantial gain. One might very much prefer that *Tea
and Sympathy* were not such a homophobic play, much as one might prefer
that Dion Boucicault's *The Octoroon* were not such a racist play, but in both
cases, perhaps we are lucky that these plays came along at all if only because
they led to other plays. By this point in time, criticizing the very obvious
prejudices in both works is perhaps less productive than understanding how
they figured in the minds of their contemporaries.

There is one moment in *Tea and Sympathy* that readers and spectators
seem to ignore, one that still rings very true: In Act I, David Harris, the
good looking young master, climbs the stairs to Tom's room to speak with
him privately. Presuming that Tom has said something to the school authorities (when it was actually someone else who reported the two of them), he
closes the room's door. Tom, the stage directions inform us, "regards this
action with some nervousness" (18). Although Tom seems to be unaware
of the accusations that have been made and the possibility that Mr. Harris
is supposedly like the janitor whom Tom's aunt has warned him about, his
immediate response to Harris is spot on: Tom may not consciously know
about what has been alleged about him, but he is aware of Harris's good
looks (36). Tom's ability to relate to the world aesthetically is demonstrated
throughout the play. Perhaps he, like Bill, finds that on some level the handsome man evokes an aesthetic response that has troubling consequences.[10]

CHAPTER 3

Albee's Untold Story

The Aftermath of Male Youth and Beauty

Where Did the Beauty Go?

In September 1959, Samuel Beckett's short one-character one-act, "Krapp's Last Tape," was performed at Berlin's Schiller Theatre Workshop along with a work written the year before by an unknown American playwright. Both were performed in German. Edward Albee, whose *The Zoo Story* rounded out that program, had never before had a play produced; he had been encouraged by Thornton Wilder and Arthur Laurents to write drama and discouraged by William Inge, whose reactions to his early efforts were less than appreciative. Nonetheless, when this pair of plays opened the following January at what was perhaps the birthplace of the serious American one-act, The Provincetown Playhouse in Greenwich Village, they were greeted with great interest, great skepticism, and a certain amount of admiration.

At this time, Beckett was a world-renowned dramatist. His cryptic *Waiting for Godot*, which had created a sensation in both Paris and London, had received much praise, although not much box office, for its 1956 Broadway premiere. Clearly, the theaters that had sprung up around the old Provincetown were much better venues for the new experimental dramas from Western Europe. Even though Godot himself would still never have never made an entrance in one of the small, downtown playhouses that collectively had become known as "Off Broadway," the two tramps who awaited him would certainly have drawn more consistent crowds there, as had the characters of Bertolt Brecht, Jean Genet, Eugene Ionesco, Brendan Behan, and Fernando Arrabal. Indeed, *The Zoo Story*, despite being set uptown on the eastern edge of New York's Central Park, was more comfortably glimpsed among the works of the foreign avant-garde, which would soon be said to comprise the so-called Theater of the Absurd.[1]

Albee would write several more short pieces for America's fringe theater before his first full-length play *Who's Afraid of Virginia Woolf?* opened on Broadway in 1962. In all of these, except *The Zoo Story*, the image of youthful male beauty would be represented by a character. In "The Sandbox," there is a good-looking young man in a swimsuit and in "The American Dream," it is the handsome identical twin of an adopted child who has been mortally abused. The well-put-together intern in "The Death of Bessie Smith" and even the younger playwright in "Fam and Yam" (the older playwright is thought to be based on Inge), both represent youthful, attractive masculinity, as does the invented child of George and Martha, that all-American blue-eyed, blond-haired (or "blue-haired blond-eyed") boy, who, never having actually been born, appears all the more vividly in the imaginations of the characters and the audience. It is significant that Albee's initial stage work seems to lack such a characterization, that the visual spectacle of male beauty is, at least at first glance, absent from *The Zoo Story*.

Or is it really? Only after reading through the dialogue many times, did I bother to go back to the opening character descriptions offered by the playwright:

> PETER: A man in his early forties, neither fat nor gaunt, neither handsome nor homely. He wears tweeds, smokes a pipe, carries horn-rimmed glasses. Although he is moving into middle age, his dress and his manner would suggest a man younger.

> JERRY: A man in his late thirties, not poorly dressed but carelessly. What was once a trim and lightly muscled body has begun go to fat; and while he is no longer handsome, it is evident that he once was. His fall from physical grace should not suggest debauchery; he has, to come closer to it, a great weariness. (11)[2]

Thus, the conflict in *The Zoo Story*, is enacted between Peter, a character who is middling in appearance and in spite of his boyishness, entering "middle age," and Jerry, a character who was once but is no longer physically attractive. The image of young male beauty, then, is never fully personified in the play but merely alluded to: Youth and physical splendor are dramatized through their ruins. Thus, the seductive specter of the handsome father and son that haunts Tennessee Williams's *The Glass Menagerie* and the menace of the "good-looking young master" whose very presence proves the real danger of homosexual desire in Robert Anderson's *Tea and Sympathy*, no longer occupy the stage. Actual male beauty, like youth, has almost ceased to be necessary. Rather, its loss and the cultural meaning of that loss seem to be that to which the playwright is pointing.

Indeed, even some of Albee's representations of attractive manhood in his early works, when compared with the more developed characterizations of 1950s homosexual playwrights such as Williams and Inge, appear to be two-dimensional, well-developed bodies and handsome faces that have been emptied of emotion, gorgeous shells signifying nothing more than gorgeous shells, like the smiling, muscled models that adorned the pages of what were then called physique magazines, marketed and sold largely to homosexual males. The man in the swimsuit, the handsome twin, the blond intern, and the younger playwright are far less real than the invented son of George and Martha. Youthful male beauty, if not extinct, has been added to the endangered-species list.

An Encounter in Central Park

Jerry and Peter, as they are described and dramatized by Albee, are not entirely opposites, nor are they very much the same. Their great similarity of course is their sex, but a major difference between them is their gender: Although they are both males, their ways of being men diverge significantly. They both claim to be heterosexual, but the (hetero-)sexuality of one appears to be consistent with societal norms, whereas that of the other is, at least in contemporary cultural terms, deviant. The two also vary according to income, social and familial status, background, and (we must assume, because we only hear about Jerry's) upbringing.

This Peter is (as is the Peter in the New Testament)[3] the "rock" upon which all—in this case, American society—is supposedly founded: husband and father of two daughters, family provider and owner of animals, albeit two birds and two cats, a "real" man, a patriarch who goes into the real world to earn real money and who carries real responsibilities. In a sense, Peter's place in the universe is as deserved as his seat on the Central Park bench to where he has retreated on this Sunday afternoon to read his newspaper; indeed, by the end of the play Peter is fighting to defend both. Jerry, however, seems to be the lone, rootless, unconnected wanderer who has strayed from the straight and narrow path. To some degree, his restive anger and intelligence are reminiscent of the Beat Generation, whom Tom Wingfield anticipates and to which Tom Lee—if perhaps he possessed a little more chutzpah—might have belonged, and yet by the time Jerry appears on stage, the Beats have become an object of laughter for conformist America, the bearded good-for-nothings who are wild and harmless and terribly peculiar—the "beatniks."

Like *The Glass Menagerie*, *The Zoo Story* offers a series of references to what would soon be construed as gay experience. "I don't like the west side of the park much," Jerry says early in the play (14). Later, when Peter feels threatened and mentions he will "call a policeman," Jerry clarifies, "You won't find a policeman around here; they're all over the west side of the park chasing fairies down from the trees or out of the bushes" (43). During his initial interrogation, Jerry deduces that Peter is married. "You're married!" he declares, to which Peter "([w]*ith pleased emphasis*)" answers, "Why, certainly"; "It isn't a law" Jerry retorts (15). Jerry also insinuates that he gets groped by men, probably in the movie theater (17), probably one of those on Forty-Second Street (33). After Jerry describes his route uptown from Greenwich Village, Peter infers, knowingly, "Oh; you live in the Village! (*This seems to enlighten PETER*)" (21). Unwilling to be pigeonholed, how-ever, Jerry refutes the obvious implication about his sexual identity. Soon, Jerry reveals that he lives in a boarding house off Central Park West and that his room is divided by a wall (of "beaverboard") to make two rooms, the second of which has been taken by "a colored queen who always keeps his door open; well, not always, but *always* when he's plucking his eye-brows . . ." (22). Later he likens toilet paper to a mirror: "always check for bleeding" (34). The references to the Rambles in Central Park, the societal preference toward heterosexual coupling, sex between men in Times Square cinemas, the gay haven of the Village, transvestitism, and rectal bleeding do not necessarily signify that Jerry is a homosexual; rather they expose his familiarity with contemporary "gay" experience, something of which Peter denies firsthand knowledge.

Jerry's description of his own sexuality seems to elude Peter's defini-tions. Although Jerry claims to be heterosexual—"oh, do I love the little ladies"—his inability to "make love to anybody more than once" suggests his lack of intimacy in the sexual act: "I love the little ladies; really, I love them. For about an hour." He offers one exception to this pattern:

> [F]or a week and a half, when I was fifteen [. . .] I was a h-o-m-o-s-e-x-u-a-l. I mean, I was queer . . . (*Very fast*) . . . queer, queer, queer . . . with bells ringing, banners snapping in the wind. And for those eleven days, I met at least twice a day with the park superintendent's son . . . a Greek boy, whose birthday was the same as mine, except he was a year older. I think I was very much in love . . . maybe just with sex. But that was the jazz of a very special hotel, wasn't it? (25)

Such an admission, with its deliberate ironies, goes far beyond the strategy of ambiguous reference; indeed it far surpasses the frankness of discourse in what was then thought to be a terribly frank play about sexuality, *Tea and Sympathy*. Not only is the unnamable named, both clinically and colloquially, but the character who names it applies it (and not in a negative way) to himself.

At the same time, the audience in 1960 must have found it difficult to understand Jerry's disclosures about his sexuality as anything other than aberrant or perverse. Even if spectators, regardless of their individual sexualities, found the notion of homosexuality as acceptable as that of heterosexuality (which at the time was rare enough, even among homosexuals), Jerry shows himself to be problematic, not merely deviant but broken. In contemporary psycho-babble, he might have been characterized or caricatured as the suppressed homosexual, whose refusal to admit his "genuine" attraction to members of his own sex resulted in his brief, seemingly forced encounters with members of the opposite sex, not unlike Laura's husband, Bill, in Anderson's play. Homosexual sexuality was generally regarded as a state of "arrested" development: A male who would normally go through adolescence with some sexual interest in members of his own sex but never "developed" beyond that, was said to be stuck in a "non-adult" and thereby "immature" state.

Certainly, Jerry might have been construed by a large part of the audience as an aging adolescent, an overgrown teenager who refused to "grow up," who, like the Beats, continued to rebel long after they had reached an age when the behavior of adulthood was "appropriate," "normal," and like the Beatniks was rather ludicrous. Peter represents the norm that Jerry resists: Although Jerry's fading good looks reflect the retreat of beauty that cannot be stopped by an ongoing adolescent rebellion, Peter's "dress and manner," which "suggest a man younger," remind the audience that the boy is supposedly destined to grow into the man. Such contradictions inherent in the characters in *The Zoo Story*, however, seem to have eluded the majority of reviewers of the original production.

Many of the reviewers reduced Peter to "normal" and most descriptions of him were either neutral or positive. Whitney Bolton in *The Morning Telegraph* called him "an indrawn, family locked, habit-formed man of distinction."[4] In *The World-Telegram and the Sun*, Frank Aston deemed him a "slight, bookish looking man." *The Journal American*'s John McClain noted he is "a conventional young man from the East Side"; *The Daily News*'s Charles McHarry, "a successful young publishing executive"; the *Variety* critic ("Burm.") echoed, "a sophisticated publishing executive." *The Post*'s Richard Watts Jr., described Peter as "a harmless young man," and *Women's Wear Daily* L.D.K. simply as "a businessman" and a "'square.'" John Beaufort in *The Christian Science Monitor* viewed him as a "bourgeois," whereas Brooks Atkinson in *The Times* saw him as "as a cultivated, complacent publisher" although less than two weeks later, he would revise this judgment to "a mild, composed intellectual." *The Herald Tribune*'s Walter Kerr managed to construe Peter negatively, regarding him as "the well-pressed modern man" and a "secure little pedant who would be at home anywhere within hailing distance of Madison Avenue."

Jerry was more difficult for the critics to characterize. The tendency was to reduce him to a simple categorical title. Several reviewers felt him to be yet another manifestation of the Beat generation. Kerr, for example, referred to him as a "beatnik," as did McHarry in *The Daily News*, Beaufort in *The Christian Science Monitor*, and Herbert Whitaker in *The Globe and Mail*. (*Women's Wear Daily*'s critic called the whole play "a 'beat'-oriented Grand Guignol tale.") Several others did the same but in different words: McClain in *The Journal American* described "an entirely unconventional man from the West Side," whereas *Newsday*'s George Oppenheimer wrote of "a young, unkempt, undisciplined vagrant, . . . the rebel . . . the young savage." *Variety* mentioned both a "volatile youth" and a "tortured youth."

The other view was to pathologize Jerry, to view him as emotionally troubled or mentally out of control. Atkinson, in his first review in *The Times*, described "[a]n intense, aggressive young man," which he revised into "an aroused, bitter, lonely young man who feels himself dispossessed by life." Watts in *The Post* characterized Jerry as "a dangerous" young man, Bolton in *The Telegraph* as a "strange, thrusting, unpredictable young man," and Aston in *The World-Telegram and The Sun* as "a hulking stranger" and "a sensitive man." A few suggested that he was clinically ill: Jerry Tallmer in *The Village Voice* records "a rabid young psychotic" and *Cue* called Jerry a "psychopath." Two writers—L.D.K. in *Women's Wear Daily* and Burm. in *Variety*—described Jerry not as an actual character based on a person but as a creation pulled from the writings of Tennessee Williams, who was thought to specialize in disturbed characters. (Burm. and Kerr threw in William Saroyan as well.) In *The Journal American*, McHarry implied that Williams was an influence here, insisting that George Maharis in the role of Jerry showed more talent than any actor since Marlon Brando debuted in Williams's *A Streetcar Named Desire*.

The repeated use of the word "young" to describe both characters reflects the original production's casting, for both actors were and thus appeared far more youthful than Albee intended. As impressive as the two performances were said to be (and there was much praise for them), they could not escape being seen as men in the first part of their lives rather than men who were entering middle age. In the case of Jerry, the majority of New York critics attributed his problems to his generational separation from Peter; only a few blamed his actions on mental illness.

None of the reviewers directly mentioned Jerry's admission of homosexuality. L.D.K notes that Jerry "is trying to escape from a world of poverty, loneliness and sexual perversion," but no one came any closer. Curiously, the same writer who branded Jerry "a rabid young psychotic," points out the same-sex theme of *The Zoo Story* as he is decrying the play. Although Jerry Tallmer in *The Village Voice* praises the first half of the bill (the production of "Krapp's Last Tape" is "inspired, inspirited, perfect"), his loathing of Albee's play is unmistakable. To an extent his dislike is based on the implausibility and contrivance of the plot, for, he contends, it is not believable that a real person like Peter would merely sit on the bench and allow Jerry to intimidate him; a real person would simply get up and leave. Still the play's message, which he sees as "murder is communication," infuriates him as well. There is even the suggestion that Tallmer despises Albee himself: "a young Villager, and comer" who "knows how to handle situation and dialogue and bring you up deftly to the edge of your seat," but "[w]hether he has anything less sick than this to say remains to be seen." While describing the climax of the play, the reviewer reflects, "We have reached the only, and violent, means of communication between sexes (sorry, one sex) . . ."

Here, less than a decade before the arrival of "Gay Liberation," the assault on Albee, the homosexual, is launched. As Stephen Bottoms indicates in *Albee: Who's Afraid of Virginia Woolf?*, at the time "Albee's homosexuality was an open secret in New York's artistic circles . . ." (101). And as in at least one other case—the 1942 review of Jean Cocteau's *The Typewriter* by fascist critic Lucien Rebatet (Krauss, *The Drama of Fallen France* 16, 22, 34)—the negative critic may be the only writer who dares point to the unspeakable.

As Things Were

The homophobic innuendo in Jerry Tallmer's 1960 *Village Voice* review emerges in a more developed form eight years later in William Goldman's *The Season*, a tell-all study of the New York theater scene that covers all the productions that were destined for Broadway between fall 1967 and spring 1968.[5] Candid, frank, and often downright nasty, Goldman was uniquely independent; because he would be reviewing for only one season in a book to be published at a later time, his discussions are sometimes more outspoken than those of contemporary theater critics, who were often limited by their publishers' editorial policies and ongoing relationships with the professional theater industry. Among the various topics covered in his book, readers will find a snapshot of how homosexuality was perceived as figuring in the world at large and in the world of the New York stage a year or two before the Stonewall riots. Indeed, the very first review is of Judy Garland's show at The Palace, complete with descriptions of its very queer audience (3–13). Throughout his commentaries on Broadway fare, Goldman

occasionally glances in the direction of off- and off-off Broadway and several
times praises Mart Crowley's production of *The Boys in the Band,* a play that
was revolutionary in its direct depictions of homosexuals. Never does he
use the word "gay" in its gay (or ought I say, post-Stonewall?) connotation.

Goldman in 1968, however, was hardly alone in condemning Albee
and other homosexual playwrights. In what John M. Clum calls a "jeremi-
ad against *Who's Afraid of Virginia Wool?*" published in *The Tulane Drama
Review,* Richard Schechner complained, "I'm tired of morbidity and sexual
perversity which are there only to titillate an impotent and homosexual
theater and audience. I am tired of Albee" (144).[6] Clum points as well to
The Times's critic Howard Taubman's 1963 cautionary article offering "[h]
elpful hints on how to scan the intimations and symbols of homosexuality
in our theater" (142). Even novelist Phillip Roth, Clum adds, incensed by
Tiny Alice in 1965, called the drama "a homosexual daydream" and mocked
the play's "own unwillingness to put its real subject [ie, homosexuality] at
the center of the action" (145). Clum provides further examples from 1960s
critics who furiously charged that the work of Albee and others on and off
Broadway was disingenuous (145–149), as do Michael Bronski (124–128)
and David Savran (*Communists, Cowboys, and Queers* 136–137). So Goldman in 1968 found himself in what seemed the best of company.

As a heterosexual Jew (Goldman admits to the latter outright and
repeatedly implies the former), his notions about sexuality and gender are
extremely illustrative of how an educated and experienced theatergoer who
was not gay might think. In addition to Judy's fans, he singles out the prem-
ise of J.J. Coyle's unsuccessful sex farce, *Ninety-Day Mistress* ("the notion of
constantly changing partners because it gets so dull if you don't is basically
a homosexual one" [61]), the tendency of some critics to like "homosexual
plays" and others to hate them (78–79), and the plot of Tennessee Williams's
The Seven Descents of Myrtle, in which a transvestite marries "a moronic
stripper in order to deprive his animalistic brother of their mother's estate"
(96). "Homosexual playwrights," Goldman asserts, ". . . are frequently at
their most perceptive when dealing with women, particularly older ones:
they understand them better; they care more for them" (79).

However, Goldman uses Edward Albee's adaptation of Giles Cooper's
Everything in the Garden as his opportunity to discuss more fully homosexuality and homosexuals within contemporary American culture. The review
begins with what appears to be an objective summary of this black comedy's
action: A middle-class housewife, who, along with her husband, is experiencing financial problems, is approached by an enterprising woman who offers
her a lucrative job as a call girl. The couple's financial success leads to a
house party in which they discover that their upwardly mobile neighbors

are doing the same, prospering through the wife's prostitution. The teen-age son of the first couple, back from his liberal prep school, objects to the prejudiced language of his parents and their guests. Later, when an alcoholic bachelor who lives next door wanders in, figures out the set up, and is about to expose them, the husbands and the enterprising women murder him (233–234). Then, Goldman's reductive conclusions are suddenly unleashed:

> This play makes three central statements:
>
> 1. All wives are whores.
>
> 2. All husbands are panderers.
>
> 3. The only wisdom lies with bachelors and young boys.
>
> In other words, *Everything in the Garden* is as clear a statement of the homosexual mystique as one could hope to find. (234–235)

What follows is an extraordinary and yet totally comprehensible set of con-clusions that reveal contemporary rationalizations about sexuality in general and about homosexuality in particular.

The problem for the homosexual, argues Goldman is that he must remain covert. Many homosexuals in show business are protected by con-venient marriages and families, but their true identities are known or sus-pected by theater insiders. Without explicitly condemning homosexuals, he sets about to expose them, not by naming them (at least directly), but by revealing their roles in the Broadway scene. Although he indicates that "the homosexual doesn't have to hide quite as much as he once did," he concedes that the current situation has not yet reached a point when a homosexual "writer or performer can come out and admit it; but dissembling is on the decline" (235). Later he adds, "the homosexual on Broadway, especially the playwright, has to dissemble: he writes boy–girl relationships when he really means boy-boy relationships" (238). Embittered by the ostracism of society at large (which is for Goldman naturally heterosexual) and the ban on his writing about his own sexuality, the homosexual playwright inevitably

> treats heterosexuals viciously. The married couples hate each other; the woman, with whom the homosexual tends to identify, is either a gentle dreamer destroyed by an insensitive man, or a destroyer herself. And the man is either a stupid stud, hot for a quick roll in the hay, or a weak, contemptible failure. (239)

Thus, the gay dramatist is not only vindictive toward the enforced subject matter, but (to make it even worse) is quite alienated from it.

As if the generalized references in the above quote were not emphatic enough, Goldman cites Williams's most recent failure (which he has already ridiculed), *The Seven Descents of Myrtle*. A "crucial speech," he tells us, "is spoken by a crude animal male, and the gist . . . is that nothing exists . . . as good, as meaningful, as fine, as perfect, as what can happen between a man and a woman" (239). (The description of this speech bears an interesting resemblance to a famous line from Williams's *A Streetcar Named Desire*, to what Stella, who has the night before been beaten by her husband, tells Blanche, who is trying to make her leave the wife beater: "But there are things that happen between a man and a woman in the dark—that sort of make everything else seem—unimportant" [321]). The statement, asserts Goldman, is not about the joys of marriage or love but about the sex act itself (239–240), and this idea, he implies, as he has done earlier, only a homosexual would propound. This leads directly into his championing Crowley's *Boys in the Band* as "a terrific homosexual play" (240). The direct insult to Albee comes at the end of the book: "those first acts of *Virginia Woolf* are marvelous bitch dialogue—not as good as Mart Crowley's bitch dialogue in *The Boys in the Band*—but still marvelous. That is the extent of Albee's skill: he writes good bitch dialogue" (411). Goldman seems unaware of the role Albee himself played in the creation of Crowley's successful script, but even so, his ultimate judgment appears to be that homosexual playwrights should write about what they really know about (i.e., homosexuals) and not about heterosexuals.

In addition to the patronizing language that Goldman uses, his points are made in a context of what may best be described as "pre-Stonewall gay panic." He explains gay men through stereotypical roles and figures—"the fashion business . . . provides a homosexual sanctuary" and "Princess [Lee] Radziwill . . . is rarely without a homosexual, and her sister, Jacqueline Kennedy has her court homosexuals too" (235)—and details how *Time* is not especially friendly to homosexuals while *Newsweek* apparently is, as is the "homosexually oriented" *New York Times* Sunday entertainment section, whose "most celebrated Sunday expert is a famous homosexual" (236). He goes on to talk about gender confusion on a societal level, about ambisexuality and cultural icons such as Rudolf Nureyev, Tiny Tim, Twiggy, and Baby Jane Holzer and Andy Warhol (236–237). Homosexuals, he warns, have a pervasive influence.

Citing *The New York Times Sunday Magazine* section, Goldman attests that the number of homosexual males in America is four million—an incredibly low estimate when the population of the United States was in the vicinity of two-hundred million (237). (Perhaps the *Magazine* section was not as "homosexually oriented" as the entertainment section.) But "homosexuals, like any minority, tend to cluster: it's easier for them; there is less resistance to them; the tensions are fewer" (235). And one of the places they cluster is in the theater. After assigning statistical numbers to homosexuals involved in the 1967–1968 season ("at least 18, or 31%, [of the total number of 58 productions] were produced by homosexuals [and] . . . at least 22, or 38%, were directed by homosexuals"), he calculates approximately "anywhere from a third to a half of the producer-director talent is homosexual" although the "percentage among the playwrights seems somewhat less, but in general more famous playwrights tend to be associated with homosexuality" (237), except for Arthur Miller, who (among the postwar generation) is "the only Jew" (238).

Amid this tantalizing homosexual conspiracy lurking in the culture and thriving on Broadway, Goldman allows that "homosexuals lead a terribly difficult life," but then undermines this idea with the following "support":

> One homosexual may complain that it is frustrating beyond mea-
> sure when, returning from a long trip, he cannot embrace his
> "wife" at the airport, but must go through the frustrating hypo-
> critical gesture of a handshake. This kind of talk may be upset-
> ting to us (we don't like to think about "that kind of thing"),
> but it often sends homosexuals into genuine despair. They are
> mulattoes in an all-white neighborhood, and it isn't easy. (238)

The trivialization through this example diminishes the actual prejudice and persecution of gay people in the 1960s and at the same time invokes the norm ("upsetting to us," "we don't like to think about 'that kind of thing'") as straight. Hence, the gay man's partner must be compared with the heterosexual's wife. The "racial" comparison ("Mulattoes in an all-white neighborhood") is obviously racist and inappropriately drawn.

Yet Goldman's most revealing statement appears in his illustration of just how friendly *Newsweek* is to homosexuals:

> Another example, and one that probably is insidious: *Newsweek*
> ran an article on men's jewelry and asked the question whether
> the wearing of it was effeminate. The answer they printed came
> from a movie star who said "no," of course it was not effeminate,
> it was fine to wear it. But the movie star whom *Newsweek* chose
> to quote is an internationally known homosexual. If everybody in
> show business knows it, surely *Newsweek* must have known it, so

> quoting a homosexual as proof that the wearing of jewelry by men
> is a normal masculine act has to be called a bit suspect. (236)

How "insidious" of the magazine to quote a queer movie star. As a homosexual, he would have no knowledge of whether or not wearing jewelry
was "effeminate" for a male. What would someone known to be queer be
able to contribute to a conversation on gender roles—especially a film actor
who played heterosexual male roles on film? After all, Goldman reminds us,
homosexuals can know nothing about "a normal masculine act."

If *The Boys in the Band* seems to speak more directly from a homosexual playwright's experience, Goldman's ideas here contradict the notions
he brings to the fore within this same chapter. He argues, for instance, that
Arthur Miller is the only postwar dramatist who is Jewish, but how many of
Miller's plays could be called "Jewish" plays? Or for that matter, how many
of Lillian Hellman's? Or William Goldman's? (I don't remember any Jewish
characters in *The Lion in Winter*, which was written by Goldman's brother,
James, although I do recall a homosexual relationship between Richard the
Lionhearted and a French prince.) Yet homosexuals, Goldman maintains,
would be better off writing homosexual plays? The ghettoization of homosexuals and their clannishness, which this straight Jewish writer ironically
accepts as the way things are, inspire in him fear and therefore must be
reduced to an understandable byproduct of life in general, the same generalized life in which biracial people try to pass for white. Indeed, "mulatto"
is a hangover from the slave-owning vocabulary of the South, in which it
was followed, through multiples of two, then four, to quadroon and then
octoroon. Such language articulates a worldview in which homosexuals (not
unlike African Americans) must not be included in the pronouns "we" and
"us." Goldman's late 1960s liberalism accepts the way the world is when it
comes to homosexuals.

"I don't know or care what Tennessee Williams's sexual preferences
are" (239) Goldman proclaims, but of course this assertion belies everything
else mentioned in his book. Indeed, the very chapter in which he states his
insouciance could not have been written if he did not "know or care" about
Albee's, and for that matter Williams's and Inge's, "sexual preferences." The
boundaries of sexuality seem even stricter than those of race: At least Goldman admits that someone could be part "black" and part "white." The exis-
tences of bisexuals and masculine homosexuals appear to be inconceivable.[7]

Ironically, Albee's attempts to explore the complexity and expose the
diversity of different performances and/or styles of masculinity was reduced
by "normal"—middle-class white male heterosexual—critics in the very simplified binaries that the playwright was trying to problematize.

Unraveling "The Story"

Critics often look to the title of Albee's first play and remark that Jerry never actually tells Peter the story of what happened at the zoo. Instead, many observe, Jerry offers a very lengthy account of his attempts to relate to his landlady and her dog. A number of contemporary reviewers refer to the play itself as a frame for the extended monologue. Yet the *The Zoo Story* is neither Jerry's prolonged rant about the woman and the dog (which he even entitles, "THE STORY OF JERRY AND THE DOG" [30]) nor yet another story left untold; it is of course the title of the play itself: *The Zoo Story*, as its name implies, is the play's story of how modern urban life transpires in a landscape where human animals are locked into unnatural enclosures, such as Peter's upscale flat, with wife, children, two televisions, and potentially antagonistic pets, and Jerry's divided space in a shabby rooming house. Moreover, the boundaries surrounding these enclosures are buttressed by even more powerful walls of class, income, education, social status, race, and—obviously—gender and sexuality. Although many others have focused on very different aspects of this play, I would like to reread the script with that final pair of blockades in mind.

Earlier I discussed how Jerry's sexuality diverged from Peter's. Indeed, the two may seem opposites. Whereas Peter's reflects a sexuality that embodies responsibility, fidelity, longevity, and normality, Jerry's discloses one of utter unreliability, continuous promiscuity, transience, and deviance. Yet what is similar in the seemingly opposed ways in which they are sexual is that both sexualities connect with signs of male masculinity. Clearly, the power of gender performance derives from its claims to articulate unambiguously the characteristics of one sex or the other. Without the binary "one sex or the other," gender performance loses much of its significance and potency. The role of the steady, caring patriarch is no more definitive of maleness than the carefree libertine; despite Goldman's allegation that "the notion of constantly changing partners because it gets so dull if you don't is basically a homosexual one" (61), there is an extensive history of male figures whose masculinity is valorized by their "constantly changing their sexual partners"—indeed, the names of two are so well known that they have made it into the English language to mean libertine: Don Juan and Casanova. The masculinity of a number of male movie stars (Errol Flynn, Clark Gable, Burt Lancaster) resided in their numerous conquests.

Yet in 1950s America, the quasi-Freudian interpretation of human behavior in modern civilization decreed that faithful marriage and siring children were the unmistakable markers of mature masculinity. The complex sexualities of Don Juan and Casanova were thus reduced to immaturity, and there was even the rationalization that the unappeasable womanizer was in fact a repressed homosexual. Nonetheless, as the 1950s passed and well into the 1960s, the image of the virile seducer, perhaps best represented by Hugh Heffner's *Playboy* magazine and its resultant franchises, thrived. Thus, rather than antithetical, the sexualities represented or, perhaps more appropriately, enacted by Peter and Jerry are competing.

Previously I suggested, contrary to Goldman, that the genuine nature of masculinity would be more apparent to a homosexual film star who on screen always played the role of "masculine" and heterosexual men; certainly such an actor would be more acutely aware of how men performed as masculine and heterosexual than an actor who was unaware of what masculine and heterosexual performance was all about, if only because his own behavior already conformed to cultural norms and he believed his "masculinity" came "naturally." The reality, as demonstrated by such Hollywood celebrities as Rock Hudson or Van Johnson, was that many males who might not be considered masculine or heterosexual off screen could easily adapt for the camera. So who was there better than a homosexual playwright for a discussion of two competing roles thought to embody masculinity?

The two characters in *The Zoo Story* compete to demonstrate who is more masculine—not who is more of a male than the other, but rather who is more of a man. This occurs in the first part of the play, in which Jerry interrogates Peter and along the way Jerry makes several startling revelations about himself. Jerry's questions and reactions seem to be more the focus of the action, but Peter (like his place in the world—his masculinity) is far better known to a 1960 audience, even a 1960 off-Broadway audience, than Jerry. For this reason, Albee gives Jerry far more to say and do than the "organization" man "in the gray flannel suit" who is quietly reading *The Sunday Times* on the park bench. (I wonder if Goldman would find it revealing if Peter was reading the entertainment section.)

Jerry's cross-examination about Peter's family and home life leads to Jerry's previously quoted statement that it "isn't a law, for God's sake" that one has to get married (15) but also to his queries about Peter's offspring:

JERRY: And you have children?

PETER: Yes; two.

JERRY: Boys?

PETER: No, girls . . . both girls.

JERRY: But you wanted boys.

PETER: Well . . .naturally, every man wants a son, but . . .

JERRY: *(Lightly mocking.)* But that's the way the cookie crumbles.
(15–16)

Every male wants a male child, admits Peter; Jerry's mocking tone implies
that Peter is less of a man for having female children. Even as Peter resents
Jerry's rather insulting innuendoes, he goes on to confide that, as Jerry has
insinuated, Peter's wife has made having a son impossible (16–17). Peter is
further diminished as a man by his choice of pets:

JERRY: . . . Hmm, no dogs? *(PETER shakes his head, sadly)* But
you look like an animal man. CATS! *(PETER nods his head
ruefully)* Cats! But, then, that can't be your idea. No, sir. Your
wife and daughters? *(PETER nods his head)* Is there anything
else I should know?

PETER: *(He has to clear his throat.)* There are . . . there are two
parakeets. One . . . uh . . . one for each of my daughters.

JERRY: Birds.

PETER: My daughters keep them in a cage in their bedroom.

JERRY: Do they carry disease? The birds. (17–18)

The illogical assignment of gender to animals—dogs are masculine, cats
and birds are feminine—is obviously understood and accepted by Peter. It
is shameful for him to admit that his house pets are "female" cats, chosen
by his wife and daughter, and (evidently worse still), "female" birds that
live in a cage within his daughters' room. Jerry's final nasty quip, clarifying
what is not, for Peter or the audience, grammatically ambiguous, implies
that Peter's female children are disease ridden and that he is the master of
contaminated (perhaps because feminine) goods.

As the questioning continues, Jerry asks Peter to define the boundary
between "upper middle-middle-class and lower upper middle-class," to tell
him whether or not bewilderment is responsible for his patronizing tone
(20), and to name his favorite authors. After listening to Peter's pompous,
middle-brow response to this literary question, Peter interrupts, "Skip it."
At the same time, he begins to *"move about the stage with slowly increasing
determination and authority, but pacing himself, so that the long speech about the
dog comes at the high point of the arc."* This crescendo of territorial takeover

and the climax of the play have already been announced by Jerry earlier: "I'll start walking around in a little while, and eventually I'll sit down." Now, as he begins to wander about to claim the playing space, he recounts his trip to Central Park, how he "took the subway down to the village so I could walk all the way up Fifth Avenue to the zoo. It's one of those things a person has to do; sometimes a person has to go a very long distance out of his way to come back a short distance correctly" (21). The geographical references hold a metaphoric resonance: If the shortest distance between two points is a straight line, the easiest way to reach the eastside of Central Park would be to cross the park from west to east. Jerry, however, has avoided the park's western edge and traveled all the way downtown in order to march directly north (against the downtown flow of traffic) to where Peter now sits. In other words, Jerry's trek has been a deliberate progress up Fifth Avenue, past the rising numbers of side streets, a "straight" march, not direct but rather "correct."

Peter's misinterpretation of Jerry's journey—his need to believe that Jerry is a Greenwich Villager—prompts Jerry's long speech about where he does live (22). The rooming house, with its small cells and captive inhabitants, sounds far more zoo-like than Peter's apartment, which Jerry has already intimated is a menagerie in its own right. As if to answer his previous (and unanswered) question to Peter, regarding the placement of dividing lines between segments of the middle-class, Jerry recites a list of his meager possessions, suggesting, among other things, his poverty and isolation. Jerry confesses a family history filled with abandonment and loss (23–24), a "terribly middle-European joke" (24) he calls it with Jewish or Slavic irony. Jerry then steers the conversation into his own sexuality, his past homosexuality (25), his deck of pornographic playing cards (26), and then back to the zoo and what happened there (27), but instead of telling "The Zoo Story," Jerry launches into the prologue of the story of "JERRY AND THE DOG" (27–29). As indicated previously, this story is not merely about Jerry and the landlady's dog but includes the landlady herself:

> A fat, ugly, mean, stupid, unwashed, misanthropic, cheap, drunken bag of garbage. . . . [S]he leans around in the entrance hall, spying to see that I don't bring in things or people, and when she's had her afternoon pint of lemon-flavored gin she always stops me in the hall, and grabs ahold of my coat or my arm, and she presses her disgusting body up against me. . . . The smell of her body and breath . . . you can't imagine it. . . . (27–28)

Jerry's disgust for the landlady is easily shared by Peter: "disgusting . . . horrible . . . unthinkable. I find it hard to believe such as that really *are*." In his "[l]ightly mocking tone," Jerry retorts, "It's for reading about, isn't it? . . . And fact is better left to fiction" (28–29). What follows is the story that consumes the central section of the play.

Jerry's remarks, however, may be more apropos than Peter (a pub-lisher) thinks, for the audience never really knows for certain whether or not Jerry is a reliable narrator. Did the face off between himself and the landlady and dog actually take place or is it fictive? We never actually find out, and perhaps it hardly matters, for the story is told to communicate something to Peter that cannot otherwise be uttered. As Jerry has put it earlier, "sometimes a person has to go a very long distance out of his way to come back a short distance correctly" (20). Perhaps the story Jerry tells is the out-of-the-way long distance that Jerry must go before coming back on the shorter, more "correct" path.

The extensive monologue is revealing: In order to enter his building and climb up to his room, he must pass not only the horrific, desirous land-lady but also her enormous dog, who is often in the entryway waiting on his own. That the dog is actually a male, not merely a masculinized canine, is made all the more emphatic by the fact that he "almost always has an erection" (30). Every day, the dog pursues Jerry across the lobby to the stairs, until Jerry finally makes up his mind to confront the animal (30–31). "I'll kill the dog with kindness, and if that doesn't work . . . I'll just kill him," says Jerry—a remark that makes Peter wince. And so, instead of going after the repellant female human (whom he can humor), Jerry chooses to make contact with the virile male animal. His "killing with kindness" requires Jerry to buy a package of hamburgers, which he sets down in the hall. The first time that this occurs, the dog "ate all the hamburgers, almost all at once, making sounds in his throat like a woman." This sudden effeminacy is followed by the dog smiling. "I think he smiled; I know cats do" (31), observes Jerry. In the language of the play, the attempted appeasement makes the macho dog womanly, like a feminized cat, and the creature, as if to assert its masculinity must continue his attack on the man who has turned him into the opposite sex.

For after the gift has been devoured, the dog turns and pursues him to the stairs. This is repeated over five successive days (31–32). Having tried unsuccessfully to make the dog love him, Jerry resolves to kill him. After purchasing rat poison, Jerry goes to buy the hamburgers and asks the man selling them not to put them in rolls. "A bite for ya pussy-cat?" asks the vendor. "I wanted," Jerry continues, "to say: No, not really, it's part of a plan to poison a dog I know. But you can't say, 'a dog I know' without sounding funny; so I said . . . : YES, A BITE FOR MY PUSSY-CAT." Again the gender coding makes it impossible for Jerry to refer directly to the "male" dog, and he loudly claims that the meat is for his "female" pussy-cat. In a time when the use of profanity on stage was severely limited, "pussy-cat" was a clever double entendre for the slang use of "pussy"; as if to make the genital identification even clearer, Jerry describes his return to the building with the murder weapon and adds that the dog was waiting, "malevolence with an erection" (32). Ultimately, the dog survives Jerry's rat poison (34), and subsequently Jerry is able to enter the building without any problems (35). The moral of the tale is this: "neither kindness nor cruelty by themselves, independent of each other, creates any effect beyond themselves; and . . . the two combined, together, at the same time, are the teaching emotion" (35–36).

This strange, often funny, often terrifying speech, which goes on for pages, sets the stage for the final part of the play, in which Jerry, as he has earlier predicted, stops walking about and sits on Peter's bench. He soon attempts to take over the bench. This in turn leads to Jerry goading Peter into a fight in which Jerry himself is—according to his own plan—stabbed to death. The decoding of the "JERRY AND THE DOG" story's oblique references to sex and gender, offers a clear explanation of the actions that conclude the play. In order to be a man, Jerry must belittle females, such as Peter's wife and daughters, cats and birds, his own "little ladies," and the repulsive and unsuccessfully seductive landlady. Females are seen, at best, as second-rate possessions and at worst as garbage to be thrown away. Jerry's sexual contact with women is contemptuous, distant, impersonal. Rather than looking to his available female landlady for contact, he chooses instead the male animal that chases him. When the "kindness" fails, Jerry sets up the kill. Why does Jerry agree, in an overly loud and formal voice, with the hamburger man that he is buying a gift for a pussy-cat? Why does "a dog I know" sound "funny"? Why lie when the object of the "gift" is "malevolence with an erection" (32)? This story only makes sense in terms of gender.

Albee is questioning the contradictions in the construct of masculinity. How, for example, is intimacy between the sexes possible if heterosexual males are required either to own and maintain females, who not being owners and maintainers themselves are inferior goods anyway, or to go meaninglessly through one after another? Both masculinities require a denigration of females and all things "feminine," even attaching "feminine" language to what is weak, unworthy, and treacherous. All real ("masculine") men are inmates in a zoo; genuine "men" are male animals, "malevolence with an erection." Because only other men are worthy of a man's consideration, real men must relate to other real men. Yet the homosocial bond is fraught with anxiety, not only because a real man must be competitive with other males and aggressive (in order to be a real man), but because the homosocial bond itself is merely one hue of male-to-male connection on a spectrum that blends into homosexuality: A real man must be heterosexual.

Jerry's sexuality is suspect: Not only does he admit that he has experienced and enjoyed sex with another male, but his description of his cell in the rooming house implies that he is still haunted by homosexuality: The room is divided "by beaverboard" (like "pussy-cat," another profane allusion to female genitalia) and shared by a drag queen whose door is always open. Homosexuals, he implies elsewhere, try to touch him in the cruisy Times Square movie houses. He hates the west (queer) side of the park. Instead of continuing the "immature" although ecstatic (homo-)sexual behavior that he tried out when he was 15, Jerry now performs what he defines as definitively heterosexual sex. Yet Jerry admits to being a very lonely man.

Jerry's very brief encounters with an unending series of women (if, for that matter, they actually exist or not) and Peter's necessary escapes from his female-occupied home, imply that isolation is not only a consequence of the construct of masculinity but a necessary result: For a "real man," Albee is suggesting, can be a real man on his own, but once another man or even another male is introduced, the attributes that make real men what and who they are must be enacted. Any sexual contact between one real man and another must end in some sort of death: either one or both of the "real men" die as real and as men, to become unreal men, males but no longer men, homosexuals, effeminates, damaged goods, or garbage.

If "playing the man" must inevitably separate men, not only from females but from each other, is the opposite then true? Just as any genuine contact between men has to end in "death," does Jerry's murder in someway provide the momentary but much-desired and much-needed proximity that Jerry so desperately seeks? Obviously, actual homicide, however close it brings Peter and Jerry, is not so much an answer to the broken construct of masculinity to which both males in the play subscribe but an inescapable outcome of it.

Reversing the Condemnation

Viewed through a lens that focuses on sexuality and gender, *The Zoo Story* appears not as Tallmer sees it, a play in which "murder is communication . . . the only, and violent, means of communication between sexes (sorry, one sex) . . . ," nor as Goldman describes Albee's later work: "as clear a statement of the homosexual mystique as one could hope to find" in which "wives are whores . . . husbands are panderers," and the "only wisdom lies with bachelors and young boys"; Albee's first play is nothing less than an attempt to critique two constructs of masculinity visible in contemporary American culture. Goldman is so personally invested in these constructs (or rather in one of them) that he is unable to discern Albee's project, much as he seems unable to glimpse Williams's. Like Tallmer, who begins his pan with an objection that in "real life" the innocent man on the park bench would get up and leave, Goldman's reading of Albee trivializes the actual subject matter by enforcing a strict, literal meaning to the script.

One of the best general descriptions of *The Zoo Story* and plays of its kind appears many years earlier, in Jean-Paul Sartre's defense of Jean Anouilh's *Antigone*. Sartre characterizes the new drama coming out of France as follows:

> Our plays are violent and brief, centered around one single event; there are few players, and the story is compressed within a short space of time. . . . A single set, a few entrances, a few exits, intense arguments among the characters who defend their individual rights with passion—that is what sets our plays at a great distance from the brilliant fantasies of Broadway. (41)

The lecture from which this is drawn was delivered in 1946 and tries to characterize the existential drama that not only Anouilh but Albert Camus and Sartre himself had written during the German Occupation; these plays would pave the way for the great absurdist dramas that would follow, by Beckett, Ionesco, Genet, and Adamov, playwrights whose works had been performed off- and off-off Broadway during the 1950s. Although the world depicted in *The Zoo Story* is not as extreme as the worlds portrayed in *Endgame*, "The Bald Soprano," or *Ping Pong*, it is recognizably not the same world in which Tallmer lives. The benches on stage do not attempt to depict realistically a clearing in Central Park. Hence, his complaint is as silly as someone asking, "Why do Estragon and Vladimir keep coming back to wait for Godot?—I wouldn't!" or "How is it possible that Mr. and Mrs. Smith don't slam the door when Mr. and Mrs. Martin arrive terribly late for dinner?—I certainly would!" His inability or refusal to read the climax of *The Zoo Story* as somehow metaphorical or symbolic is equally preposterous.

At the same time, Goldman's and others' opinions about homosexual playwrights and their plays would be laughable if they were not so dreadfully bigoted and grounded in what most people thought of as commonsense. Just because a script includes male characters who cast aspersions on women or are represented as crass brutes does not necessarily indicate that what these characters say and do is endorsed by the playwright. I think one could make a good argument today that the characters in the *Agamemnon* of Aeschylus suggest that women are evil and conniving and that men are either courageous, powerful, and proud or womanish because instead of directly fighting, they conspire and connive, but I doubt that Goldman would agree because his own values to a great extent coincide with the patriarchal views of the writer and original audience of the *Oresteia*. He would probably argue that the trilogy was a foundational work of Western Civilization and should not be reduced to such simple ideas; yet more than forty years later and with six decades' worth of feminist criticism, modern readers and audiences can easily glimpse in the very obvious dramatization of male superiority the need to suppress females.

This notion that homosexuals should write only about homosexuality was not consistent with the history of Broadway criticism. After all, no one had ever criticized heterosexuals like Lillian Hellman or Robert Anderson for scripts that depicted female or male homosexuality. The paranoia of white, liberal, straight male critics about some cultural war in which homosexuals were insidiously producing scripts in order somehow to trick heterosexual audiences, echoes a society-wide fear of changes in the constructs of gender: Their call for "honesty"—homosexuals should write about their problems, not ours—is merely a call for segregation. With the debut of *The Boys in the Band*, there was suddenly a whole new category of drama according to these men, "homosexual" drama, written by homosexuals and authentically depicting the problems of homosexual culture. Presumably, if (normal) audiences knew they were going to see a "homosexual play," they could separate themselves from the subject matter or decide not to see the play. Yet in retrospect, Mart Crowley's groundbreaking script seems rather didactic and hollow in comparison with Albee's best work. In the twenty-first century it is obvious that Albee's "bitch dialogue" is so much more brilliant than Crowley's.

In writing about the sudden appearance of gay plays in New York, Savran mentions Frank Marcus's *The Killing of Sister George* and Charles Dyer's *Staircase* as well as Crowley's hit (*Communists, Cowboys, and Queers* 136). David Savran observes that Tennessee Williams suddenly found himself outflanked. The language of "obscurity" and "indirection" on which he had relied for thirty years was abruptly outmoded. For the first time, Williams was able to speak openly in the theater about his sexual practices. Yet the theatrical language at his disposal was no more capable of articulating his subjectivity and desire than the idiom of *Tea and Sympathy* had been twenty years before (137).

Savran is suggesting that the supposedly new openness in which gay subject matter could be dramatized rendered Williams speechless. Yet Savran himself is aware that the gay plays of the 1960s "perpetuate negative gay and lesbian stereotypes" (136). The valorizations of these stereotypes on stage were no doubt appealing to the straight male critics that took issue with Albee and other writers who openly critiqued heterosexuality.

At the same time, however, who could appraise straight culture better than someone who was forced to conform to its demands, even as he or she resisted them? And if the postwar theater can be said to have begun before the war had actually ended, with *The Glass Menagerie*, who but a homosexual playwright would have dared to comment on the bizarre contradictions of "normal" sexuality that the majority of those in the audience cherished or at least were told to cherish? As I tried to make clear in the first chapter, those gay people who saw the first production of *The Glass Menagerie* were offered a number of clues from the script as to Tom's sexual identity. If the rest of the audience did not catch on, it was in part because they did not wish to. The "frankness" of *Tea and Sympathy*, at least in its presentation of homosexuality, did not go beyond what the American public thought about it in the first place. Similarly, the critics of the 1960s wanted to see homosexuality depicted on stage in a manner that openly confirmed their beliefs about it—which of course was so much more pleasant than being confronted with the problems inherent to their own lifestyles.

In *The Zoo Story*, the beauty of men is portrayed as dangerous though ephemeral. The loss of youth and beauty turns males into little more than the gender construct of manhood that they have chosen to follow. Without the handsome young male, whose attractive qualities often mitigate and even eclipse the particulars of his gender role, masculinity is visible as a set of attributes that may be applied to male and female alike, and to animals and inanimate objects. Of course, in a male-centered culture, masculinity is only potent when it appears to be the "natural" outgrowth of being male. That which seeks to expose the contradictions in and arbitrary "nature" of masculinity, is thus identified within the culture as threatening. Williams's work, which from 1944 on sought increasingly to question the culture's assumptions about gender and sexuality, was branded false, whereas Anderson's attempt to deal with variations within the performance of masculine gender was acknowledged (because in part its controversial ending attested that it was better for Tom to learn his true sexuality from a woman than to question it) to articulate significant truths. In the case of Albee, whose assaults on such American institutions as marriage, the family, religion, and ageism and racism were clear, the heterosexual male critical establishment, regardless of individuals' politics and age, banded together to expose him for what he was; in so doing, their criticism gave way to highly contradictory and irrational rants of 1960s sexism.

The next generation would make the Beats, who would emerge as heroes, seem tame. They would challenge almost everything that for their predecessors was sacred, necessary, and timeless. With an increasing destabilization of the conformist culture, came blatant defiance of the restrictive constructs of gender, sexuality, race, government, religion, family, and capitalism itself. In part, such disruptive defiance was inspired and nurtured by the theater works that had come before.

Although much has and can be made of the dramatic text of *The Zoo Story*, Bottoms's assertion about *Who's Afraid of Virginia Woolf?* might be extended to the shorter play—both are better appreciated and realized when played on stage, for like *Virginia Woolf*, *The Zoo Story* is about performance— the performance of manliness over the shallow grave of male beauty.

CHAPTER 4

Complicated Masculinity

The Beauty of Montgomery Clift

Playing Roles

When Edward Albee's first play opened at the Provincetown Playhouse in 1960, George Maharis, who played the role of Jerry, was just 22 years old—a substantial discrepancy from the playwright's character description:

> A man in his late thirties, not poorly dressed but carelessly. What was once a trim and lightly muscled body has begun to go to fat; and while he is no longer handsome, it is evident that he once was. His fall from physical grace should not suggest debauchery; he has, to come closer to it, a great weariness. (11)

As I suggested in the previous chapter, the critics of the original production obviously saw Maharis not as the once-handsome man sliding into middle age but as the handsome youth Maharis actually was—a deranged youth perhaps, even a "beatnik," but clearly not a man who had suffered the "fall from physical grace" that the author specified.

At the time, however, there was in fact an actor—a brilliant actor—who might have played the role as it was written and done it justice, someone who had worked on stage, starred in films, and who by 1960 could have easily personified the characterization as Albee had conceived it. Although he would have never considered appearing in such a play in a tiny Off-Broadway theater for a minimal salary, and although his behavior would have made him difficult, if not impossible, to work with, Montgomery Clift might have created the quintessential Jerry: His talent, his background, and his former gorgeous looks would have made him ideal.

Clift certainly had the "great weariness" for which the part called. By 1960, he was slowly careening toward the end of a once-promising career.

This long descent, which Robert Lewis, a founder of The Actors Studio and one of Clift's mentors, called "the slowest suicide in show business" (LaGuardia 4), ended with Clift's death (from cancer) at age 45. Many would construe Clift's decline as additional proof of how the greatly talented were inevitably doomed. Certainly his protracted, downward trajectory, fueled by alcoholism and other personal problems, was not unique in American culture: The Romantic story of the artist as victim of society is hardly new, and the list of those to whom this narrative has been applied is so long and so well known that it hardly bears recitation.

But beyond this indisputably appropriate way of making sense of Clift's troubled existence, there was far more to Clift than the estranged, self-destructive artist. There was, indeed, Clift himself and all that his life brought to his ability to perform on stage and screen. The beautiful outer shell—the exceptionally handsome face and lean but athletic physique—was undeniably a factor is his appeal, and yet unlike so many other young men in Hollywood with pretty faces and attractive bodies, the external functioned as a mere component of a sensitive and compelling instrument. Clift defined himself not as a star but as an actor. The inner conflicts in his characterizations and the struggle to resolve them made him seem to possess a rather different way of acting as a man—a way that was palpably more intriguing and more complicated than the more familiar modes of performed masculinity. His creation through his characters of a sensitized, intelligent manhood, apparent in his first screen role, when he was cast opposite that icon of rugged masculinity, John Wayne, demonstrated the effort required within the male persona to hold onto and maintain a gendered identity.

Clearly Clift's own struggles greatly contributed to the dramatization of his characters' struggles on stage and screen—at least early on. Ultimately, however, his real-life conflicts, which gave him the nervous, edgy quality that had made him the actor he had been, would prove too heavy a burden for him to carry, and in his last few screen appearances very little remains of the beautiful young man whose grace and ambivalence charmed audience members of both sexes.

Nevertheless, in his later stage and early screen appearances, Montgomery Clift's performances seemed to point to a present in which the kind of definitive manliness embodied by Wayne and other contemporary paragons of machismo no longer rang true. In the aftermath of World War II and the Holocaust, when nothing was certain, Clift stood out as an emblem of a more problematic but authentic masculinity. As such, he would influence a generation of actors—the other two stars included in this section, Marlon Brando and James Dean, openly admitted their debt to him—and, perhaps even more significantly, generations of audiences.

Performing the Myth of Identity

What goes into creating an identity? The diverse constructs that make one who one is are numerous. In the case of Montgomery Clift, there was a plethora of factors to be considered.

Edward Montgomery Clift was born in 1920, along with a twin sister, called at the time Roberta. His father, William Clift, came from people who knew who they were: William's father, Colonel Moses Clift, son of a religious Baptist who had fought for the Union, had remained loyal to the South and ended up in Chattanooga after the Civil War. A passionate lawyer, he and his family held a distinct place in Southern society (Bosworth 6–7). However, Montgomery's mother, Ethel (nicknamed "Sunny") Fogg, had been raised as an adopted daughter by a déclassé couple in German-town, Pennsylvania. On her eighteenth birthday, ready to start at Cornell as a freshman with a scholarship, Sunny was told by the physician who had attended her birth—a Dr. Montgomery—that she was actually the illegiti-mate descendant of Colonel Robert Anderson, the Union commander who had defended Fort Sumter, and of Montgomery Blair, Lincoln's postmaster general. The match that had resulted in Sunny's birth had never been made legal; on learning her actual parentage, however, Ethel or Sunny embarked on a lifelong quest to be recognized by the relations whose genealogy she carefully charted (10–11).

At Cornell, where Sunny met William Clift, she hid her background; when pressed, she invented an exotic past. The Clift family, however, was not impressed. Sunny and William married in 1914 without his family's blessing (12–13). In 1919, they had a son, Brooks, and a year later, the twins arrived. Sunny decided to raise the three in a way befitting her upper-class relations, who refused to recognize her (13), and also in a highly uncon-ventional manner, in which the three children were turned into triplets with the same hairstyles and clothing, as well as education, despite their age and gender differences (18). They were kept apart from other children and schooled at home. She was afraid of others inquiring into the children's and her own background (22).

Montgomery Clift was clearly named after Sunny's maternal grand-father, but without the sanction of the Andersons, she refused to disclose even to her children her actual descent. Monty's twin sister, Roberta, had been named for William's favorite sister, but after the rift between Sunny and William's family widened, she gave the girl her own given name, Ethel, which neither of them especially liked (26). Sunny never discussed her celebrated relatives with her children until 1964 (50), although she gushed quite openly to others about her brilliant (and unnamed) relations. But her disclosure had been preceded by her husband's sixteen years earlier: In 1948, William had confided the family secrets to Brooks, who had in turn told his younger brother (46–49).

Actor Kevin McCarthy told Patricia Bosworth that Monty never discussed his family and childhood, not even with his closest friends: "His family—where he came from—was shrouded in mystery." Indeed, all three of the Clift children had buried their pedigrees and their childhoods, but for Monty details of his past sometimes re-emerged in sudden rushes of memory (36). Unwilling to invent, as his mother had, a past for himself, Monty repeatedly asserted that he could not recall his early life, which he deemed to be unimportant. Of course, the contradiction here is relevant: While feigning any real knowledge of who he was, the actor attempted to live in a present in which all that had formed him was reduced to insignificance. In a sense, his mother's hording of ancestral details, and her use of naming and renaming her children to hide, and at the same time disclose, who she was and who they were, diminished and simultaneously time amplified the potency of those things that ordinarily would go into creating a familial identity. Ultimately, Clift would stage his own revolution against his mother's pretensions of aristocracy. Raised to be a little prince, Monty would later act like a true vulgarian—but that would come years later.

Certainly, one aspect of Monty's early life that played a vital role in the formation of his own identity was having a twin of the opposite sex; Bosworth describes how he and Roberta-Ethel, also known as Sister, shared a room and were close companions. Their separateness from their older brother was perhaps most obvious when Brooks tried to talk with them about sex, which disgusted them (38–39). Brought up to look and act the same, Monty and Sister were a sexually ambiguous pair. He was pretty, whereas she was big and strong (26). His gender ambiguity seemed plain to other boys who tried to befriend him, such as Ed Foote, who found him "conceited and self-involved" (28) like his mother. Ed preferred the pleasant fellowship of Brooks (29). Ned Smith, whose "first reaction [to being told that Monty would be visiting in the summer] was 'what do I want that damn sissy actor around for?'" (51). Although Ned became a friend of Clift's, he later described for Robert LaGuardia how Monty would sometimes "speak in this whispery, pansy voice . . . I hated all the pansies that went along with being in the theater" (21).

As Smith's remarks imply, Clift's identity was further compounded when he went on stage at the age of 13. In 1933, he became a child actor, performing in a Sarasota, Florida production of As Husbands Go and then appearing in a variety of plays on and off Broadway between 1935 and 1945. At first his performances seemed very comfortable, almost effortless, as if he belonged on stage. Eventually, however, this ease was complicated by his desire to be a great actor. Mentored by some of the major stage performers of the day, including Mary Boland, Alfred Lunt and Lynn Fontaine, Frederic March and Florence Eldridge, and Patricia Collinge, Monty strove for excellence and truth in acting. Lunt in particular coached the young Clift to create his characterizations by focusing not on what the character said or did but rather on what lay under the dialogue and actions (70). The search for the "inner truth" in acting had been best described by Constantine Stanislavski earlier in the twentieth century. His teachings would influence a number of companies during the ensuing decades, most notably New York's Group Theater, which blended and sometimes corrupted the maestro's methods, combining them with social-activist politics. LaGuardia portrays the males who led the Group Theater as homophobic, consumed by "a decidedly warped, super-masculine mood" (38). By the time Lee Strasberg emerged as guru of The Actors Studio, displacing Harold Clurman, Elia Kazan, Stella Adler, Sanford Meisner, and Robert Lewis, the school had become a requirement for American actors. And even though Clift attended only a few sessions there, by the late 1940s critics and audiences thought of him as a practitioner of "The Method"; nonetheless, he carefully distanced himself from many of Strasberg's more invasive exercises.

At the same time that Clift was becoming an actor of depth and expression, he began to understand that his sexuality transcended the boundaries set by American culture at the time. According to Bosworth, Sunny had surmised by 1939 that "he was addicted to little boys. It shocked me. . . . His father was furious. 'How can a son of mine stoop to this?' . . ." (Bosworth 66). Yet according to Brooks Clift and many others, Monty was not definable by the term *homosexual*: Asked about his brother "being a fag," Brooks retorted that Monty wasn't: "Monty disliked effeminacy" (67), he noted. Yet one of Clift's lovers, named "Josh" by Bosworth, affirmed Monty's conflict about who he was: "One of the things that was starting to torture Monty back in 1940 was that he had to hide his sexual feelings. He despised deception, pretense, and he felt the intolerable strain of living a lie" (74). This lover's apologia implies that Clift was a regretfully closeted homosexual. Still, who Clift was and whom he slept with challenges post-Stonewall reconstructions of sexuality. Obviously, Monty slept with men, but he slept with women as well. Perhaps engaging in a world in which heterosexuality was the norm compelled him to strike up relationships with women—or perhaps, given that he could have slept with whomever he wanted, he chose to sleep with women some of the time. His brother's characterization of Monty as a bisexual (67) may have been spurred by Brooks's own need to distinguish Monty from "a fag," but what if, given all we know, it is nonetheless accurate?

Just as it is difficult to name in twenty-first-century language the sexuality (or rather the sexualities) of the ancient Greeks, Montgomery Clift's sexuality cannot be neatly explained in modern terminology. Clift lived in a "pre-gay" time when males who slept with other males sometimes referred to themselves as "gay." Yet American culture at large did not admit knowing what "gay" and "straight" meant. The general consensus was that what we now call "straight" was normal and what we now call "gay" was criminal, a mental illness, or a perversion. As society prescribed that "men" should marry "women," the whole notion of heterosexuality was, somewhat irrationally, if not desperately, assigned to what (at least in part) made a male a man. In such a context, is it accurate to say that males attracted to other males slept with females because their own masculinity hinged on heterosexual coupling, or could one propose that for many males (and for many females), the seemingly rigid limits that had defined personal sexuality no longer applied?

In other words, Clift's identity was Clift's identity: Trying to claim who and what he was as one thing or another, defeats any investigation of what sexuality—or for that matter, identity—can be. Bosworth seems to agree with Brooks, that his Monty was "a bisexual," sleeping with "both men and women indiscriminately" (67); LaGuardia, however, while admitting that Clift did sleep with females, explains that his inclinations were stronger toward males and that sometime after he made A Place in the Sun (1951), "Monty's sex life had become wholly male oriented" (125). In a paper delivered to the New York Psychiatric Institute, William Silverberg, Clift's psychiatrist, offered a case study that, despite its supposed anonymity, described the actor as "asexual" (Bosworth 209).

Clift's sexuality seems rather contradictory. In addition to Brooks's claim that Monty disliked effeminacy, Edward Dmytryk recalled Clift remarking at a party, "[L]ook at that disgusting fag"; Dmytryk at another party saw Monty "making love to" the same man whom he had called a "fag" (Bosworth 67). Tennessee Williams, who had met Clift when he acted in You Touched Me (which Williams had adapted and written with Donald Windham) asserted, "Monty disliked me because I was so open about being gay and he wasn't" (102). At the same time, Clift found the hyper-masculinity of John Wayne and Red River director Howard Hawks disgusting. He explained to record producer Ben Bagley, "The machismo thing repelled me because it seemed so forced and unnecessary" (109). Clift even thought of his own hairiness as a detriment, going "monthly to an electrologist . . . to have the thick pelt of hair removed from his shoulders and chest." Frank Taylor, once a story editor at MGM, recalled, "In a bathing suit he looked like a monkey" (168), and Bruce Robertson-Dick, who had taken Monty fishing in Maine noted, "I don't recall he ever swam—I had the feeling he was embarrassed at being so hirsute" (246). Clift would probably have protested that rather than being labeled as one thing or another, he was what he did, rather than what other people said he was. At the same time, however, his inner conflict as to who and what he was were never really resolved. While shooting *The Search*, immediately after *Red River*, he agonized over his use of the word "dear" while addressing the young Czech boy whose mother was thought to have been killed in the war (LaGuardia 65): Was it too effeminate for Clift's soldier character to utter? Did it make him sound like a "pansy"?[1]

Whatever his sexuality, Clift projected a certain androgyny in performance. "He was so ambiguous sexually it was a relief," press agent Mike Mazlansky told Bosworth. Much of his secret life was lived in New York City (139). Flirtations gone wrong could be hushed up from inquiring gossip columnists, and Clift's lawyer could arrange that an incident on Forty-Second Street that ended in an arrest could be expunged from the police records. While the general public was unaware of Clift's private life, Clift himself tried to make sure that most of his friends were unable to connect the disparate pieces of his existence. "What floored me," a former male lover of Clift's told Bosworth, "was Monty's ability to keep every single relationship separate and apart from every other relationship. I don't think any of his other friends knew about us, but then I didn't know any of his other friends" (75). Longtime friend Jeanne Green noted that "Monty led many lives. . . . We were only part of one of them" (106). Ned Smith told LaGuardia, "[H]e really had no circle of friends, just friends in corners" (20). Ultimately, LaGuardia suggests, Clift came to isolate "himself more and more with a little family of people, each of whom filled a certain need in his life" (129). What we now call "compartmentalization" became Monty's modus operandi. Certainly, Sunny had taught him this method of dealing with the world, not merely by example but also as a method he was forced to develop in order to survive her oppressive supervision. Thus, he was able for years to convince himself, as well as others for a while, that despite the sexual ambiguity inherent in his acting and his own refusal to admit to being one thing or another, there was no evidence to link him with anything that would definitively characterize his sexual identity.

In moving away from his family, Clift chose to de-class his patrician image. He used profanity (Bosworth 95; LaGuardia 75), began drinking heavily (Bosworth 229), and caroused. Although this helped him separate from them, many detected that this behavior was not so much proletarian as affected. Marlon Brando quipped that Clift had "a Mixmaster up his ass" (59), a comment that no doubt referred not only to his restraint and inhibitions but to his sexuality as well. If Clift at first believed that he could manage to present himself by refusing to reveal himself, his strategy recalls Williams's depiction of Tom in *The Glass Menagerie*; Tom's lack of admission about himself does not serve to save him from being identified but becomes instead the very sign of his obvious difference. Indeed, Tom

Wingfield was not so far off from Tennessee Williams himself and his own early sense of identity. Yet ultimately Williams, at least by the time he met Clift after the war, proved too "openly gay" for Monty.[2]

Performing on Stage

In an article that appeared in *The New York Times* on January 27, 1935, producer Theron Bamberger wrote about the four child actors who were currently appearing in his Broadway production, *Fly Away Home*. These young players had received positive responses in the press; Montgomery Clift, "whose years on the planet number just under fourteen," is described as "completely inexperienced, in a professional sense" (X2). This was sort of true, for Clift had appeared only once before in *As Husbands Go*, an amateur production in Sarasota, Florida, about two years earlier. When the Clifts returned to New York in the fall of 1933, Brooks was sent to boarding school, and Sister attended Dalton in Manhattan. Sunny and Monty began making rounds to auditions; eventually she registered him with the John Robert Powers Model Agency. She hoped his modeling might bring him to the attention of the theatre agents and producers who had so far ignored him (Bosworth 40). During the summer of 1934, the two stayed in a house in Sharon, Connecticut, where Sunny heard from a neighbor that Bamberger was trying out a new comedy over in Stockbridge, Massachusetts and was looking for a boy for one of the roles.

The play ran successfully in the Berkshires and transferred to Broadway, where it ran nearly seven months. Monty and the other kids in the cast were mentioned and praised, but reviewers focused on the star, Thomas Mitchell, who carried the show. Clift shortly after was cast as one of the princes in the Cole Porter-Moss Hart musical satire, *Jubilee*, in October 1935. The show was highly successful and featured Mary Boland and Melville Cooper along with a host of singer-dancers and character actors. Monty was never mentioned in any of the reviews. After *Jubilee*, he was cast in a week-long production of *The Road to Paradise* at the Alden Theatre in Jamaica, Queens. The play, which was reviewed by *Variety* (July 8, 1936) was deemed "a weakie" and clearly unworthy of Broadway. "Star [Lenore Ulric] works hard to lift it along, but it appears too thin." As for Clift and the others in the play, the reviewer wrote, "Supporting cast is competent."[3]

So far, young Clift's career was not a success: Sometime in 1936, he was enrolled at Dalton where he lasted less than a year. In late June 1937, he was in Newport, Rhode Island with family friends (Bosworth 51). Ned Smith recalled how later that summer, a local boy who was interested in breaking into the theater approached Monty for advice. "Monty didn't seem that interested in the conversation," remembered Smith, "but as he advised him he assumed an almost theatrical air" (52). The boy would go on to appear in the chorus of *Pal Joey* a few years later and became a well know Hollywood star. His name was Van Johnson. Despite his limited stage experiences, Clift had come to regard himself as a member of the New York theater world. It did not apparently matter to him that he had at first received some polite reviews and had then been ignored; his sense of worth and self-importance resided in the notion that he was a Thespian and a professional.

When Clift returned to the theater in January 1938, he had a relatively small part, appearing in a single scene of a terrible play with some famous leads. *Yr. Obedient Husband* was produced by Frederick March, who also starred in the comedy, along with his wife, Florence Eldridge, and Dame May Whitty. The show closed within a week, largely because the script was judged badly written. Thus, many critics looked for something—anything—to like, and in addition to Eldridge and Whitty, many singled out the boy who played young Lord Finch: "There is an excellent performance in the minor role of an eager young nobleman by Montgomery Clift, who plays with a surprisingly successful suggestion of shyness," noted Richard Watts Jr. in *The Herald Tribune*.[4] *The Brooklyn Daily Eagle*'s Robert Francis echoed "particularly excellent." John Mason Brown in *The New York Post* added that "[w]ith the exception of Montgomery Clift, who gives a charming performance of young Lord Finch," the cast seemed "out of place" in Queen Anne's London. Sidney A. Whipple in *The World-Telegram* concurred that Clift "was as charming as possible," while Robert Coleman in *The Mirror* called his performance "neat," and John Anderson in *The Journal American* noted Clift's was "the best performance." Although Brooks Atkinson in *The Times* never referred to Clift, this badly written vehicle and his role in it would be remembered.

Initially, the memory of this performance would not help Clift, whose next appearance, in *Eye of the Sparrow*, in May 1938, would be held up in contrast. Richard Watts, who had used the word "excellent" with regard to Lord Finch, grumbled, "I am afraid that he makes us who praised him in his earlier appearance look a little foolish." Robert Coleman also noted that Clift, like the other actors in this play, had "won salutes in good plays," and made "the best of a bad engagement."[5] Henry A. Whipple, who had emphasized Clift's "charm" as Lord Finch, lamented that he deserved "a better part and much better direction." Yet Whipple, in reviewing Monty's next role, in *Dame Nature*, which opened later in September 1938, announced that "The acting was excellent. Young Mr. Montgomery Clift is seen as the too-young father. Those who remember him in 'Yr. Obedient Husband' will realize that here he has a role made for him and one which, thanks perhaps to Worthington Miner's good direction, he handles capably and surely." One of the ironies here is that very few would "remember him" from a play that had run less than a week—mostly just a handful of theater critics, who could and did keep that performance alive. It is at this point that Clift the child actor actually becomes a member of the Broadway scene and a denizen of the theater world.

As such, he was rewarded for his role in *Dame Nature* with good notices. Atkinson in *The Times* finally mentioned him and positively. Watts was no longer afraid to be seen as foolish when he stated, "Young Mr. Clift has an enormously difficult characterization to manage and on the whole he handles it excellently, although there are times when he makes the youthful father too neurotic for comfort." Joe Morella and Edward Z. Epstein, in their study, *Rebels: The Rebel Hero in Films* (1971), cite this review and suggest that this "neurotic acting style" may have been the reason that Clift was taken out of *Life With Father* (37) after only five rehearsals. Brown in *The Post* remarked that Monty "plays earnestly"; Anderson in *The Journal American* called his acting (along with that of his costar's) "simple and sensitive"; *Variety* mentioned his "clever performance."[6] Burns Mantle, in *The Daily News* declared him "one of the younger and more wholesome juveniles."

Thus, Clift found a place on Broadway—a role, as it were, and an established identity. He became a familiar show-business commodity, a known entity, like a leading lady, a character actor, or an ingénue, someone to notice and look at, someone to be aware of. A year after condescending to Van Johnson's questions, his inflated notions of himself begin to coincide with his life. Yet Clift remained a working actor, who struggled to find parts to play and was often obliged to perform material that was less than brilliant. One might argue, in fact, that none of the plays in which he had thus far appeared was especially good, which seems to have been at times not a bad thing for him. In the spring of 1939, he received good reviews for his work in Karel Capek's *The Mother*, one of the playwright's deservedly unknown pieces. Alla Nazimova starred in the title role. Whipple, reviewing *The Mother* in *The World-Telegram*, admitted that Clift was one of his favorite actors, and *Variety* called his performance "sincere and direct."[7]

A year later, Clift appeared in Robert Sherwood's *There Shall Be No Night*, a topical script on the Soviet Union's invasion of Finland that was promptly praised (it won a Pulitzer Prize) and then forgotten; he played the soldier son of Alfred Lunt and Lynn Fontanne. By the spring of 1940, the war in Europe was raging and France was falling. This was to be the first of several portrayals by Clift of young soldiers—portrayals that began on stage but would continue onto the screen. Eclipsed by the Lunts and Sydney Greenstreet, a debuting Elisabeth Fraser, and Richard Whorf, Clift nonetheless won the notice of the dean of the New York critics, Brooks Atkinson, who asserted, "Montgomery Clift has grown up to the part of the son and plays it well." Now acknowledged by *The Times* as an up-and-coming actor, no longer "one of the younger and more wholesome juveniles," Monty was working with some of the best in the business. The show played in New York for a year and then toured for eight months, closing on the road when Sherwood had supposedly received a call from President Roosevelt, who thought the script too controversial (Bosworth 75). It was by now 1942; America had entered the war.

Working with Alfred Lunt had made Clift aware of how much effort should go into playing a character. An increasing focus on detail and on adding specifics to a role became hallmarks of Monty's style. He even took dance and singing lessons, in imitation of Lunt but also in an effort to broaden his own range. Indeed, his next part was in a curious piece that had won an award from the now defunct Group Theatre, *Mexican Mural*, the title of which referred to it being composed of four separate sketches (called "panels"), each set during Carnival in Vera Cruz. Through this production, Clift formed four friendships that would significantly influence his life and his career. The first and second were with actor Kevin McCarthy and his wife, Augusta; both would remain very close friends with Clift over the next decade. The third was with a Russian actress with a German accent, known as Mira Rostova, who would become Clift's acting coach and confidante and would eventually follow him onto film sets. The fourth was with the show's star, singer Libby Holman. Monty's relationship with Holman, which would end with his death in 1966, was romantic, erotic, and intimate, and through it he reenacted his relationship with Sunny, for Holman was at least sixteen years older than he; unlike Mrs. Clift, Holman had a well-known scandal-ridden past.

These relationships helped fire Clift's desire to separate from his family. These friends would become members of his new family, each one playing a particular role in his life as Clift played a different role with each of them. With McCarthy he was a close buddy and an ambitious fellow actor; with Augusta he was a sympathetic and sometimes flirtatious gallant; with Mira he was a probing perfectionist; and with Libby he became an errant son eager to commit whatever sins he could aspire to. And while *Mexican Mural* was, at least for the players, a success, Clift in particular found much praise in the press; Atkinson in *The Times*, George Freedley in *The Morning Telegraph*, and even Ralph Warner in the doctrinaire *Daily Worker*, singled him out among the strong cast. Anderson in *The Post*, however, was keenly aware of what made Clift so much better: "Montgomery Clift plays the young man with fine perception and great effectiveness. If his vocal inflection and gesture remind us of Mr. Lunt, so too does the greater quality of concentration in a young actor of unusual promise."

According to Bosworth, Monty continued in Lunt's footsteps in his next role as the petulant son in Thornton Wilder's *The Skin of Our Teeth*. Stephen Cole told Bosworth, "Opening night he sounded *exactly* like Alfred Lunt. . . . You know—the Midwestern drawl, combined with an English accent. Whenever he felt nervous he'd hide behind a Lunt imitation." When Cole mentioned this to him, Clift replied that it might be true, "but isn't it better that I imitate the best actor in the world than the worst? Supposing I sounded like Johnny Weissmuller?" (85). In Wilder's madcap comedy on human civilization, Clift appeared again with March and Eldridge and also the legendary Tallulah Bankhead; perhaps impersonating Lunt was his way of standing up against these very strong personalities, who were at war with director Elia Kazan. Clift kept out of Bankhead's crusade against the director. He remained on good terms with Kazan, whose association with The Group Theatre (like Robert Lewis's) had grounded him in "The Method." Monty's friend, Bob Ardery, who introduced him to Kazan, was well aware that the director was homophobic. "Kazan didn't like homosexuals," Ardery told LaGuardia. "I explained to him that Monty wasn't, that he was simply a very nice, well-bred boy, and that didn't make him a fairy" (38). Clift was aware of Kazan's prejudices, and onstage and off, the young actor played himself very straight and extremely polite. He was obviously convincing. Ardery and Kazan persuaded Clift to move out of his family's apartment "because the image of the 'nice boy' turned off directors and producers in the theatre" (39).

Reviews of *The Skin of Our Teeth* were extremely positive; the play itself, which would go on to win a Pulitzer, came at a time when America had been in the war less than a year, and its broad and sometimes dry humor was regarded with relief, as was its optimism. Cast as the son Cain, later called Henry, to March's and Eldrige's father and mother of all humanity characters (Mr. and Mrs. Antrobus), Clift went from (as critic John Beaufort in *The Christian Science Monitor* put it) "spoiled brat to fascist menace" between the first and third acts, only to be reclaimed as a member of the family of man by the end. There were many strong notices for him in spite of the star competition: "Montgomery Clift plays the part of Cain with proper violence," wrote Atkinson; he "suggests perfectly the sullen waywardness of the killer in Cain," echoed Anderson; and Kelcey Allen in *Women's Wear Daily*, called him "excellent as the truculent . . . boy . . . whose sadistic tendencies make him resemble a hoodlum of the storm trooper variety." Once again, Freedley, who had written so glowingly in *The Morning Telegraph* on Clift's performance in *Mexican Mural*, now pronounced that "Clift's Cain, who regains his soul and his peace of mind, was as brilliantly acted as you would expect from this rising young actor. His growth as a player has been steady without backsliding." The critical reception acknowledged his skill and rising stardom and even pointed to his ongoing (and suddenly flawless) body of work.

Under the influence of Kazan, Clift vowed to remain a New York stage actor although Hollywood was beginning to show interest. In 1943, when offered a role in MGM's *Mrs. Miniver*, he refused to sign the customary seven-year studio contract. In January 1944, he was cast as George Gibbs in City Center's revival of Wilder's *Our Town*. Because *Our Town* had premiered less than ten years before, critics and audiences were familiar with the original production, and the comparisons between Clift and the first George were all flattering (as noted by Willella Waldorf in *The Post*). In this reprise, playwright Marc Connelly made his stage debut as the narrating stage manager, and Martha Scott, on loan from Hollywood, played George's sweetheart and bride, Emily. What is clear from the reviews of The City Center performance was that Clift, who was brilliantly cast in a role truly worthy of him, was nonetheless regarded as a member of the "supporting cast," as is stated by Edgar Price in *The Brooklyn Citizen* and implied by John Chapman in *The News* and Burton Rascoe in *The World*.

In his next three roles Clift would play a soldier, a part that he had first played in *There Shall Be No Night* with Lunt and Fontanne. In April 1944, he opened in Lillian Hellman's acclaimed *The Searching Wind*, appearing as a wounded corporal whose parents promoted appeasement before the war. Fourteen months later, he would play an enlisted man who, due to nervous fatigue, is returned home in a maddened state, in Elsa Shelley's *Foxhole in the Parlor*; it was the end of May 1945—just two months after the debut of *The Glass Menagerie*—and Clift's impassioned rant about the war impressed critics, even though Shelley's script did not. And the following September, Clift headed the cast of *You Touched Me*, which Tennessee Williams and Donald Windham had adapted from a story by D.H. Lawrence and reset in World War II; here Clift played a returning R.A.F. Pilot, a role that required him for the first time to play a confident adult man. His ability to play all these parts made him, at a time when the war was ending, an actor who could fit into the current Broadway and Hollywood dramas; in fact, Howard Hawks, who would direct Clift's first film, had seen his performance in *You Touched Me* (Bosworth 107, LaGuardia 53)[8] and recognized that he would be perfect for *Red River*.

Although Sherwood's *There Shall Be No Night* had picked up great press, none of the critics who wrote on the Hellman play seemed to associate Clift with his 1942 role; none of them even mentions it. Instead, reviews for *The Searching Wind* emphasize the sensitivity and power of Clift's performance. In addition, there came appreciative evaluations of his status as an actor: The ever-complimentary Freedly observed, "Clift is splendid as usual." Kelcey Allen added, "He is one of the most gifted of our younger actors." Howard Barnes (*The Herald Tribune*) called his characterization "the very stuff of fine acting," and Edgar Price declared him "one of our most able juveniles." Yet his next project, *Foxhole in the Corner* was inevitably compared with the Hellman play and his role in it. Rowland Field quipped in *The Newark Evening News,*

> Montgomery Clift portrays the tormented soldier victim, as a follow-up to the similar part he played in Lillian Hellman's "The Searching Wind," not so long ago, and his new role, let it be said, seems a lame facsimile of its arresting predecessor. If Clift is to be typed in this sort of thing from now on, he deserves better treatment in Broadway.

Many reviewers mentioned Hellman's play. *Variety* noted, "Montgomery Clift, who gave a splendid performance in 'The Searching Wind' does an admirable Dennis."[9] Robert Garland referred to it as well in *The Journal-American*, as did Chapman and Allen. Herrick Brown (in *The Sun*) and Waldorf both observed that not even Clift's incredible performance could save this script. Arthur Pollack (*Brooklyn Eagle*), who thought Miss Shelley a "feeble and fumbling dramatist" called Clift's "one of the finer performances of the season." However, the usually admiring George Freedley protested that Monty's "restraint rendered a somnolent play more soporiphic" and that he "was frequently inaudible."

Freedley reiterated this complaint twice, first when he reviewed the opening night of *You Touched Me* and then a month later, with the publication of "Additional Comments," in which he wrote, "What the last row of the balcony thinks of Mr. Clift's performance would be interesting if impossible to know." Ward Morehouse, in *The Sun*, enjoyed Monty's characterization but admitted, "at times he is inaudible." Another appreciative critic, Garland, nevertheless joked that Clift,

> at the beginning of the war . . . [,] was Cpl. Samuel Havens in "The Searching Wind." In the middle of the war he was Cpl. Dennis Patterson in "Foxhole in the Parlor." And now that the war is over, he is Flight Lt. Hadrian Rockley in "You Touched Me." Equity, or someone connected with the theatre, has had him promoted. And rightly!

There was no way that these critics could have known that this would be Clift's last New York theater appearance for nine years. Yet they could see that something was different. Some of the immaculate stage technique was dropped. Before each Broadway performance of *Fly Away Home*, Monty had

"Sunny climb to the last row in the gallery to make sure his voice could be heard" (Bosworth 43). What would Lunt and Fontanne have done if young Clift had become an "inaudible" soldier for them? And had Clift, as Garland perhaps unintentionally intimated and Field had anticipated, played this young soldier role so many times that neither the critics nor Clift was interested in it? Or had something else occurred?

Performing on Screen

Mira Rostova, who had first worked with Monty in *Mexican Mural*, began coaching him for roles beginning with *The Searching Wind*. "Actually," she told LaGuardia, "it was the preliminary probing that Monty really loved; performing on stage frightened him" (51). Of course, this was not originally true. Clift appeared to have been born to play on stage, but having worked with Lunt, his acting suddenly seemed more intense as well as a little derivative. On the first day of rehearsals for *The Searching Wind*, "director-producer [Herman] Shumlin . . . told Monty that if he closed his eyes while Monty was reading he could hear Alfred Lunt talking." After much effort by Clift, "Lunt was still there, but the similarity was no longer so startling" (46). Suddenly the ease with which he had previously navigated the stage turned problematic. Mira and Monty "would engage in endless discussions of choices and character motivation; they would pick apart every line of dialogue" (51). This intensive study eventually eradicated what Monty had picked up from Lunt but at the same time seems to have erased his once meticulous projection.

For *Foxhole*, Robert Lewis joined Monty and Mira. The three created an intricate subtext and often engaged in lengthy discussions about Stanislavski. "It was one of the most beautifully worked-out performances of his career," remembered Lewis (Bosworth 96). The raves Clift received for this role may not have saved the show, but they certainly proved how amazingly a well thought-out preparation could add to a badly written script.

You Touched Me, in which Clift starred, added yet another dimension to the "new" Montgomery Clift. He had Mira come along to the Boston try-outs, where they secretly sat in his dressing room and "spent hours discussing his performance." He changed blocking without notice and "spoke certain lines so softly he could hardly be heard—'so the audience listens more intently,'" he wrote to Patricia Collinge (Bosworth 102). LaGuardia reveals that the rest of the cast came to resent his "selfishness and incommunicativeness." He would move set pieces about without consulting the stage manager. "If he didn't like the direction," recalled fellow actor, Neil Fitzgerald, "he would change things to suit himself" (49). Robert Lewis tells us that Monty's goal was to cut "every speech that was longer than a grunt . . ." (Qtd. Hoskyns 49). LaGuardia also suggests that in his efforts to portray his character's "pure machismo," Monty developed "the personification of virility," a distinctly "heterosexual" characterization:

> He managed to convince the audience that he was unmitigated male sexuality without making a vulgar display of himself, as most other actors of his age and type would have. . . . He used inner silence, unusual pauses in his speeches, awkward body movements. He spoke so quietly that at times he was practically inaudible[,] . . . an exceedingly selfish aim . . . (50)

This pattern—the extensive and often secretive preparation with Mira, the need to control the production and to alter the script from a rather self-centered perspective—followed Clift into the movies. However, for his first screen role, Monty found himself a newcomer, under the care of veteran director Howard Hawks, who had seen him in *You Touched Me*. LaGuardia suggests that Clift's lack of experience before the camera and his insecurity about it allowed Hawks to exert a strong and positive influence. Without his coach and having been cast opposite John Wayne, who was at ease in the movie-making process, the director was able to gain Clift's trust (54–55). Hawks had a reputation for taking young actors in hand and making them stars; although Monty would never allow real proximity, he did listen to Hawks, perhaps out of the same kind of fear he felt for the homophobic Kazan (57) and perhaps because he was so new to this kind of acting.

The Western genre was an inclusive one, for it managed to contain B movies and Saturday afternoon serials as well as more highly regarded works. Wayne, for example, had been cast as a lead in Raoul Walsh's larger-than-life (shot on seventy-millimeter stock) *The Big Trail* (1930) but trudged on through the 1930s in scores of budget and low-cost pictures (most of them Westerns) until he appeared in John Ford's *Stage Coach* (1939), which was not only popular but deemed an artistic success. With a career that would span nearly two hundred films, current associations with Wayne may focus on his roles as gun-toting, macho patriarch and frontier tough guy, "an embodiment of authority, masculinity, love of country, and other allegedly endangered American virtues" (Campbell 466), an image popularized by Wayne himself in his later years and, after his death, by right-wing and ultra-conservative ideologues. In reality, *Red River* was the first Western in which Wayne played this character (Sanderson 40); in all of his appearances in 1930s Westerns, Wayne almost always appeared as a spirited young cowboy.

Howard Hawks was an incredibly versatile director who had started in silent movies and then moved easily into talkies, working in numerous film genres: adventure, gangster, screwball comedy, foreign intrigue, war, film noir, romantic comedy, and action; *Red River* was his first Western. Prominent throughout his many works, regardless of genre, Hawks had an obvious interest in the nature of gender and sexual identity. He twice put Cary Grant in drag (*Bringing Up Baby* and *I Was a Male War Bride*), developed a series of strong-willed, fast-talking heroines (turning *The Front Page*'s male cub reporter into a spunky female), and despite the censors, managed to weave a visible strand of sex throughout most of his films.

Shot in Arizona between March and November 1946, *Red River* went $1,250,000 over budget (Bosworth 108), and the shooting was plagued by weeks of rain. Several scenes were rewritten to include the stormy weather. The script's climax, which originally resulted in the death of Wayne's character, was also revised (109). The plot had come from "The Chisholm Trail," a Western serialized by Borden Chase in *The Saturday Evening Post*. In *Red River*, Tom Dunson (played by Wayne), an aspiring rancher, abandons a wagon-train going West to settle cattle lands in Texas. Shortly after, the love of his life, a girl named Fen (Coleen Gray), dies in an Indian attack. Now at the banks of the Red River, Dunson and his pal, Groot (Walter Brennan), see the smoke from the wagon train in the distance. After fending off Indians all night, Dunson finds a boy, Matt Garth (Mickey Kuhn), who lost his parents in the same attack. Because the boy has no one and is fast on the draw, he takes Garth with him south to the Rio Grande.

Fourteen years later, Garth fights in the Civil War, and now, played by Clift, returns to help Dunson prepare for the longest cattle drive ever planned, from Laredo into Missouri. Along the way, they pick up a gunslinger, Cherry (John Ireland), who signs on for the drive. Throughout the drive, Dunson brutally pushes on, striking those who disobey him with a hard justice. He and Garth, who is temperamentally more tolerant, eventually clash over Dunson's use of violence, and finally, backed by the cattle men, Garth deposes Dunson, who rides off on his own. The drive then follows the Chisholm Trail into Kansas. When the herd finally reaches Abilene, Dunson confronts Garth, and they fight. Their battle to the death is interrupted by Tess (Joanne Dru), a woman who has known them both and is in love with Garth. Her protest, that father and foster son love each other too much to murder each other, leads to their reconciliation.

Tess, although not really relevant to the film's plot, does become meaningful in this context. She and the other two women in the narrative are in fact connected: When leaving Fen, Dunson gives her a serpentine-shaped bracelet worn originally by his mother. Later, after the wagon train has been destroyed by Indians, Dunson realizes that she has been killed when he discovers the bracelet on the arm of an Indian he has knifed. When Matt returns from the war, the bracelet is on his arm; it later appears, much to

Dunson's surprise, on Tess's arm, after Matt has left her behind en route to Kansas. The use of the snake image, only one of various strategies through which the male characters can discuss the taboo subject of sex, is obviously inspired by Eve.

Tess may first appear as a virgin, but Matt presumes, due to the party she is traveling with ("women gamblers"), that she is a prostitute, a presumption that Tess resents. After Matt removes an arrow from her arm and sucks the poison from her wound, she slaps him. Once she has Groot tell her about Matt's life, however, she feels sudden compassion for him, and in spite of her wound goes to talk with him. The implication is that the next morning she is a virgin no more; yet Matt abandons her to continue the drive. A week later, Dunson, now in pursuit of his foster son, arrives at the spot where Tess's wagon train is stopped. Aware he intends to kill Matt, she tries to argue that Dunson is wrong to go after him. Dunson is clearly attracted to her and even propositions her, offering half his fortune if she will give him a son. Tess says she will, but only if he ends his hunt for Matt, which Dunson refuses to do. During this conversation, Dunson notices the bracelet on Tess's arm and recalls his own leaving Fen.

Jim Sanderson, writing on "*Red River* and the Loss of Femininity in the John Wayne Persona," suggests that "Tom Dunson, the classic Wayne Westerner loses the feminine, thus determines his fate, and tries to escape his fate by regaining some femininity" (40). To an extent, Matt embodies Dunston's feminine side (42), which explains perhaps the transfer of the bracelet from Fen to Matt. One might put this idea more emphatically, that three times in the narrative, males literally abandon the feminine: Dunson leaves behind his mother, then forsakes Fen, and Matt deserts Tess.

Sheila Ruzycki O'Brien goes back to Chase's serialized novella to compare the Tess in the published story with the Tess in the film. The former is a calculating conniver who manages to manipulate men for her own success—a "selfish, sexy, and destructive female so common in U.S. narratives during and after WWII, particularly in *film noir*, but also in detective and other fictions" (184). We may recall Brigid O'Shaughnessy in Dashiell Hammet's *The Maltese Falcon*, the most famous film version of which was released in 1941 (in which she was played by Mary Astor), or the wily Phyllis Dietrichson (played by Barbara Stanwyck) in *Double Indemnity* (1943). In contrast, Tess in *Red River* is not exactly one of Hawks's strong, nontraditional heroines, like reporter Hildy Johnson, played by Rosalind Russell in *His Girl Friday* (1940), but a more likeable though less powerful intermediary, more like Matt than Dunson (184–185).[10]

Graham McCann finds the film had much immediate relevance to the period when it was shot and later released: "In terms of American history, the new, 'softer' individualism of Matthew Garth (finely articulated in Clift's subtle performance) must defeat the old, aggressive individualism of Tom Dunson" (45). (Morella and Epstein call *Red River* "*Mutiny on the Bounty* on horseback" [37].) Indeed, Chase's Tess is something of a nineteenth-century version of the self-serving Marie Derry, whom Virginia Mayo portrayed in *The Best Years of Our Lives* (1946). In the absence of her flier husband (Dana Andrews), Marie has made a life for herself by manipulating men, using sex to get what she wants, obviously betraying her soldier husband. Similarly, as originally conceived by Chase, Tess, until the end of the serial, would have appeared a menace to returning soldier Matt.

Indeed, Matt and most of the men on the cattle drive, Dunson acknowledges, belong to the younger generation who have come back from the South's defeat, and the drive itself may be their redemption, an opportunity to better themselves and their families and to rise above the horror they have endured. This opportunity is made clear in Dunson's speech, just before the men sign a contract to complete the drive, and is reiterated mid-picture when Dan Latimer (Harry Carey Jr.) is killed during a stampede; even the legalistic Dunson is willing to forego the fact that Dan, who did not fulfill the contract by completing the drive, should be paid in full. Clift, whom Hawks had seen in one of his returning soldier roles on Broadway, was still the returning soldier. The Western mythology was useful in retelling the story of the boys coming home, of a new generation displacing the one that had, it was popularly believed, allowed the war to happen.

With Clift's stage performances, there is nothing beyond the reception that remains; it is possible to get a sense of what he did on stage through critical notices and spectator anecdotes. While these are invaluable for understanding how Clift's performances were received and construed, the performances themselves lie beyond what is clearly visible. With his films, however, it is possible to view now what he did—albeit out of context but nevertheless firsthand. Our ability to watch Clift's roles on film allows us to gain a closer knowledge of his acting.

In the case of *Red River*, Matt Garth is a tough yet sensitive young male who differs from his father-mentor in his ability to act primarily through his intellect. Unlike Dunson, ruled by anger and emotion, Matt considers not only what is good for himself but also the greater good. There are moments, of course, when Matt's emotions lead him to action, such as when his own anger against Dunston's plan to hang two men cause him to rebel, but the script clearly shows that this rebellion is preceded by numerous observations by Matt of Dunson's unjust sense of justice. There is also Matt's intense attraction to Tess, which is anything but rational, and his stubborn decision not to flee Abilene before Dunson confronts him. What he feels for Tess is part of a larger construct of love accepted in the cinema in which opposites attract as violently as they repel; his choice to face his foster father seems inevitable in the way in which the film is constructed: With Dunson as thesis and Matt as antithesis, how is it possible for them not to clash head-on? The ongoing question of Matt's masculinity, as opposed to the ongoing statement of Dunson's, is raised during the fight itself: "Won't anything make a man of you?" Dunson shouts, trying to provoke him. Is the returned soldier, sensitized by his wounding experience, any less manly than his forefathers? The answer, of course, must be no.

Or rather, the answer must be Montgomery Clift and his performance. In *Red River*, without Mira and Bobby Lewis, left to trust in and follow the director, and with no power to change the script or filming, we see perhaps the purest of Clift's screen roles: Monty is acting. Seemingly aware that acting for the camera must be far smaller and more minimalist than acting on stage, he appears to shed his Broadway projection and body language; no one watching his first film would even associate his performance with Alfred Lunt.

One aspect of the screenplay that helped Clift was the paucity and terseness of his lines. There are no long speeches for him to utter, as in *The Searching Wind* and *Foxhole in the Parlor*, and no excess of lines for him to cut or pronounce softly as in *You Touched Me*. He allows his facial expressions, gestures, and movements to speak far louder than his words. In one scene in particular, the one in which Matt is reunited with Tess in an Abilene hotel room, he manages to show fear, suspicion, relief, affection, erotic arousal, and assertiveness; he has only one line—in response to Tess's indication that Dunson hasn't give up his hunt, Clift murmurs almost inconsequentially, "I didn't think he would." As a character of few words, Clift's Matt Garth is immediately more complex than other screen actors might have made him because everything the actor does implies a highly wrought subtext.

From his first scene, as the grown boy now back from the war, Clift uses his eyes, which dart back and forth as Dunson and Groot quip. Later, the night before the drive begins, as Dunson declaims on what he expects from the men who sign up, Matt calmly surveys the cattle hands. When three men desert the drive, Dunson is about to ask Matt to bring them back. Wayne even starts to say, "Matt get—" but changes his mind and asks Cherry. Matt's glaring eyes, the only part of his face visible as he drinks from a cup, keep Dunson from issuing the command. Later, after he has left Dunson behind, Matt listens to Groot speculate about how quickly Dunson can catch up with them and his eyes again widen over a cup. Once he finishes drinking, he hides his face with his hand, so only the eyes can be seen, and then reveals a distorted expression as his fist grazes his chin. When Tess comes to speak with him, following her conversation with Groot about Matt's life, he watches her talk, his eyes widening and narrowing. The incredible subtlety of Clift's performance relies, to a great extent, on his focus, on whom he listens to and when, on how his eyes can swiftly go off to distant thoughts and then suddenly return to the immediate moment; perhaps the clearest instance comes when Dunson announces how he will punish the deserters, when Matt's eyes shift to what seems to be the abstract and then back to the concrete.

The voice, although it may be underplayed, remains nonetheless highly expressive. From his first scene, Clift gives Matt slight and unpredictable breaks in his voice. For example, once Cherry and Matt have had a shooting match, Cherry says, "I take it I'm hired." "You're hired," Clift responds, but instead of merely repeating John Ireland's tone, he injects a barely discernable flutter under "hired." When Dunson says he is going to hang the deserters, Matt replies, "You're not going to hang them," his voice unable not to quiver in spite of his great control. A moment later, however, the same voice becomes surprisingly adamant: Dunson asks who is going to stop him, and Clift steadily retorts, "I will." Clift's sudden voice changes are used brilliantly throughout the film: Having prevented Dunson from shooting the cowboy whose accidental upset of the pots and pans has prompted the stampede, Matt rasps, "You'd've shot him between the eyes." Matt later puts a gun into the hand of one of the men whom Dunson would have hanged and growls, "Go on and use it."

Even more powerfully, however, Monty's lines occasionally sound very flat, not as if his character is devoid of emotion but as if Matt is restraining himself, fighting to keep emotion out of his voice. At some point early in the drive, cowhands find a good water source on the way to another spring. Rather than allowing them to remain, Dunson stubbornly prods them on to the next watering hole, some three or four miles beyond. Matt pleads, with a shudder in his throat, that the "men are beat," but Dunson tells him to move on. "Move on," Clift repeats, in a tone that is clearly meant to show nothing but which, of course, shows how much Matt is unwilling to let others see him disagree with Dunson's command. Finally arriving outside Abilene, Matt and Buster are greeted by a welcoming party from the city. In addressing them, Matt's voice goes surprisingly flat, as does his presence, and later the same night, as he sits with Melville, the man who has bought the herd (Harry Carey Sr.), discussing how Dunson will soon find him, his fear and suspicion lie beneath the surface and seem almost, but not entirely, suppressed.

Perhaps the most potent aspect of Clift's spoken performance resides not in what he says but in what he does not say. The use of pauses and silences make his gestures and facial expressions all the more significant. A good example of this comes just before Clift tells Wayne, "The men are beat": He pauses. The lack of speech here, which allows the audience to follow Matt's thoughts as he considers broaching the subject of giving the

cowhands an unexpected break, is lucidly revealing. What's more, throughout the film Clift not only offers silence before and after lines, but also
sometimes will stop a beat within a line. Rather than speaking himself, Matt
is quiet as others speak, and thus sometimes all the more readable. He has
wonderful pieces of business with rolling and smoking cigarettes. From his
first scene, Matt is putting tobacco into papers, lighting the rolled cigarette,
and usually offering it to Dunson, who smokes it. Only later, once he has
taken command, does Clift smoke his own. In addition, he has a peculiar
gesture—placing his fingers on his nose—that immediately calls attention
to something inner, something unspoken. We see this first when Cherry
asks to see Matt's gun[11]; the moment during which he considers the request
(Dunson taught him as a boy not to trust anyone) is marked by a touch
to his nose. On the trail, Cherry comments, "If I tangled with Dunson, I'd
have to take you on too." Before answering (that he would find Dunson "a
handful by himself"), Clift touches his nose again. The panoply of nonverbal
cues includes half-smiles, playing with a straw, a stride, an array of gazes and
deep stares, and the use of his hat (when Groot tries to tell him how he's
been missed)—these tiny particulars all add up to a marvelously intricate
performance, each small element creating qualities of that larger, invisible
construct, the character.

   This method of acting had been originally taught to Clift by Lunt, and
his subsequent work, in spite of his earlier imitative style, allowed him to
learn from directors (especially Robert Lewis and Elia Kazan) whose notions
of performance included such detailed portraiture. According to LaGuardia,
Hawks had sensed Monty's insecurities regarding his lack of experience—
Clift had never even sat on a horse before—and worked with him even
though for Hawks Monty's obsessive development of a subtext seemed like
"baloney" because the director believed it left no room for spontaneity (55).
As a stage actor Clift felt obliged to play the lines, especially in the scene
when he actively confronts and then deposes Wayne, but Hawks, aware of
how overpowering Wayne could be, instructed him to "[u]nderplay the first
part of the sequence, throw the lines away as if there was something more
important going on in his mind" (56). The result was the miraculously taut
scene in which Matt Garth takes over the drive.

   Yet for Clift, making *Red River*, which went on for months, and dealing with Hawks and Wayne, whose machismo infuriated him, was not an
enjoyable process. To some degree, the actor's aversion to their displays of
masculinity contributes to Matt's resistance of Dunston and his reticent but
ultimately decisive performance of a more sensitized masculinity. Clift saw
the final result only when the feature was released in September 1948. He
had feared for many months that it would prove a miserable failure and that
he was terrible in it. Ironically, neither was true. It was a great first film for

him, but the public would regard it as his second film because the movie he made next, *The Search*, would be released six months earlier.

Making Movies

Clift sought stardom without the usual restrictions. He was one of the first actors who refused to sign a long-term contract with a studio, preferring to choose his films and directors on his own. Such autonomy was unheard of in the mid-1940s, and initially, Clift looked for and participated in productions in which other aspiring cinema actors would never have appeared. Two of these were *The Search* (filmed 1947, released 1948) and *The Big Lift* (filmed 1949, released 1950). Both were shot on location in postwar Europe and featured non-actors as well as European players; in both, Clift returned to the role of soldier.

The film he co-starred in between these two was very different, a Hollywood-made, period drama derived from Henry James's *Washington Square*, called *The Heiress*. Based on the 1947 Broadway hit by Ruth and Augustus Goetz, the film version would cast him opposite Olivia de Havilland. *The Heiress* (filmed 1948, released 1949) was shot indoors on soundstages. Clift, far from being a soldier, played a fortune hunter.

Yet the soldier roles stand out as indicators of how Clift was perceived by those who made the movies and by those who watched them. In the public eye, he was identifiable as the young male injured by war, no longer a boy, not yet a man, like the three stage soldiers he had portrayed and like Matt Garth—and also like Robert E. Lee Prewitt in *From Here to Eternity* (1953) and Noah Ackerman in *The Young Lions* (1958), the two soldiers he would play later. These characterizations explain some of Clift's enormous appeal, especially during his early screen years. Indeed, one might argue that his success as Morris Townsend, the mercenary suitor in *The Heiress*, and as George Eastman, the duplicitous suitor in *A Place in the Sun* (1951), relied on the audience's desire to see him as a well-intentioned male in transition from youth to maturity who should be forgiven his flaws.

Despondent as he finished *Red River*, Clift was approached by Fred Zinnemann, a young director who had previously shot documentary shorts. Monty was interested in the feature Zinnemann wanted to make and asked for a script but received instead an outline of it when he returned to New York (LaGuardia 61). Although he liked the idea of a film about concentration camp survivors, Clift found the screenplay's omission of references to the Nazis' Final Solution unacceptable, and he thought the dialogue overly sweet and artificial. Nonetheless, the role offered what he thought would be a great acting opportunity. When he arrived in Zurich in April 1947 to begin

filming indoor shots in a studio, he brought Mira Rostova, never mentioning to Zinnemann or anyone else why she had come (Bosworth 114–115).
The result was disastrous: Mira's presence on the set and her apparent influence over Monty provoked Zinnemann, who eventually banished her, but
as with *You Touched Me*, the two worked together in private, in a dressing
room or hotel suite (LaGuardia 64). At the same time, Clift would rewrite
the stilted and saccharine lines allotted to the American soldier (Bosworth
116). These revisions infuriated the producer, whose son and another writer
had composed the dialogue. Ultimately, Monty's contract expired, and he
refused to re-sign unless the producer allowed him all rewrites (LaGuardia
63). In this particular case, Clift was probably right: The screenplay with his
changes won an Oscar, but a precedent had been set; now as he advanced
toward stardom, Monty felt entitled to question both writers and directors.

The plot of *The Search* contains two separate though related stories
that are connected toward the end. One, narrated by Mrs. Murray (Aline
McMahon), who is the head of a United Nations facility for displaced children somewhere in Germany, begins with a small unnamed boy (Ivan Jandl)
who has run away and is presumed drowned. Sometime after, a Mrs. Malik
(Jarmila Novotna) comes to a refugee center, looking for her child from
whom she was separated while interned in a camp. At first, a British officer
is able to match her description with an identity card, but as it turns out, the
child claiming to be Karel Malik is actually hiding his own Jewish identity
and has adopted her son's name. She soon reaches the UN facility where
Mrs. Murray is able to identify the boy Mrs. Malik is seeking as the one
whom they believe was drowned. Greatly despondent, Mrs. Malik falls ill
and remains at the facility while recovering, eventually becoming a worker
at the home, which is now sheltering Jewish children bound for Palestine.

The second story begins with the arrival of the escaped boy into
a ruined German city about forty miles away. Here, he sees a GI, Ralph
Stevenson (Clift) eating his lunch in a jeep. Steve, as he is called, gives the
boy half his sandwich, and when he has devoured it, Steve offers him the
other half. He brings the child back to where he is billeted, to a comfortable
suburban house near the bombed-out city. Terrified, the child tries to escape,
but gradually Steve and his friend, Jerry Fisher (Wendell Corey) win his
trust. Over the next few weeks, the boy (to whom Steve gives the name of
Jim), has begun learning English. Steve becomes attached to him and wants
to take him back to America. Yet the boy's mind is bothered by the arrival
of Jerry's wife and son; he is suddenly reminded of his own mother and sets
off to find her, believing that a factory in the city was the last place he saw
her. He is mistaken and wanders into the countryside, where Steve eventually finds him and explains that from what he has learned, the boy's mother

died during the war. Ready to leave for the States, Steve brings Jim to stay at Mrs. Murray's facility, where ultimately, he and his mother are reunited.

The sentimentality and pathos in the script are offset by Clift's finely nuanced performance. While Aline McMahon and Jarmila Novotna play their parts emotionally and the young Ivan Jandl is heart-wrenching (he was awarded a special juvenile Oscar), Monty's Steve is an ordinary young man who finds himself in an unusual circumstance. There was not much to draw on from the script's characterization: We know that Ralph Stevenson lives in New York City and will return there, that he is an engineer of some kind, and that his mother resides in Baltimore, but some of the crucial background material that was available to Clift for Matt Garth was significantly absent. The screenplay's blank spots, however, became Clift's canvas; he and Mira would spend hours filling in the empty spaces. In rewriting Steve and developing his character, Clift used his own knowledge and his keen ability to observe. The generalized characterization became, through his research and analysis, very specific.

Unlike the usually silent Matt Garth, Clift's Steve is a garrulous young man. As soon as he begins to address the boy, offering him the sandwich, he starts a conversation largely with himself. He quickly learns that the child speaks no English, little German, no French or Italian; Steve's ongoing speech, although it sounds like an attempt to communicate, becomes his thinking out loud: Not only does Steve ask the child questions, but he answers them as well. His anxiety about what to do with the boy manifests itself in words spoken to no one else. The dialogue opens wider when he brings the child home and Jerry joins the two. As the story progresses and the boy—now Jim—learns English (and unbelievably well in a short time), he is able to converse with him.

This talkative soldier is likeable and well intentioned. He can be playful and serious. Instead of the half-smiles allowed by Matt, Steve actually laughs out loud a number of times throughout the picture. Rather than keeping silent in moments of stress, he chatters through them. He can raise his voice in anger—as he does when Jim begins to demand they find his mother—and he can do things that are not carefully thought-out—such as threatening Jim with a hypodermic needle and then feeling guilty when he realizes that the boy has been hiding a tattooed number from Auschwitz on his arm. Yet he is capable of remorse and also of articulating it; when he lies to Jim, claiming he does not know where his mother is (an inaccurate military report alleges she died), the remorse plainly, although subtly, disfigures his otherwise likeable face, and a few moments later, when Jerry's wife asks, "You mean you haven't told him?" Clift's features contract in a spasm of dread.

This U.S. Army "good guy" does not (unlike both Clift and Matt) smoke: The chatty soldier chews gum, a habit that immediately identifies him as an American. He likes the radio and at one point turns up the volume on a late-1940s jazz rendition of George Gershwin's "S'Wonderful." He uses an electric razor that he steers nimbly about his face and celebrates the memory of President Abraham Lincoln, who represents how the ordinary American is capable of rising to greatness.[12] For Steve, as played by Clift, is just that, a tribute to the decency of the ordinary American.

He is also asexual. Unlike the smoldering Matt, Steve shows no sparks around women. There is no evidence of him being heterosexual or homosexual. To a great degree, his sexual neutrality seems the result of the script, but Clift's refusal to engender Steve as a macho man is clear. In contrast to wiser and older Jerry, who has a wife and a son, Clift remains boyish. In a way, his decision to take the boy back to America is irrational and odd, almost like a teenager's loyalty to a found pet. As noted earlier, Clift was especially concerned about his utterance of the word "dear" when calming the runaway Jim after Steve has told him his mother is dead. The usual word that the character uses to address Jim is "lad," a choice that seems neutral if archaic. Clift obviously feared that his improvised "dear" might tip the balance on the audience's view of his sexuality. Only homosexuals, he reasoned, were accustomed to using the term with another male. In a film in which Jerry's wife admonishes her son's sudden burst of weeping with, "Jim isn't crying—Jim's a big boy," the weight of gender and sexual identity, though not obvious, remains oppressive.

Despite Mira's banishment and his own battle with the producer over the script, Clift enjoyed the process of making *The Search*. He felt Zinnemann considered his ideas and incorporated much of what he had come up with. His next film, however, would be entirely different, for his next director, William Wyler, was reputedly an authoritarian movie-maker and had his own way of running a production. The entire shoot of *The Heiress*, even the exterior shots, took place on Paramount's sound stages. Whereas Hawks had at least listened to Monty's "baloney" and Zinnemann had drawn from the actor's preparations, Wyler had no interest in discussing the particulars of the role of Morris Townsend. In his hotel room and on-set dressing room, Clift again worked with Mira on each scene; he was shocked that Olivia de Havilland, who would win an Oscar for her performance as Catherine, would simply come onto the set in the morning with nothing more than her lines memorized, ready to be directed by Wyler (Bosworth 127).

As in the rehearsals and the run of *You Touched Me*, Monty became more concerned with his own performance than with relating to the other actors: "I had a sense," recalled de Havilland, "that Monty was almost entirely thinking of himself and leaving me out of the scene. It was difficult for me to adapt to playing that way. But my having to adapt to him, and not his adapting to me, was really part of my character, so in the end it worked" (LaGuardia 71). Indeed, much of de Havilland's brilliance in her role hinged on her character being able to believe that a man who actually has little regard for her loves her deeply.

Based on James's *Washington Square*, *The Heiress* concerns an unmarried and rather plain girl, Catherine Sloper (de Havilland) who will eventually inherit from her father, a medical doctor (Ralph Richardson), a substantial income. Awkward in social situations and uncomfortable among strangers, she is befriended, then courted by an extremely handsome and charming but impoverished man, Morris Townsend (Clift). Certain that Townsend is really interested in his daughter's fortune, Dr. Sloper opposes the marriage. He takes Catherine to Europe for six months, but on returning she announces her intentions to marry Morris. Dr. Sloper then tells her what he has suspected—that the only reason a man like Townsend would be interested in her is her money. Catherine refuses to believe him and decides to break with her father forever. She plans an elopement with Morris, but on learning that she is rejecting her father's money, Townsend fails to show. Dr. Sloper dies shortly after, and Catherine comes into his fortune. Years later, Morris returns, explaining why he left Catherine—he claims he was ashamed to separate her from her family and her inheritance. He pledges his love again, and when he once more proposes, Catherine insists that they elope that very night. However, when he turns up to take her away, she bolts the door and darkens the house.

The role of Morris Townsend must have had a certain resonance for Clift: He, like the character, had been brought up with a taste for the finer things, and during the depression, his gentility far outreached the family's money. He too had been "finished" abroad and was well versed in European culture. Both men were hiding something, Townsend the secret reasons for his wooing, Monty the true nature of his sexuality and sex partners. Perhaps most significantly, Monty and Morris were both handsome and charming young men who played the role of the handsome, charming young man in public: They were both actors. For the first time, Clift's screen role was playing someone who was consciously playing a part. In spite of the problems working with de Havilland, not to mention his fear and disapproval of Ralph Richardson's incredible precision (and bizarre, often distracting stage business [LaGuardia 71]), Clift's performance remains sensational.

One of the genuine challenges in the role is to persuade the audience, for at least half the film, that Morris Townsend may be indeed, in love with Catherine. In *Washington Square*, James never actually resolves what motivated Townsend, but in *The Heiress*, at least in the stage version, the truth that he is a mercenary suitor becomes extremely obvious by the beginning of the second act. Clift had to make the audience fall in love with him, just as Catherine does, and remain in love with him for as long as possible. In this he succeeds admirably. Wyler shows Morris Townsend to be incredibly handsome—so handsome in fact, that even before we see him ourselves, we watch Catherine seeing and then listening to him, before he enters the frame. Her expressions of attraction and fear are startling, and when we finally observe their source, we understand why she is feeling what she is feeling.

Perhaps the truly insightful aspect of the Goetzes' dialogue (they wrote the screenplay as well as the play) is that it provides two kinds of speech, a sometimes florid, rather polite discourse, used for social interaction, and a plain, more intimate language, spoken in private. Interestingly, Dr. Sloper speaks the former, whereas Catherine is only able to sustain the latter. Townsend, however, a true player, is fluent in both. He is able to socialize in words of propriety, but he can also leap into a plainer, seemingly more direct and honest discourse. When Morris finds that the young lady whom he has met is uncomfortable making social niceties, he becomes instantly more colloquial, speaking more candidly, at least in style. He even takes on some of the awkwardnesses that define Catherine's nervousness, allowing them both to laugh about them. Later, once he has come to call on her several times, he maintains his polite chatter around Catherine and her chaperone, her meddling aunt, Mrs. Penniman (Miriam Hopkins), but alone with each he descends to a more ardent and supposedly spontaneous level. Clift clearly understood that he was portraying a man who was not what he seemed, who was playing being in love and doing a good job of it.

In mid-nineteenth-century costume, Monty suddenly looks rather dashing. His usual slump and the drag in his walk are not apparent. Wyler ingeniously managed to frame shots so that Clift's usual saunter (which would prove so appealing to the factory girls in A Place in the Sun) is hardly visible; likewise, the director allowed Richardson all his theatrical histrionics and gestures but only filmed part of Dr. Sloper's upper body (LaGuardia 71). Clift's height is contrasted with de Havilland's petiteness. During their courting scene, he towers over her and is bowed slightly forward, making de Havilland repeatedly bend slightly backward. As a cat with a mouse, he permits her to escape only to trap her in a doorway. He then proposes.

The proposal scene, in which the usually poised Morris plays a young man in trouble, is almost moving: He gets Catherine to take pity on him and to accept him; she is even drawn into the act of being in love. Convinced that she is truly loved by a man other than her father, she feels an affection that she has never felt before. In the scene between Townsend and Dr. Sloper, in which father abuses suitor and vice versa, Morris tries to play off the paternal feelings he expects to find. Yet with Dr. Sloper, Morris has encountered a father with few paternal feelings, whose cold estimation of his daughter and her suitor are not colored by the usual emotions of love. Ironically, Clift's Townsend is so compelling and Richardson's Dr. Sloper is so punctiliously cruel, not only to Morris but to Catherine, whom he dismisses as a nonentity with a bank account, that Clift's character seems all the more credible.

Morris's visits to Mrs. Penniman and his pleasure in enjoying the comforts of the Sloper home may sway the audience from sympathy with him; the screenplay retains only a few moments of a longer scene in the stage script, but there is enough in it—the drinking of Sloper's brandy and pilfering of his cigars, the maid telling Townsend that the wine will be served (as he has requested) at room temperature—that viewers can easily detect his motives. Still, Catherine's return and her reunion with Morris are tender and passionate. Although anyone who thinks about the plot cannot avoid arriving at the conclusion that she will be jilted once he knows what she plans, Clift is so engaging in these scenes that many may strongly wish not to accept the inevitability. The telling moment, after Catherine says that she will reject her father's money and then implores Townsend to take her away immediately, is met with a slight pause and then an almost believable, "Very well, we'll do it." During this pause, Clift looks down, his eyes sweeping across the ground, and then looks up. Again, we may wish to believe him until he exits through the end of the garden without once turning back.

Clift watched the rushes daily and thought he was not "doing his best work" (Bosworth 127). Nonetheless, what survives, six decades later, is nothing short of splendid. Regardless of the problems he encountered while making The Heiress, his performance, as well as the performances of the other leading actors, remains startling. And Clift was back on familiar turf: He had played well in a costume piece with March and Eldridge and had excelled in domestic dramas.

In his next appearance, Clift would play a role almost opposite to the one in The Heiress: In The Big Lift (1950), Danny McCullough, a guileless U.S. Air Force sergeant assigned to the Berlin Airlift, falls prey to a German beauty, Frederica (Cornell Borchers), who wants to use him to get to the United States. Danny is a trusting young man who is ultimately all-too-willing to overlook Frederica's past, even when his older, gruffer friend, Hank Kowalski (Paul Douglas), shows him her dossier that indicates her dead husband fought with the S.S and her father was a Nazi party member. Frederica tries to explain the lies she has told (she previously claimed the husband was drafted into the regular army and her father murdered for protesting the book-burnings) by asking Danny to understand the misery in which she and the rest of the German people have been living; soon, as he becomes aware of the Germans' suffering, he proposes and she accepts him.

Kowalski, although a rabid anti-German, has a Berliner girlfriend, Gerda (Bruni Lobel). Unlike Frederica, who like thousands of others toils in the city's ruins, gathering up the rubble of the bombed buildings, Gerda works in a lunch wagon at Templehof Airfield, where she has come to know many Americans. Gerda readily admits her paternalistic fatherland has been horrible—she even disparages her Nazi father—and shows an interest in democracy and change. Eventually she makes the tough-talking Kowalski treat her with respect, and when, as they wait outside the mayor's door at City hall, Danny announces to Frederica that he has learned (from one of her neighbors) that she only wants to marry him so that she can reach her German lover who is now in St. Louis, Gerda explains that many Germans, taught by the Nazis that the ends justify the means, have to change their ways.

This romantic pretext, however, is surrounded by the story of the Air Lift itself, which has been re-enacted by members of the U.S. Air Force. Indeed, except for Clift and Douglas and the German actors, members of the occupying forces play all the other roles in the film. Woven through the love story, director-screenwriter George Seaton provided a wealth of facts and data about the Air Lift. The film, unfortunately, is both didactic and filled with very bad amateur performances. An obvious piece of Cold War propaganda, *The Big Lift* would eventually be of great interest to scholars of the American occupation of Germany. G. Schmundt-Thomas includes it as one of three films that depict relations between the male occupiers and frauleins, whereas Ralph Stern carefully decodes the messages the movie contains about shifts in U.S. and German identities. Yet cinematically, *The Big Lift* has much difficulty holding itself together.

Nonetheless, Clift's performance seems unusually natural, as if he is merely playing himself, especially in contrast to the men in uniform who really are playing themselves. In fact, as with his later theater and previous film appearances, he has scrupulously overprepared. His contract specified that Mira be allowed on set. As before, her presence infuriated the director, who tried to banish her; Seaton even had his wife take Mira to lunch, so he could shoot an important scene without her. Unable to get her to leave (Clift threatened to leave himself), Seaton went on to badmouth Clift around Hollywood (LaGuardia 77). Yet Clift's acting here, even more than in *The Search*, has an extraordinary ordinariness to it. Whereas Borchers, Douglas, and Lobel are all obviously performing, Clift's ease in front of the camera is almost constantly clear. Sometimes he looks as though he should be in a different film, one made a decade later in the style of Cinéma Vérité.

If Ralph Stevenson was the epitome of the "good-guy" American Joe, Danny McCullough is the guy who is too good for his own good: From the first moment he sees Frederica, when she presents him with an award for having been aboard the ten-thousandth flight into Templehof, his eyes reveal his desire for her. Clift makes Danny awkward and ardent: Posing for a photo, he gets to kiss her, and they repeat this for other reporters. He takes her phone number, but making several flights a day, he is unable to remain in Berlin long enough to get to see her. An Associated Press (AP) correspondent (played by an actual AP correspondent) asks if Danny will allow him to follow him for a story; when it becomes evident that this will permit Danny to see Frederica, he consents. The timing in this scene is exacting: Clift's initial reaction of unwillingness is suddenly pierced by a moment of realization indicated by a small movement of the eyes—a barely discernable but pivotal instant, following which the character suddenly justifies his taking part in the project.

The other professional players in the film are not so subtle: Douglas blusters, Borchers (who is still very good) makes an overly obvious face when Danny disparages the Nazis, and Lobel delivers her lines either so earnestly or so good-humoredly that one wishes at times to pinch her. The servicemen are simply awful. Yet Clift is able to pull off a number of cinematic turns—incidents that could only be written into a screenplay—with a nonchalance that nearly makes them credible. For example, while sitting in civilian dress in a café, Danny watches as policemen enter to check identity papers. How does he hide? Why, by drifting onto the bandstand to join the quartet singing "Chattanooga Choochoo" in English, of course. And when they slip back to crooning in German, he starts providing sound effects. Only in a movie, one may think, but Clift's performance here illustrates why spectators believe movies.

There are myriad moments when Clift refuses to overplay his role. Asked by the AP reporter about how he likes his job, Danny's eyes suddenly enlarge and his voice flattens as he pretends to describe how wonderful it is. When he and Frederica are stopped in what they think is the Russian sector and soldiers address him in German, she quickly explains that her husband was shot in the throat during the war and cannot speak. Danny utters an anguished moan, which is almost hilarious. Later, at a coffee house, listening to swing, Frederica observes that this sort of music is considered "hot" in America, and Danny replies, "Smooth, in the groove, hot." A lesser actor would charge the lines with emotion, but Clift lets them roll off his tongue casually. Later, alone in her room with a sleeping Danny, Frederica deliberately awakens him although she makes it appear to have been accidental. Danny, who has been running from the authorities all day and is clearly knocked out, stirs, claiming he was merely dozing. Clift gives him a wonderfully crooked smile as he lies to her.

As with some of his earlier screen roles, however, Clift is just as convincing while he is silent and reacting. Perhaps the most powerful part of *The Big Lift* occurs with the sequence in which Frederica admits that she has covered up her past and ends with his marriage proposal. Through six short intervening scenes, Danny wanders the streets of the city. He is first approached by a child black marketer, whom he ignores. He then passes an alley in which many homeless children live; next an elderly lady in a shabby coat, who is pushing a dilapidated baby carriage, crosses his path. He watches as a uniformed man kisses his wife good-bye as he leaves for work—their home is a rundown freight car. Finally, he is confronted by two men who bring a large canister of garbage to the curb, where there suddenly appears a crowd of people eager to pick through it. Clift's body language and movements are enough to tell us that he has begun to sympathize with the plight of the Berliners. This sympathy allows him to forgive Frederica.

Rather than having the soft-hearted Danny represent all Americans, Seaton uses the character as an antithesis to Kowalski's hatred of his former foes. During the film, Kowalski softens toward the Germans, coming to terms not only with the democratic Gerda but also the ordinary people on the street. Danny, the dupe of the conniving Frederica, ultimately admits that Kowalski must have been right about her and everyone else. Surprisingly, Kowalski replies, "No, we were both wrong," and adds that "the answer lies somewhere between," that is, in a synthesis of Danny's sympathy and Kowalski's distrust. The Cold War moral, naturally, is that as bad as the Germans may have been and are, they are not the Russians. In a film where the Reds are seen as devious bunglers rather than insidious enemies, the "Krauts" (as Kowalski calls them) pose the lesser evil.

When Danny returns to the States, he may have learned, as Henry James's Americans often do, how to remain both sympathetic to the plight of others and protective of himself. The contradiction in Danny's character is that his vulnerability makes him attractive and engaging to others but also susceptible to their schemes. Kowalski's self-protective mechanisms—his ethnic bigotry, aggressive sexism, and raw brutality (he beats a man nearly to death until Danny pulls him away)—are, however, not only (even to Kowalski's view) excessive, but also ostensibly unnatural for Danny. Audiences had seen Clift reconcile with John Wayne, attempt unsuccessfully to adopt a son, charm, then jilt a woman, only to be jilted himself, and now suffer a broken heart: All of these roles, however, would be eclipsed by Clift's next performance, in which his character's ability to charm and deceive would be fused with a fierce, unexpected vulnerability.

Stardom

Montgomery Clift's next cinematic appearance begins with him facing oncoming traffic along a busy highway. He is wearing a dark leather jacket (and when he turns, we also see a T-shirt), his arm stretched toward the road as he thumbs a ride toward the approaching cars. After the credits disappear, he finally turns, and the camera comes in close on his angular, sunlit face as he looks at something off camera that puts him for a moment into a state of awe. Again, with the camera behind him, we gaze on what he has been gazing on: a billboard of a dark-haired bathing beauty reclining in her swim suit, with the company name of "Eastman" printed boldly below. An unusual horn honking at him[13] draws his attention to a young woman in an open Cadillac convertible whizzing past: She becomes even more obscure as she speeds into the distance. His eyes, however, are drawn now to the roadside arrival of what appears to be an old truck transporting caged chickens. He picks up his suitcase, gets in, and smiles broadly, like a man who would have preferred to ride with the woman in the Cadillac but is willing to take whatever has come his way.

Beginning with this opening sequence in A Place in the Sun, Clift's character follows in a long line of poor young men who, in their attempt to climb the ladder of success, must commit acts that are punishable by law. Unlike Julien Sorel in The Red and the Black, he seems to regard the horrors he contemplates with misgivings, but very much like Stendhal's anti-hero, he is ultimately betrayed by his own passions. And although readers may admire Sorel for his psychopathic brilliance, Clift's George Eastman in the end seems something of a victim of society. Nonetheless, as George, Clift for the first time assumes the lead role in a Hollywood film. Throughout, his thoughtful subtext becomes the audience's primary concern: Reading his tone and expression, his gestures, posture, walk consumes much of the spectator's attention. Here, finally, we glimpse on screen at close range the individual continuously creating his own gendered identity: George Eastman is an ambitious, troubled male who is constantly struggling to perform credibly as a man.

A Place in the Sun was Clift's first real starring role. Although his name had always appeared above the title, after Wayne's in Red River and after de Havilland's in The Heiress, and first for The Search (for which he was nominated for an Oscar) and The Big Lift, his new film would put him first before two other well-known movie actors, Elizabeth Taylor and Shelley Winters. Based on Theodore Dreiser's An American Tragedy, A Place in the Sun (1951) transposes the novel's America of the 1920s into post-World War II America. Although the war is never mentioned in the film itself, it is alluded to, for example, by the veteran's medal and wounded leg of the prosecutor who appears toward the film's end. Clift's character, George Eastman, is in his 20s, and as the director's son mentions in his commentary on the DVD version, during the time when the film was made and first viewed, audiences assumed that George had served during the war even though he never mentions it. Essentially, all we learn of his past is that he is the nephew of the man who manufactures the swimsuits advertised on the billboard at which he gazed. His late father, a religious fanatic, and his mother, who continues to run an urban mission, made him participate in their activities until, at the age of 14, he left home and made his way in the world, working as a bellboy, a caddy, and an elevator operator. Through a chance meeting with the wealthy Eastman uncle in Chicago, George is offered an opportunity for a better job. The scene on the side of the road that opens the movie is George hitchhiking across country to where the factory is located.

Although Dreiser set his book in New York state, the geography in the film is never explicit. The film does retain the setting of Loon Lake, where the wealthy Eastman family vacations, but the Loon Lake pictured in the film is not readily identifiable as the Adirondacks—it looks more as if it is out west, where of course the actual shooting location was. McCann characterizes George as "the poor western boy wanting to become the prosperous 'Eastman'" (51), and yet without any knowledge of where the movie is set, the possibility of George going west from Chicago rather than east is just as likely, or maybe more likely given the postwar rush to California. Perhaps "Eastman" refers not to the geography of the United States but to the metaphor contained in the title, for no matter where one may be, the sun always rises in the east, which is where George must turn (as he does toward the end of the opening sequence) to find his place in the sun.[14] The America of big business, of money and power, of middle-class and working-class people, of inequality for most and of justice for those who can afford it—this pervasive construct, the movie seems to say, could be anywhere in the United States; in a sense, by not specifying where the events take place, A Place in the Sun attempts to enlarge on the "America" particularized in An American Tragedy.

The plot concerns George Eastman's introduction to the Eastman factory and family. Although clearly from a different class than his relatives, George seems a hardworking young man, eager to succeed. He is put on an assembly line with female workers but is later promoted to an office job; later still, his uncle invites him into the family-held administration. Warned by his cousin that as an Eastman he cannot fraternize with the factory girls, George secretly meets with one who has been obviously eying him, the plain, blousy Alice Tripp (Shelley Winters). They go to the movies, stroll about a sleazy side of town, and for George's birthday Alice plans a dinner for two in her boarding house room, for which George is very late. Alice is hurt; she also reveals that she is carrying George's baby.

The reason he is late is because he has been to his uncle's party, where he danced the night away with Angela Vickers (Elizabeth Taylor). The dark-haired beauty, who resembles the billboard swimsuit model at whom

George stared in the opening sequence, is the same girl who whizzed by in the Cadillac and honked its distinctive horn at him. He has seen her since then—at his uncle's home, arriving at high-society events in the city, and in the factory parking lot—but at the Eastman party, she sees him. Drawn by his solitariness (no one will talk to him, so he withdraws to the billiards room to shoot pool), Angela is fascinated by how different he is from the young men she knows. She goes after him, dropping by his boarding house, taking him to parties (where he is suddenly accepted), and inviting him to her family's posh summer home on Loon Lake for his vacation.

George is torn between Alice, who becomes emotionally clinging and manipulative, and Angela, who now provides the light that illuminated his features as he faced the Eastman billboard. His place in the sun is beside her, even as Alice is unable to find a doctor who will perform an illegal abortion. Listening to the radio, which reports a number of vacation deaths over the weekend, George conceives a plan to murder Alice.[15] He is able to convince her that he should spend the first week of his vacation with his family at Loon Lake because it will gain him a promotion. All goes extremely well: His uncle promises a position in administration, Angela's family and friends all seem to like him, and Angela has fallen deeply in love with him. When a photo of Angela and George appears in the newspaper, Alice shows up at Loon Lake train station and phones George at Angela's house, threatening to come over unless he picks her up immediately. Claiming his mother is ill, George leaves and assures Alice they will find a place to get married in a nearby town the next morning. Yet the next morning city hall is closed for Labor Day.

He calms her by saying they can marry the next day; in the mean time they should enjoy the holiday by staying at a lodge on the other side of the lake and have a picnic once they arrive. On the way, George pretends his car has run out of gas. He urges Alice to come down to the lake with him, so they can eat their sandwiches, after which he will go for gas. He finds a boat to rent and rows them out into the lonely waters. Unable to perform the murder and yet unwilling to accept a future with Alice, George struggles with his conscience, finally choosing to return the boat to shore. Alice asks that he wait, so they can enjoy the moment, but her description of what their future together will be like horrifies George, who snaps at her and then withdraws to the bow. Desperately, Alice rises and moves toward him, even as George tells her to sit. Thus the boat overturns, and Alice, who cannot swim, drowns. George makes his way back to Angela's, obviously shaken but plainly determined to cover up what happened. When the police come, George flees but is soon arrested.

At trial, George is defended by his uncle's lawyer (Fred Clark), who believes in his innocence. Nonetheless, the district attorney (Raymond Burr) is able to convince the jury that George planned the murder and carried it out. Sentenced to die, he awaits his fate on death row. His mother and a Catholic priest encourage George to tell the truth about what happened. In their presence he cannot sustain his innocence and admits to being guilty. Later, Angela arrives, still in love with him, to say farewell. While blinding remembrances of their kisses play in his head, he walks the corridor to the electric chair.

Those familiar with Dreiser's works may detect the film's absence of his sometimes heavy-handed didacticism. Bosworth explains that "[e]ver since the blacklist, all the major studios were terrified of doing anything that could be construed as un-American" and adds that director George Stevens "kept toning the characters down, making them and the story more romantic" (163). LaGuardia puts it in even stronger terms: "Stevens decided to throw social commentary out the window in favor of success insurance. Now he wanted a compelling love story, with little to do with Dreiser's book" (79). Yet Steven Cohan, in his brilliant analysis, *Masked Men: Masculinity and the Movies in the Fifties*, points out that Joan Mellen, in her book, *Big Bad Wolves: Masculinity in the American Film*, had (without even referring to *A Place in the Sun*) managed to describe the dynamic of its social commentary: The film, he tells us, "aptly demonstrates her contention that fifties Hollywood cinema interiorized social dissent to focus instead on male sexuality" (229). In other words, much of what Dreiser had in mind—issues of class, gender, economics—remain in the film but are manifested in a different way, through a characterization that deconstructs the central image of patriarchy and its use of class, gender, and economics. Throughout the production, Clift, who had carefully read *An American Tragedy*, argued with the director about his performance and the performances of the other players, especially of Shelley Winters, in terms of what Dreiser had had in mind in the novel. He felt that Alice, as directed, was not sufficiently sympathetic.

Director George Stevens, was, like Howard Hawks, not only a veteran who had started in silent films and leapt into talkies, but also had worked successfully in a variety of genres. His (sound) credits included *Alice Adams* (1935), *Swing Time* (1937), *Gunga Din* (1939), *Penny Serenade* (1940), *Talk of the Town* and *Woman of the Year* (1942), *The More the Merrier* (1943), and *I Remember Mama* (1948). He also had headed the film unit that documented the Army's landings in Normandy in 1944 and the allies' opening of the Dachau concentration camp. Characteristic of Stevens's work in general and of *A Place in the Sun* in particular were the pensive, delayed tempoes, slow dissolves, and the use of superimpositions that lingered over transitions from one scene to the next. The director combined a very vibrant realism with expressionism. In this film, the combination of the two helped to reinstate many of the key ideas that Dreiser had introduced through the then-suspect (leftist) use of naturalism. In fact, Stevens had worked hard to convince Dreiser, who had died in 1945, to give him the rights to film the novel.[16] Like Clift, Stevens was very independent and stood up to the studios, retaining full artistic control of his work.

As in *The Heiress*, Clift portrayed a character playing a role, someone whose performance of himself was intended to communicate with and influence others. As a good-looking hitchhiker, he immediately attracts the audience's gaze, as well as Angela's. His own gaze takes in and admires the billboard and all it symbolizes as well as Angela's fleeting profile in the luxe convertible. When he enters the factory, he endures the scrutiny of the security guard and then of Mr. Eastman's secretaries. Later that evening, after he has bought a suit, he visits the Eastmans' home, where his tweed outfit makes him appear totally out of place, especially to Eastman's tuxedoed son (Keefe Brassell) and glib, gowned daughter, who look at but fail to see him; when their friend Angela arrives, she ignores him as well. His first day on the assembly line elicits audible sighs from the factory girls and a wolf-whistle as he strides sensuously into the room. Alice gazes at him; he never gazes back but appreciates her interest, inevitably taking advantage of it when they accidentally meet in a movie theater balcony, which is swarming with petting and lust. He continues to gaze upon Angela until, finally at a party, she begins gazing at him, at which point his feigned insouciance takes over.

Not only is George cognizant of his own beauty, but he also is aware too of how it can mitigate his social interactions. In *A Place in the Sun*, Clift becomes the handsome young man whose looks, along with his performance of honesty, draw affection or at least sympathy: George is the guy down on his luck, the well-intentioned eager beaver willing to work harder than the job demands, the obvious candidate for success—at least this is who he claims to be. In reality, however, he is simply the man who will use virtually anything he can muster—his youth, his intelligence, and his male beauty—to get ahead. To a certain degree, this intention is what makes him a man—not a boy willing to dissipate his assets for pleasure but an adult male, capable of weighing his options, investing himself in success, and creating a plan for the future. Boyish though he may appear, George represents a postwar America that would do what was necessary in order to succeed in a world that had survived the war and stood ready to replace the former imperial powers.

Ironically, George aspires to erase all the signs that draw Angela to him: He wishes to be like the young men whom Angela already knows. Yet as he succeeds in becoming like them, he is preoccupied with what he will do with Alice. Angela arrives at his rooming house just as George is contemplating Alice's "accidental" drowning. Her car's horn rouses him from his murderous thoughts, but as soon as he comes down to Angela's

car, her gaze recognizes his formidable anxiety, which she construes as yet
another sign of his difference, attributing his troubled eyes and expression
to his being very deep. Indeed, for Angela his struggles appear to hint at
an interiority absent from most men his age. This is what in fact attracts
her to him.

At this point, he suddenly realizes that his gaze has been more than
reciprocated: "You love me," he tells her, as if it is a tremendous, undeserved
surprise and his only solace. Before Alice turns up at Loon Lake, George
seems carefree enough, even playful, but with her phone call he is suddenly
thrown back into conflict. Again, Angela, who believes he must go see his
ill mother, finds his inner turmoil fascinating. When George finally returns
to the Vickers's house, the African-American housekeeper is first to see him;
her gaze notices that he looks horrible, and she even asks, "Are you well?"
Clift immediately gives George a new face and answers he is fine.

In the wake of Alice's drowning, all George wants is to be alone with
Angela, but the partying atmosphere and his acceptance by the young people
at the lake make it impossible. Later, when he tries to escape the crowd, he
encounters Angela's father (Shepperd Strudwick), who wants to have a man-
to-man talk with him about his interest in Angela. With Angela listening
just beyond the room's windows, George recites his history, which might
have been written by Horatio Alger: a poor boy raised by street missionaries,
working at an early age, fighting to make his way up. At first, the audience
may think George's defensive responses will earn Mr. Vickers's contempt,
but of course, George is playing his strong suit, for he is an embodiment of
The American Dream and a very appealing one at that. Most convincingly,
he has the mannerisms and vocal inflections of someone who is being abso-
lutely candid. Mr. Vickers awards his performance of honesty by consenting
to their eventual marriage.

Finally alone together, George cryptically tells Angela that something
terrible has happened and that people will soon be saying awful things about
him. Alone with her in the woods in the convertible, he seems, despite
everything, to be happy, but the audience knows that this is transient, for
they have listened to the radio that was left at the dock as George and
the others zoomed away in the Vickers's speedboat, seen the headlines in
the local papers, and watched as the young people at the house joke about
the reported murder. Even as George and Angela rush to their momentary
privacy, the presence of the police is made obvious when Angela gets a
speeding ticket before reaching the woods; as they converse and hold each
other, sirens blare in the background. Finally it is time to leave. On reaching the Vickers's home, George is aware that the police are about to come
for him. He asks Angela to enter the house first, alleging that he will be
along shortly. Instead he runs.

George's actual role in Alice's death is never made clear. Having watched the capsizing scene, the audience knows that he did not intend for the boat to overturn. Yet once it does, do George's actions make him guilty of her drowning? He tells the court that after the accident, he was dazed and cannot remember. The prosecutor, however, makes a convincing argument that whatever George says is suspect because of the numerous lies he admits to having told previously. Certainly, on death row and in the gaze of his mother (played by the soon-to-be blacklisted Anne Revere) and the priest,[17] he does acknowledge that he is guilty of not having saved her, and when Angela comes to see him, he tells her that he is guilty. Yet just what is the character guilty of? Claiming to be a decent, upstanding young man? Debauchery and fraud? Taking advantage of a vulnerable girl and then luring her to her death? Or murder? Or is George Eastman, like the protagonist of Dreiser's *An American Tragedy*, a victim of circumstances—in this case, of the circumstances as they have been constructed by a cruel American culture?

As George Eastman, Clift once again deploys an extraordinary range of subtleties in his acting. In many of the scenes, Stevens places George in the shadows, such as when he makes love to Alice and when she returns to his waiting car after she has learned the doctor will not give her an abortion, and in both scenes the audience can only hear the tight desperation in his voice. At the same time, we often view the back of George's head, as in the scene in which George phones Alice to tell her he will spend his first week of vacation with the Eastmans. Although the camera comes in for a close-up as Alice listens on her end, George's back faces the pay phone in the hallway, and the audience sees his stooping posture through the door of his room as they hear him lie about where he will be. At other moments, we watch George as he listens and reacts to someone facing him; Alice's long speech, indicating that she is in trouble, is shot over Alice's shoulders, as Clift's almost still face attempts to stifle the emotion George feels.

Through much of the picture, the camera observes from a distance, especially in the scene in which George arrives in his tweeds at the East-man mansion; his discomfort in his plush surroundings is evident from Clift's walk, from his taking a seat and squirming as his relations make small talk, from his tight-lipped attempt at pleasant conversation. The camera comes in for a close up only when Angela, whose signature honk has sounded a few seconds before, enters the room, and George's sudden recognition of her is palpable on his face. Stevens uses this strategy again, as George and Angela dance into the night at the Eastmans' party. We watch them move in the distance, across a great room, and then dance out of the frame through a large doorway, only to catch a close-up of the two a moment later.

Taylor had never before worked with an actor like Clift. She regarded *A Place in the Sun* as "my first real chance to probe myself" (Qtd. Bosworth

166), her first opportunity to be an actress instead of a teenage star (she was 17 when production began). Monty was totally committed to working out characterization, and while rehearsing with Taylor (whom he used to address as "Bessie" or "Bessie Mae"), he sometimes played her character to demonstrate his ideas about Angela (166–167). In a short documentary,[18] George Stevens Jr. interviews an older Taylor, who vividly recalls how Monty's character made him shake uncontrollably and had sweat pouring down his forehead, not as if he were playing George but as if he were George.

"Stevens commanded Monty to keep Mira out of his way," notes LaGuardia, and this "made Monty edgy and distrustful" (80). Yet again, he worked with Mira in his dressing room, and when his interpretation of his role differed from Stevens's, Clift would argue with the director, who was used to getting his own way eventually. One demand that Stevens made, however, was that George "conjure up some awesome, terrifying emotion" as he crosses down the prison corridor to the death chamber. Clift's flat, almost passive expression, which Stevens fought him on and lost (Bosworth 169), and his calm, anesthetized gaze forward never reveals who George really is—if, in fact, he is anyone.

Perhaps the enigma of the character is the most impressive aspect of what Clift achieves. Who is George? We get glimmers of the inner identity from time to time, but he shows us just a precious few. His excitement at the promise of the billboard and the alluring taunt of Angela's drive-by freely play across his features, and so does the horror of the drowning murder he contemplates, as his shocked, repelled expression is countered by the sharp darting of his eyes back and forth. When George and Alice, passing along an unsavory street on their way from the movie theater, stumble upon some missionaries, including a boy, who resembles him, singing a hymn, George goes pale and looks genuinely appalled. Yet when he trembles uncontrollably on the witness stand and beads of perspiration drip from his brow, in full gaze of the jury considering his case, spectators may wonder if this is George Eastman authentically or merely in performance, just as his "sincere" story to Angela's father is too good not to be performed (even if it is all true).

Critics have construed the role of George Eastman in various ways. Some commentators make sense of Clift's performance in A Place in the Sun as the beginning of a long line of rebel male characters in postwar films. Morella and Epstein, for example, claim that the film "exemplifies his rebel hero image" and that he "was tremendously relevant to the youth of the early fifties. . . . He was a man rebelling against his fate without knowing how and questioning why" (58). McCann, in Rebel Males, points to Clift's onscreen ambisexuality:

[H]e was not another Gable or Tracy—a traditional, tough, taciturn leading man; he was rather remote, displaced, a loner, and
somewhat androgynous in his appeal. He represented a new kind
of man for the 1950s; a man who refused to make judgements
on sexual preferences. He reflected the loneliness, the emotional
dislocation, the smouldering hostility, and the quicksilver charm
that soon became characteristic of an entire generation of actors.
(47)

Although McCann sees Clift in this film assume the role of a needy child
around women (52), he consistently uses the term *man* to describe George
Eastman.

Steven Cohan, however, regards Clift's early roles, as well as those of
Brando and Dean, as performances of boys who try unsuccessfully to play
men. Cohan recognizes that during the war, the troops overseas had been
referred to as "The Boys," but he also finds that

[o]n both sides of the battlefield, many of these soldiers were
literally boys who never became men, so the term "boys" evoked
innocence and loss as well as immaturity and loss. . . . Yet
because the term did not correspond to an actual age group,
but included school children, adolescents, college students, and
bachelors [as well as soldiers], "boy" was also an indeterminate
gender category functioning, through its absorption of all the
male "vices," to regulate the masculinity of grown men. (237)

As such, Clift is only the first of a line of grown boys who furtively and
disastrously fight against the construct of 1950s manhood (which Cohan
sees as characterized by "the breadwinner ethic of hegemonic masculinity"
[239]). He describes "Brando, like his rival Clift, as a boy masquerading as
a man" (241).

Although much of what Cohan says is extremely insightful and revealing, I disagree with him on this; if anything, I would reverse his description:
Brando, like Clift, is a man masquerading as a boy. As Kylo-Patrick R. Hart
maintains, in his speculation about gay male spectatorship of Clift's films,
"Clift became the first actor of the era with whom audiences identified rather
than looked up to" (73). Thus, his appeal to some spectators—especially to
young men disaffected and disillusioned by the war—was immediate. He represented *un homme manqué*, an adult male unwilling both to accept the rigid
definitions of American masculinity and to see himself as non-masculine,
whose vulnerability and sensitivity could not be relegated to effeminacy,

though it was deemed immature, childish, and lacking in the grown-up manly wisdom that accepted and exemplified the prevalent construct of masculinity. In social terms, in both his real and performed lives, his refusal to conform to gender norms and his persistence in rewriting manly identity constituted a rebellion, albeit one that often was presented as a romantic act of failed rebellion. Nonetheless, for those young men watching and identifying with Clift's performance, the critique and questioning of "the breadwinner ethic of hegemonic masculinity" was sufficient, for Clift was a man and Clift was like them.

Epilogue: A Final Turn On Stage

It may be unfair to end this discussion of Clift's performances on film here, for he went on to make twelve more movies. However, by the time *A Place in the Sun* premiered in 1951, a staunch competitor had appeared on the scene. Clift's rivalry with Brando had begun in New York when they both were appearing in Broadway plays. After Clift had left for Hollywood, Brando would score his greatest stage triumph as Stanley Kowalski in Williams's *A Streetcar Named Desire* (1947). Four years later, both would be nominated for an Oscar for best actor, Clift for *Sun*, Brando for the film version of *Streetcar*. Clift was no longer the unique eccentric young actor on the screen, and after Brando, there would be a succession of unconventional male stars who seemed to follow in their wake.

True, many of Clift's later roles were amazing, and he twice received Academy Award nominations, but the person who Clift was in life was about to undermine Clift the actor. Around the time he finished *Sun*, friends and family began to notice he was drinking heavily. He consulted a psychiatrist who seemed to have a bizarre hold on him and who could not—or would not—stop his drinking. When production began in California for Alfred Hitchcock's *I Confess* (1952), his drinking became worse—he actually passed out at a dinner party Hitchcock had thrown. By the time he began shooting *From Here to Eternity* (with Zinnemann in 1953), Clift would show up drunk on the set (LaGuardia 108).

He appeared heavily dependent on Mira Rostova as well: Karl Malden, who played the detective in *I Confess*, heard Hitchcock attack Clift's coach: "Monty doesn't need that little pigeon!" Yet "Hitch" tolerated her on the set, "because whether she believes it or not, I know bloody well more than she does" (Bosworth 216). Although Mira came out to the West Coast for *From Here to Eternity*, helping Monty prepare his role before shooting began, Zinnemann refused to allow her on the set, and with his psychiatrist's encouragement, Monty had Mira return to New York (LaGuardia 108). Clift was becoming more difficult to work with.

In the spring of 1954, Clift left Hollywood to work on an off-Broadway production of *The Sea Gull* by Anton Chekhov. He had talked, earlier in his career, of assembling a company of actors to perform in a script of substance on stage, and in a way, this show would make good those intentions. The play was mounted at The Phoenix, one of the few remaining New York theaters to continue doing the classics. He included in the cast two of his closest associates: Mira Rostova would play Nina; Kevin McCarthy would play Trigorin; and the two of them, along with Clift (who would appear as Constantin), collaborated on the translation.

In one of the kinder reviews, Brooks Atkinson wrote in *The Times* that it was "an interesting performance." Extolling the brilliance of the script, Atkinson tried to explain how the play had been written for a "permanent company" in which the "individual performances" would seem "more integrated." He allowed that as Americans, "[W]e shall have to be satisfied with the mixed styles inherent in the work of good actors who are not accustomed to play together." At the same time, he complimented a number of the actors, including Judith Evelyn (as Mme Irina Arkedina), Maureen Stapleton (as Masha), and those in smaller roles, including Sam Jaffe, Will Geer, June Walker, and others. He noted that "Montgomery Clift's lonely, brooding Constantin, her [Arkedina's] unhappy son, is beautifully expressed without any foolish pathology. It is more American than Russian, but so is Mr. Clift, for that matter." Certainly, there was praise here, but at the same time Atkinson seems to be pointing to an aspect of Clift's acting style that perhaps had been less noticeable before: Monty's "honest" performances did not transcend the immediate limitations of time and space from which the actor himself had emerged. Unlike Brando and many others, Clift did not believe in taking on foreign accents or mannerisms. He was bound to roles that he could play as an American.

Atkinson was less kind when it came to the two remaining players. He found Monty's acting coach, Mira Rostova as Nina, "handicapped by a heavy accent" and by "a florid style alien to the whole spirit of Chekhov." He also noted that Clift's great friend, Kevin McCarthy, as Trigorin, lacked "the worldliness or worldly corruption" of the character and added that he did not "suggest any of the qualities of a writer. These important parts," he concluded, "are inadequately played, which is a pity."

Although Atkinson was grateful for any American production of *The Sea Gull*, which had not been seen in New York since the 1930s, when Lunt and Fontaine had headed a Broadway version of the play, much of the optimism with which Clift had looked forward to his return to the theater diminished considerably. Although he had acquitted himself well in this limited run, the two to whom he was closest had been exposed to the critics' disdain. The bad reviews were ultimately more harmful to Mira, who subsequently made her career as an acting coach who rarely appeared on stage. McCarthy, however, would have a long career as a film and television actor. Clift went back to making movies.

What Montgomery Clift brought to his film roles was a sense of performance, not so much a sense of his own performance, as some actors tend to do, but of his characters as performers in life. No doubt his own life, in which he was performing much of the time, informed his sense of characterization. Likewise, his personal life and ideas about his own gender and sexuality, informed the way his characters performed their masculinity. Cast against John Wayne, Ralph Richardson, and Paul Douglas, Clift's characters embodied younger men. Identity, he had been brought up to see, was a matter of self-construct: Sunny taught him that names could be changed, ancestries erased, and socioeconomic factors discounted through good manners and breeding. Similarly, the boundaries of sexuality and of gender could be moved, crossed, even dissolved.

If some believe Clift was "a boy playing a man," they are perhaps confused, for Clift—like most adult males—was an adult male playing a man. The difference between his performances and Wayne's, Richardson's, and Douglas's was that Monty always showed that manhood is a performance, whereas the others presented masculinity as if it flowed naturally from them. His noticeable vulnerability is not begrudgingly admitted, nor is it encrusted in a persona of power and control, nor embedded in a matrix of class: Clift's characters are men who are aware that they are acting the role of men before other men; in front of women, Clift's characters, such as Steve in *The Search*, Danny in *The Big Lift*, and George in *Sun*, become childlike, boyish perhaps, harkening back to an earlier developmental stage from which all males (and all men) supposedly emerge. If Clift's onscreen identities continue to seem especially genuine and honest, they are so because they allowed him to express publicly what he practiced and hid privately.

Hence, Clift's performances, which clearly present masculinity as performance, complicate what was accepted as an essential truth, that all Americans knew, even if they could not articulate it, just what a man was. A man could be beautiful, a quality reserved for women on screen up until Clift, and soft, and nonaggressive. The intellectual was no less a man than the action hero. A man like the men Clift played could call into question every certainty the audience held about masculinity, conjuring up a competitive masculinity that cast doubt on what had been thought to be intuitively "known."

CHAPTER 5

Doing and Undoing Masculinity

The Early Performances of Marlon Brando

Introduction

If any single male actor can be said to represent postwar American masculin-ity, it would have to be Marlon Brando. His range was wider and his oeuvre, larger than either Montgomery Clift's or James Dean's, his career surpassed and outlived theirs, and even after he had stopped acting, he remained for many the quintessential screen actor of his—and for some, for all—time. Moreover, somehow, while playing roles that in many ways were to define contemporary manhood, he managed to complicate the gender ideals that he was supposedly upholding by creating within his characterizations thor-oughly honest depictions of the instability of gender itself. With his need to problematize deliberately the masculinity his roles demanded, Brando was one of many who led a generational challenge to what it meant to be both a man and a male.

Whereas Clift has had relatively few biographers, most of whom were careful in their research, Brando has had many, many of whom have not always been so. In her 2001 biography of Brando, Patricia Bosworth, whose biography of Clift remains a definitive source on his life and work, included minimal information about Brando's private activities and his sexuality: "I chose not to deal with these subjects," she notes (212), referring the reader to Peter Manso's extensive (and sometimes highly speculative) *Brando: The Biography* (1994). There are literally dozens of books on Brando's life. My personal favorite was a tome entitled, *Brando Unzipped*, an apparently self-published exposé, in which the author would have us believe that the list of Brando's sex partners ran longer than the New York City telephone direc-tory. If one-fourth of what is stated in the book were true, Brando's exploits would expand the meaning of the phrase "sexually active" to pandemic proportions. As of this writing, there has been no definitive biography of Marlon Brando.

At the same time, much, probably too much, has been written about Brando. Although some of what has come before is very good and very insightful, a large part of it is pure silliness: tell-all's about his sex life, trivializations of his work, and reifications of the very publicity he supposedly loathed. (I write "supposedly" because even Brando writing or talking about Brando adds to the myths about himself, even as he tries to dispel them.) Tempting as it has been to consider him in the context of his private existence, I have chosen to write on Brando's performances—not only his acting performances on stage and screen but, as Judith Butler might put it, his performance of gender as part of those performances.

To understand how Brando influenced his original audiences, we must look away from all we now know (or at least from what we think we know) about Brando behind the scenes; theater and film audiences in the 1940s and 1950s often did not know what to make of Brando, and details about his life released at the time probably confused them even more. He was a movie star who frequently defied movie star behaviors, an inexplicable oddball, or (to use a term from the period) a genuine "kook." At the same time, he brought to his roles an intensity and authenticity that were difficult to dismiss: Perhaps the one indisputable truth about Brando was his extraordinary presence on the screen.

A key part of his presence was his on-stage and later on-screen creation of male characters whose performances of masculinity somehow suggested that the gender construct was neither consistent nor natural. As Susan Bordo asserts, his "portrayals of macho consistently maintained a highly self-conscious, critical edge . . ." (111). She continues, "His ambivalent manhood would eventually inspire a generation of actors and directors . . . bent on 'deconstructing' macho rather than playing it straight" (111–112). Part of what Brando deployed in order to derail traditional masculinity was, according to Bordo, "an emotional expressiveness, a willingness to portray male *need*, helplessness, dependency" that was markedly different from the masculinity of the "violent action hero" (112).

Of course, not everyone liked Brando's acting. Even on Broadway, some failed to appreciate what he could do well and focused instead on his limitations and flaws. On the screen, where audiences experienced him with what at least appeared to be a greater immediacy, such limitations and flaws were blown up, enlarged, so that comedians who did celebrity impressions, such as Frank Gorshen, could easily caricature him. Naturally, what they imitated was what they and their audiences saw on screen, so they were imitating Brando imitating Stanley Kowalski, Terry Malloy, or Mark Antony. Yet Brando himself was a mysterious being, lurking somewhere behind his performances, whom audiences often believed was identical with his characters. We may never clearly know who he was, but we can certainly re-examine some of what he created.

Brando on Broadway

Young Marlon Brando, born in Omaha on April 23, 1924, arrived in New York in the spring of 1943. Classified by the draft board as 4F due to an injured knee and poor eyesight, he worked a variety of menial jobs. The following fall, he began classes at the New School, where he studied with Stella Adler, who, in addition to having worked in the Yiddish theater, had been one of the Group Theatre's primary players. In 1934, she and her then husband, one of the Group's founders, Harold Clurman, made their way to France and studied with Constantine Stanislavski, the first acting teacher to develop a method (often called "The Method") of teaching acting. Adler, as part of the Group's inner circle, had found herself at odds with Lee Strasberg, whose approach to acting centered on affective memory, a technique based on some of Stanislavski's early writings. Stanislavski himself was by now at odds with such ideas, believing that instead of relying on memory, actors needed to work more from their imaginations.

During his time at the New School, Brando appeared in a variety of roles—including parts in George Bernard Shaw's *Saint Joan*, John Millington Synge's *Riders to the Sea*, and a stage version of *War and Peace*, adapted from Leo Tolstoy's novel and directed by German émigré, Erwin Piscator (who had worked—or at least tried to—with Tennessee Williams). In early 1944, young Marlon appeared in two different roles—one youthful, the other ancient—in Gerhardt Hauptmann's *Hannele's Way to Heaven*. He repeated this performance later that year when he joined Piscator's summer troupe on Long Island. Agent Maynard Morris, who had come to see the show one evening, approached Brando after the final curtain. The following fall, Morris and another agent at MCA, Edie van Cleve, sent Brando to Broadway auditions.

The kind of training and ideas imparted by Adler were not widely in practice on the professional stage, where hams freely mixed with more sensitized players. In a world where song-and-dance man Eddie Dowling could play a character at least two decades younger than himself in the drama, *The Glass Menagerie*, and where a former matinee darling, such as Laurette Taylor, could turn in an exquisitely detailed—or to put it more ironically, a thoroughly Stanislavskian—performance as Amanda, the assortment of acting styles visible on stage at the time was quite amazing. This was the context in which Marlon Brando first appeared.

Brando was cast in what would become a hit that season, John van Druten's *I Remember Mama*, directed by the playwright and produced by Richard Rodgers and Oscar Hammerstein II. In this nostalgic drama, replete with family humor, Brando played the adolescent son, Nels, not a major role but not exactly a walk-on. However, the cast was large, starred stage favorites Mady Christians and Oscar Homolka, and featured a number of polished players. Most of the reviews do not mention Brando and many more simply list him as a cast member or refer to his character without giving his name. However, Robert Garland, in *The Journal-American*, described a "teen age youngster, Nels, puffing his first cigarette quite openly in public" and added, "The Nels of Marlon Brando is, if he doesn't mind me saying so, charming."[1] A few other reviewers commended his performance, along with those of the other children in the play, but no one other than Garland singled him out. Despite their apparent obliviousness to Brando, the critics would recall him in this long-running show when he turned up, sixteen months later, in a bomb by one of America's leading dramatists.

Truckline Café was Maxwell Anderson's postwar critique of failed matrimony. Set in a West Coast road stop, the play awkwardly detailed the comings and goings of men and women who, because of the war, had been unable to remain in their marriages. The notices were merciless to both Anderson and director Harold Clurman. Not surprisingly, the reviews praised the efforts of the large cast, which included Kevin McCarthy, Virginia Gillmore, Karl Malden, Lou Gilbert, and of course Brando, who played a vet who murders his unfaithful wife and then confesses to the crime. Garland, who had pointed out Brando in *I Remember Mama*, calls the show "a bit-player's fiesta" and states "Brando has himself a high old actorial time" and "distinguishes himself in this, his second professional part." Burton Rascoe in *The World-Telegram* asserted that most of the acting was indifferent "[e]xcept for a brief bit by Marlon Brando as the former soldier who blew his top" and the performances of McCarthy, Malden, and June Walker. Several critics, including Ward Morehouse in *The Sun*, Louis Kronenberger in *PM*, and an unnamed reviewer in *The Christian Science Monitor*, called his performance "effective," whereas others extolled him: "[T]he role of [Tory McRae's] unforgiving husband is acted with force and decision by Marlon Brando," wrote Kelcey Allen in *Women's Wear Daily*; "Marlon Brando is exceptionally fine as the tense, neurotic killer," proclaimed the *Newark Evening News*; and "Marlon Brando is remarkably good," remarked Arthur Pollock in *The Brooklyn Daily Eagle*.

Robert Coleman in *The Daily Mirror* indicated that " 'Truckline Café' didn't stir the first nighters to anything resembling enthusiasm till its third act when Marlon Brando won robust applause with a virtuoso performance as the regretful wife killer," and similarly, George Freedly in *The Morning Telegraph* observed, "It was Marlon Brando who walked away with the show with his brilliant portrayal of the deceived husband. His scene of anguish after killing his wife was really terrific and he deserved every round of applause his exit earned." Yet this ovation and his performance were ignored by George Jean Nathan in *The Journal American*, Howard Barnes in *The Herald Tribune*, John Chapman in *The Daily News*, and Lewis Nichols in *The Times*.

Brando's work in this ill-fated play had obviously made an impression on some critics, but there remained a few who chose not to notice him. Because the cast was so large, they could easily avoid discussing a performance that in some way made them uncomfortable. In his next role, however, no critic could avoid writing about Brando: He was cast as Eugene Marchbanks, the dreamy poet who falls in love with a married woman, in *Candida* by George Bernard Shaw. The title role was to be played by one of the great leading ladies of the American stage, Katherine Cornell, who had already played the role several times on Broadway, most recently in 1942 opposite Burgess Meredith as Marchbanks.

Critics were divided over just how well Brando had done. On the negative side, Rascoe in *The World Telegram* alleged, "Nobody can ever do Marchbanks properly. . . . Maybe Miss Cornell should put on pants and play Marchbanks, even if she has to wear whiskers. Mr. Brando did as well as he could. . . ." Morehouse in *The Sun* opined, "Marlon Brando isn't very successful in his projection of the poet, Marchbanks. He isn't eloquent or sympathetic or dominating or exasperating. He is just weak. And at times he is almost inaudible." Nichols in *The Times* protested that, as Marchbanks, Brando "emphasizes the weakness and banks the fire, the result being a somewhat monotonously intoning poet. His version is not believable, it fails to prove, among other things, why Morell [Candida's jealous husband] should pay any attention to him." *The Brooklyn Daily Eagle*'s Pollock obviously enjoyed Brando's performance but found it out of his range, pointing to his strong work in Anderson's flop:

> He is going to do a great many similar roles [i.e., to the one in *Truckline*], it is likely, for he has a talent for them, and he will get over his sleep-walking technique in time. It does not suit all characters. As the Byronic young man in Shaw's imagining he makes the boy seem only seven or eight years old, and he favors sweetness more than light, but he is good just the same, sensitive and understanding, if not quite articulate enough for the best of Marchbanks.

Even at this early stage of Brando's career, critics were beginning to place him in a particular category, to delimit the types of roles he should and should not play.

Some of his reviews were mixed. Coleman's in *The Daily Mirror* saw that "Brando's poetic, romantic, Machiavellian Marchbanks [was] uneven— excellent at best, but marred, sometimes by poor timing, which seems to be attributable to diction trouble." Kronenberger in *PM* admitted that "the role is a trial and a test, and in his own soft, poetic-looking way, Mr. Brando was at times most effective. He always, moreover, held your interest. But the part was not altogether sustained, nor was the interpretation particularly successful." Barnes in *The Herald Tribune* made the inevitable comparison: "Brando is no Burgess Meredith, but he makes the final act . . . exceedingly satisfying"; and so did Rowland Field in *The Newark Evening News*: "Brando [is] a new Marchbanks and a good one, if not as outstanding as Burgess Meredith's portrayal. . . ."

Yet a substantial minority of critics offered accolades, starting with *The Journal American*'s Garland, who had previously spoken of Brando glowingly and now turned the comparison to Brando's advantage:

> I had thought that the Eugene Marchbanks of Mr. Meredith was the Eugene Marchbanks for whom his creator had been waiting. As a matter of fact, I remember saying so in print. But in the [*sic*] late April of 1942, I had not sat in the presence of the Eugene Marchbanks of the [*sic*] Marlon Brando who played it yesterday. Young Mr. Brando stepped right out of the stage directions.
>
> [T]he fresh excitement of the current reproduction stems straight from the Eugene Marchbanks of Marlon Brando [whose] Marchbanks is superb.

In *The Daily News*, Chapman agreed, "Brando managed to make something different, something a little more understandable out of the trying role of Marchbanks, the baby poet" and pointed to the actor's understated but concentrated performance:

> Mr. Brando achieved a believable, love-sick individual by play-ing very quietly. I felt that his intensity was within him, where it should be, and not spread all around outside. For the second time this season . . . the young man has shown himself a player of promise.

Vernon Rice in *The Post* found Marchbanks, the character, capable of "caus-ing a wave of nausea to pass through any audience" but that Brando's ver-sion did not do so, insisting, "[H]e continues to be the promising young actor he was in his two previous plays." "A very fine actor," offers Allen in *Women's Wear Daily*.

Pollock's commentary on Brando's proper roles perhaps anticipates our own ideas about him. Shaw may not seem the sort of playwright with whom we would associate Brando as an actor, and in retrospect casting him in *Candida* may sound very strange, but in the 1940s, Shaw (who incidentally was still alive) was regarded as one of the major twentieth-century dramatists. Brando's training was in the classics—some work in Shakespeare and Molière but also much more in what was then thought of as the "modern repertoire," which included Henryk Ibsen, Anton Chekhov, and of course, Shaw. In fact, after Brando abandoned Broadway for Hollywood, he made a brief return to the East Coast in 1953 and played the foolish but glorious military officer in a summer stock production of *Arms and the Man*.

At the same time, we may find it difficult to comprehend how Brando fit into a cast that included Cornell, as well as Mildred Natwick and Sir Cedric Hardwicke, all Broadway veterans from an earlier era. Brando is currently thought of as one of the first of a whole new generation of actors. Clearly, in spite of all his training with Adler, he was still obliged to perform professionally with players who had had radically different backgrounds in and philosophies on acting. To a degree, some of the complaints about Brando as Marchbanks reflect how critics, who were used to one style of playing, tried to make sense of his, and the silence from four influential critics probably hides a deeper problem with his performance. True, a few critics liked his Marchbanks, but the majority seemed to find him jarring, especially in a Shavian context.

The next show in which Brando appeared, in September 1946, was described as an agitprop pageant. Written by Ben Hecht and directed by Luther Adler, with music by Kurt Weill, *A Flag Is Born* raised money for the American League for a Free Palestine. Set in a European graveyard, the play brought an elderly Jewish couple, Tevya, played by Paul Muni, and Zelda, played by Celia Adler, face to face with David, a suicidal young man, who has managed to escape what we now call the Holocaust, played by Brando. After viewing together the march of Jewish history from biblical times to the present, David decides, despite his bitterness, to fight for a Jewish state, whereas Tevya and Zelda join their departed ancestors in the cemetery. The script was overstated, repetitive, and reductive, and the piece ran an hour and forty-five minutes without an intermission. Muni, who had been a major star in the Yiddish theater and then in Hollywood, was roundly praised for his performance in this propagandistic work, and critics were extremely respectful of the cause that the play represented, but few actually appeared to have enjoyed the show.

A few reviewers singled out Brando. Once again, Garland of *The Journal American* mentioned him in particular, now as "the bright particular

star of the Ben Hecht pageant. . . . His David is enduring in the memory."
Beaufort in *The Christian Science Monitor* also praises his acting:

> Marlon Brando, who controls his force as an actor with an intui-
> tive sense of inner restraint plays the shadowy figure of a modern
> David. Mr. Hecht has permitted his old people almost too much
> garrulity, but he has treated David with terseness. This quality is
> astutely caught in the economy of Mr. Brando's playing.

Women's Wear Daily's Allen called his performance "sincere and eloquent."
  Yet there were those again who seemed to dislike Brando's acting,
such as Rice in *The Post*, who summarized, "Marlon Brando was called upon
again to provide some dramatic fireworks." William Hawkins in *The World
Telegram* called Brando "a sternly hopeless David whose accusations sear
when his bitterness bursts out," and Chapman in *The Daily News* carped,
"Marlon Brando portrays the young man and he, too, has bitter things to
say." Freedly in *The Morning Telegraph* conceded that Brando "was deeply
touching," but then complained that he only "at moments realizes" the
role. He adds,

> His scene of denunciation of the complacent ones has a mag-
> nificence about it. However, he badly needs work on his voice
> for he is straining it unnecessarily and someday will pay for it.
> He has too much promise of development as an actor to neglect
> his primary instrument of expression.

The gist of Freedly's criticism goes back to technique and to how Brando's
performance contrasted with his costars'. What kind of actor either wastes
his voice or mutters inaudibly? One, Freedly suggests, without adequate
stage training. For all his sincerity and power, Brando struck some critics as
unprofessional, a newcomer who needed to conform to the rules of the stage.
  Early in 1947, Brando was cast in a translation of Jean Cocteau's
L'Aigle à deux têtes, opposite Tallulah Bankhead. As the play toured out of
town, it changed names from *The Eagle with Two Heads* to *The Eagle Has
Two Heads* and then to *Eagle Rampant*. Yet the play's title was the least of
its problems. It was hardly one of Cocteau's best works, and the role of Stanislas, which Brando played, had originally been written for Cocteau's close
companion, Jean Marais, whose beauty quickly faded as soon as he opened
his mouth; consequently Stanislas did not say a single word throughout the
entire first act even though he was on stage most of the time. This suited
Bankhead but not Brando. Moreover, the reviewers were unkind to Brando.
Bankhead asked Clift to come to one of the performances, hoping that he

might step into the role; because the two had already worked together in *The Skin of Our Teeth* (directed by Elia Kazan), Clift was not willing to repeat the experience. Eventually, Brando left the cast to be replaced by Helmut Dantine, who opened the play on Broadway, where it was panned and quickly closed.

Brando's big role came toward the end of 1947 in Tennessee Williams's masterpiece, *A Streetcar Named Desire*. The play was directed by Elia Kazan, one of the founders of The Actors Studio, who originally tried to get John Garfield for the role of Stanley Kowalski and then considered Burt Lancaster although neither was willing to accept a run-of-play contract. When it made its debut, *Streetcar* seemed to belong to the character of Blanche DuBois, a high school teacher who has lost both her job (for having slept with a male student) and her family's southern mansion ("Belle Reve"). She leaves Mississippi to join her married sister, Stella, in New Orleans. Stella's husband, Stanley, quickly catches on that, despite her attempts to appear genteel, Blanche's personal life has been rather unsavory. At the same time, his common manners and working-class values repel her. Blanche tries to make her sister sever her ties to Stanley and simultaneously flirts with Stanley's best friend, Mitch. Eventually, Stanley is successful in putting Blanche in her place, drawing his wife back to him and revealing to Mitch Blanche's sordid past, but the violence in his victory culminates in his raping Blanche while Stella is in the hospital having his child. Stella is placed in the awful position of having to choose to believe her sister, who insists she has been sexually assaulted, or her husband, who maintains that Blanche is crazy. In the end, Blanche is taken to a state mental hospital.

Like most synopses of great works, the above reduction of *Streetcar* is hardly adequate and dreadfully simplified although it offers a sense of the "plot" that evolves through the interactions of the characters. Because Blanche gradually deteriorates as the play progresses and because she goes through a wide variety of emotions, the role is difficult. In the original production, Jessica Tandy created the character, and she received very positive reviews and about an equal number of mixed ones. (Karl Malden played Mitch and Kim Hunter, Stella.) Yet giving the play to Blanche, as the first critics and audiences clearly did, in many ways distorts and even alters the piece. Ultra-ladylike Blanche is meaningful only in juxtaposition to macho, proletarian Stanley. Each embodies extreme and supposedly opposing constructs of gender. Although Blanche may be construed as almost a parody of femininity, Stanley is a caricature of masculinity. Each is a performer of what many Americans at the time believed to be the defining characteristics of gender. What differentiates them, however, is not so much a set of polar opposites as a collection of identical traits that each performs differently.

The brilliance of *A Streetcar Named Desire* is in its determination to critique and thus destabilize what audiences think they know about the sexes and sexuality. In the play, Stanley may be brutal, but he is no more savage than Blanche, who is willing to destroy his marriage and social position. Blanche may be more vulnerable, but she is no more sensitive than Stanley. In the end, what distinguishes him from her is not sex but power, for Stanley's rape of Blanche is violence in the guise of sex. Of course, in 1947, such considerations were hardly part of American cultural discourse. Williams's play was far ahead of its time, as Woody Allen's film *Sleeper* (1973) implies: Part of the time traveler's gender re-education requires Allen not only to perform as the winner of a Miss America pageant but also to play Blanche to Diane Keaton's Stanley.

The part of Stanley Kowalski would make Brando's career, propelling him from Broadway to Hollywood, and for the first time earn him general praise from the critics. Yet some of the praise was tempered with reluctance. Richard Watts Jr. in *The Post* stated his position very clearly: "I have hitherto not shared the enthusiasm of most reviewers for Marlon Brando, but his portrayal of the heroine's sullen, violent nemesis is an excellent piece of work." (However, Watts continues, "Even finer is Karl Malden. . . .") Kronenberger in *PM* exhibited a similar reticence: "No one is likely to underrate Marlon Brando's brilliant performance of the brother-in-law, the more astonishing for being like nothing else he has ever played."

Other critics emphasized the savage aggression inherent to Brando's performance of Stanley. *The Morning Telegraph*'s Freedly, for example, indicated,

> Marlon Brando has genuinely justified our faith in his acting for
> he is giving the best integrated performance of his young life
> as the tough-talking, tough-acting Steve [*sic*]. Anything more
> brutal could not have been endured not less be right.

Barnes in *The Herald Tribune* mentions how he "is brutally convincing as the brother-in-law who forces her [Blanche] on the night her sister is having a baby." Beaufort in *The Christian Science Monitor* concurred that Brando "acts Stanley with uncompromising brutality, bereft of all compassion." As *The Daily News*'s Chapman saw it, "Mr. Brando is magnificent as the forthright husband, in his simple rages, his simple affections, and his blunt humor." In *Women's Wear Daily*, Thomas R. Dash called Brando's Stanley, "properly uncouth, unmannered and violent and can explode in a convincing fit of anger." In *The Sun*, Morehouse thought the role was Brando's "finest work to date in his characterization of the slow-witted, virile, uncompromising young husband." The implication throughout these evaluations is that Stanley is the kind of role Brando could do well—the inarticulate, highly emotional, irrational brute, capable of physical violence—not unlike (as Freedly would no doubt readily admit) the murderer in *Truckline Café*.

Although Garland gushed as usual in *The Journal American* ("Here . . . is our theatre's most memorable young actor at his most memorable"), Brooks Atkinson in *The Times* gave prominence to Tandy and disposes of Brando, Malden, and Hunter in a single paragraph, calling their performances "of very high quality—all act not only with color and style but with insight." The little he says about Brando places him with the critics mentioned above, describing his Stanley as "the quick-tempered, scornful, violent mechanic. . . ."

Stanley was Brando's most admired stage performance and would eventually become one of his great achievements on film. There would be many more great on-screen achievements, but Stanley Kowalski was his final gift to Broadway audiences. Following the run of the play, he would effectively leave the stage and make movies. All in all, it was a high note to go out on.

Des Hommes Manqués: Unsexed Males

Brando went to Hollywood to shoot a screen test.[2] The results were not in themselves spectacular—he plays a small-time crook opposite a young woman with a big nose who wants him to take her away with him to someplace new—but his emotional power and mix of tough guy with vulnerable young man are apparent. Moreover, in the interview portion of the test, his warmth and spontaneity are immediately clear. In his first film, *The Men*, directed by Fred Zinnemann, who had already worked with Clift in *The Search*, he would use all these qualities.

Like *The Search*, which told a story intended to inform Americans about displaced persons in Europe, *The Men* strove to show the nation the problems of wounded soldiers who had returned home as paraplegics. It was also filmed, at least in part, on site, at the Birmingham Veterans Administration Hospital in Van Nuys in the San Fernando Valley. For research, Brando had himself admitted and posed as a paraplegic; at first he was not detected and was quickly befriended by the men in his ward (many of whom would appear in the film). Here he discovered what would be carefully dramatized in the film: These men had come home to their wives no longer able to have sex with them. They were "men" who had fought for their country and yet were no longer able to perform sexually as males and thus could not be regarded as genuine "men."

Brando's peculiar ability to perform manhood fit the character well. Lieutenant Ken Wilozek bravely leads his men into what turns into an

ambush in which he is injured permanently. Many months later, in the
hospital ward, a young woman named Ellie (Teresa Wright) turns up and
asks Dr. Brock, the physician in charge (Everett Sloan), if he will allow
her to see the man to whom she is engaged. Brock asks her to come back,
and he begins to wean Ken off painkillers and presses him to begin physical therapy. He also takes Wilozek from his private room into a ward filled
with other paraplegics in various stages of recovery. Ken begins to open up
and commit himself to getting better and even warms to the idea that his
fiancée still wishes to marry him. Yet his inability to walk and his sexual
impotence doom their relationship, as does his need to do everything for
himself. Their wedding night ends before any direct mention of consum-
mation is uttered, when the young husband forces Ellie to admit that she
is sorry she married him. He returns to the hospital, where he feels safe.
Dr. Brock, however, is unwilling to allow him to hide from his life and,
following Ken's drunken-driving accident, agrees with the Paralyzed Veterans
of America's (PVA) counsel's decision that he cannot stay. In a final scene,
Ken returns to his wife, ready to try again, this time allowing her to help
him up the steps leading to their home.

There is much lecturing in the film—as with *The Search*, the film's
well-meant attempts to tell rather than show are occasionally contrived and
tedious. However, Brando is responsible for much of the showing, and his
performance is outstanding for its searing pathos. In the role of a male who
questions his manhood, he manages to produce a characterization whose
physical limitations do not destabilize his masculinity; even without an
operational phallus, Ken Wilozek and his fellow paras are still men. Thus
masculinity is extended, the audience accepts this surprising modification to
gender definition, and the film tastefully breaks off (unlike *Coming Home*)
without going into detail about what their sexual relations will be like.

Our first glimpse of Brando comes at the opening of the film, where a
close up of his face—alert and cautious—dominates the screen. The camera
pulls back a little and his military gear—helmet, uniform, weapon—appear
as he raises his hand to signal his men to follow him. While the credits
roll, we watch the long line of soldiers following him, first into the camera,
then in profile, and finally marching to a fence through which they carefully
pass. They press up against a cinderblock wall; Brando's character pauses as
he looks round a corner. Raising his hand again, he begins to beckon the
troop to follow him when suddenly shots ring out and, just when he falls
face up, a mildly ironic voiceover describes in the first person how he could
not feel his legs and how he was afraid he would die although now (as the
shot fades into his face in a darkened room) he fears he will live. In shadow,
his head turns and his lit features tightly scowl with pain. A nurse enters
with medication, administers it with some water, and wryly comments on

how he has let his Silver Star fall to the floor. She turns out the light, and when she opens the door, his darkened features, slightly eased, are suddenly illuminated for a moment until the door is shut.

His subsequent dialogue is minimal; after he falls in battle, visibility is limited. Yet Brando's face shows us so much of what is going on inside the mind of Ken Wilozek, his anger, hurt, and terror, that we begin to sympathize with him. Brando's eyes, his slight and occasionally sudden expressions tell so much more than any dialogue could. Indeed, the next scene, in which Dr. Brock holds a meeting in the hospital's chapel to explain to the wives and mothers of these wounded soldiers the extent of their injuries, plays like a scene from 1930s "documentary" drama—awkward and obvious. Much of the acting is in keeping with the scene's didactic tone. There is little subtlety in the questions and reactions of this obviously "representative" (racially, ethnically, and economically mixed) group of women, and Sloan's Brock seems to overplay the curmudgeon he has become.

This marked contrast, between Brando's performance and those of Sloan and Wright, brings to mind an earlier reaction to Brando's stage work. Beaufort in *The Christian Science Monitor* had indicated that in *A Flag is Born*, Brando's character (David) was written with a certain "terse-ness." "This quality," Beaufort offers, "is astutely caught in the economy of Mr. Brando's playing." This spare playing is exactly what appears in much of Brando's scenes in *The Men*. Perhaps Brando's detailed approach to act-ing eluded many of the critics who saw him on stage (or simply annoyed them), but his "economic" use of his instrument becomes highly visible and effective for audiences who experience him on screen.

Through much of this film, in which he plays a character who is not only half-paralyzed but also emotionally crippled and reticent, Brando allows his eyes to do much of the talking. In a scene in which Norm Butler, one of his fellow paraplegics (Jack Webb), cynically attributes to financial reasons the motives of a nurse who has married one of the injured soldiers, Brando, who is faced away from the conversation, widens his eyes, listen-ing. Shortly after, when one of the soldiers, the muscular Angel, bids him good night, Brando's right eye opens wide, then closes in reply. And in the next sequence, as Wilozek considers grabbing the strap over his bed to pull himself up, his pupils aim themselves overhead and next focus on the unseen bar. In his first attempt, he stretches to reach for it, his eyes nar-rowing, then closing in pain, and fails. After fainting and being revived by Norm, he tries again, this time with his entire face clenched.

In a subsequent scene, the cynical Norm brings a girlfriend to the ward. Her dialogue makes it obvious to all (except Norm) that she indeed is after his money. Although Brando's face is shown in profile, his eyes make it clear that he sees through her feigned interest in his friend. When his ward-mate, Angel, suddenly dies, the nurse announces his passing first by clearing Angel's bed of its linens. Her actual verbal pronouncement comes with Wilozek shown from behind, but the quick rigidity of the back of Brando's head, neck, and shoulders shows his shocked response.

Brando's performance in the wedding scene, in which he again has little dialogue, anticipates the break-up scene that will follow. After a long montage sequence of Ken exercising, practicing walking, and rehearsing his marriage vows, we watch him and Ellie in the same chapel where Brock earlier addressed an audience of wives and mothers. Now Brock is Wilozek's best man and stands aside as Ken rises from his wheelchair for the ceremony. His eyes fixed on Ellie, he reaches across to her as the justice of the peace requests they join hands, at which point he loses his balance and falls back into the chair. Again, the eyes and face are fixed with determination as he stands once more. Yet the stare he offers Ellie as the ceremony proceeds is filled with doubt.

Another of Brando's acting techniques apparent in *The Men* is anticipated by the same Beaufort review cited above when he speaks of Brando's "force as an actor with an intuitive sense of inner restraint." Chapman in *The Daily News*, describing Brando's performance as Marchbanks, made the same point: "[H]is intensity was within him, where it should be, and not spread all around outside." This sense of interiority, the feeling that what the actor was expressing was only one aspect of some larger mass of feelings inside, permeates a number of Brando's scenes in his first picture.

For example, in the scene in which Wilozek is taken from his private room into the ward, we can feel the character's internal anger rise. Brando raises his voice and then, when his bed has reached its designated place, he hides in it, still fuming. Norm, who played by Webb appears as a bearded paraplegic with an open smile, wheels over to ask Wilozek if he would like to join the PVA, but before he can finish his spiel, Brando has rejected the offer. "I'm not a joiner," he rasps. As the other men on the ward start ribbing him, Ken continues to close his eyes, effectively hiding from their gaze and taunts. One of the patients, whose radio has been blaring a swing arrangement of Schubert's "Marche Militaire," turns up the music, which sends Brando clutching for his temples. In an eruption of anger, he throws his water pitcher across the room, drenching the offender. Web wheels back, flinging another pitcher at him.

And in a subsequent scene, Ellie enters the ward (empty of all but Wilozek), and in the darkness seeks Ken's bed, awakening him. At first whimpering, then plaintively, he tells her to leave him, and then moves his bed linens so she is forced to look at his legs. His voice becomes throaty as he bursts into tears. Suddenly the lights come on—the ward members follow the paralyzed man who has just wed one of the nurses. Wilozek covers

his face but soon looks out at the bride unwrapping the ward's gift to her:
A rolling pin, symbolic of a wife attacking her husband. All laugh as Ken
averts his eyes. The others leave; the lights dim once more. Now, with his
face in darkness and Ellie's bathed in light, he seems suddenly drained of
emotion. His answer to her desire they get back together is a flat, "I don't
know," and a sigh.

This moment-for-moment intensity, this progression of behaviors, all
motivated and all underplayed, is typical of Brando's on-screen brilliance.
His sudden bursts, which never come out of nowhere, are ominous. Later
in the film, after Ken has left Ellie and returned to the hospital, he ends up
in a bar with another ward member. An older man who is obviously inebri-
ated and who tries to compliment them for what they did during the war,
drunkenly praises the two. As they mock him, the drunk lays some coins
on their table and walks away. Wilozek calls him back: "Come here, I want
to apologize," he calls. The man turns, reapproaches, at which moment Ken
slugs him in the face. Such an explosion, although totally credible, comes
like a flash of lightening.

Yet another aspect of Brando's performance of Wilozek is the deadpan
humor that is not always funny but remains highly revealing. Ken's replies
to the drunk in the bar—"Could I marry your daughter?" he asks in a
seemingly serious tone before slugging him—illustrate what would later be
associated with Harold Pinter's comedy of menace, black humor. It is the
violent deadpan of an age of skepticism.

Finally, the way in which Brando listens often betrays more than what
his character says. In a scene with Angel in the gym, Wilozek asks him what
he will do when he leaves the hospital. Angel answers that he will not get
married but will be fully occupied taking care of his mother and his many
sisters and brothers. Because the audience already knows (through Ellie's
conversation with Brock) that Ken is an orphan, his slightly taut smile as
he listens to Angel discloses his own dilemma—that without marriage to
Ellie, he will have no family, no one to take care of.

All the details of Brando's performance in this film are subtle and
small, and the emotions within his characterization seem quite genuine. His
acting appears authentic, especially in contrast to the amateur actors with
the actual infirmity and the professional actors, including Sloan, Webb, and
Wright, whose style of acting appears more identifiably theatrical (or perhaps
more obviously cinematic). Although the screenplay by Carl Foreman would
(along with the film itself) be nominated for an Oscar, the dialogue in *The
Men* is often clumsy. "I'm not marrying a wheelchair," Teresa Wright has to
say at one point, "I'm marrying a man." (She later regretted doing the film
and never spoke well of Brando.) Everett Sloan as Brock must announce,
"The word 'walk' must be forgotten. It no longer exists." Poor Jack Web,

the would-be ward intellectual is given, "Normal is normal and crippled is crippled, and never the twain shall meet." Even Howard St. John, as Ellie's less-than-sympathetic father, is not spared: "You've signed a contract to be his nurse for the rest of his life," he intones. All of this, of course, is written in the service of a noble cause, much like the diatribes allotted to Paul Muni in *A Flag Is Born*. Although *The Men* has its moments, the film is most interesting as a precursor to Brando's next screen role, which would be Stanley in *Streetcar*.

Brando and Kazan: A Streetcar Named Hollywood

As Ken Wilozek in *The Men*, Brando plays a male who, despite his limitations, is able to build for himself a working construct of manhood. That this manhood is a construct is made plain by the film itself and by the actor's sensitive and often conflicted exploration and development of his character's identity as a man who, at least in one sense, can never regain his manhood. In the film version of his Broadway triumph, Stanley in *A Streetcar Named Desire*, Brando instead of sustaining a seemingly seamless and instinctive masculinity, performs a manhood that proves no more natural than the charade of femininity put on by Blanche. Although many would misread his Stanley as the quintessence of machismo and would even mistake Brando's performance of Stanley for Brando playing himself, the film strategically first invites the audience to sympathize with Stanley and then later to feel growing antipathy toward him. This turnabout is aided in large part by some of the changes made in the screenplay.

The Motion Picture Code required numerous alterations to the play-script. Brando himself, who was wary of repeating the role he had done so long on Broadway, waited until a screenplay was written that met the censors' demands and at the same time was acceptable to director Elia Kazan. One major enticement in the film production was the replacement of Jessica Tandy with Vivien Leigh, whose Oscar-awarded performance of Scarlett O'Hara made her the logical cinematic heiress to the role of the aging Southern Belle. Brando and Tandy had not gotten along backstage or on stage; Leigh offered him the opportunity to rethink Stanley, even as Hunter and Malden would again play Stella and Mitch. Perhaps this allowed Brando to focus on character rather than on the many cuts that Williams's play now suffered: The language and subject matter were toned down, all mention of Blanche's brief marriage to a homosexual who committed suicide was cut, and much of the overt sexuality between characters, notably Stella and Stanley, was left on the cutting room floor.

Yet the greatest revision came at the film's end, for the Code required that Stanley be punished for his rape of Blanche. Rather than closing (as does the play) on a tableau of the married couple and their new child, the screenplay has Stella taking the baby upstairs to Eunice's apartment, vowing that she will never go back to Stanley. Of course, she has made a similar move earlier, only to return to her husband, so there is no guarantee that her resolve will last, but this change and others are sufficient to turn Blanche into the victim and Stanley into the villain, rather than the victor, in their sexual tug of war.

Initially, the movie asks the audience to view Blanche as a creature apart from the world they know. In her very first moments on screen, beginning with her flight from a crowded railway platform and into the New Orleans train station, Leigh appears to be in a different shot than everyone else, almost as if she had been photographed separately with the people behind her projected onto another screen. Once she has taken the streetcar and arrives in the Latin Quarter, her body language exhibits extreme discomfort while she searches the neighborhood. Her response to being told that she has indeed arrived at Stella's home is emotionally articulated, with outrage and disappointment and with total obliviousness of those around her. In the next sequence, she lingers in the shadows of a bowling alley, eventually drawing Stella into the darkened bar.

Stanley is first viewed very briefly, surrounded by other men, engaged in some sort of ruckus, brightly lit. When he returns home, in the following sequence, he finds Blanche there. His nonchalance and evident informality look "normal": effortless, natural, without any of the "affectations" we have already observed in Blanche's speech and manners. The film thus seems to establish the authenticity of Stanley's masculinity as opposed to the artificiality of Blanche's femininity. Whereas Brando's Stanley appears to have no problems being viewed by others, either as he tussles in the crowded bowling alley or replaces his drenched T-shirt before his sister-in-law's somewhat curious eyes, Blanche lives in constant anxiety of being the object of people's gaze: The light must be filtered, the make-up and costuming must be perfect, and the observer—male or female—has to be charmed by the object's conversation.

Thus, Stanley's abrupt inventory of Blanche's trunk may be construed as clumsy yet genuine. Rummaging through her clothing and jewelry, he is bringing to light the different components that make her who she is, thereby exposing her as a sham. His invasiveness, which extends to her love letters, may seem crude, but the audience is for the most part able to locate his behavior as consistent with his "masculine" clumsiness; he is ready and willing to give her back her letters (unread) and even seems hurt by her

extreme reaction that she must burn them now that they have been tainted
by him. Perhaps a tough guy with a beating heart, Brando's Stanley initially
appears as the more likeable of the two.

Blanche is not merely portraying femininity—she is striving to perform that construct beyond "womanhood," to the supposedly rarefied role
of "lady." The class associations with that term significantly influence her
struggle with Stanley, who claims to be nothing more (although nothing
less) than an "ordinary Joe." Class discrepancies between the two are noticeably present in the scene mentioned previously, in which Stanley seemingly
naively voices his contempt for Blanche's "solid gold" dress, large "dia-
monds," and "expensive" furs. Only another woman, the film implies, can
discern Blanche's false accessories, for it is Stella who identifies the trunk's
contents as cheap imitations. Stanley's insistence on having the wardrobe
appraised may signal his defensiveness about his own class identification, but
it also may be forcing the issue of what and how women "know" things as
opposed to how men arrive at an "objective" understanding.

Yet another aspect of Blanche's construct is her age. Although Leigh
was five years younger than Tandy, the camera allowed for a more intimate
exploration of her facial features. Williams' play itself does not make Blanche
Leigh's age—which at the time was 37—but age becomes an important factor in Blanche's character in the film. The scene in which Mitch submits her
face to a close examination under direct lighting emphasizes that Blanche's
preoccupation with her age is not merely a neurotic, culturally inspired
fixation: Streetcar, the movie, makes it all too clear that Blanche in fact is
significantly older than her sister.

An older Blanche must engage in a more literal battle against the
years. She is not only performing a gender and class but an age, and so in
addition to her masquerade of femininity and gentility, she must perform
the masquerade of youth. Certainly, they are all intimately connected: The
cultural myth that men do not age while women do is obviously at play
here, and whatever Blanche's age may be, her obsession about how old she
appears is indicative of how prevalent that myth is. The real difference
between stage and screen versions, however, is that on screen, Leigh under
Mitch's merciless scrutiny really does look old, shockingly so.

The screen version thus pits a younger man against a mature woman,
an opposition with interesting implications in theatrical casting. Indeed,
during the late nineteenth and first half of the twentieth centuries, the European stage had allotted certain male roles to be played by mature women.
The unspoken presumption was that males in their youth were somehow
similar to grown-up women. In opera, of course, there were (and still are)
an array of "trouser roles," but the practice did not end there. Such female
players as Marguerite Jamois and Sarah Bernhardt, for whom the role of

the male teenage heir to Napoleon's throne was especially written, traditionally represented Shakespeare's Hamlet and Alfred de Musset's Lorenzo. Falconetti, whose most memorable role remains Joan of Arc in Dreyer's silent film, also appeared in male roles, and although this practice was far less prevalent in the United States, the role of Peter Pan, a boy stuck in adolescence, had been portrayed by Maude Adams (who had also played the doomed Duke of Reichstadt), Jean Arthur, and, just a few years after *Streetcar* was released, Mary Martin. True, Stanley Kowalski is no Hamlet, but the apparent juxtaposition of him and Blanche suggests a certain equality or at least equivalence between the two.[3]

It is tempting to liken Blanche to a transvestite. The drag queen's strategic use of illusion to create "femininity," is mirrored by Blanche's efforts to look like a pretty young lady. Nonetheless, Williams resists drawing characters whose sex and gender identities do not correspond according to contemporary norms. He is more concerned about questioning how "natural" gender can be for those whom society expects to perform a particular gender than in asserting that gender performance is composed of acts that may be performed by anyone regardless of his or her sex. Although he demonstrates that males are capable of womanly behaviors and vice versa, and that the factors supposedly distinguishing one gender from another are largely arbitrary, Williams focuses here on the ways that males as men and females as women are to some degree prisoners of their gender.

Although much of the film appears to depict Blanche's construction of youthful, refined femininity, Stanley as played by Brando clearly engages in performing (and thus constructing) a particular version of masculinity. As noted earlier, the audience may at first wish to view Stanley as "naturally manly" or "simply masculine," but Brando's characterization clearly depicts a male who is as astute and detailed a performer as Blanche: His costuming, gestures and actions, use of language, and choices of props are every bit as intentional as hers, although he substitutes grime and sweat for her makeup and perfume. His tight and torn undershirts, his form-fitting jeans, satin bowling jacket, and silk pajamas—these are his versions of Blanche's gilded dresses, rhinestone tiaras, and small-time furs. He is overtly crude in what he says, whereas she is excessively polite; her actions are small, often whimsically delicate, just as his are frequently large, deliberately violent. He is, no less than his sister-in-law, a creature acutely aware of living in the gaze of others—of other women and other men. Whereas Blanche clearly euphemizes, obfuscates, and tries to use guilt to control others, Stanley plays plainspoken, direct, and primitively sincere.

Simultaneously, Brando's Stanley, despite his heavy armor of machismo, often displays an emotionalism that contradicts his alleged masculinity. The famous, often-imitated scene, in which a drunken Kowalski, having started a fight with his poker buddies and driven his wife and sister-in-law out of the apartment, begins bellowing his wife's name, is perhaps the most obvious example. Still, there are plenty of examples to add: The ruckus at the bowling alley, the poker party itself and the fights that ensue, the stories of Stanley smashing windows and light bulbs, his vicious exposure of Blanche's past, and his rape of her, make it impossible to view Stanley as a "real" man. Even as Brando's Stanley alienates the audience, he reveals the "truth" about masculinity: Manhood is every bit as much a put-on as femininity. While incorporating Simone de Beauvoir's perception that "[w]omen are not born but made," he implies that men too are constructs.

As noted in the previous chapter, in *Masked Men: Masculinity and the Movies in the Fifties*, Steven Cohan discusses Clift, Brando, and Dean (among others) in a chapter entitled, "Why Boys Are Not Men" (201–263). Cohan refers the reader to a statement by Joan Mellen in *Big Bad Wolves: Masculinity in American Films*: "The assumed definitions of the male sex role were challenged as films discovered the male capable of sensitivity and an open expression of tenderness, feelings that in the forties were ridiculed as effeminate" (192, qtd. by Cohan 203). Cohan, however, attributes this shift in the representation of masculinity not to the inclusion of "effeminate" feelings but to the youth of these actors:

> Far from following the critical consensus, then and now, that the new stars were simply feminized (and hence "lesser") males in contrast to big "he-men" like [John] Wayne, I claim that their disruptive status as "boys who are not men" summarizes an important reconfiguration of masculinity in movies of this period because their "new look" challenged the conflation of "gender" and "sexuality" underwriting the symbolic economy with which "boys" were made legible as the opposites of "men." (203)

To an extent, Cohan is correct in identifying this adversarial face off between boy and man; his statement remains particularly pertinent to an analysis of Clift's and Wayne's juxtaposition in *Red River*. Nevertheless, in *Streetcar*, Brando's Stanley is never contrasted with an older, "more masculine" male because none of the other male characters seem to be a genuine threat to Stanley; as I point out above, he is set against a mature woman, a figure that was in some culturally traditional sense his equivalent in a variety of ways. And one might add to Cohan's thesis that even in the case of Clift versus Wayne, the mitigating factor is never another male (such as Walter Brennan's or John Ireland's characters), but a woman, in the form of Joanne Dru's Tess. Is the implication that Tess is more of a man than either Dunson or Garth? Is her intercession necessitated by the homosexual anxiety that simultaneously connects and separates the two men? Or is she a walking example of a woman who has some masculine characteristics, just as Dunson and Garth exemplify men with some feminine characteristics?

Rather than what Cohan calls "feminizing" masculinity or breaking it into a boy/man divide, the performances of Clift, Brando, and Dean call into question not merely the masculinity of the old guard but the entire idea of masculinity. Instead of acting as "boys" in the presence of "men," all three tear at the fabric of machismo, exposing holes in the construct and to some degree widening and deepening the notions of what may constitute a performance of manhood. Such performances do not in any way promise that the young man portrayed will ultimately join the established male order; on the contrary, just as Clift at the happy ending of *Red River* will never become Wayne, Dean will never grow into Raymond Massey in *East of Eden*. Brando, at least in his early career, never encounters a truly effective male adversary but nonetheless manages to portray the performance of masculinity as a struggle that is often not successful.

Williams's gift as a homosexual playwright lay in his ability to dramatize and comment on cultural institutionalizations of relationships between people. In *Streetcar*, he critiques heterosexual marriage and courtship (prominent themes in *The Glass Menagerie*). As an "outsider," he was perhaps ideally situated to observe the contradictions in societal norms, the enforcement of which had marginalized him. Moreover, in the postwar period, virtually all discussion of sex (especially discussions as public as those in theater and film) revolved around heterosexuality. When *Streetcar* opened on Broadway, it was one of the few dramas that dared explore sexual issues, and Williams was regarded as a dramatist who boldly raised such matters; by the 1960s, of course, heterosexual male critics would attack Williams, William Inge, and Edward Albee, as incapable of attaining an objective understanding of heterosexual relationships and of women merely because they were gay. Nonetheless, throughout the late 1940s and into the 1950s, Williams was regarded as a playwright who wrote adult plays for adult men and women.

Although one of the most provocative lines from the original script—Stella's "There are things that go on in the dark between a man and a woman that no one can . . ."—was cut from the screenplay, the idea itself is loudly proclaimed by Stella's decision to descend the staircase and return to her bellowing husband. The cinematic glamorization of the intimacy between them and Eunice's remarks to Blanche that imply that the brutality women suffer from men is a small price to pay for the "love" they receive, establish a precedent that, as I suggest above, undermines the "justice" dispensed at the end of the film: Just as Eunice always goes back to Steve, Stella will probably go back to Stanley. For many in the audience, the passion enacted by Stanley and Stella more or less reinstates the cultural assertion that heterosexual marriage and family are at the hub of human life. In a sense, Williams's original ending—with the happy couple and baby—was so disturbing that it better represented the dramatist's own analysis and condemnation of the status quo.

If critics and audiences were not prepared to see past Williams's lurid narrative into the realm of gender critique, they were certainly no more ready to comprehend Stanley's masculinity as Brando's performance of excessive masculinity. In this role, the actor functioned as a male impersonator, subordinating (as any good actor must) himself to the character, drawing on whatever he possessed that could contribute to the characterization, and creating (as Adler had taught him to) through his imagination this personification of machismo. That it was completely over the top somehow eluded, at least on a conscious level, those who first wrote about the film, but the anxiety prompted by the film of Streetcar, most visible perhaps in televised comedians of the era dully shouting, "Stella! Stella!" in parody of Brando's performance, was evident.

One aspect of Williams's dramaturgy that discomforted and titillated audiences was his showing characters in various stages of undress. (Again, this became an object of humor later in the 1950s when Mad Magazine satirized the film of Williams's The Rose Tattoo by depicting all the cast members in their underwear.) Both Stella and Blanche appear in their slips and robes, and Stanley is famously shown in and out of his undershirts, torn or otherwise, a guise with which Brando would be associated until the end of his life. The focus on his body had started in The Men, in which Ken Wilozek exercised bare-chested, and continued through Streetcar, in which the actor's muscular torso became representative of his character's masculinity; although Brando's body would figure less prominently in his third film, Viva Zapata! it would be used far more noticeably in the three films that followed.

Brando as Not-Brando

In his first two screen appearances, Brando had played roles that made use of his physical and speech characteristics. That critics and many others mistook him for Stanley Kowalski is, in its own way, a tribute to how "natural" his portrayal of Stanley was, but at the same time such a misreading stands as an acute reminder of how much film spectators wish to conflate the actor and his or her role. (Throughout his life, Brando repeatedly refuted the notion that he was anything like Kowalski.) His attraction to his next film role was perhaps strengthened by the necessity of having to alter himself in order to play the revolutionary Mexican leader, Emiliano Zapata.

This would be Brando's second film with Kazan, a director whose politics and method of directing were extremely problematic. I examine these aspects of Kazan's life and career and their influence on Brando in the final segment of this chapter with reference to the third and final film they would make together, *On the Waterfront*. At this point in the discussion, however, if only to explain the contemporary background of the screenplay of the Zapata film, I should indicate that Kazan, who had been attracted to leftist politics in the 1930s and 1940s, had slowly withdrawn from radical political life as the House Committee on Un-American Activities (HUAC) began to investigate Communists in the entertainment industry. Kazan's private and public testimony before HUAC came in the first half of 1952, around the time when *Viva Zapata!* was released, and the film shows signs of his pre-informing ideological maneuvers.

Ultimately, Kazan would identify himself as an anti-Communist liberal, and this positioning, unique to the late 1940s and to the1950s, was shared by screenwriter (and novelist) John Steinbeck. Steinbeck's revision of Zapata's life served both as an adventure story and as a warning against Stalinism, which throughout the world (including America) had become the policy of virtually all Communist parties. Steinbeck wrote and Kazan brilliantly directed a film that was every bit as didactic as Zinnemann's movies but seemingly less obviously so. Brando was apparently oblivious to the movie's message, perhaps because so much of his performance required him to become someone totally different from himself. Despite his own allegedly left-leaning politics, he was possibly too busy creating a role to consider the implications of the film itself.

Viva Zapata! opens in the office of Mexican president Porfirio Díaz: A delegation of peasants from Morelos Province asks the leader to punish the plantation owners who have taken their land. As he placates them, Díaz observes one outspoken man, and looks for him on the list of delegates; Diaz circles his name: Emiliano Zapata. With Zapata picked out as a troublemaker and the land still in the hands of the ranchers, the peasants return to Morelos and eventually join forces with a rebellion against Díaz, who is soon replaced by revolutionary politician Francisco Indalécio Madero. Zapata, now a general, goes back to Morelos and marries the upper-class girl whose family previously denied his proposal. Madero tries to make peace with the peasants, but his administration is corrupt, and General Victoriano Huerta soon replaces him in a coup d'état. Zapata and his armies join with Pancho Villa, and after occupying Mexico City, Villa makes Zapata head of Mexico. Yet when a delegation from his own province comes to visit him, complaining of the abuses of Zapata's brother, Zapata recalls how he once stood before Díaz and relinquishes power. Before he leaves, however, he confronts his aide, the elusive journalist Fernando, who began as an emissary for Madero but then shifted allegiance to Zapata. Zapata finally understands that Fernando has always been attracted to power and that his lust for revolution—his only emotion in an otherwise calculated existence—lacks any human compassion and feeling. Later Zapata, once again in charge of a vast army, is lured into a governmental trap and murdered.

The script subordinates many of the finer points of characterization to both the political message and the film's plot. Brando's performance, which earned him his third Oscar nomination for leading man, is extraordinary, and he spent much time creating the Native-American peasant and much effort as well. Many of the other major roles, such as the would-be revolutionary Machiavelli, Fernando (played by Joseph Wiseman), Zapata's brother, Eufemio (Anthony Quinn), and Zapata's old friend and confidante, Pablo (Lou Gilbert), represent political positions and ideologies; the roles are enlivened by the acting rather than developed by the script. Many of the minor parts are gems: Jean Peters, who in spite of her top billing appears only occasionally as Zapata's wife, Josefa, is feisty and intense; Harold Gordon as Madero shines as an idealizing but ineffective politician, and Frank Silvera as Huerta seems the incarnation of evil; and Mildred Dunnock, in a cameo as Josefa's proper mother, is wonderfully sympathetic as she tries to supervise her daughter's polite conversation with the peasant. Yet for all its talk about humanity and what makes people human, *Viva Zapata!* often fails to depict people as people.

Steinbeck's screenplay, in spite of its warnings about the dangers of creating heroic leaders, is an antithesis to Bertolt Brecht's 1947 play, *Galileo*, in which the title character remarks, after a former student proclaims he is heroic, "Pity the land that needs a hero." Brecht, of course, was a self-proclaimed Communist writer who had developed his epic theater in stark contrast to the agitprop drama and social realism that had swept the Soviet Union and influenced leftist dramatists in America, including the Group Theatre's Clifford Odets, in whose "Waiting for Lefty" Kazan had appeared, as well as leftist novelists like Steinbeck. Unlike Brecht's work, *Viva Zapata!* invites the audience to translate the past into the present—to look at something that happened in a different time and place as somehow analogous to contemporary America—and to take its rather generalized political pronouncements at face value. The film also attempts to sweep the themes into a final resolution, in which the heroic image of the slain Zapata is mythologized so that the people, who are now capable of leading themselves, may draw strength from it. In Brecht's *Galileo*, *Mother Courage*, *The Good Woman of Setzuan*, and *The Caucasian Chalk Circle*, spectators are distanced from making heroes out of individual characters and must confront a lack of resolution that becomes a source for the audience's subsequent political discussion. Ironically, for all its condemnation of the absolutist personality cult of Stalin, Steinbeck's script is written in the very format that Stalin prescribed: social realism. As such, the film succeeds on a narrative level (or on what Brecht would call an "Aristotelian" level). The political demagoguery is awkward and obvious.

One way in which *Viva Zapata!* betrays itself is in its inconsistent performances. The film was shot in southern Texas, which stands in quite well for Mexico, but only a few of the actors, including Brando, attempt Mexican accents. Although Mexicans and Mexican-Americans were hired as extras and in nonspeaking roles, most of the "country people" whom we hear come from the Actors Studio and have New York accents. Although Brando strove to create the peasant hero, through his posture and movement, the use of his eyes, and his gestures, most of the other players seem only vaguely aware that they are portraying people who are so incredibly different from themselves. Thus, while Brando's Zapata and Anthony Quinn's Eufemio, Emilio's corrupt brother, stand out as authentic, the cast is mainly composed of American actors in a film about a place called Mexico before World War I. Likewise, the construct of Mexican identity, which is crucial to the film's subject matter, is merely alluded to and never really dramatized.

Nonetheless, the movie's most significant flaw is in its equating Zapata's inability to ignore human suffering and his intuitively violent responses to it with a political standpoint. Again, Brecht's Galileo is similarly plagued by an irresistible curiosity with regard to scientific inquiry, but the playwright and even the character make it clear that this irresistible need for discovery derives from an emotional appetite rather than an ideological position. In this film, most of the characters' politics are in fact fueled by their irrational desires: Eufemio's "grab-what-you-can" laissez-faire; Madero's cowardly liberalism; Pablo's compassionate collaborationism; and Fernando's blood lust for revolution. If Zapata is romanticized, as Steinbeck and Kazan would have him, as a man who instinctively cannot bear inhumanity, he becomes less a political figure and more a passionate martyr; indeed despite the film's warnings against making someone a heroic leader, he is by the end a saint in the tradition of *The Greatest Story Ever Told*, and his followers grant him not only immortality but the possibility of a second coming.

Because of all these disturbing aspects of *Viva Zapata!* Brando's acting seems less significant than it otherwise might have been. As I earlier implied, his Zapata is a masterful characterization that he embraced whole-heartedly. With the use of make up and other devices, he managed to change his face; his body too seems less developed, almost scrawny at times, and the ways he walks, stands, and sits are not recognizable from his earlier roles. According to Kazan, Brando was directed to invent Zapata: "a peasant does not reveal what he thinks," Kazan told him. "Things happen to him and he shows no reaction." He mentioned too "a peasant's watchful wariness, the illiterate sense that words can entrap" and added, "Zapata doesn't romanticize women" (qtd. Bosworth 84). Brando clearly submerged himself in this role, and the results are startling. When he first appears on screen, he is revealed by a withdrawal of those surrounding him. His fellow countrymen begin to leave their audience with President Díaz, but he refuses to move. At first glance, even after first hearing him, Brando is not immediately recognizable. Only after watching and listening intently does the spectator begin to recognize, faintly as it may appear, the actor behind the mask. True, the mask at times does slip, but overall, the audience is obliged to recognize how good Brando is at not being "Brando."

Inevitably, one must ask, If he is good, it is in service of what? As a vehicle for politics, *Viva Zapata!* remains a highly compromised film. As a tale of action and events, it succeeds as a rousing narrative. As a statement of postwar masculinity, it adapts previous versions of manliness into a Cold War code thereof: Brando's Zapata is an idealist who impatiently waits for justice. He leaves even more unsaid than Ken Wilozek and Stanley Kowalski, for he is a man of action rather than of language. Simultaneously, as Kazan directed, he "doesn't romanticize women," whose lives occupy a different realm of existence that is necessarily less real than the realm inhabited by men. Even in the crowd scenes, females are separate from their male counterparts: They try to tempt Zapata with food and other offerings, they adulate him, and when he falls, they heap flowers upon his corpse. In the one scene in which they do play an active role, hiding explosives in their market baskets, which they set down in front of the door to an enemy garrison, they are able to succeed because the male soldiers find it inconceivable that females can ever pose a threat to them. Jean Peters goes from a playful, spirited upper-class girl to a drab wife whose prescient nagging that Zapata should not go on the mission that takes his life foretells her wailing as his widow.

The character Zapata, not unlike Brando himself, operated in a world of males and manhood. Although there were plenty of women in their lives (Zapata was said to have had twenty wives and Brando confessed to a far greater number of female sexual partners), both supposedly had their most meaningful relationships with other males.

De Evil dat Men Do: Brando and the Bard

Imagine, if you will (as Rod Serling used to propose), a major American movie studio, with more stars than in all the heavens, assigning to the writer/director of the most wonderfully witty backstage screen comedy the script of an Elizabethan classic, to make a film that was to include some of that studio's major names (if not talents), along with some assorted major talents from beyond that studio's walls. . . .

Of course, there is no need to strain one's imagination, for in 1952, *All About Eve*'s Joseph L. Mankiewicz began shooting Shakespeare's *Julius Caesar* at Metro-Goldwyn-Mayer. The film featured a bizarre assortment of actors, including James Mason as Brutus, Edmund O'Brien as Casca, and Louis Calhern as Caesar, with Greer Garson as Calpurnia and Deborah Kerr as Portia, and it starred the veteran English Shakespearean actor John Gielgud as Cassius and, in the role of Mark Antony, Marlon Brando. As ridiculous as this may sound, and as ridiculous as the film itself now appears, MGM's *Julius Caesar* was nominated for five Academy Awards, including Brando's fourth consecutive nomination for best actor.

The film is, to be kind, the essence of middlebrow American sensibility and, to be cruel, an absolute disaster. In his authorized autobiography, written with Robert Lindsey, Brando offers a single paragraph about *Julius Caesar*, concluding, "[F]or me to walk onto a movie set and play Mark Antony without more experience was asinine" (174). Nonetheless, at the time he took the role quite seriously, finding in it a challenge that he tried to meet head-on. The very idea of Brando "doing" Shakespeare prompted Jerry Lewis, Milton Berle, and Sid Caesar to impersonate Stanley Kowalski declaiming, "Friends, Romans, and countrymen, lend me your ears." The casting was, of course, terribly funny, but in reality Brando was an actor who had never publicly performed the early classics; he may have read the plays in high school, played in Shakespearean scenes in classes with Stella Adler and Robert Lewis, and studied the bard in his offstage breaks on Broadway, but he had little background as a classically trained actor. As usual, he found a way through the production, creating a characterization that, despite its virtues, seems as incongruous as the performances of the other cast members.

Such incongruity should come as no surprise: Mankiewicz had never been associated with artistic cinema; he was, on the contrary, a remarkably artful writer, producer, and director of commercial successes. As wonderful as his best work is—and some of it is nothing short of brilliant—the very notion of him as a high-culture auteur seems somewhat naïve. And so, Mason, while suppressing his more contemptuous side, became a weak Brutus (who is, after all, the play's protagonist), whereas Brando, with his well-developed body and his suddenly articulate although odd elocution, became the focus of the film. Supposedly Brando and Mason loathed each other, and Brando's retort to George Cukor—that if he was looking for someone to play the alcoholic husband of Judy Garland in *A Star Is Born*, he should look no farther than Mason—was intended as an insult, even though the role of Norman Maine was one of Mason's finest.

There are two ways to look at Brando's performance in the 1952 production of *Julius Caesar*: One is to watch him in the context of the production as a whole, in which he acquits himself favorably; the other is to regard
his scenes in isolation, at which point he seems a strange actor indeed. As
critics had argued when he was back on Broadway, he was an actor whose
silences were more eloquent than his speeches, some of which were mumbled
to the point of being indecipherable. The pain in his voice as Ken Wilozek
and the grit and grime of Stanley Kowalski's rants was suddenly gone, and at
first the only voice Brando could muster was his own. Unfortunately, with
his slight lisp and high register, the recording sent to MGM to show his
readiness to play Antony was not recognizable as Brando's. Always ready to
meet a challenge, Brando worked harder on his oratory and came back with
a second audition record that producers in Hollywood thought was in fact
the voice of Laurence Olivier. During the shooting of *Streetcar*, Brando had
amused Vivien Leigh by doing an imitation of Olivier's great speech from
the movie, *Henry V*. After viewing *Julius Caesar*, Olivier himself observed
that Brando's "Friends, Romans, and countrymen" eulogy resembled the way
in which a very bad Olivier might have delivered it.

Although there were only two scenes in *Viva Zapata!* in which Brando
had bared his chest (the wedding night and his final goodbye to his wife),
Mankiewicz made use of Brando's body throughout the film. In a time when
historical epics often promoted the physiques of movie stars, Brando joined
Victor Mature, Yul Brynner, Charlton Heston, Paul Newman, and many
others as Classical musclemen.

Because his voice was far better than everyone had feared it would be
and his body looked the best it ever had, Brando dominated the picture.
His behavior on the set made him some enemies, including Mason and
Mankiewicz, and a few friends, including Calhern, Garson, and Gielgud,
who, attracted to Brando, worked with him on his diction, metrics, and
delivery. It was rumored that Sir John (who had been arrested in a public toilet shortly after his being knighted) made a recording of Antony's
speeches, which Brando followed in his own performance. Gielgud's own
performance in the film is impressive, but as with Brando's, it comes amid
the assortment of incompatible acting styles that each actor brought to his
or her role. Certainly, his Roman-styled toupee and over-sized togas did not
help him. Whatever fondness he may have had for Brando during the shooting, Gielgud later abandoned in a flurry of catty but amusing comments.

"Asinine" may be too strong a word to characterize Brando's attempt
at Mark Antony, but it fits perfectly to describe the film as a whole. The
delusional chutzpah that MGM could throw together a cast and a director
and a lot of money for sets and costumes and then end up with a decent

version of a Shakespeare tragedy stands out quite comically today; it might have been something that Evelyn Waugh or Aldous Huxley had invented for their satires of Hollywood.

With regard to masculinity, Brando now qualified as genuine beef-cake. The defiant young man he had played before is curiously absent from his performance as a supporter of the old guard, just as it is absent from Shakespeare's script. However, his next film, which was in its own way as disastrous as *Julius Caesar*, would solidify his image as a figure of rebellion.

Uneasy Rider: Brando in Gear

The peculiar conflation of the biblical/classical epic hero and the rebel-lious young man is anticipated in Kenneth Anger's 1964 short, *Scorpio Rising*. Whereas Mellen calls it a "paean to male sexuality" (281), Pauline Kael's capsule review in *The New Yorker* put it best: It's about "homocycle motorsexuals." Shot with a shaky handheld camera in strangely diluted color, the film follows a gang of motorcyclists, who are either playing Hells Angels or actually are Hells Angels, through one of their wild excursions. Cut into the film are a number of clips, including one of Brando in full gear, smirking across a television screen as Johnny in *The Wild One* and also scenes from Family Films' "The Living Bible: Last Journey to Jerusalem." The sound track uses popular songs from the 1950s and early 1960s, beginning with the credits, behind which adolescent heartthrob Ricky Nelson croons, "Fools rush in where angels fear to tread." Under scenes from "The Living Bible," in which Christ is shown leading a parade of disciples, Anger plays the early rock ballad, "I Will Follow Him," and even innocent lyrics, such as, "Is it really me you love or is it just an act?" (from "The Point of No Return"), figure as bawdy innuendo.

Anger's use of the savage motorcycle gang's regalia, along with Brando's wardrobe as a restless young rebel in *The Wild One*, is an example of some of the appropriations that occurred during the late 1950s and early 1960s in homosexual photography and pornography: Touko Laaksonen, who was known as "Tom of Finland," whose first images of men were influenced by the uniformed Nazi soldiers with whom he fought (Finland having been allied with Germany during the war), had been drawing brawny, almost voluptuous men in T-shirts and tight jeans (like the ones Brando had worn in *Streetcar*) and in leather jackets, boots, and caps (which Brando modeled in *The Wild One*). *Scorpio Rising* is not so much a display of masculinity as a conscious exhibition of the signs of masculinity. The males depicted (unlike those of Tom of Finland) appear at times dwarfed by what they are wearing and their rough play occasionally seems, in contradiction to their outfits, childish and silly. Similarly, the insinuation of homosexuality lurking under the homosocial behavior shown in the film, much of it rather juvenile, invites the early-1960s viewer to recognize some of the contradictions inherent in contemporaneous constructs of masculinity.

The Wild One, filmed a decade earlier, may not be the best of Brando's films, but thanks to Julius Caesar and a score of later turkeys, it is certainly not the worst. Brando himself denigrated it—largely because it had been so severely censored. Decades later he wrote in his memoir-autobiography, "[I]t looks dated and corny now; I don't think it has aged well" (178). It is in many ways a product of the studio system at its worst, a film that was initially intended to confront the issue of social violence but was changed and cut into what many (particularly those involved with the film itself) thought was a negligible product. The plot revolves around a motorcycle gang that takes over a small, rural town. As Johnny Strabler, the leader of the B.R.M.C.—the Black Rebels Motorcycle Club—Brando plays a young man who superficially appears indifferent but, underneath his disdainful mask, has intense feelings and desires. Nevertheless, for all of Brando's complaints about this picture, it has become one of his "signature" movies for two good reasons.

First, Brando related to the role immediately. Unlike Ken Wilozek, Stanley Kowalski, Emiliano Zapata, Mark Antony, and Terry Malone (the protagonist in On the Waterfront), Johnny did not require him to change his voice, face, hair, body, or movement. In his autobiography, Brando admits that "[m]ore than most parts I've played in the movies and onstage, I related to Johnny" (178), and notes that the character's resentment of authority, a result of early abuse, had led him, like Brando, to become "arrogant" and adopt "a pose of indifference to criticism" (178–179). Brando further reveals,

> He [Johnny] had been so disappointed in life that it was difficult for him to express love, but beneath his hostility lay a desperate yearning and desire to feel love because he'd had so little of it. I could have just as easily been describing myself. It seemed perfectly natural for me to play this role. (178)

Such a confession is unusual from an actor who frequently tried to differentiate himself from his roles. His insistence on not being confused with Stanley, for example, was often repeated in interviews. Here, however, he confesses how very much he identified with the character.

Second, despite critical pans, spectators were drawn to the film and Brando's performance in it. Perhaps the reason that The Wild One resonated so deeply with audiences was that it was one of the few movies that, as Brando ultimately put it, touched on what he later recognized as

> the budding social problems that a few years later exploded vol-
> canically on college campuses and the streets of America. Right
> or wrong, we were at the beginning of a new era after several
> years of transition following World War II; young people were
> beginning to doubt and question their elders and to challenge
> their values, morals, and the established institutions of author-
> ity. There was a wisp of steam just beneath the surface when
> we made that picture. . . . I simply happened to be at the right
> place at the right time . . . (178)

In other words, Brando came to believe that the film anticipated the wide-spread political unrest that rocked the United States from the mid-1960s through the 1970s. The confluence, then, of the right actor finding the right part served, at least in this context, to authenticate Brando's performance, despite the movie at times looking "dated and corny." For all its shortcom-ings and Hollywood absurdities, enough remained in the script to suggest some of what the original scenario made explicit.

David Savran, in *Taking It Like a Man: White Masculinity, Masochism, and Contemporary American Culture*, regards as central the figure that Johnny and Brando himself represent, the white hipster who defies the system. To be sure, Johnny is a far more simplistic version than the more complicated rebels produced by the writers of the Beat generation, in whom Savran is more interested. Yet for the vast majority of Americans who did not read the Beats, a movie like *The Wild One* was the most palpable expression of protest against what Savran calls "the normative masculinity of the 1950s" which beat a "retreat from the more independent- and entrepreneurial-minded masculinities that preceded it" (47).

Even if Johnny is "pure" Brando, the film was plagued by many prob-lems early on. The script, which had originally attracted him to the project, was altered numerous times due to fears of how the censors would receive it. There were many, not just those within the studio (Columbia Pictures), who, from the top down, desperately fought to clean it up and rename it. By the time the film was completed, the screenplay had lost much of its more controversial material and seemed to have little to say beyond telling the story of a town overrun by gangs over the course of one awful weekend. The action drowned out much of the social commentary, and many who saw it thought it glorified the aggressive behavior that it supposedly condemned. Few actually responded to the cultural critique that we now see plainly in

The Wild One: The film was banned in Britain and widely condemned across America as excessively and gratuitously violent.

Brando had come aboard thinking that he was playing not just a troublemaker but also a rebel, a loner, and a sexual outlaw whose past had made him who he was. He even expanded his characterization by emphasizing Johnny's sensitive inner conflicts, making the character more like himself. Although he felt disenchanted by the end result and resented all the compromises that went into the production, he never completely dismissed this role as he would Mark Antony.

Some of the corniness to which Brando alludes is evident in the way that Johnny claims to have been changed by a particular girl: "She got to me," he says impassively in the voiceover at the very beginning. One narrative strand of the film rests on the Hollywood cliché that all that is needed to fix a troubled and confused young man is the love of a good woman, in this case, a waitress named Cathy (played by Mary Murphy), daughter of Frank, the town's ineffective chief of police (Robert Keith). Although the end of the film seems to leave this aspect of the narrative unresolved, the opening voice of Johnny more or less seals this plot from the start. The closing frames show Johnny riding out of town on his motorcycle, but the audience has already learned that he must return for a scheduled hearing.

However, Johnny's usual apathy about sexual attraction is made clear in two short scenes with a young woman called Britches (played by Yvonne Doughty). In keeping with her moniker, she is shown wearing slacks and her hair is cut short, and yet her bulging sweater, with her name sewn onto it, makes it clear she is flaunting her female sexuality. In the first scene, Britches, who has arrived with a rival gang of which the B.R.M.C. was once a part, tries to remind Johnny that she has not seen him in a year, but when she asks how he has been, he snubs her, remarking, "Still swinging." Later that night, when both gangs have started drinking heavily, Britches finds him again and drunkenly requests, "Sing me a song. Buy me a beer." When he points out she already has a beer, she answers, "I'm singing—I'm really singing. I'm on the Christmas tree." Johnny tries to break from her, but she continues, "Remember the night? . . . We really got ourselves hung on the Christmas tree, didn't we?" Even while he struggles to get away from her, she appeals to him, "I won't get on your back." Striding away, he asks, "What do you want me to do, send you flowers?"

These interchanges are curiously linked to conversations he has with rival gang leader and former friend, Chino (played by Lee Marvin). On arriving in town, Chino spies a motorcycle trophy (which was previously stolen from a competition) lashed to Johnny's cycle and moves to take it. When Chino sees Johnny, he greets him, "Johnny, I love you. Let's you and me have a beer, and I'll beat the living Christmas out of you!" They fight, supposedly over the statuette, which has by now been given to Cathy to hold, and in the midst of the tussle, an irate local citizen, soon to turn vigilante, tries driving his car through the street, now crowded by the gangs. Chino and his friends stop the car, which nearly hits someone, and pulls the driver out. Frank separates Chino and the driver and is ready to arrest them both when a local points out to him that the driver, named Charlie, an influential man in town, will be furious if sent to jail. Frank caves in, letting Charlie go, but he incarcerates Chino. This inequality enrages Johnny, who comments on it. "Johnny don't like nobody on his back," quips Chino. Later in the film, now freed from his cell by the gang, Chino greets Johnny once more with, "Johnny, I love you. Let's you and me have a beer, and I'll beat the living Christmas out of you!"

The use of "back" and "Christmas" connect what Britches and Chino say, and although Britches's lines very obviously suggest a sexual tie, Chino's do so rather subtly. Moreover, the trophy over which Chino and Johnny struggle has been featured earlier, when Johnny has first met Cathy in the café and offers it to her as a gift. (The trophy recurs in the film, and I discuss it shortly.) Throughout *The Wild One*, human contact is expressed almost exclusively through violence, even in what in a cornier and more dated picture would be the romantic scenes between Johnny and Cathy. Johnny's spurning of Britches is tantamount to his fight with Chino, both of which are in turn similar to Johnny's attempt to overpower Cathy physically and his heated speeches to her. In fact, much of the motorcycle gang's violence appears to comment on what society calls romantic love.

Because so much of the contemporary critical and official outcry was focused on the depiction of violence, it may be instructive more than half a century later to witness, in a totally different time, just what that violence consists of. The B.R.M.C. members are men who work during the week and on weekends act out their frustrations and disappointments. A major part of their violent responses to what they encounter is parody—instead of simply smashing the social conventions against which they are rebelling, they frequently make fun of them, imitating them in a way that, through the ridicule of laughter, belittles them. For example, at the beginning of the film, as the gang rides into a cycle speedway and disrupts the races going on, a voice from a loudspeaker demands, "Please don't cross the track." One gang member climbs up the tower from where the voice emanates, mimicking, "Please don't cross the track! Don't get hurt! Blood makes everything so slippery!" As the gang surrounds the winners' stand, pretending to admire but actually mocking the significance of the gold-plated trophies, a policeman approaches and warns them to leave. "We want to watch the thrilling races, Daddy," says the same gang member, this time in a child's voice.

Throughout the movie, the gang members take on their targets by burlesquing them. When they arrive in town, they drag race, but their game is upset when an old man in a Model A swerves onto the sidewalk. "Hey, help this man out," cries one of the locals, trying to open the car door. "Help the man out!" cry the gang members over and over, as they surround the car, open it up, pull out the driver, and hoist him above their heads. Shortly after, when Johnny has decided they will wait for Crazy, who was injured in the car crash, gang members strike up a conversation with Cathy's uncle, who owns the bar and grill across the street. "Don't fight boys," he tells them as they start to grab each others' beer bottles, "Plenty more where this came from. It's ice cold too." "Hey, doc," one of them counters, "where do we eat?" "Why, right there at Bleeker's Café," he answers. "You got steaks?" asks a second gang member. "Kansas City steaks?" asks the first. "We serve good meat," he assures them. "Where's the motel?" asks the first. "Well, the hotel is right over there," says the café owner proudly. "Hey," says the first gang member, as if truly impressed, "they got a *hotel* here!" Once in the cafe, they chat with Jimmy, the old man tending bar. The gang members ask him chummy, seemingly innocuous questions, in a caricature of small talk, allowing him to voice his opinions, at which they loudly laugh. As Johnny tries making time with Cathy, the gang's conversation deteriorates to jive, studded with words like "pops," "crazy," "man," "cool," "daddyo," and "rebop," until it dissolves through double-talk into a rhythmic bebop of nonverbal sounds.

This tendency to pretend to be engaged in normal social interactions, only to make fun of them while supposedly performing them, persists throughout the film. Always mocking authority and conventions, the gang members deploy a menacing humor. As day turns to night, Johnny's and Chino's followers descend into drunkenness, and their humor becomes more violent. Their violence, however, retains an element of social satire. As local citizens form vigilante groups, gang members smash the windows of a formalwear shop, exposing the mannequins neatly dressed as bride and groom. They later invade Mildred's Beauty Parlor: One member emerges wearing a rag mop as a wig, while others appear cone-headed with steel drier tops over their heads, and they all begin to dance, some alone but many others with each other. This display of leather-jacketed men jitterbugging in pairs is an obvious take off on heterosexual interactions. Subsequently, as Johnny searches for Cathy, who is hiding from him, he comes upon a snack stand that has been taken over by gang members, some wearing dresses, others in outlandish hats and one in a false beard, breaking windows and throwing things into the air. The absurdity of this attack and its significance to those engaged in it become evident when Chino, now sprung from jail, screams out, "Storm the Bastille!" as he rushes back toward the jail building.

What made the violence so terrifying to and objectionable for the original spectators is, at least in part, this parodic assault on the ordinary niceties and customs of life as they knew it. There is anarchy in the comedy, a quality that Antonin Artaud identifies in the Marx Brothers' *Horse Feathers* in an addendum to *The Theatre and Its Double* (1938). At the same time, *The Wild One* extends the disruptive comedy into what Artaud called "The Theatre of Cruelty," in which the emotional impact caused by the portrayal of violent acts makes the audience reevaluate their understandings of the world as they know it. What makes Chino's call to storm the Bastille so poignant is how it harkens back to a much earlier depiction of choreographed violence, the spectacle of the carmagnole in D.W. Griffith's *The Orphans of the Storm* (1922). Set during France's horrific Reign of Terror, the film depicts a crowd of maddened Jacobins performing their destructive dance as evidence of just how evil Robespierre's supporters were.

In contrast to the others, Johnny seems a brooding, stoic presence, capable of erupting at any moment but for the most part taciturn, even reserved. Although he occasionally acknowledges the humor in some of his friends' words and pranks, he more often presides over them as a quiet presence. As noted earlier, Brando was aware that he was creating beneath the tough exterior of Johnny, a more sensitive, needy soul. One prop that manages to offer a glimpse inside him is the trophy stolen during the cycle meet at the beginning of the film. As his cohorts mock the races, Johnny looks on curiously as the cyclists whiz by them, and his attention is captured momentarily when one of the fans starts cheering for a particular driver. At the winners' stand, gang members disparage the array of gilt statuettes given as prizes, but Johnny gazes at them, indicating how he sees the trophies as symbols of the crowd's cheers and admiration. One gang member, Pigeon (played by the uncredited Alvy Moore), no doubt observes Johnny's interest because he steals one of them for Johnny. Another gang member points out that it is only an award for second place, adding Pigeon must think Johnny is only second rate, but Johnny takes the prize and conceals it in his jacket.

When the gang is forced to leave, Johnny ties the statuette to his front fender and handlebars. He offers it to Cathy but she declines the gift as too personal coming from someone who has only known her a few minutes. He lashes it again to his cycle, where Chino sees and tries to take it. During their fight, it is given to Cathy again, but when she learns that Johnny did not actually win it, she gives it back to him, calling him a fake—a fake like her father, the useless policeman whom Johnny loathes. Much later in the film, after the hoodlums have taken over the town, Cathy is chased by cyclists who, in one of the film's most terrifying scenes, form a thundering circle around her. She is saved by Johnny, who then attempts to take her by force but then relinquishes her. After a heated argument, in which

Johnny assumes she thinks she is better than he is, there is a moment of reflection as the two try to talk to each other. "You were going to give me that statue—will you give it to me now?" she asks. When he asks her why, she cryptically replies, "I just wondered if you still wanted to give it me."

What does the stolen trophy represent? Certainly it stands for something Johnny wants, the adulation of others, recognition of his value, validation of his existence. It also becomes a token of his regard for others—an object to win a girl's affections, which he denies to his former buddy, Chino. At the close of the film, after Johnny has been found not guilty of causing Jimmy's death (the film's legal resolutions are so complicated that they defy recounting), he is set free and rides out of town with his fellow cyclists. Yet sometime later, he is back at Bleeker's Café, where Cathy and her father are drinking coffee at the counter. A county sheriff's car pulls up outside, and Frank rises, exits, and crosses the street as the officers emerge. Following a moment in which Johnny waits to see if he will be arrested again—he has been warned not to come back to this county—he watches as the officers get back in their car. Then, in complete silence, he struggles with himself, rises and heads for the door, but stops, removing the trophy from his jacket. He turns around, comes back to the counter, sets down the trophy, and pushes it slightly in Cathy's direction. With the camera fixed on his face, his previously impassive features turn into a slight smile, which she returns. The camera pulls back as he exits, Cathy and the statuette watching his departure. Glancing neutrally at Frank and ignoring the patrol car, he mounts his cycle and leaves. He drives off into the distance as Cathy comes out in time to see him disappear into the horizon.

As I argued earlier, this parting shot of the lone rider on the open road is contradicted by the sheriff's warning that if Johnny does not return for the hearing, he will be in serious trouble. Yet the romance story does much the same: Johnny, who has been "got to" by the girl, offers her, in the gift of the trophy, the thanks he is unable to articulate. Whatever it once stood for, it now represents a piece of himself that he is willing to share with her.

In a sense, Brando's Johnny is contrapuntal to the more rambunctious gang members of The Wild One. He is both the tough thug and the tender-hearted man. Of course, even John Wayne manages to hint that there are some emotions inside—if he did not have any, he would have nothing to suppress—but even more than Clift in Red River, Brando plays a man as someone who constantly lives at two extremes, the extreme of tough, active masculinity and the extreme of conscience-driven, compassionate manhood. The two exist within him in conflict, allowing him to perform a gender role that breaks from tradition and looks forward to a world in which having to be a man may not be such a terrible oppression.

In the end, of course, the love of a good woman may neutralize the threat that Johnny appears to pose. In Savran's terms, the lack of a genuine agenda ("What are you rebelling against, Johnny?" asks someone; "What d'you got?" Brando replies) translates not into an empowering challenge of gender and social norms but into a pathology of violence: The gang's "rebellion is coded as an Oedipal conflict rather than a political project" (57). Nonetheless, as the snippets of *The Wild One* inserted into *Scorpio Rising* demonstrate, the film's parting shots do not entirely erase the defiance of the earlier scenes.

The Contender

In spite of his success as Zapata and his not totally preposterous attempt at Mark Antony, the early roles that made Brando a star were those in which he played men who looked and spoke a lot like ordinary Americans, men like Ken Wilozek, Stanley Kowalski, Johnny Strabler, and Terry Molloy in the 1954 hit, *On the Waterfront*. Later in the 1950s, he would take on parts like Zapata that would require heavy makeup, prostheses, and/or accents, but his performances as Napoleon in *Desiree* (1954) and as Sakini, an Okinawan houseboy in *The Teahouse of the August Moon* (1956) were perceived as stagy, and his sudden leap into a musical comedy, as Sky Masterson (with a very strange New York accent) in *Guys and Dolls* (1955) was seen as just short of catastrophic. Even his drawling Texan military officer in *Sayonara* (1957) appeared stilted. Only the German soldier in *The Young Lions* (1958) pleased critics and spectators in the last six years of the decade.

Yet Terry Malloy was, despite the film's shortcomings, a brilliant role for Brando. With his thickening build and broken nose, he truly looked the part of a punchy ex-boxer, and he could play through the pauses in the character's speeches; his face and body could express what was going on inside the character well before the character could articulate it. The simplicity of the role allowed him to improvise and create and to build more complexity into Terry Malloy than the script contained.

The script itself was far more politicized than *Viva Zapata!* It glorified the dubious position of the informer. By the time production started, both director Kazan and screenwriter Budd Schulberg had appeared before HUAC and named names. Brando was acutely aware of Kazan's testimony. Between takes on *Julius Caesar*, Mankiewicz had caught Brando weeping about what he should do if and when he saw Kazan again (Bosworth 88). Initially, he refused to appear in the film that Kazan brought to him, but goaded by his agent, Jay Kanter, and Sam Spiegal, the producer of *On the Waterfront*, he agreed to play Terry Malloy (99). Brando maintained that during the filming, he was ignorant about the film's Cold War political implications:

> [W]hat I didn't realize then was that On the Waterfront was really a metaphorical argument by Gadg [Kazan's nickname] and Budd Schulberg: they made the film to justify finking on their friends. Evidently, as Terry Malloy I represented the spirit of the brave, courageous man who defied evil. Neither Gadg nor Budd Schulberg ever had second thoughts about testifying before the committee. (195)

In retrospect, we may find it difficult to believe that anyone, especially Brando, could not have been aware of who and what Terry represented. After all, he had become a supporter of the leftist Jewish underground in Palestine as a result of his part in A Flag Is Born, had worked on Henry Wallace's presidential run in 1948 (which The Party supported), and attended the 1949 Waldorf Astoria World Peace Conference—an event condemned as a Communist front (Bosworth 77). As mentioned earlier, Kazan's betrayal had troubled Brando in 1952 and caused him to reject the role in On the Waterfront when it was first offered. (It was then given to Frank Sinatra, but when Kanter talked Brando into ignoring the politics, Spiegal happily let Sinatra go.) Once the film opened, word circulated that it was Kazan's apologia for "squealing." By the 1960s, this interpretation appeared in print and has remained, more than half a century later, the widely accepted view.

Perhaps, as with Viva Zapata! Brando's immersion in this role inoculated him from understanding what Schulberg and Kazan intended. Brando probably "got it" when Kazan showed him the final cut; as he later recalled, "I was so depressed by my performance I got up and left the screening room. I thought I was a huge failure, and walked out without a word to him. I was simply embarrassed for myself" (199). Possibly, Brando was actually upset by how Kazan had used him to express an idea that the actor found repulsive; here was one of the great performances of his career, expansively researched, finely thought-out, and brilliantly alive, created to make a case for "singing like a canary."

Kazan might have argued that a betrayal of the Stalinist ideology that he had witnessed in The Group Theatre in the 1930s and early 1940s, when he had for a brief time been a Party member, was no betrayal at all. He remained until his death unapologetic about his HUAC testimony, which had made it possible for him to continue making movies. To a degree, the expediency of his naming names was in perfect keeping with the way that he practiced his art. Whatever needed to be done to achieve the right product was justified. Such an approach to movie making led Kazan not only to befriend the House Committee but also to work things out with the Mafia, which controlled the New Jersey waterfronts where he would begin shooting. At the same time he remained unrepentant, insisting that he had only named names that others had already given to HUAC. Kazan himself does not seem to have held much of a political perspective at all. Instead, he invested heavily in the notion that the ends justified the means both in negotiating with political adversaries and with actors.

Whatever worked is what Kazan would use. If this included telling little Peggy Ann Garner that her father had been shot down over France so that she would appear heartbroken for a scene in *A Tree Grows in Brooklyn* (1943), then so be it. "It's not a nice thing for a director to do," Kazan laughingly admitted about tricking the young Miss Garner, "but you know I think finally a film director has to get his shot no matter what he does. We're desperate people . . ." ("Elia Kazan: A Director's Journey").[4] Such justification certainly implies that Kazan had no real ideologies or doctrine, just a rampant desire to succeed no matter what the cost. During the filming of *Viva Zapata!* Kazan told Anthony Quinn that Brando had been slandering him behind his back, and he told Brando that Quinn was doing the same to him. In reality, neither had said anything about the other, but Kazan used their now inflamed mutual animosity in the scene in which Zapata must attack his brother for taking the peasants' lands. If their fight looks convincing on screen, there is good reason for it. (Quinn and Brando believed Kazan's lies for several decades.) Similarly, while shooting *East of Eden*, Kazan appropriated the discomfort that Raymond Massey felt around James Dean's seemingly casual approach to acting and amplified it so that the father–son relationship that they portrayed would be infused with the actual tension between the actors.

Such an approach to direction, in which the deliberate manipulation of players is justified by the performances they give, places the director in a dictatorial role; of course, Kazan had learned how to direct through the "Stalinist" principles of The Group Theatre—principles that would later be sharpened into ruthless and exploitative techniques by the Actors Studio at its worst. He also lived in a time when some established artists defended themselves by collaborating with the congressional witch-hunt in order to save their careers, which became increasingly despotic. Jerome Robbins, for example, named names, supposedly because the HUAC threatened to "out" him as a bisexual, and became an extraordinarily important and at the same time a pitiless, tyrannical choreographer. The figure of the older artist as tyrant was hardly a new one in modern times, but in the 1950s such tyranny was particularly in keeping with the ideas of "art for art's sake" and the depoliticization of art in contemporary culture.

Even in such an allegedly apolitical context, however, *On the Water-front* cannot avoid gesturing toward witch-hunt politics and, perhaps even more meaningfully, operates within the cultural framework of sexual politics. The plot attempts to detach an older version of masculinity from a newer one: Johnny Friendly (Lee J. Cobb), the mob boss who controls the waterfront workers, has assembled a "brotherhood" of males under him who extend his power and maintain loyalty toward him. Those who defy Friendly are treated savagely, beaten, or even killed. Foremost among his supporters is "Gentleman" Charlie Malloy (Rod Steiger), the college-educated older brother of Terry, who has become a failure since being defeated in the ring years before. Friendly has become their surrogate father, favoring them and offering them opportunities to succeed. Such an opportunity comes one night when Terry is asked to lure a young dockworker, Joey Doyle, out of his apartment so some of Friendly's "men" can "talk" to him. Both Terry and Doyle raise pigeons (a symbolic reference to "singing"), and when Terry calls up to Joey's window that he has recovered one of Joey's birds, Joey agrees to meet him on the roof. Instead, Terry lets the bird loose and goes back to find his brother, only to see Joey falling as two shadowy figures retreat into the night. This is a world of men in which power and profit determine what will happen.

Because Terry believed that Joey would not be harmed physically, he now begins to feel uneasy in Friendly's manly world and looks beyond it. He becomes infatuated with Joey's sister, Edie (Eva Marie Saint in her movie debut), who wants to know who killed her brother, and he ends up at a church meeting led by the parish priest, Father Barry (Karl Malden), in which the cleric exhorts those in attendance to speak out about what is really happening on the waterfront. Joey, we learn, was murdered because he was about to testify against Friendly's organization. Terry has actually been sent to the meeting by Friendly, who wants to know what is being said, but when thugs burst into the church with clubs, dispersing those within, he leads Edie out to the street.

Thus the film divides the "old boys' club" run by Friendly from the stevedores, their families, and the priest who serves them. When a man named Dugan, who, encouraged by Father Barry, gives secret testimony to the city's crime commission, is killed on the job, Terry is further drawn away from Friendly's circle of males and into the realm of those who have been exploited by it. Ultimately, he confesses to Edie the unwitting role he had in Joey's death, and is then urged by his conscience to do what Joey and Dugan could not, to appear in a public session and reveal what Friendly and his organization have done.

This is the act of betrayal that Schulberg has Terry commit, and although it is romanticized in the film, it seems rather brave in context. Terry must choose between the men, who by this time have murdered Charlie as well, and the rest of humanity. Nonetheless, the Friendly mob is hardly comparable to The Party, and if Friendly is Stalin, he is a rather small-time Stalin; although branded in the neighborhood as a stool pigeon, Terry's "singing" performs a valuable service. It also makes him a new kind of man, who can stand up for himself and others instead of exploiting those who cannot resist, who can appreciate the pain of others and act compassionately. And if the film stopped at this, it might have been an easier film to watch.

True to form, however, Kazan looks for a grand gesture at the end. Just as Brando's Zapata becomes a mythic martyr, he makes Brando's Terry a martyr for the cause. Thus, having taken down Friendly and his cronies, the stubborn or perhaps merely addled Terry goes down to the docks and taunts Friendly. Unable to resist retaliating, Friendly and his men beat Terry to a pulp while the frightened dockworkers do nothing to help him. Terry eventually emerges from this assault—Friendly is afraid that killing him will result in his immediate arrest—and leads the stevedores, who suddenly insist that they will work only if Terry is allowed to work too, to the loading dock. His walk to the pier is wobbly, with all the stumbles and blurred vision that the subjective camera allows, but finally he arrives, all at once inexplicably steady, strong, as if miraculously recovered.

Yet the key subject here is Brando's performance in *On the Waterfront*. As a male playing a male performing masculinity, the actor once again was able to infuse the macho tough guy with a vulnerability and compassion often missing from earlier film characterizations. In a scene set in the hold of a ship, Charlie catches Terry reclining and reading a girlie magazine, in which Charlie too shows some interest. He conveys to his brother Friendly's demand that Terry listen in on the church meeting. Afraid to be viewed as a "stool pigeon" by the longshoremen at the meeting, Terry tries to get out of the assignment. "Stooling is when you rat on your friends," says Charlie. This scene is counterpoised with one that follows the attack on the church, in which Terry leads Edie to safety. Suddenly, he becomes gentle, protective, and respectful. Brando's genius in this scene comes in an improvised bit that occurred when Saint accidentally dropped one of her gloves: Terry tries on the glove and gets a feel for what it is like to wear it before returning it to Edie. He also advises her to let him walk her home because there are too many men in the street "with only one thing in their mind." Here, the consumer of cheesecake, who has stood with his brother and the other mobsters by objectifying women, is suddenly transformed into a caring, considerate mensch, who seems to sense what it must be like to be a member of the "opposite sex."

The cab ride in which Charlie must either talk Terry into not testifying or deliver him to his executioners is the scene that spectators recall most vividly. Here, as earlier in the picture, Charlie invokes the brotherhood, not only the one between himself and Terry, but also the band of men that makes up the Friendly mob. The acting between Steiger and Brando is intense: detailed, deeply internal, and emotional. Throughout earlier scenes, the audience has picked up enough information to know that Charlie was responsible for making Terry throw his last fight—Terry almost admits it when he is confronted by the crime commission lawyer who meets him on the roof of his building. Thus, when Terry tearfully assigns the blame for his fall to Charlie, we are not so much shocked by the revelation as struck by how Terry has changed enough to be able to accept this horrible realization. At this moment, the value system suddenly shifts from "Do it to him before he does it to you" (a sentiment Terry himself has expressed to Edie early on) to a Christian selflessness in which Charlie will literally give his life for his brother's. Once again, Terry's conversion from macho thug to sensitive man is established by the actor's willingness to expose a softer side of masculinity.

Brando's capacity for expressing such a "softer" side was viewed by Kazan as ambisexual: "I think the trick, the wonderful thing about him, is the ambivalence again between a soft, yearning . . . [pauses to find correct word] . . . girlish side to him and a dissatisfaction that's violent and can be dangerous"[5] ("Elia Kazan: A Director's Journey"). Is the display of behaviors traditionally excluded from manhood, as Mellen has suggested, necessarily a display of femininity, or are such behaviors indicative instead of an immaturity, a boyishness as opposed to manliness, as Cohan asserts? Or are these behaviors, which some have viewed as "feminine" and others as "boyish," manifested through Brando's characterizations in such a way as to widen the definition of what is "proper" to the male?

In a way, these are all rather silly and reductive concerns because masculinity is not in fact derived from a cogent and consistent set of traits or performance acts. If that were the case, then being a man and being a woman would be very easy. Construing someone's gender is, like the reading of a poem, an interpretive act that relies heavily on cultural values that are inevitably in some way arbitrary and contradictory. Likewise, the performance of gender always takes place within a specific cultural context, so that the individual performative acts themselves signify locally and in the present but not cross-culturally or through time. A man who cannot fight back his tears may be thought of as girlish by mid-century Americans, or childishly hypersensitive, but in other places and times, that is, in different cultural contexts, the act of "not fighting back tears" becomes the act of weeping openly, something that is manly.

In our constant spectatorship of others' performances of gender, we can never find a truly definitive performance: There is always some aspect that does not exactly fit—or to put it another way, because the ultimate test of gender is intuitive (we naturally "know" whether someone is masculine or feminine), we tend to accept some indicators of gender and discount others. With regard to Terry Malloy in *On the Waterfront*, then, we view the result of incorporating a variety of acts that were not previously associated with the performance of masculinity as masculine because we spectators have accepted Brando, or what we perceive to be Brando, as masculine.

The problem is, of course, that Terry, like Zapata, becomes a superhuman figure who rises to lead the ranks of ordinary males. Unlike Zapata, who dies, the failed boxer, the self-admitted bum, is resurrected to shepherd his flock into their new working environment. All at once, the notion of the common man, or common men, in charge, is eclipsed by the phenomenon of the hero; of all Brando's early characterizations, Terry Malloy is the one who is most in danger of becoming like the mobsters he has replaced. As long as the working world is defined as belonging exclusively to men, there is always the possibility that the rules of "brotherhood" will come back into play.

Conclusion

What made Marlon Brando so emblematic of masculinity during the postwar era was his consciousness of and discomfort with who and what he was. Granted, Montgomery Clift's performances of manhood disclosed a clear uneasiness, but Clift's characters seemed usually able to reconcile their conflicts, whereas Brando's left profound doubts about his masculinity in particular and about masculinity itself in general. In the Age of Anxiety, when those emerging from the war and those who had been too young to serve in it found themselves enclosed within a paranoid, repressed society that equated conformity with normality, dissatisfaction, and resentment of what was called "normal" simmered, sometimes, as Brando himself recalled, beneath the surface. In a way, the theater was a better medium to express such dissidence if only because there was much less heavy-handed censorship on Broadway than in Hollywood, but the movies were a mass medium that enjoyed far wider circulation and attracted audiences from all classes and locales—not merely an elite in New York City.

In the 1950s, when the personal lives of stars were still scrutinized and often controlled by the studios, Brando, like Clift, avoided signing with one studio and remained a free agent, often exhibiting what was then considered eccentric, nonconformist behavior and keeping his private life comparatively quiet. Clift's lifestyle proved untenable: He burned himself out of an acting career and drank himself into very bad health. When he died in 1966, he left empty a role in a film that Elizabeth Taylor had won for him, in John

Huston's *Reflections in a Golden Eye*. Brando took over the part and gave a peculiar performance of a closeted homosexual military officer, but the entire film was peculiar so he fit right in. If Clift had lived, he would probably have been too far gone to play the repressed officer, which probably was too close to who Clift really was anyway. By this point, Brando's career suddenly soared with a second wave of extraordinary characterizations in some incredible pictures, including the title role in Francis Ford Coppola's *The Godfather*, the American male in Bernardo Bertolucci's *Last Tango in Paris*, and Kurtz in Coppola's *Apocalypse Now*. There also were many other roles into the first year of the twenty-first century.

Yet the Brando who became a cultural phenomenon and an icon of masculinity was the early Brando, the roughneck with feelings, who swaggered and simpered, mixed his machismo with something that men had not shown before, at least not on screen. This girlishness, as Kazan construed it, or this boyishness as others have called it, this refusal to conform to gender norms in an era of conformism, even as Brando demonstrated that he was perfectly capable of playing a "man" in contemporary terms, made it possible for spectators to recognize that performing masculinity might not be as restrictive an activity as society at large decreed it was.

The young Brando was a beautiful looking man. Sometimes his roles demanded that he change his appearance, but with most of his characters, audiences could still catch glimpses of the handsome face and muscled body. No where was his beauty more blatant, perhaps, than in *Julius Caesar*, in which Mankiewicz took advantage of the actor's classical profile and sculpted physique. With his hair clipped like Augustus's and his frame in a scanty peplos, Brando made the back cover of Bob Mizer's *Physique Pictorial* (Winter 1954–1955), the first and in many ways most influential of the early physique magazines that featured photos of partially unclad men for the pleasure of other men. He also appeared in *Tomorrow's Man* (September 1955) and *The Body Beautiful* (August 1957). At least among homosexual readers, he had earned the title of beefcake.[6]

Before Elvis Presley became the musical inspiration to an entire generation, Brando had won the respect of those segments of postwar audiences, who, like himself, sought separation from much of what had come before and virtually all that was going on at the time. Both rebellious, both sporting dangerous good looks and showing blatant male sexuality, Brando and Presley commanded the attention of female and male fans. Yet it was Brando who served as a model for the next icon of a new masculinity to come onto the screen, James Dean, who had stalked Brando (as well as Clift) in New York and actually made contact with him in California. Dean would supplant Brando as the movies' new hot male superstar and thus would influence

Presley, but Dean's life and career were even shorter than Clift's—so short, in fact, that his three film appearances and early death would catapult him into America's popular cultural mythology by the mid-1950s. Brando would live on, both as a myth and man and in time, would eventually come back to what he had always said he had wanted to be, an actor.

CHAPTER 6

Beauty Forever Young

The Brief Career of James Dean

Although both Montgomery Clift and Marlon Brando had begun by playing juvenile roles on stage, by the time they appeared on screen they were young men: They initially appeared as veterans of the war who were changed by their experiences and as such appealed to an audience composed not merely of returning servicemen but of the larger population that had awaited their homecoming. However, as the 1950s wore on, a new generation of movie-goers who had been children during the war were looking for characters to whom they could relate. Coming of age in a time when the fabric of postwar society seemed to be tearing apart, they sought truths about themselves and where they stood, how they perceived, and what they wanted. Many were not interested in joining a society built around what William H. Whyte would call "The Organization Man"—a society that required conforming to what seemed by now well-worn norms. These skeptical late adolescents were the first wave of a youth culture that would eventually sweep across America.

Brando and Clift certainly appealed to those coming of age, but both were adults, albeit young adults. The first postwar star, however, to per-sonify teenage angst was James Dean, who, although in his early 20s, could still believably play a high school student. Dean's characters embodied the contemporary rebelliousness of youth and a genuine dissatisfaction with the status quo. Their contempt for the hypocrisy of middle-class life and their often violent attempts to express themselves authentically made him a gen-erational hero.

In a way, it may seem unfair to compare Dean, who only made three pictures and died at the age of 24, with the two actors who preceded him, who both made many more films. Some have justified his place in this trinity by his posthumous fame; as soon as his death was announced, his image took on an almost mythic significance, making him more than just a generational hero but a hero to all youth in succeeding decades. This argument may justify his being remembered, but it precludes any serious discussion of his performances.

Dean began starring in films after Clift and Brando had already arrived. He knew their work well and admired them both, to the extent that, had he lived today, he would have acquired the title of stalker. Although he was frequently compared by critics and others to Brando, there was relatively little in Dean that actually seemed to echo Brando, aside from the method acting that he embraced, despite his indignation with Lee Strasberg's dissection of a role he had performed at the Actors Studio. Elia Kazan, who had been a founder of the school and who had worked extensively with Brando, was able to draw on Dean's own use of "The Method" while directing him in his first major role, as Cal in *East of Eden*. Yet the outcome was totally different from what Kazan had achieved with Brando in *A Streetcar Named Desire*, *Viva Zapata!*, and *On the Waterfront*. Nonetheless, it was evident to most moviegoers that Dean belonged in the same category as Clift and Brando if only because, like them, his acting looked and sounded and felt like nothing else movie audiences had previously witnessed.[1]

Likewise, Dean's portrayals of masculinity seemed somehow to relate to those of Clift and Brando. Initially, Clift had been cast against someone who would become one of the most popular 1940s versions of manliness, John Wayne, the male movie star with no doubts about his own manhood. In *Red River*, director Howard Hawks had set Wayne's infallible and often brutal masculinity in sharp contrast to Clift's more compassionate and reasoned version. Wayne would go on to become even more John Wayne in the 1950s, 1960s, and 1970s, but in the 1940s, through Westerns, war pictures, and even light fare, such as his turn with Claudette Colbert in the 1946 romantic comedy *Without Reservations*, Wayne remained for better and worse the action-oriented super hero who always intuitively knew the manly (and thus, correct) thing to do.

If Wayne upheld the image of an instinctively masculine male, Humphrey Bogart, one of his contemporaries, performed a masculinity that was far more existential: In a sense, Bogart's characters seem fully aware that the gender construct itself is, like so many other social and cultural constructs, arbitrary and absurd. Instead of clinging to the codes that Wayne appeared to perpetuate, Bogart's roles revolve around the notion that one must choose one's own version of manliness. Perhaps best personified by Rick in *Casablanca*, the self-made, self-centered male inevitably finds a cause to which he must commit. Like the protagonists of Bogart's postwar films noirs, the man *engagé*, in the midst of danger and chaos, eventually finds himself doing the manly thing. However, as Joan Mellen points out, the assertion of whatever masculinity the Bogart characters create, always shows itself as superior to femininity, no matter how imaginative and resourceful it may be (152–161). Whether played by the feisty Lauren Bacall (who became the actual Mrs. Bogart) or another actress, the films' heroines are only too happy to acknowledge Bogie's pre-eminence.

During the war, Wayne and Bogart were exceptional. The more typical image of males on screen was that of the average young soldier. Bravely fighting for democracy, GI Joe came in a variety of ethnicities and types; whether he was proletarian or patrician, Irish or Italian, Jewish from Brooklyn or Nordic from Minnesota, the American serviceman was usually pure of heart and strove to put on a brave front. The relative youth of the majority of the troops often turned war into the proving ground of manhood. Suddenly, the late adolescent had to be taken seriously. The "boys," who for the most part looked and behaved more like Mickey Rooney than Wayne or Bogart, suddenly had to be regarded as men. This quick conversion was made necessary by the conditions of the time, but it would resonate through the next decade as young men (and later young women) struggled toward their majority. In the end, it would contribute to the youth culture of the 1950s and 1960s.

Clift's postwar performances point both to the absurdity of Wayne's (and others') enactment of a rough and intuitive masculinity and also to the problems of sustaining the self-determining concept of manhood that Bogart's roles exemplify. Up against Wayne, Clift is able to hold his own, but as the intervention of Joanne Dru illustrates, he never really overcomes Wayne, not even in the final physical battle that erupts near the movie's conclusion. The film ends on a distinct note of ambivalence: Hawks is prepared to accept Clift's rendition of masculinity but is not ready to discard Wayne's. Throughout his early career, Clift demonstrates how difficult it is to sustain a credible masculinity.

Brando, unlike Clift, portrayed males who were ready to follow the old-school masculinity of Wayne and others, only to fail in doing so. The macho antics of Stanley Kowalski in A Streetcar Named Desire result in his inability to hold onto his "manly role" as husband and father, even with his resounding but hollow defeat of the "feminine" wiles of his sister-in-law. Having Blanche contained in an insane asylum may temporarily stabilize Stanley's sense of masculinity, but ultimately her exile cannot help him preserve it. After all, how can anyone be "masculine" without the competitive (and necessarily "inferior") construct of the "feminine"? In the end, Brando's tough guys (Terry Malloy and Johnny Strabler included) have to crack; such breakdowns unleash a fleeting sense both of what masculinity is not and what masculinity might be.

More than anyone, James Dean embodied the complex and warring components of what masculinity might be. In his first two features, East of Eden and Rebel Without a Cause, he played adolescents, and in his third,

Giant, he began as a sensitive late adolescent who grew into a thwarted middle-aged man. Because he was in his early 20s but looked younger, he could take on roles (such as Jim Stark in *Rebel*) that both Clift and Brando had outgrown. As with such stage characters as Tennessee Williams's Tom Wingfield, Robert Anderson's Tom Lee, and Edward Albee's Jerry, Dean's youth or at least his semblance of youthfulness, allowed him to deconstruct and explore the gender of his characterizations and at the same time remain an object of desire. The effectiveness of such a strategy was made clear by the extraordinary success of the novel embraced by the evolving youth culture, J.D. Salinger's *The Catcher in the Rye*, published in 1951.

The notion of men on screen as objects of desire probably dates back to the beginning of cinema itself, and yet the first emphatic proof of male star power came with the career and death of Rudolf Valentino. In the mid-1920s, however, Valentino's attractiveness to women proved threatening to heterosexual men, who questioned his masculinity because he flaunted his sexuality so blatantly for the cameras and spectators. Any man who was "too" pretty could not be a real man because he inevitably provoked in other men a recognition of their own attraction to him. So, ironically, Valentino, who held an obvious allure for an extensive following of women, was castigated as an effeminate and even a homosexual. Subsequently, men who were pretty enough to be recognized as such by straight males would ground their manhood in some of the more traditional activities that were associated with masculinity. Still, in the 1930s, overly handsome actors like Cary Grant, Tyrone Power, and Errol Flynn sometimes proved difficult for some heterosexual men to accept, and rumors about their sexuality continue to circulate to this day.

Far safer were those male actors who did not seem dazzlingly gorgeous, such as John Wayne himself, Humphrey Bogart, Spencer Tracy, James Stewart, Henry Fonda, Gary Cooper, Joel McCrea, and many, many others. Such stars might be desirable to women, but men could like them without having to admit that they were desirable. Even the teen-aged box office winner of the late 1930s and early 1940s, Mickey Rooney, posed no real threat to his male audiences.

Thomas Hine sees Rooney as a significant phenomenon in the prewar movie era: "One secret to his allure was that it seemed he would never grow up at all." Juxtaposed with the wisdom and abilities of Judge Hardy in the Andy Hardy series, Rooney seemed as though he would never "acquire the patina of age and authority that virtually defined the character of the judge" (100). Few if any of his fans associated him with the glamorous women he dated and married; for the public he was the perpetual teenager. Hine contrasts Rooney with the young Frank Sinatra, "the first true teen idol," who "was admittedly a far more sexual figure," but then qualifies that "in his early years, [Sinatra] seemed so thin and vulnerable, crooning in his bow tie, that his female fans wanted to mother him . . ." (104). What separated Dean from these earlier late-adolescent stars, of course, was the war.

A generation later, Dean's three performances would prove something of a threat to male spectators. Both mature adult males and females might look at Dean in *Rebel* and shudder, much as they had at Brando in *The Wild One*. Although the upheaval wreaked by the troubled teen would be resolved, the power of Dean's anger, violence, and despair was never suc-cessfully purged from the audience's experience. Thus, late adolescent and young adult spectators related easily to the at-times expressionistic displays of Dean's concentrated emotions; he was indeed showing them visually what they believed they were feeling. Adults might scoff at the melodramatics and reductiveness of the plot and characterizations (especially of the adult roles) in *Rebel*, but the feelings generated through and by the plot resonated deeply with the younger generation.

As noted earlier, Dean himself had been heavily influenced by Clift (especially in *A Place in the Sun*) and Brando (especially in *The Men*), rec-ognizing their profound depth of characterization and the raw enactment of emotion in both performances. He was also in awe of their ability to maintain their characterizations through a medium that, by its very nature, was pieced together from fragmented scenes and often shot out of sequence. Yet, however much he appreciated these actors, he was hardly in a position to replicate their performances—the limitations of his own instrument, both physical and vocal, made it impossible for him to do what they did. Thus, Dean applied their technique to himself and to what he could do. The end product carried him through three films and proved so breathtaking that his fans, then as now, rarely bothered to look past his performances at the virtues or ills of the movies themselves.

If they had, they might have recognized that certain narrative ele-ments seem to surround Dean's three starring performances: His characters are always loners, alienated from social institutions like the family, school, and community; they are always pitted against a father or patriarchal figure; they find solace in the company of an attractive female; and they are not fully grown-up. (Even Jett Rink, whom we see as a man in his 50s toward the end of *Giant*, remains an overgrown teenager.) Although some of these elements are present in early Clift and Brando films, they seem to have been requirements in Dean's films. True, Dean made only three movies, but there is some evidence that the next two movies he would have made, *Somebody Up There Likes Me* and *The Left Handed Gun*, both of which were ultimately filmed with Paul Newman (whose male presence on screen was far less threatening to other men), locate themselves within the familiar parameters that marked the first three. Like Clift and Brando, Dean would have had to adjust his performances to his age eventually—but in Dean's case, that eventuality never came.

True to Mies van der Rhoe's dictum, less is more. In Dean's case, the little there was, made it far easier for the late actor to be reduced to a legend. And although men and women who actually knew Dean and biographers who did not, have put into circulation more and more details to humanize their by-now mythologized subject, the specifics are more often than not subsumed by the larger-than-life image of the martyred boy who had to die young. The more we know, it would seem, the less we understand. In an effort to make sense of Dean's performances, I reserve comments on his life and afterlife until later.

Nonetheless, Dean's performances critiqued much of what was wrong with traditional masculinity (as had Brando's) and at the same time personified a masculinity that lay ahead. The specifics grew out of the holes in his failed attempts at traditional gender performances, in Dean's failure to "live up to" the rules that governed manhood: deep emotion, unreasoned violence, a capability for tenderness, even the possibility of deep—even erotic—affection for other males.

Early Attempts

Although, as mentioned in the previous chapter, the number of tomes on Brando's life and career has been vast, the literature on Dean is large but eclectic. Much of it is highly reiterative—with regard to such a short life, there were only so many stories to tell—but over the years, some of those closest to Dean have told their stories more than once. For example, John Gilmore, a friend and occasional sexual partner, wrote on "the real" James Dean in 1975, only to tell more in 1997 in a new memoir. More industrious, William Bast, a close friend, sometime roommate, and sometime lover, came out with his first biography in 1956, and then offered updated versions of it in 1975 and 1992, and finally, in 2006, wrote his tell-all, in which much of what had been left unsaid in the earlier books was articulated. Dean's girlfriend from his time in New York, Liz Sheridan (who would become famous playing Jerry Seinfeld's mother), told bits and pieces to a few biographers and then came out with a revealing memoir in 2000. This gradual release of sexual information has been due in part to shifting morals over the decades following Dean's demise; what could not be written in the 1950s became easier to express as the decades wore on. Yet all of the volumes dedicated to Dean, either by those who knew him firsthand or by those who have studied him, have preserved an ongoing interest in his legend while mentioning many of the same facts and events.

The facts are relatively simple: Born February 8, 1931 in Marion, Indiana to Mildred Wilson, who after becoming pregnant married Winton Dean, James spent his first six years in Indiana. His father, a dental technician, moved the family to Santa Monica, California in 1937, where three years later James's doting mother succumbed to cancer. James was especially close to his mother, who spent much time with him, grooming him to be artistic and sensitive, and her loss (which he at first refused to accept) prompted his father to send the boy back to Indiana, where Winton Dean's sister and brother-in-law raised him on a farm near Fairmount.

After high school, James went back to California, enrolling in classes at Santa Monica City College and staying, at first, with his father, who had since remarried, but the two could not get along. Gradually, he moved out, applied to law school at the University of California at Los Angeles, and began attending workshops with stage and screen actor Stuart Whitmore, who taught him and his fellow students (one of whom was Dean's roommate, William Bast) some of the basics of method acting. Dean soon dropped out of college and began attending television and film auditions. It was during this time that Dean became friendly with John Gilmore, who was, like Dean himself, an occasional hustler. One of Dean's girlfriends was the daughter of famed television comedienne Joan Davis, but in California he was unable to make much headway in the entertainment community. He managed to find a few television roles (singing in a Pepsi Cola commercial, playing the apostle John in a religious drama), and eventually became the protégé of advertising executive and former producer, Rogers Brackett.

The relationship between the young actor and the older man was sexual as well as professional. Some of those who knew Dean and had met Brackett describe the latter as an old queen. Dean found a few bit parts on the West Coast but decided in 1951 to go to New York, a trip that was paid for by Brackett, who had a home in Manhattan as well as Hollywood. In New York, Dean found a few odd jobs: For one, he was in charge of testing the various games for the game show "Beat the Clock," a métier at which he was too good; he was far more agile than most of the contestants. During his years in New York, he met and had an affair with dancer Liz (nicknamed Dizzy) Sheridan. William Bast came East for a while, and the two roomed together for several months.

After attending open calls for plays, Dean was cast in 1952 in *See the Jaguar*, a drama in which he played a troubled boy. The show received poor reviews, although Dean was singled out by several critics. This in turn led to some television roles, one with Hume Cronyn, whom he enraged by constantly changing the director's blocking, and some off-Broadway parts. Finally, in 1953, after auditioning at The Actors Studio, he became a member. Yet director Lee Strasberg's response to the first scene Dean presented there was so critical that the aspiring actor never performed for Strasberg again although he did attend workshops at the Studio. In 1954, he appeared as the pandering Arab boy in an adaptation of Andre Gide's *The Immoralist*. Again, his reviews were positive, but unwilling to remain in the cast for long he accepted an offer by Kazan, who was directing *East of Eden* at Warner Brothers. Although he would return to New York for television appearances, he would never perform on stage again. During the remaining months of his life, he focused on making movies, telling a number of people that he ultimately wanted to direct films.

Unlike Clift and Brando, Dean had a very limited career in the theater. His Broadway productions numbered two, and he did not remain in either of them for very long. In the case of his first play, *See the Jaguar* by N. Richard Nash, his short run in the show was hardly his fault. Nash's earlier drama, *The Young and Fair* (1948), had been well received, but his latest offering did not sit well with critics, some of whom thought the play was written in verse and others of whom believed it to have been composed in florid prose. Set in a mountain community, the play "amounted to an incredible fable," as John Chapman tried to explain it in *The Daily News*, "about a boy who was kept in an ice house by his mother for 18 years, and when he got out he was sweet but simpleminded."[2] Most of the people in the community assume that the boy knows where his late mother has hidden a substantial sum of money and attempt to coerce him into revealing the secret; only two people sympathize with his plight, a "brawny but high-minded country school teacher" played by Arthur Kennedy, noted Chapman, and the animal-loving daughter of the owner of the local general store, played by Constance Ford. By the end of the play, the boy has been put in a cage into which the well-meaning daughter had hoped to place a locally caught Jaguar, and the protesting school teacher, who liberates the boy, is shot dead by the mob. Chapman allowed that "[a]s the boy, James Dean is very good."

Other critics seemed to agree with that evaluation. Whitney Bolton in *The Morning Telegraph*, wrote, "[A] young actor, James Dean, making his Broadway debut, is overwhelming as the boy brought from the icehouse into a world incomprehensible to him." Lee Mortimer in *The Daily Mirror* added that "[n]o show is complete without a character actor who thefts the show," naming Dean as one of two. *The Herald Tribune*'s Walter Kerr concurred, "James Dean adds an extraordinary performance in an almost impossible role: that of a bewildered lad who has been completely shut off from a vicious world by an overzealous mother and who is coming upon the beauty and the brutality of the mountain for the first time." Richard Watts Jr. in *The New York Post* thought, "James Dean achieves the feat of making the childish young fugitive believable and unembarrassing," while William

Hawkins, reviewing for *The World-Telegram and The Sun* allowed that Dean was "gently awkward as the ignorant boy." George Freedly of *The Morning Telegraph* felt that Dean "acted the mentally retarded boy with sweetness and naivete [sic] that made his torture singularly poignant." Only *The Times's* Brooks Atkinson failed entirely to mention Dean.

Two years later, in his review of *The Immoralist*, a stage adaptation by Ruth and Augustus Goetz (who had also adapted *The Heiress*) of André Gide's novel, Atkinson did name Dean (as one of the "African villagers") but said nothing about his performance. Luckily, most of the New York critics did pay attention to him even though he played a minor character. As with James's novella, *Washington Square*, Gide's book had to be heavily reworked (and also somewhat sanitized) for the stage: The Goetz's *Immoralist* concerns Michel (played by Louis Jourdan), a young man who has managed to repress a homosexual indiscretion at school, and Marcelline (played by Geraldine Page), a young woman who has always loved him. In spite of his past, Michel marries her, but their honeymoon through north Africa makes it all too clear to Michel that he is a homosexual; an encounter with a seductive servant boy, Bachir (played by Dean), demonstrates his attraction to males and to the sordid world of sodomites. He finally admits the truth to his wife, who is now pregnant with their child, and the two return to France, to live out their lives together.

In a world in which Robert Anderson's *Tea and Sympathy* was regarded as a sensitive portrayal of gender and sexuality, *The Immoralist* appeared strikingly didactic; it also strove to do what *Tea and Sympathy* (which was then running on Broadway) never dared to do—that is, to depict a homosexual character in a sympathetic (although perhaps pitiable) way. "Its appeal," concluded Robert Coleman in *The Daily Mirror*, "is likely to be limited— limited to those interested in sociology." Coleman appeared to have had no inkling that homosexuals enjoyed going to the theatre. Other critics found the script downright repellant or merely badly written. Yet, as with *See the Jaguar*, an unsatisfactory script made reviewers more aware of the talent on stage.

There was considerable acclaim for Geraldine Page and some, a bit more tempered, for Louis Jourdan. At the same time, many of the lesser characters drew praise as well and were complimented for their roles in this cautionary tale. Coleman, for example, said Dean's performance as "a venal panderer" was "excellent," while *The Tribune's* Kerr stated that Dean made "a colorfully insinuating scapegoat." Watts in *The Post* condemned the subject matter and alleged, "James Dean is realistically unpleasant as the slimy [homosexual]." Others followed suit, including *The Brooklyn Eagle's* Louis Scheaffer ("Dean makes a vivid impression as a completely immoral young Arab"); *Women's Wear Daily's* Thomas Dash ("Dean is sly and rascally as a roguish and blackmailing houseboy"); and *The World-Telegram and The Sun*'s Hawkins ("It is James Dean as the houseboy who clearly and originally underlines the sleazy impertinence and the amoral opportunism which the husband must combat").

Only Freedly in *The Morning Telegraph* seemed genuinely to appreciate the play and found Dean's rendition of the role particularly sensitive: "James Dean gives the best masculine performance in the role of the Arab boy, a part which could easily have become extremely offensive with less good acting and direction." Such an observation implies the critic's own desire not to condemn the subject matter itself and not to accept stereotypical characterizations of homosexuals.

Directly opposed to Freedly stood George Jean Nathan, whose review in *The Journal American* was entitled, "Grim Fairy Tale." The title is revealing about Nathan's disapproval of homosexuals. Almost a decade earlier, Nathan had recommended to Eddie Dowling that he produce Tennessee Williams's *The Glass Menagerie* despite the critic's suspicions that Williams was queer, and Nathan later condemned the playwright in his column; in this case, he used his column to share his views on "the changed theatrical attitude toward homosexuality." In spite of some occasional flashes of liberalism, Nathan referred to Michel's sexuality as an "abnormal urge." He further proclaimed that "the subject of homosexuality has already had too much stage airing to be any longer in the least scandalous," and that the subject was "not so very different from those of the plots in which the husband is found to be psychopathically given to murder, or congenitally insane, or some other social defective." Nevertheless, he manages to go on for many paragraphs, even as he protests that the subject of homosexuality is of little relevance and hardly sensational: "It has, in a word, become impossible theatrically to shock people who have been sitting in the world's electric chair for now so long and waiting for the current to be turned on at any minute." The immediate implication of Nathan's diatribe is, why even bother to talk about homosexuality at all? Predictably, he fails to mention it by name even once.

After leaving the cast of *The Immoralist* only three weeks into the run and before departing for Hollywood—during the weeks when he was probably making some of the New York screen tests for *East of Eden*—Dean participated in a reading of Ezra Pound's translation of Sophocles' *Women of Trachis* presented at The New School. The only review appeared in *The Brooklyn Daily Eagle*, and Sheaffer's critique is largely devoted to the translation itself, which was published in *The Hudson Review* around the same time. Although Scheaffer did not completely embrace what he called Pound's "curiously harmonious blending of modern humor and old tragedy," he complimented the performances of Anne Jackson (as Daianeira) and Eli

Wallach (as Herakles) but mentioned Dean ("as the son") only in passing. It would be his final stage performance.

Not only were Dean's stage appearances few, but he also never played a lead role in the theater. True, some of his television roles were prominent, but at the time the little box was considered a popular medium far less artistic than cinema. Although Clift and Brando had attained stardom on Broadway, Dean would have to wait until his image flashed across the silver screen.

Et in Arcadia Ego: The Trouble with Paradise

The film *East of Eden* is based on the final two chapters of John Steinbeck's epic novel of the same name and is set in California just before America entered World War I. As the title implies, despite the modern setting, the book and the screenplay (by Paul Osborn) contain numerous allusions to the biblical tale of Adam and Eve, their ejection from the garden, and the fatal conflict between their sons, Cain and Abel.

The plot concerns Adam Trask (Raymond Massey), a well-to-do farmer in Salinas, and his two sons, Cal (James Dean) and Aaron (Richard Davalos). Adam considers Aaron, the older of the two, the perfect son but finds himself repeatedly disappointed with Cal. Aaron's fiancée, Abra (Julie Harris), feels sorry for and a little frightened of Cal, whose spontaneous and often irrational actions complicate his relationship with his family. Cal discovers that his mother, Kate (Jo van Fleet), whom he has been told died when he was a child, is alive in nearby Monterey, and he tracks her down to the bawdy house where she presides as madam. Unaware of who he is, she has him ejected.

Meanwhile, Adam has become fascinated by the idea of sending chilled vegetables by rail across country, and he brings his sons and Abra to visit an icehouse that he is buying. At the icehouse, Cal climbs up to the loft where he sees Aaron and Abra together and overhears their discussion of him. In a rage, he suddenly opens the chute, sending down large blocks of ice onto the ground. Over dinner, Adam reprimands Cal, making him read Bible verses, which he does resentfully. That night Cal returns to Monterey and tries again to see his mother but again is thrown out.

On his return home that night, Cal glimpses through a window his father happily experimenting with ice and a head of lettuce. Eager to gain Adam's approval, he throws himself into helping with the project, loading the lettuce and ice into box cars, and even improvises to speed up the process using a coal chute (which he has appropriated from some unwitting delivery men) that allows the vegetables to move faster from wagons to the processing table. When Adam realizes that the coal chute was stolen, he expresses his disappointment in Cal, even as he compliments him on his innovative idea.

A far greater disappointment, however, comes as Adam and his sons and Abra are looking at a new automobile. The county sheriff (Burl Ives), who earlier confirmed for Cal that his mother was indeed the proprietor of the brothel, informs Adam that the shipment of lettuce has been returned even before it reached the East Coast; the vegetables, which were in direct contact with the melting ice, have rotted. Dismayed, Adam forsakes his dream, believing that others will figure out the way to make it come true.

Adam is broken in spirit; again, in an attempt to win his father's respect, Cal plans, with the help of Abra, to rally Adam's morale with a surprise birthday party. He tells her about the party while they are at the local fair, where he has agreed to meet her and Aaron but before his brother has turned up. Previously, Cal has succeeded in meeting with Kate and has received the sum of $5,000 from her. He has invested this money in beans, in hopes that America's recent entry into the war in Europe will raise the prices of crops, and plans to give his father this money at the party to replace the fortune he lost. As they talk, temporarily stranded at the top of the Ferris wheel, Abra is moved by Cal and kisses him, but she quickly denies the feelings she has, insisting she loves Aaron. Their discussion is interrupted by an angry exchange below between a German friend of the family and a crowd of locals intent on blaming all Germans for the war and its atrocities. Aaron, a confirmed pacifist, stands steadily beside the family friend, but when violence seems imminent, Cal climbs down the Ferris wheel and begins pummeling the mob members.

The birthday party begins well enough, but even before Cal can present his gift, Aaron, by now jealous over his fiancée's feelings for Cal, announces their engagement, much to Abra's surprise. The gift of the money suddenly seems anticlimactic, and worse still, Adam refuses it, condemning Cal's speculation as having unfairly profited from the labor of the poor bean farmers. Cal attempts to embrace his father, who cringes at his son's desperation. Cal then flees, followed by Abra, who in turn is followed by Aaron. Aaron orders her back into the house and tells his brother to keep away from her. In response to his being rejected yet again in favor of his brother, Cal vengefully takes Aaron to Monterey and flings him into Kate's room. He then returns home.

A day later, the sheriff arrives to tell Adam that the formerly tee-totaling Aaron has been drinking all night in Monterey and is about to leave on a train to enlist in the army. Shocked by his son's uncharacteristic behavior, Adam, Abra, and Cal rush to the train station as the train slowly pulls away. Adam spies Aaron, obviously intoxicated, in one of the carriages, and when Aaron turns to confront his father, he breaks the window in a bout of mad laughter. Adam suffers a stroke.

In the final scenes, Cal is contemplating leaving Salinas. Urged by Abra to talk to his now-paralyzed father, Cal is finally able to reconcile with him as Adam begs him to stay and take care of him.

Here we can see all the components of the Dean character: the lonely young man who feels an outcast at home, in school, and in the world at large, who struggles against his father and finds comfort through a girlfriend. Although the plot itself in many ways recalls the Genesis narrative, the combination of author Steinbeck and director Elia Kazan suggests the possibility of what proved true in their earlier collaboration, *Viva Zapata!* Kazan's personal political agenda (also apparent in his collaboration with Schulberg in *On the Waterfront*) may be discerned in *East of Eden*. Cal may be a younger version of Kazan, who like Cal (and like Dean) had had a distant relationship with a hard-to-please father; he is then also the boy who tries to do good even though people characterize his actions as bad, condemning him without really knowing him. In this reading, the director would have a need to demonstrate that the man unjustly accused of doing wrong has a likeable soul and is, at base, a good human being; perhaps this explains why Kazan filmed *East of Eden* in a way that appeared to show people engaged in an age-old struggle with such psychological depth.

Indeed, depth is the central visual trope in the film. This was Kazan's first Cinemascope movie. Instead of acquiescing to the inevitable horizontal that the wide screen allowed, Kazan strove to use the screen much like a perspective painter, who would try on canvas to emphasize a progress of largely vertical elements increasingly farther away. There are, of course, a few exceptions, shots showing, in true Cinemascope fashion, wide, flat fields and long, rolling landscapes, but these are relatively few. For much of the film, Kazan, who was never before considered an especially visually oriented director (he was instead regarded as an actor's director), carefully composes the frames to include a foreground and background that anchor the view of the figures between them. The effect is stunning—a truly amazing feat in a mid-1950s film that requires intimate groupings rather than constant panorama. A concrete sense of depth pervades the movie as soon as the credits end.

As the movie's theme music climaxes over the director's name, the panoramic coastal view cuts sharply to a side view of a vacant lot on a run-down street. An unpainted gate faces the ocean as children play and men mend nets, paint boats, and a woman, perched on the fence, watches as Kate, dressed in black, gloved and veiled, crosses into the frame from the viewers' left. The lens follows her walking into three-dimensional space, past a tree, which lingers in the shot, past some fishing nets stretched out to dry, which remain in the shot, into a wider street that narrows into a distance. There is a new shot, with Kate crossing the new street, moving in front of a car parked at the curb and behind a signpost (which has its back to the camera and thus cannot be read). As the camera pans to follow her, Cal is suddenly discovered sitting on the pavement watching her walk toward and then past him. Two men on the sidewalk foreground the next shot, in which Kate passes them as Cal rises, follows for a few feet, pauses, then continues. Kate passes a building, actually a cutaway of the bank interior, suggested by vertical windows and a glass door. The interior is foregrounded by the ample scrollwork around the elaborate teller's window; behind Kate and the teller sits an older woman with spectacles.

Yet this technique is more than just an interesting way to open the film; it sets up its central visual metaphor. Through a succession of scenes, we are repeatedly reminded that the characters are located in a space that lies behind and also before them, contextualizing each moment in the same way that Vermeer contextualizes the figures in his paintings. Some of the more memorable moments include the scenes in the icehouse loft, where large, translucent frozen blocks foreground both Cal and the young couple, Abra and Aaron; the subsequent dinner scene, in which the camera confronts the dining room through the sparse Edwardian parlor, framing it within the arched proscenium (complete with period pocket doors) leading from one room to the other; Cal's success in gaining entry into the back rooms of the brothel, where he and the reluctant bar maid (Lois Smith) stare down a dark corridor which splays out in front of them; the conversation in the sheriff's office, which is foregrounded by what appears to be an iron stove and backgrounded by a cellblock which holds two prisoners. Although these moments stand out, there are an almost countless number of shots between them that are composed in the same way. Even the film's final scene, in which Cal sits by his bed-ridden father, ends with the camera withdrawing from the bed alcove (another proscenium) and rising.

Not only was this Kazan's first film in Cinemascope, but it was also his first in color—in this case, WarnerColor rather than Technicolor. The latter, which was the more established process, required cumbersome cameras capable of recording three film copies, each in a different color. WarnerColor, which was based on the one-film process developed by Kodak during World War II (and named Eastman Color), used a simpler, smaller camera. In many instances, films shot in WarnerColor (or MetroColor or any of the other Eastman-based processes) lacked the intense saturation of vivid color associated with many of the Technicolor productions of the past, such as MGM's *The Wizard of Oz* (1939) or Fox's wartime musical *The Gang's All Here* (1943).

Certainly, the portability of the Eastman-based camera made it far easier to shoot on location rather than confining filming to a soundstage.

Thus, the opening sequence described earlier (with Cal following Kate) could actually be filmed in a place that resembled the Monterey of 1917, which was Mendocino, and Cal's moments in the bean field could be shot in an actual bean field. In these scenes, sunlight infuses the screen with a brilliance that bleaches out much of the natural color. Kazan extended this sense of muted color throughout the film, through costumes that were either dark and somber (such as Kate's and Adam's street clothes) or pastel (such as Abra's frocks and Cal's beige sweater and light trousers). Perhaps his goal was to allow the subdued shades and hues to recall faded sepia photographs from earlier in the century; perhaps it was his way of differentiating his Bible-based film from some of the more lavish biblical epics of the period (such as Cecil B. DeMille's 1949 Technicolor *Samson and Delilah*), through toning down the larger-than-life palette; or perhaps Kazan understood that the broad, archetypal plot itself needed to be colored with the pigments of the ordinary lest the film be reduced to melodrama.

Clearly the director's reliance on the detailed style of acting associated with The Method had prepared him to work toward performances that transcended the epic proportions of the story, performances activated through the seeming "trivia" of psychological realism. Rather than retelling the Eden myth in overly broad, DeMille-like terms, with grandiose dialogue, wooden acting, and tantalizing displays of flesh, Kazan domesticizes it so that the conflicts between father and son, brother and brother, mother and child, are recognizable and on an all-too-human scale. True, there are times when the emotions displayed, especially by Dean, seem over the top, but these are all psychologically justified in spite of their apparent flamboyance.

In the previous chapter, with regard to Brando, a few examples of Kazan's practices as a director of actors emerged. His manipulation of Peggy Ann Garner in his first feature both upset the child star and brought out a performance that worked brilliantly (Peggy Ann was awarded a special Oscar for *A Tree Grows in Brooklyn*). Likewise, his setting Brando against Anthony Quinn and vice versa off the set during the filming of *Zapata*, made for some fierce on-screen conflicts. His approach in *East of Eden* was similar.

Kazan recognized in James Dean yet another property that he could develop and use in this picture. He was aware of Dean because of their mutual interest in the Actors Studio even though Dean had only performed there twice, once in an audition and then in the scene that Strasberg had picked apart. True, Kazan had probably heard that the Goetzes had hated working with him on *The Immoralist* and that Jourdan along with most of the cast had found him unbearable. Director Herman Shumlin, who gave into Dean's demands and his need for attention, had been replaced out of town, leaving Dean with a hostile new director. In a way that would repeat itself both in his first and third features, Dean was befriended and to a degree protected by the female lead—in this case, Page, who recognized both his talent and his terrible insecurity.

Kazan never really liked Dean personally (Spoto 147), but his instincts about actors and Dean's screen tests told him that Dean was the right choice for Cal, and Kazan's ability to read people let him see how Dean could be managed. Thus, Kazan set about cultivating Dean for the new film.

His previous film credits were distinctly minor, but Kazan must have known at least some of his work on live and recorded television, which was extensive. If Clift and Brando could claim the New York theater as their training grounds, Dean's credits on TV bore evidence that he was a natural in front of the camera. As with his few stage performances, Dean was constantly his own worst enemy, expressing his insecurity through a defensive arrogance that alienated most of his fellow actors. Hume Cronyn, who became infuriated when Dean kept stepping beyond the marks set by the TV cameraman during rehearsal, warned Kazan about him. Kazan was not surprised and willingly acknowledged that he could handle the actor (Spoto 149).

Of the two surviving screen tests that I have seen, one features Dean with Paul Newman. What remains of it shows the two clowning around with Dean jokingly making sexual advances to Newman, who, although thrown, laughs them off. Newman was originally considered for both the Cal and Aaron roles.[3] The other test is of a scene that in a different form would later be shot for the film but was eventually cut and replaced; this test, along with the discarded scene, features Richard Davalos, who played Aaron in the film, and from the time the film was being planned up until the final cut, it was considered central to the plot. Both the Newman/Dean test and the Dean/Davalos test are in black and white and were shot in New York.

The Dean/Davalos test consists of a scene that would have come after Cal's second return home from Monterey, later on the same night when Adam and Cal have clashed over his unrepentant Bible reading. The early part of this test has Dean seated on his bed facing Davalos so that we see only his back as he cites the many times that Adam has favored Aaron. At the end of this conversation, Dean lies down on the bed and turns away, holding his arms by his head to hide his face. Davalos then rises from his bed, crosses to Dean's, and asks, "What have you ever done to deserve Dad's love?" This provokes Dean, who rises and threatens Davalos as he spars in his direction. Instead of fighting, Davalos reminds him of Adam's preoccupation with shipping the lettuce and asks him what he has done to help him. "Just show him that you love him," he repeats as the scene digresses into playful wrestling on the floor between their beds, with Davalos on top, tickling Dean and asking him to promise to show Adam how much he cares. Eventually this turns into a pillow fight and the two settle down beside each other to go to sleep.

In this test, Davalos is adequate—he certainly doesn't have the presence of Paul Newman—but Dean is already creating Cal. Remarkably, even with his back to the camera, even with his face and much of his body hidden, Dean's posture, his squirming and abrupt movements, make him interesting to watch. His lines, which he often was accused of mumbling, are clear and movingly articulated. Although Kazan had never seen Dean on Broadway, the actor's capabilities seem evident.

The version of this scene cut from the picture follows much of the test's dialogue although the use of movement is very different. Shot in color, this scene begins with Davalos on his bed and Dean turned away, toward the camera; the light in the room makes Dean's face, which is closer to the camera, appear darker than Davalos's. As Cal makes the same complaints about Adam rejecting him for Aaron, it is difficult to see Dean's features, as if the dialogue is emanating from the darkness itself. Dean then moves to his bed, which is no longer parallel to Davalos's, sits down and starts playing the recorder. Davalos rises and approaches him, ultimately posing the question regarding what Cal has ever done to deserve Adam's love. There is no wrestling, no physical contact here, but in this version, Cal thanks Aaron for his advice.

The scene was also reshot, beginning with Cal's recorder playing, with the lens on Dean entirely. This partial version allows the spectator to study Dean's performance closely: We can see the anguish and the longing, the intense need to be loved, all playing over Dean's face. This take alone indicates just how brilliant an actor Dean could be. His voice is now fine-tuned, carefully adjusted, fragile at moments, vulnerable at others, filled with a rising tension throughout the first part of the scene. His gestures, never random or arbitrary, express an inner hurt.

This scene was removed and replaced by a scene mentioned earlier, in which Cal, returning from Monterey with the sheriff, spies his father happily experimenting with the lettuce and ice; this brief encounter is meant to be the inspiration for the coal chute scene that follows. Although it works and is far briefer than the scene that was cut, the absence of the bedroom scene robs the film of the interaction between the two brothers. Indeed, without the scene in place, we are left wondering about how Cal really feels about Aaron and vice versa. The affection between the two characters is never visible elsewhere. Even without the brawling on the bedroom floor and their bedding down together, the scene as revised for the screen version still carries a strong indicator of fraternal love, which is missing from the movie as a whole.

Although Davalos's acting often feels thin, without substance, Dean's seems to acquire the kind of depth that Kazan had found in Brando's, and although both Massey and Harris were capable of holding their own, Kazan did not shrink from exploiting how the actors related to each other. Raymond Massey, a veteran stage and film actor, was rather conservative, if not businesslike, in his craft. He came to the set having learned his lines and ready to begin shooting. Dean, however, had a problem with his lines (he probably suffered from dyslexia), and frequently wanted to explore each scene anew, sometimes through improvisation. When Massey complained about Dean to Kazan, the director assured him that he would talk to Dean; nonetheless, when Kazan did talk to Dean, he encouraged him to keep doing what he had been doing, which continued to exasperate Massey. The friction between the actors enhances the subtext of anger between the two characters. In the party scene in which Adam refuses to take Cal's money, Kazan kept the cameras rolling as Dean suddenly improvised an uncomfortable embrace of Massey, whose cringing frame and shudders of repulsion feed into the heart-rending moment. Kazan had previously accompanied the young actor to his father's home, had witnessed firsthand Dean's distant and uncomfortable interactions with his father, and thus could draw on the actor's feelings (Spoto 157).

Julie Harris was in her late 20s when she signed on to do *East of Eden*. She had appeared on Broadway in 1950 as Frankie, the adolescent girl who cannot understand her place in her family in *The Member of the Wedding* and reprised the role in the film version (1952). She received a Tony award for playing Sally Bowles in John Van Druten's dramatization of Christopher Isherwood's *Berlin Stories* (1951), entitled *I Am a Camera*, which was the basis for the film (1955) she made after *East of Eden*. If Kazan allowed Massey to become progressively more outraged by Dean, he also gave his blessing to Harris's growing friendship with the younger actor. As he had done backstage in *The Immoralist*, Dean enlisted the leading lady, much as he had Geraldine Page, as a confidante. Impressed by his talent and moved by his sadness, Harris became the calming confidante who made it possible for filming to go on. (He would find Elizabeth Taylor an equally sympathetic costar in *Giant*.)

Throughout production, Kazan was free to flatter and cajole Dean, to feed his deep need for attention, and to give him the impression that the film revolved around him. That Kazan resented his position at times shows through in his ultimate disdain for Dean himself. Ever the consummate director, Kazan squeezed out as much emotion as Dean could show by seeming to be Dean's best friend. Only at the end of shooting, when the film was essentially wrapped and production had ceased, did Dean experience the terrible panic brought on by the dissolution of the fictional worlds of the production and of the film itself. Kazan became distant.

The image of young manhood in *East of Eden* emerges at the end of the film; rather than an alternative to traditional masculinity, Cal's performance of the gender serves as a replacement—it is gentle, forgiving, nurturing. Unlike the outcome of *Red River*, in which Wayne's character puts Clift's character's initials into the ranch's cattle brand, symbolizing the old masculinity joining forces with the new, *East of Eden* depicts an older masculinity on its deathbed and a new masculinity trying to bring it back to health. In the case of Adam, we have already learned from the self-centered nurse who was left to attend him (Barbara Baxley at her most abrasive) that he has very little time left. What will replace the manliness of the first man? Dean's characterization promises something better.

Life With and Without Father

Dean's next picture, *Rebel Without a Cause*, was a very different project from Kazan's. Originally conceived as a vehicle for Marlon Brando, who by 1954 was too old to play the lead teenage role, the film was supposed to be based on a 1944 psychological study of the same name about a troubled youth, by Dr. Robert Lindner. All plans for the film were shelved for eight years until director Nicholas Ray, shocked by the outbreak of criminal activity among middle-class teens, expressed his interest in making a film on this subject. He submitted an outline, "Blind Run," but because Warner Brothers had owned the rights to Lindner's book since 1944, Ray's treatment was retitled. Clifford Odets was originally named as screenwriter but was replaced by Leon Uris; then the studio gave the script to Irving Shulman, who argued with Ray about the final scenes. Desperate because he was scheduled to begin production in a few weeks, Ray asked Stewart Stern, whom he met at a party, to revise the screenplay. Warner Brothers regarded it initially as a B picture and had announced that it would be shot in Cinemascope but in black and white (*Rebel Without a Cause: Defiant Innocents*).

By the time the film was ready to shoot, however, not only had *East of Eden* opened with glowing reviews for Dean, but MGM also had released its own saga of juvenile delinquency, *Blackboard Jungle*, which was enormously popular despite its sensationalization of youth violence. Thus, Jack Warner increased the budget, insisted that the film be in WarnerColor,[4] and made Ray reshoot the scenes already shot in black and white (*Rebel Without a Cause: Defiant Innocents*).[5] Suddenly, Dean's new film was announced as a major motion picture.

By the time *Rebel* was released, in October 1955, less than a month after Dean's death, Warner Brothers feared that audiences would stay away because of its star's untimely demise. Such fears proved totally baseless.

Unlike Kazan, Ray, who had worked on the screenplay, saw his role not as the central authority in charge of filming but as one of a team working to make the movie look and feel as authentic as possible. In contrast to *Blackboard Jungle*, *Rebel Without a Cause* would not be filmed exclusively on soundstages and the back lot: The scenes set in and around Griffith Park Observatory were shot on location; likewise, for the scenes set in an abandoned mansion, an actual abandoned mansion (actually owned by J. Paul Getty and ironically the same one that was used as Norma Desmond's in *Sunset Boulevard*) was used. The school in the film was Santa Monica High.

In a way that recalls how Fred Zinnemann directed Clift in *The Search*, Ray frequently consulted the actors and others who had been brought in as extras, some of whom had been or still were gang members. The atmosphere was collaborative. Drawing on the cast's personal experiences, Ray brought to life a screen version of teenage angst that was vivid, meaningful, and at times almost too real.

Rebel Without a Cause concerns Jim Stark—the last name is an anagram of Trask (which had been Dean's character's surname in *East of Eden*), and the first name is what Dean himself was called—a high school senior, who appears beneath the opening credits, in jacket and tie, laid out on the sidewalk in front of a comfortable-looking house. He is drunkenly playing with a clockwork monkey that bangs a pair of cymbals. Jim ends up clutching the toy and then covering it with some stray piece of paper as he himself falls asleep.

When the credits end, Jim is still drunk but awake in a police station. He is dizzy and as the policeman pats him down, he begins giggling. Sent to stand in the waiting area, he wobbles and has to take hold of the wall. Meanwhile, in an office visible through its glass windows, Judy (Natalie Wood), a girl about the same age as Jim, is tearfully explaining to a plain-clothes officer, Ray Fremick (Edward Platt), why she has fled her home: Her father and she have been quarreling because he seems unable to cope with her becoming a teenager. In another office, a younger teen, John (Sal Mineo), nicknamed Plato, is seated with a black family maid (Marietta Canty), who appears to be his caretaker. Another plain-clothes officer asks him why he has shot a neighbor's puppies. When the younger teen is sent back to the waiting area, his companion notes that he is shivering. Jim offers the boy his coat, but the boy refuses.

Jim's parents (Jim Backus[6] and Ann Doran) arrive, along with his grandmother. In the same office in which Judy was interviewed, Jim sits in the same chair in which she sat; he finds that she has left her compact and, unnoticed, slips it into his pocket. While Ray tries to question Jim, the parents and grandmother argue about the boy. They have just moved to the area, having fled Jim's previous misdemeanors in their previous hometown. Aware that Jim's behavior is a result of the family's dysfunctional relationship, Ray takes him into his private office and talks frankly with him. Jim initially doesn't want to respond and attacks Ray physically, but Ray is strong enough to floor him. Jim gets up and speaks with Ray, acknowledging that his parents are driving him crazy. Ray gives him his phone number and encourages him to give him a call when he needs to talk to someone about his problems.

The following morning, the family has breakfast, and Jim emerges from his room in coat and tie, ready for his first day at his new school. As he goes toward his car, he catches sight of Judy (who happens to live next door) and tries to offer her a ride to school. She refuses, and as he goes back to his car, a convertible filled with teenagers pulls up, driven by Buzz Gunderson (Corey Allen). They are raucous and dressed in blue jeans. They trade remarks with Jim, who seems unfazed by their taunts.

At school, Jim learns that the junior and senior classes will be visiting the park observatory that morning. He also runs into Plato, who recognizes him. The students are already seated as Jim enters, settling into a seat two rows behind Judy and Buzz and friends, one row in front of Plato. The planetarium show is beginning, a narrated display of how the world will end in the ultimate explosion of the cosmos. As the narrator points out the constellations, Jim hears the teens in Judy's row making noises, and he contributes a moo. Then as the show draws to its frightening close, driving Plato under his seat, the lights come on and the students stampede out.

Jim lingers by the console that controls the star projection, but Buzz and his friends are waiting for him by the turnstiles at the exit. When Plato tries to leave, they drive him back in. He follows Jim upstairs to a balcony overlooking the parking lot, where Buzz and the gang are now gathering around Jim's car. With Jim watching, Buzz takes out a switchblade and cuts into one of Jim's tires. Jim comes down, unwilling to fight, but he is provoked once Buzz calls him "a chicken." One of the gang members tosses Jim his knife and reluctantly he is drawn into a fight. As the two spar around an outdoor telescope, Jim eventually disarms Buzz and then throws down his own knife. He agrees to meet him later to settle this through what Buzz calls, "a chickie run."

Before leaving for his confrontation with Buzz, Jim encounters his father at home. Dressed in a frilly, flowered apron, he is bringing Jim's mother, who is not well, a plate of food, which he inadvertently drops on the floor. Jim asks him for advice about showing up for the challenge that

Buzz has set up, broaching the issue as "a matter of honor," but his father is unable to give him an answer. Jim leaves.

At the appointed site, two stolen cars are faced, side by side, toward the edge of a bluff overlooking the ocean. The "run" is a race to the precipice, with each driver jumping from the vehicle before it careens over the drop off, the first to jump being called "chicken." As the run is readied, Jim and Buzz chat, the latter indicating that he actually likes Jim. "Why do we do this?" Jim asks him. "You gotta do something," Buzz answers. Meanwhile, Plato, who has arrived on motorbike, tells Judy how Jim is his best friend and invents details about their relationship.

During the "run," Jim is able to jump before his car goes over the edge, but a strap on Buzz's leather jacket catches itself on the interior door handle and Buzz is killed. All but three of the gang members who have shown up drive away. Judy stands looking down into the ocean. The three friends of Buzz who have remained threaten Jim and then leave. Jim extends his hand to Judy, who has drifted perilously close to the edge, and pulls her back to where he and Plato are standing. Later, after Jim has driven her home, he returns the compact that she left at the police station.

At home, Jim discovers his parents in the living room waiting for him. His return precipitates a loud argument between the three of them: Jim wants to go to the police and report what has happened, but his parents object. His mother insists that he should stay out of the matter, so Jim appeals to his father to back him up. When the father equivocates, Jim erupts in anger, dragging his father to the sofa where he begins to throttle him. He then bolts, arriving at the precinct just as the three gang members who earlier threatened him are leaving the station. Inside he looks for Ray, who is not there.

He meets Judy outside her house and the two drive out to an old house that Plato has mentioned to Jim, an abandoned mansion within sight of the observatory. At the same time, the three gang members are looking for Jim, whom they blame for Buzz's death and whom they believe has talked to the police. They run into Plato, pulling him from his bike, and steal his address book with Jim's house number and street. They appear at Jim's home and hang a live chicken from the front door. Later, when Plato comes to warn Jim, Jim's father tells him that his son is not at home. Plato concludes that Jim is in the old mansion that he pointed out to him earlier.

Judy and Jim are in the mansion. When Plato arrives, they pretend to be a newly wed couple who are inspecting the property and refer to Plato as the realtor. After showing them the house, Plato leads them down to the emptied swimming pool, where they chase each other. They then settle into an arbor. By now, Plato is no longer the realtor—he has become their son. He falls asleep, and Jim covers him with his coat. Judy declares her love for Jim, and the two proceed into the house once again leaving Plato. The three gang members have sighted Jim's car at the mansion and pull into the drive. The first person they find is Plato, who awakens as the three gang members surround him.

Plato manages to run into the house and hide beneath a piano. He has been carrying with him a gun, the same one that he used earlier to shoot the puppies. In the darkness he manages to elude the gang members, but overcome by panic, he comes out and is suddenly confronted by one of them, at whom he fires. Upstairs, he encounters Jim and Judy, whom he feels have abandoned him. He even tries to fire at Jim, but he fails and runs out of the house, toward the observatory.

Eventually Jim and Judy catch up with him. By now, the area surrounding the observatory is filled with police. Jim and Judy slip into the same door through which Plato entered, carefully attempting to make contact with him. Ray has arrived on the scene with Jim's parents, and Plato's family maid turns up as well. Jim assures Plato that he has not abandoned him and gets him to show him his gun. Promising to give it to back him, Jim takes it and removes the magazine. He then returns it to Plato and refers to all the people outside, who he says like Plato and want him to come out. Skeptically, Plato allows Jim to lead him out of the building, but suddenly frightened by the lights trained on him, he takes out his gun and runs. He is shot by the police.

Jim breaks down as his friend falls. Howling in grief, he tells the police that the gun was not loaded. Jim's father comes forward and embraces his son. Jim introduces Judy to his parents, who seem changed. His mother is about to say something but defers to his father. As the sun rises and the camera backs away, there is the feeling that a new day has come, that life has changed, and that Jim and Judy will go on.

This summary, which leaves out a great many pieces of the film, suffices to describe the plot. In its time, the film was regarded as controversial despite the fact that Warner Brothers submitted each scene to the censors and even did a lot of self-censoring. For example, Judy is brought into the precinct for some reason that is never explained; the studio feared that if she had been picked up for walking the streets late at night, audiences might assume she was a "streetwalker." Likewise, Plato's invitation to Jim to come with him to the mansion and stay the night was not to be seen as a homosexual advance, although the audience had already noted that taped to Plato's locker door is a headshot of Alan Ladd. Similarly, the studio was careful to cover up the possibility that Judy's father's sudden aversion to his daughter's affections was due to his own attraction to her. And because it was inconceivable at the time to show two teenagers experiencing sexual attraction, Jim and Judy are never alone long enough for anything to "happen." (Douglas L. Rothgelb cites these and other censorship issues in his commentary on the DVD version of *Rebel*.) Nevertheless, the film has continued to insinuate most of what the studio tried to hide.

Yet beyond these lurid details, the movie was hardly as radical as it seemed. After all, the director set out to explore why teens like these, from "good families" (as the film's poster put it), should engage in criminal acts, only to blame the contemporary family as the cause. Jim is driven to act as he does by his passive father's refusal to perform the masculine role. Judy too is the victim of her father, of his refusal to deal with his own feelings about her. Plato, on the other hand, seemingly has no parents at all. The causal factor throughout the film is the dissolution of the family as a social unit. Is there an alternative? True, we watch as Jim and Judy and Plato form a pseudo-family in the mansion, but this is doomed to fail given the circumstances of life in the 1950s, just as Buzz's admitted affection for Jim (and Plato's for Jim) must fail as well.

In a reappraisal of *Rebel Without a Cause*, published nearly two decades after it was released, Peter Biskind examines the film from the perspective of what appears to be the New Left, considering (to a certain extent) class and sociological units. Biskind sees Plato, not Jim, as the real rebel without a cause: Plato, "with the form of rebellion but without its content" dies a martyr to Jim's reconciliation with adult society (35). To save Plato, Jim takes on the characteristics of a father figure, who, like Jim's own father, must lie and manipulate to get Plato to do what he believes is right. In a sense, Plato's rebellion, which emerges as a result of his mental illness, is emptied of its meaning largely because it is pathologized.

Yet without the stigma of madness, Plato's words and actions clearly demonstrate the failure of the nuclear family whatever its social status; his own parents never appear, and the adult married couples whom we do see, Jim's parents and Judy's, are in themselves indictments of heterosexual coupling, in which women must be subservient to men, who must provide the leadership among the pair and over any children that issue from it. Thus, the pairing of Jim and Judy is intended to be seen as a normal step in their maturation, a "natural," socially acceptable development between normal teenagers, as opposed to the subversive, antisocial, and homoerotic behavior of Plato. Plato's death not only valorizes the Jim-and-Judy connection but also reconciles Jim with his father, who is suddenly in command of the family, even capable of good-naturedly silencing his formerly shrewish wife. Perhaps it is worth recalling how, early on, Jim tells the only admirable adult in the film, Ray, that he would like to see his father "knock Mom cold," a surprisingly violent way of saying that his father should take control and one that Ray has no problem understanding.

The hint of homosexual attraction from Plato toward Jim could not be obscured by the censors, largely because the younger boy's desire to be close to Jim and to "be" like him are recognizable signs of how he feels. Whether or not Plato (or Mineo, who played the role) was conscious of any sexual stirrings in the character may be debated, but in the context of the spectrum containing homosocial and homosexual feelings, Plato's feelings fall closer to the latter. This may have passed the censors and perhaps many in the audience (because at the time people generally did not talk or write about homosexuality), but even when the film was released, those who looked for such innuendoes and wrote about them, had no problem picking up on those in this film: "Note daring treatment of unusual love triangle in James Dean's REBEL WITHOUT A CAUSE," urged Dal McIntire in his regular column, "Tangents," in the homosexual journal ONE.

It is difficult to argue with Biskind, but when Joan Mellen suggests that "Dean's rebellion in the film is thoroughly emasculated by the backsliding notion that firm authority offers the solution to a tormented, alienated adolescent's quest to discover how to be a man" (213), she is perhaps ignoring the power of the depicted image itself, which in spite of the literary trappings of a tidy dénouement (not to mention the careful use of the symbolism of classical tragedy), supersedes the heavy mechanics of the plot. The teenage audience is far less likely to recall Jim at the film's close, walking into the dawning construct of empowered masculinity accompanied by his female partner, than the Jim they have witnessed all through the movie, the angry Jim who tries to attack Ray and later beats his hands into Ray's desk, the principled Jim who regards the "chickie run" as a point of honor, the desperate Jim who howls at his family, "You're tearing me apart!" and the tender Jim who befriends Plato and awkwardly approaches Judy. Jim the loner, Jim the "father" of Plato, Jim the son who cannot bear to see his father in a frilly apron—these are the images that teen spectators retained.

Hence, *Rebel Without a Cause* and Dean's role in it have become emblematic of a younger generation that seeks to assert its own authenticity as it separates itself from the falseness of those who have come before. The truly revolutionary aspects of the film lie not in what it intends to say but in what, in spite of the censors and the conventional ideas of those who wrote and directed the picture, it cannot help but show. Dean's performance throughout the film sears its way through the superstructure of plot. As even Mellen admits, "Throughout he was portrayed as a young man with a varied and complete sensual nature, capable of accepting his own vulnerability and more emotionally complex than any screen male of the seventies" (21).

One moment that critics seem to gloss over is the encounter between Jim and Buzz. They are about to race, ostensibly to determine which of them is more of a "chicken," but in their short exchange, Buzz acknowledges not only that he likes Jim but that their competing in this way has little to do with the "point of honor" Jim tried to describe to his father: Asked by Jim, "Why do we do this?" Buzz replies, "You gotta do something, don't ya'?" Rather than express their mutual admiration, which might result in a close male–male pairing, they must engage in activities that will make one of them the "chickie," that is, both the coward and the "chick," a 1950s slang for "girl." (This play on words is revived when Plato finds Jim at the mansion and knocks at the door, demanding to know who is inside; "Just us chickens," a giggling Jim responds.)

The proof of genuine masculinity, then, is not the homosocial or, worse still, homosexual bond, but the bond that establishes one person's power over another, in which the former is the man and the latter is the woman. Buzz's "friends" accept him as their gang leader; Plato accepts Jim as a substitute father; and Jim longs to have a father he can look up to. Once Ray has knocked Jim down, he looks up to the older male. Instead of acting on their mutual attraction to each other, Buzz and Jim can only sublimate what they feel through death-defying combat, which ultimately proves destructive, quite literally for Buzz and also for Jim, who is confronted by the specter of having caused his potential friend's death. In the world as it is constructed, males must remain competitive, lonely, and distant in order to be men.

At the same time, all that happens following Buzz's fatal crash belies an unquestioning obedience to the codes governing masculinity. Jim's kindness to Judy, his affection for Plato, his attempt to form a family, even as he mockingly re-enacts the traditional fatherly role in the nuclear family structure, all these occur once the gang leader is no more. In true gang fashion, Jim would be acknowledged as the next leader of the pack. However, Jim's guilty affection for Buzz makes it impossible for him to replace him. As the night wears on, there is for a short time a period when everything wrong with society ceases to operate. Of course, this short time stops, as soon as Plato's subversive refusal to trust in the very authority that Jim has previously mocked, which in turn leads to Plato's annihilation.

To judge *Rebel* on what its creators wanted to show, rather than on what the movie actually does show, is to equate the film with its supposed narrative. Yet cinema, like dramatic theater, is never completely reliant on telling a story; making real a fantasy, whether it is sustained or short-lived, is just as important, and perhaps in some cases such as this, even more so. Ultimately, audiences carry away with them what appeals most to their imaginations. No matter what the film seems to say, viewers will recall Judy's tribute to Jim when she confesses her love for him; she wants "a man who can be gentle and sweet, like you are. . . . And someone who doesn't run away when you want them. [*sic*] Like being Plato's friend when nobody else liked him. That's being strong." These lines, incidentally, were added during production by Ray himself (Frascella and Weisel 184). This is the manhood that much of the film promises, a manhood performed by Dean with great emotional turmoil, great joy, exceptional power, and much focus. We may hope that, as the sun rises over the observatory, Jim will someday, somehow attain this form of masculinity, which lies somewhere beyond the horizon, as yet merely glimpsed but never completely visible.

More than Brando as Johnny in *The Wild One*, the Jim Stark in 99% of *Rebel Without a Cause* seems very much like the hipster whom Savran describes in *Taking It Like a Man*:

> The figure of the white rebel male is . . . so important historically because of its condensation of fears circulating around questions of masculinity, male sexuality, race, and social class. Unlike the normative middle-class working man/husband/father, the hipster is a hybridized subject, a product of cultural miscegenation, a cross-dresser, neither completely white nor black, masculine nor feminine, heterosexual nor homosexual, working class nor bourgeois. (52)

Given the film's ending, Savran concludes that Jim, Plato, and Judy are ultimately untenable: "[A]s subjects produced by and mimicking perpetually dysfunctional Oedipal triangles, all three remain irreducibly split . . ." (64).

Giant Manhood

In his next and final picture, Dean once again played the role of an outsider, Jett Rink, in the screen version of Edna Ferber's mammoth novel about Texas, *Giant*. Again, he was juxtaposed by a patriarchal figure: Bick Benedict (played by Rock Hudson), heir to one of the largest cattle ranches in the state, who also served as his rival for a beautiful woman (Elizabeth Taylor). The inclusion of a rival for Dean's character was not new in this film—Cal and Aaron were rivals for Abra's love and Jim and Buzz for Judy's—but what was new here was that Dean's character did not succeed in his suit; indeed, in *Giant* the beautiful woman is already married to the rival, who also happens to be the major representative of the status quo and thus, in spite of his age at the beginning of the film, the chief enforcer of the patriarchy and its values.

Ferber's novel caused a sensation when it was first published in 1952: Many in Texas felt that she had satirized the nouveau riche who made many millions in the oil business, drawn unsympathetic sketches of the wealthy cattlemen who had preceded the new millionaires, and critiqued the caste system that made Mexican-Americans untouchables. Yet the movie was directed and written in part by George Stevens (who had earlier directed Clift in *A Place in the Sun*), who seemed far more sympathetic with the state and its history. Although he had purged much of the social commentary from his rendition of Dreiser's *American Tragedy*, here he retained the message of prejudice against Mexicans that Ferber had included in the book. Sadly, that message was far less powerful than Dreiser's had been, and in the movie seemed rather tacked on to an epic plot that, with its sweep of melodramatic action (capably enhanced by Dmitri Tiomkin's score), never actually embodied the politics it claimed to espouse.

Unlike *East of Eden* and *Rebel Without a Cause*, *Giant* is a rather disappointing picture, in part because it is based on a middlebrow bestseller with rather superficial characters and themes. Because it was directed by the great George Stevens, there is much in it that makes it almost bearable to watch many decades later. Elizabeth Taylor gives a strong, although somewhat static, performance, and Rock Hudson is often less than wooden. Many of the character actors—Chill Wills, Mercedes McCambridge, Dennis Hopper, Jane Withers, Earl Holliman, Caroll Baker, and Sal Mineo—turn in very fine performances, and the costumes and sets look great. Yet despite the music and the photography, the movie seems rather dead, too willing to aim its Cinemascope lens at the broad, seemingly endless Texas plains, those infinite horizontals that too frequently flatten the work as a whole.

And then, of course, there is the last performance of James Dean, which doesn't exactly fit in with many of the other performances. Dean is for the most part quite good, but he is only interesting in some of his scenes. Stevens's unwillingness to develop the character Dean was given, undermines what Dean could and did do on camera. In the end, although he had enormous respect for Stevens's accomplishments with Clift, Dean found that he could not get along with the great director, who had little wish to get along with him.

The basic plot of this epic story begins with the romance of Texas cattleman Bick Benedict (Hudson) and Leslie Lynton (Taylor), the daughter of a Virginia physician who is selling Bick a horse. In spite of their differing views on the world and politics, the two marry and travel to the old homestead in West Texas, where they are greeted by Bick's older sister, Luz (McCambridge), who eyes her brother's new wife with suspicion. In fact, the two women do clash, and their feud is ended only by Luz's sudden death after being thrown by Leslie's horse.

In her will, Luz has bequeathed a small portion of the ranchlands to the lone cowhand, Jett Rink (Dean), who helped her during the weeks when Bick was away courting Leslie. Bick, aided by several prominent men in the county, tries to pay Jett twice the value of what the property is worth, but he refuses on the grounds that he finally has something of his own. From conversations between Bick and others and also from the dialogue between Jett and Leslie, it has become apparent that Jett, the son of an impoverished rancher, feels that he has been excluded from the wealth in Texas, to which he believes he deserves a fair share. We note that Jett is more sensitive than Bick, that he is shy, introspective, and interested in improving himself.

A few years pass: Bick and Leslie have three children, while Jett continues to hunt for oil on his few acres. Ultimately he is successful and drives all the way to the Benedict house, where a party is going on. Covered in oil and already drunk, he climbs to the family's porch, where he proclaims his new riches and flirts with Leslie. Bick, enraged, punches him but is restrained by some of the guests. Jett gets up, bids them goodbye, but before leaving, he attacks Bick and then drives off.

As the years pass, Bick's son (Dennis Hopper) decides he wants to be a doctor, a decision that Leslie defends. He attends medical school and then works at a local clinic, where he meets a nurse, Juana (Elsa Cardenas), of Mexican descent, whom he marries. Bick, who throughout the film has failed to correct Leslie's genteel treatment of the local "wetbacks," is shocked and is only partially reconciled to their match. Meanwhile, one of his daughters has decided to marry a cowhand instead of going to college abroad. The youngest daughter, Luz (Caroll Baker), is intrigued by their enormously wealthy neighbor, Jett Rink, who is set to open a luxury hotel with its own airport in another part of the state.

Luz gets a job helping to publicize Jett's project. There is an announcement of a grand opening to which every prominent Texan, including the Benedicts and their friends, have been invited. Determined to show the upstart oil baron that they are every bit as good as he, if not better, Bick organizes a private plane to fly them all to this event. At the grand parade, preceding the ceremonial dinner, Luz rides in an open car behind Jett's; she wears a crown as the queen of the opening. Both Bick and Leslie, who by now has lost all sympathy for Jett, are appalled, and later that evening, Luz argues that Jett is actually a very likeable person, an enterprising entrepreneur whom she admires. However, when Bick's son and Mexican-American daughter-in-law arrive, she tries to use the hotel's beauty parlor, which refuses to serve her. Enraged, her husband goes to confront Rink himself, who is just arriving at the banquet. Drunk, he has his two bodyguards beat up the enraged husband; he is then challenged by the father: Bick draws Jett into a wine storeroom just off the dining room, but instead of fighting him, his disgust for Rink leads him to topple all the wine shelves, bringing hundreds of bottle shattering to the floor. Much to Luz's chagrin, the Benedict party leaves the gala, and Jett proceeds to make his big speech.

Ironically, Jett is so drunk that when he is introduced to thundering applause, he cannot even get up from his seat. Instead, his head drops to the table, where he lies unconscious. When Luz, who has blamed her parents for disgracing her at the event, finally comes downstairs to the now-empty dining room, she realizes that Jett is really a pathetic wreck of a man. Disillusioned, she accompanies her parents and sister-in-law back home.

Yet on the way back, when the family pauses to eat lunch at a road-side restaurant, they look on as Juana is insulted by the staff and then as a Mexican family is told to leave the place. In a great rage, Bick attacks the owner, who fights back and knocks Bick out. Once home again, Leslie indicates that she has never been so proud of her husband as she is now.

This synopsis is reductive to an extreme—it is difficult to retell a film that runs two hundred minutes in a few paragraphs. Nonetheless, it demonstrates that Jett Rink is not the leading male character; for the first time, Dean was not going to be the film's major star. He accepted this part readily, interviewing with Stevens several times before he was actually cast. He felt a clear affinity for the role. However, he was not prepared for the way Stevens worked, which differed markedly from how Kazan and Ray directed. Stevens shot a lot of film, reshooting scenes from virtually every possible angle, and then served as his own editor, piecing the movie together over a period of many months. Thus, the process of shooting took much longer than it had when Dean had worked before. He became tired, easily bored, and somewhat antisocial. He also argued with Stevens about his having to get into make up at six in the morning on days when he was not scheduled to act on the set, something that Stevens expected him, like all the other cast members, to do.

As a result of this friction, Dean found himself in less and less of the film. Although he had been eager to play a character that develops and ages over several decades, there was little if any continuity between the sensitive malcontent Jett Rink, who discovers oil, and the one who, years later, has become a powerful, alcoholic egotist. Dean was especially embarrassed by his final scenes in the film, when Rink, now in his 50s or 60s, is discovered drunkenly mumbling in the darkened banquet hall by young Luz; he even begged Stevens (according to Caroll Baker) to focus the camera on Luz's face rather than on him, which Stevens did (*Memories of Giant*).

As with his previous two films, Dean's character was a loner whose performances of masculinity did not conform to the social norms. Early scenes in the film identify him as a have-not who is eager to improve his own lot. His shyness, especially around Leslie, seems endearing, and his ability to recognize Bick's sister as his boss suggests that her "mannish" performance of femininity does not threaten him. Given *East of Eden* and *Rebel*, audiences probably expected to see Dean finally play the man his earlier roles, as well as this one, appear to anticipate, a man whose performance of masculinity was markedly different from the conventional performances offered by Bick and the other male characters in the film. What they encountered instead was a complete failure of a man—an adult male who has never genuinely matured.

Indeed, as Ferber must have been aware, the plot required the figure of *un homme manqué* if Bick were, in spite of his previous prejudices and failings, to emerge as heroic. The film does not lampoon his quick-to-act, double-fisted masculinity, and in the end the ultra-civilized Leslie responds positively to his angry violence because it is unleashed in the service of a good cause (although it does nothing to further that cause). Thus the coarse cattle baron becomes the prototype of Texan manhood, much as John Wayne had done.

Unlike Wayne, Hudson came perilously close to looking attractive. His off-screen homosexuality caused him to marry and to try to imitate the performances of what was then viewed as authentic masculinity, even as he continued to live a gay life.[7] Yet if Hudson was handsome, Dean was beautiful in a way that threatened to expose the deep gap allegedly separating the homosocial and the homosexual. Such a man, *Giant* alleges, cannot really be a man. Sensitivity and vulnerability is only for females such as Leslie, who as a woman naturally comes by them. It is never explicit just why Bick has from the beginning of the film such enormous hatred for Jett; an obvious reason is their difference in class, but with all the film's implications about gender and sexuality, another possible reason may lie in Jett's physical beauty, and its potential threat both to Bick's masculinity and to his marriage to Leslie, who is clearly attracted to Jett.

There are a number of good scenes in which Dean is featured, but he has relatively few lines. In the scene in which Bick and others offer him money for the land that Luz has left him, Dean sits listening, playing with a lasso. The actor also gave Jett the high-pitched giggle of Jim Stark, which he injects into some of his dialogue through the early part of the picture. As usual, his presence does not always require dialogue; a silent Dean on camera speaks far more eloquently than Hudson. Unfortunately, all his method acting, all his brilliance, all his subtlety cannot save the film from going to Hudson and Taylor.

Conclusion

By the time *Giant* had been pieced together by Stevens and premiered, James Dean had been dead for more than a year. Just as Dean, as a young boy, could not accept his mother's death, many of his fans continued writing him letters addressed to Warner Brothers, as if he were secretly alive. Some who did believe that he had perished when his Porsche Speedster had collided with another car, wrote the studio too, demanding that Stevens not cut any of Dean's scenes from the film, even threatening the director. As with *Rebel Without a Cause*, the death of one of the leading actors did not keep moviegoers away; if anything, Dean's now-extinguished brilliance brought audiences into theaters.

Giant, despite the way it may look today, made out well enough on its own. Dean was nominated for an Oscar (his second posthumous nomination) for best actor. Hudson also was nominated in the same category although the Academy Award went to Yul Brynner (for *The King and I*). The film was nominated in eight other categories, including best picture, but won only one award, for best director. The returns at the box office were very good.

Dean's three major films capably illustrate just how well he managed to create characterizations through which manhood was refracted, much like white light through a prism, and thus deconstructed into separate components, all of which had to be regarded as varying hues of gender. He could be violent and tender, irrational and reasonable, silent and demonstrative; and he could demand his audience's eyes, not only because he played with genius on the screen but also because he appeared young and beautiful. Those who did not experience an attraction to his appearances on film at least admitted admiring him and wanting to be like him, which according to Sedgwick's homosocial/homosexual spectrum is an admission of attraction. To a degree, Dean filled a void that young Americans were only beginning to recognize that they felt.

This in part explains the phenomenon that followed his death on September 30, 1955, the replacement of the person and actor James Dean with the legend that, although based on his image, reduced that image's significance to a few simple meanings. After he died, fans ransacked his apartment in Los Angeles, eager to get their hands on anything that he had once touched. Newspapers, magazines, and television coverage rehashed his fatal accident. What had been a very talented but very troubled person was elevated to a perfect mythical hero. With a certain morbidity, the car in which he was killed was sent around the United States; gradually his worshippers took souvenir pieces of it until the shattered vehicle ceased to exist.

Similarly, except for the James Dean we encounter in memoirs, such as those mentioned earlier, there is very little of the actual James Dean left. True, his films survive, but in the face of his supposed tragedy, one must be careful not to do what 1950s film critics did, which was to equate the actor with his roles. Before there was the James Dean whose image now haunts posters and advertisements and even videos, there was a gifted boy from Indiana who was desperate to become an actor. As with any actor, his peculiar personality and experiences infused his understandings of the parts he played. If he had grown older as Clift and Brando did, we would probably have recalled the early part of his career as his golden period; how much longer it would have lasted is difficult to know. Yet eventually we would have had to look back on those years with nostalgia for the young James Dean, as opposed to the perhaps less than splendid older James Dean.

Of course, such a view of Dean is not possible. Many of those who worship his image have probably never seen all—or even any—of his films. Nonetheless, he has remained recognizable as some sort of symbol of youthful rebelliousness who died young. Such a death, as in so many cases of American celebrities, is turned by popular culture into martyrdom.

Dean's legacy, however, should be much more complex. Dean himself was complex, contradictory, conflicted. He had, as today's popular psycho babble would put it, many issues. He was very insecure and at the same time could be terribly arrogant. He could be downright vindictive but was also somewhat passive aggressive. He apparently had a very large ego. At the same time, his three movie roles reflect some of his own awareness of how the human personality was a highly complicated construct, especially in his performances of males performing masculinity. Much of what he portrayed on screen cries out against the conventional enactment of manhood. Occasionally, spectators thought they glimpsed something better.

Valentino left behind a large fan base of admiring women; Dean's fans, however, had always included males, and after his death this remained the case. The massive devotion to Dean suggests not that Dean's appeal to other males was sustained by his performing a safe masculinity—in part based on exclusive heterosexuality—but that the same outright ambisexuality apparent in his performances allowed other males to recognize his beauty.

CHAPTER 7

All About Dick

Physique Magazines and the Career of Richard Harrison

The Postwar Male Body

In both postwar high and popular culture, images of males were repeatedly embodied by young men whose masculinity incorporated certain sensitivities, vulnerabilities, even defects. The wartime images of servicemen and postwar images of veterans, which proliferated in both theater and film, set the tone for a revised construct of manhood. The youthfulness of those depicted in some ways permitted a general appreciation of their beauty and of their other-than-traditional masculinity.

To a degree, these subjects' masculine gender and "normal" sexuality were ensured by their identification with the armed forces; if they had served, then they had to have been "real" men. Thus, heterosexual male viewers could relate to photos of soldiers bathing naked on a beach or one bare-chested sailor tattooing another as examples of the war experience. As the title of Marlon Brando's first film proclaimed, the paraplegic vets who had literally lost their virility were indisputably *men*. Hence, the display of the muscular bodies of Ken Wilozek and his ward mate, Angel, did not suggest to the straight male observer anything more than a welcome valorization of these injured vets' manhood.

Indeed, as the war was ending, a ward of men at Walter Reed Hospital, each of whom had lost a leg, went through the seemingly bizarre rehabilitation of forming a cross-dressing dance team, the "Amputettes"; they performed in outfits inspired by Carmen Miranda and in gay nineties costumes, much to the amusement of other patients. A chorus line of amputees in drag may sound like an outrageously effeminate form of entertainment, not to mention therapy, but David Serlin relates their acceptance and success to the homosocial rituals of all-male, often homophobic institutions, including the military (149–151).[1] In this context, their performances were viewed as "normal."

Alongside (and in many ways connected with) the highbrow New York stage and the mass appeal of Hollywood movies, a subculture of men who were sexually attracted to other men was emerging. To an important degree, homosexual men who had successfully served in the war felt the same kind of valorization of their manhood as other vets. Those who had not been weeded out at induction and who had managed to remain in the military, ultimately receiving an honorable discharge, came out of the services having proven themselves the equals of "normal" men. Just as black soldiers had to return to the deplorably racist stratifications of American society, "gay" veterans had to suffer the consequences of their own "differences."

The postwar period became an age of conformity. In this light, we may look back on *Tea and Sympathy* and recall its attention to normative "male" behavior, and to the glass unicorn that loses its horn and can thus pass for a "normal" horse, and Jerry's "abnormal" behavior compared with Peter's. Homosexual men who had successfully served their country had managed to do so by conforming to the rigid, though somehow more relaxed, definitions of masculinity prevalent during the war—by hiding any signs of their sexuality and by carefully performing their gender. If theater audiences related easily to the notion of looking for signs of normalcy, we can keep in mind the Cold War witch-hunts that began in the late 1940s, some of which sought to identify government workers who were "sexual perverts," namely homosexuals. Yet the idea that one could identify homosexuals derives from an earlier scrutiny, the one involving volunteers and conscripts before they were inducted into the armed forces, beginning in 1941.

Even before Pearl Harbor, a set of procedures and criteria had been put together to weed out recruits who seemed to exhibit "homosexual" characteristics. These were devised and put into place by prominent psychiatrists eager to serve the government, perhaps the best known of whom was Harry Stack Sullivan, himself a practicing homosexual, and remained in place during and long after the war[2]; however, as part of the postwar congressional mission to scrutinize and cleanse the government of subversives, hundreds, if not thousands, of federal employees were fired because of their sexuality. Following World War II, a wave of homophobic paranoia spread across the United States. The so-called Cold War inspired not only anti-leftist purges but also an inquisition in search of all that appeared to threaten American values, especially American masculinity, including homosexuality.

It is no wonder, then, that homosexual men who actively campaigned for gay rights during the period were especially intolerant of men who exhibited what they and the rest of society regarded as signs of queer behavior. The Mattachine Society and its publications, as well as the editorial staff and readership of the homosexual journal ONE, commented negatively on men who appeared effeminate.[3] By and large, these early homophile-movement periodicals argued for assimilation and persistently avoided discussing some of the core differences between gay people and society at large. Michael Bronski notes how these publications, although deliberately addressed to a gay audience, rarely if ever discussed the day-to-day realities of the gay life: "Looking through old issues," he quips, "you get the feeling that homosexuality is an intellectual pursuit rather than a sexual orientation" (146). Indeed, these early journals seem highly political and polemical but only tangentially gay.

Such tendencies toward a "normal" looking, conformist masculine construct are often reflected in the more popular magazines printed for homosexual audiences, notably the physique magazines that first appeared in the early 1950s. Unlike the physical culture magazines that had been popular since the turn of the twentieth century, physique magazines were not genuinely concerned with the science of bodybuilding or with diet, exercise, or weight lifting. They primarily presented photographic images of the unclothed male body. Beginning with *Physique Pictorial* in 1951, gay male readers could chose from an array of digest-sized monthlies and bimonthlies that displayed attractive young men. Post office regulations and general rules of decency necessitated an obscuring of the male genitals—swimsuits and ingeniously designed pouches known as "posing straps" took the places of fig leaves—and although such magazines were confiscated and their publishers hauled into court, they remained far more popular and better distributed[4] than the more serious homophile political journals. Visually, the photographs conveyed many of the same ideas about gender that the journals maintained, and yet at the same time, there was more of an indication in these magazines that most gay men at the time were more acutely aware of what constituted gender performances.

The photographs of scantily clad muscle men that were discovered in Tom Lee's drawer, in *Tea and Sympathy*, were probably clipped from such magazines or ordered from advertisements found in their back pages. Jerry, from *The Zoo Story*, would have noticed the numerous issues of such magazines for sale at newsstands, both in Times Square and in his own Upper Westside neighborhood. Although Plato in *Rebel Without a Cause* was probably too young to buy any of these publications (except perhaps through the mail), he would not have found a portrait of Alan Ladd like the one that hung in his locker, but he might have been able to locate beefcake pictures of Guy Madison and Tab Hunter—and even of Brando as Mark Antony.

Perhaps because the physique magazines illustrated objects of homosexual desire, they gave more of a sense of gay life than the serious journals. They were sometimes playful and irreverent, whereas *The Mattachine Review* and *One* remained for the most part circumspect and somber; even in their

lighter, sometimes satirical moments, both journals adhered to a party line.
Gradually, many of the physique magazines withdrew from the pretext that
they were printing photographs for art students and devotees or that they
were really concerned with bodybuilding rather than beefcake. Because they
were in the business of selling magazines—magazines that heavily advertised
the sale of additional photographs and other products—those who ran the
physique magazines were interested in the gay audience as members of a
consumer group. They thus came to address their audience as members of
a cohesive subculture.[5]

In this and the following two chapters, I examine the careers of three
men who modeled for and participated in the production of photos that
appeared in physique magazines in the 1950s and 1960s and of other photos
that sold through magazine advertising during this period. As contributing
creators of what amounted to early pre-Stonewall pornography, their images
provide a glimpse into the evolution of postwar masculinity, especially into
how masculinity was constructed by homosexual men.

Selling Naked Photos

Nudes became a genre of photography, much as they had with traditional
graphic arts; throughout the nineteenth century, photographers produced a
number of academic nudes and nude studies made for other reasons, such
as medical, geographical, and anthropological documentation. However, the
first photographer known to sell male nudes to a homosexual audience was
Baron Wilhelm von Gloeden, a minor Prussian aristocrat, who for health
reasons had settled in the village of Taormina, Sicily. He and his male house-
guests reputedly indulged in wild, drunken orgies with local boys. When von
Gloeden's family fortune was lost in 1888, he acquired a camera and began
taking pictures of the boys in the village (Goldman 238).

Most of von Gloeden's photos featured the nearly naked boys in classical settings. These he marketed to travelers on the grand tour, who often
stopped in the idyllic fishing village and bought his photographs as artistic
souvenirs. At the same time, he also marketed naked photos of the same
boys to men such as Oscar Wilde and Friedrich Krupp, whose sexual interests
were aroused by such pictures (242). These would be chosen from catalogue
sheets. As Thomas Waugh points out in *Hard to Imagine*, surviving catalogues show that von Gloeden established a "two-tiered" system: For the
general public, he offered a series of prints showing "tasteful" poses, facial
portraits, and landscapes; for "special" collectors, the shots all included the
boys' genitals. Waugh also concludes that the more explicit shots were less
likely to carry von Gloeden's signature (83).

Looking back on von Gloeden's career, many art critics from the 1970s onward hailed him as a true visionary and as an artist who publicly challenged the morality of his age. The truth, however, is far more complicated; in an age when pedophilia might easily lurk behind what many believed to be "Art," as it did in the work of Charles Dodgson (aka Lewis Carol) or J.M. Barrie, von Gloeden pursued two kinds of photography: idealized depictions of youth and what we would now call child pornography. He knew how not to mix them together. Although his more exalted guests might be shown his entire collection (and even carry some of it home in their diplomatic pouches or in luggage that slipped unopened through customs), his ordinary clientele wanted "proper" and "innocent" photos. People at large simply did not know about von Gloeden's "sexual" pictures; they probably would have been repelled by them.

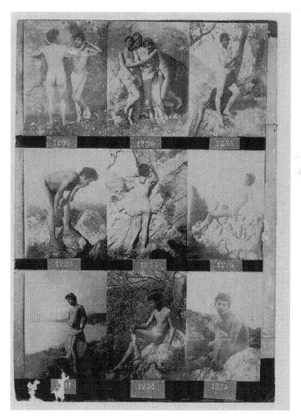

Figure 7.1. A page from one of von Gloeden's "tasteful" catalogues.

This double standard in photography survived well into the twentieth century. With the increase of mass media, including books, newspapers, and magazines that were capable of cheaply reprinting photographs, the proliferation of nude or near-nude male images escalated. All of these had to conform to contemporary standards of taste and decency. Photos of near-naked boys, however tastefully done, were by the close of World War I viewed as indecent or at least highly suspect. Thus, the pictures in the books and magazines devoted to physical culture were all of adult males who were not completely naked. Trunks or shorts, leopard-patterned briefs, posing belts, or fig leaves (as in the case of strongman Eugene Sandow) covered the genital area, much as they had in the nineteenth century cabinet cards of nearly nude wrestlers. If the model was not wearing one of these garments when photographed, it would be drawn onto the print by hand.

Ostensibly, all photographers who wished to show "more" were relegated to the category of pornographers. In the 1920s, these photographers could not advertise their work publicly, even as physical culture magazines began to allow their advertisers more liberty with the photographs they used. Ads in a February 1925 issue of *Muscle Builder*, for instance, show a variety of photos that are noticeably more revealing: Accompanied by hard-sell, macho rhetoric, one photo depicts a well-developed man in swim trunks that display a prominent bulge (5), and two others feature men who appear to be nude (35, 42). All of these ads are for bodybuilding courses, but they illustrate that the readership was becoming more tolerant of and perhaps more excited by the spectacle of male beauty, at least when it was invoked in the name of manhood.

However, physique photographers by the mid-1930s had evolved a strategy similar to that of von Gloeden. Using versions of pictures that, at least as presented, appeared to conform to the laws of decency, they placed ads (usually small ones) in the back pages of physical culture magazines, heretofore reserved for supplements, training courses, and gyms. For example, in the January 1936 issue of *Strength and Health*, there is a notice with a photo that takes up one-third of the far right column (39). This tiny ad is for the work of the Ritter Brothers, two New York City bodybuilders who sold naked photos that they had taken of themselves. The photo in the ad itself shows them in posing straps. The catalogue for which the reader could send (for $1) also showed the brothers Ritter in straps although these had obviously been painted on. However, the actual photos would arrive either with "the paint-ons" gone or with the paint-ons done in watercolors that were easily removed.

By 1940, there was an increasing number of advertisements like this. For example, in the back pages of the issue of *Strength and Health* from February 1940, a reader could find ads by photographers Dick Falcon and Robert Gebbé (39), Don Rolando (also known as Ron Rolando) and Ermitage

Figure 7.2. Advertisements from *Muscle Builder*, February 1925.

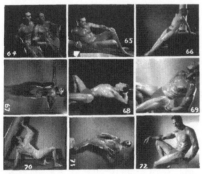

Figure 7.3. Top: Ad for the Ritter Brothers, *Strength & Health*, January 1936. Bottom left: a page from the Ritter Brothers' 1936 catalogue. Bottom right: the actual photo (in center on catalogue sheet).

Studios (57), Al Urban (58), and Edwin Townsend, whose main model Tony Sansone was marketing his nude books (60). Dick Falcon, a body-builder himself, began photographing others in the 1930s, whereas Robert Gebbé (shortened from Gebhart) moonlighted as a photographer while he danced on Broadway and designed hats. Al Urban began as a commercial photographer but started advertising his physique studies in the back pages of physical culture magazines in 1937. Urban's patrons would receive an appropriately censored catalogue sheet and the option to purchase pictures. (If a former customer happened to have missed Urban's ad, he would receive a letter from the photographer with the same photo on the letterhead.) The actual photo in Urban's ad would arrive without posing straps. Similarly, Don Rolando's customers received a noticeably retouched catalogue, and those who wrote to Ermitage would be required to sign a form indicating that they were over the age of 21, would only use the photos for their personal use, and that they were one of the following: "doctor, artist, art student, collector." Those interested in Sansone could buy his book, *Rhythm* directly by mail. As Sansone's ad seems to imply clearly, *Rhythm* featured pictures of him (by Townsend) completely naked. In most of them, however, rather than painting in posing straps, Townsend used an air brush to obscure the pubic area although at least one photo depicted Sansone's private parts.

This arrangement of finding advertisements in the back of physical culture magazines, sending off, and then ordering from catalogues became more difficult in the late 1940s. Sending such materials through the mail became punishable by jail, as Al Urban and Los Angeles photographer Bob Mizer ultimately learned in 1947 when both were arrested (the former on the East Coast, the latter on the West) and served time for selling what were deemed lewd pictures. Although Urban stubbornly continued to sell photographs of men who were completely naked (for which he was repeatedly prosecuted), Mizer's incarceration led him to avoid nude subjects for nearly two decades. The result of Mizer's decision to require his models to wear actual (as opposed to painted-on) posing straps—even sometimes for shots that did not require them—serendipitously led to a totally new kind of publication that would become known as *Physique Pictorial*.

Mizer had originally founded the Athletic Model Guild (AMG) in 1945. The ostensible reason, or rather the reason given, for the enterprise was to publicize some of the good-looking, well-built young men, many of them vets, who flocked to Hollywood after the war. Many, according to Mizer, welcomed this promotion in the hope that it would help them to get into the movie studios. Having befriended some of the bodybuilders on Muscle Beach (at the time located in Santa Monica), he began taking photographs and like others in the same field, began in 1947 to advertise in the back pages of *Strength and Health*. He was careful, as von Gloeden had been, to separate his nude photos from those in which the models wore posing straps. Indeed, as Wayne Stanley indicates, in mid-1947, when his premises were raided, all of his nude shots had been moved elsewhere (12–13). Nonetheless, the puritanical prosecutor and judge managed to find some of Mizer's posing-strap photos offensive:

> [T]he prosecutor's primary focus was on that type of image in
> which the model appeared young (an allusion to children),
> was aggressively posed (an allusion to sexual availability), was
> heavily oiled (an allusion to carnally excited perspiration), and
> was covered only by an extremely immodest posing strap with
> a very generously filled pouch. Such an image was alleged to
> be obscene, not for what appeared but for what appeared to
> appear. (13)

Clearly, the case centered not on *what* was and was not shown but on *how*
what was shown was shown. Pleading not guilty and citing his first amend-
ment rights (14), Mizer was found guilty and sentenced to a year on a
prison farm.[6] In 1950, the U.S. Post Office threatened *Strength and Health's*
publishers that unless they removed the ads for physique photos that lined
their back pages, they would lose their second-class mailing permit (15).

Sometime after the expurgation of such ads, Mizer conceived of a
publication that could be sent through the mail and would showcase samples
of his work and that of other physique photographers. All pictures would
conform to the same standards that had applied to the *Strength and Health*
ads, although now the ads (as well as the photos in them) could be larger.
In May 1951, Mizer created *Physique Photo News*, an eight-page booklet, the
cover of which was addressed to "Mr. Photo Collector":

> Six physique photography studios have joined together to bring
> you this brochure. Because of its wealth of photographs you will
> want to keep it for reference or pass it on to an interested friend.
> A substantial return from their advertisements will encourage
> these and other photo advertisers to continue presenting this
> miniature magazine which will be sent you free of charge.

Mizer offers advice on the easiest way to order the photos and mentions that
the booklet was originally to be printed by *Iron Man* magazine, which still
carried advertisements for physique photographs, but that because of *Iron
Man's* new publication, *Body Culture*, other arrangements had to be made.
(In actuality, *Body Culture* had already premiered in 1949. Perhaps *Iron
Man's* editors wanted to avoid participating in Mizer's publishing venture.)

The studios, in order of appearance, were Spartan, Russ Warner, Bruce
of L.A., AMG, Al Urban, and Richard Caldwell. Although the photos in
most of the ads are small, allowing for displays of several pictures, they
are still noticeably larger than the ones in the back-page ads in *Strength
and Health* and *Iron Man*. Only Urban's ad for "Sculpture in Bronze" is a
genuine large-sized enlargement. The back cover featured a painting by

George Quaintance, who had done covers and illustrations for a number of physical culture magazines and was now creating art work that revealed a little more of the male form; this and other works for "private connoisseurs" could be purchased through AMG. In its own way, Quaintance's painting of men skinny-dipping in a stream recalls the photos published in *Life* of nude servicemen bathing and at the same time adds a camp eroticism.

Physique Photo News was obviously aimed at a homosexual audience. "Mr. Collector"—a male who sought pictures of nude or near-nude males, neither for scientific nor artistic reasons—was encouraged to participate in the physique photo trade. Readers who repeatedly perused the back pages of physique culture magazines now had a publication entirely their own. Small though it was, the magazine was devoted solely to the exhibition and procurement of those photos without the mediation of articles about physique culture. Mizer, who had been unjustly prosecuted for allegedly presenting sexual content in his pictures, now appealed to an audience interested in finding just that. He had produced the first magazine specifically intended for a gay male readership in the United States.

Six months later, the magazine appeared under the title *Physique Pictorial*, which, according to Mizer's explanation in the issue, was a better name because the offerings included photos as well as paintings. The second issue was longer—twice as long, in fact, as the previous—and included more studios. Urban took up two pages, as did the art and photos of Quaintance, who also contributed the front and back covers. This issue of the magazine provided more ads with larger photos. Mizer's need to avoid further obscenity charges is reflected in this declaration:

> Physique Pictorial is not a closed enterprise and any legitimate studio can be represented in it. However, it was necessary to deny space to some firms that have had a bad customer relation record—who have misrepresented the merchandise they sell, or have failed to when customer [sic] sent money.
>
> No new advertiser is accepted until he has been thoroughly studied and you may feel confident in sending your order that he intends to see you fully satisfied.

This carefully coded pronouncement provides some insight into the caution Mizer felt it necessary to exercise. The advertisers, he implies, had been fully vetted. Mizer was more direct in his next issue, in February 1952. Articulating his "policy regarding nude photography," he specifies,

> Even though we recognize that there is a widely legitimate use by artists, sculptors, etc. for nude photographs, PHYSIQUE

PICTORIAL cannot carry the advertisement of any photographer which makes these available by mail or other public carrier
(such as express).

Reiterating postal practices, he reminds readers that magazines are forbidden from carrying ads for such pictures. Rather than risk violating the law,
he tells us, the studios offering photos in Physique Pictorial, avoid "that
questionable 'borderline' where art leaves off and pornography begins," by
exercising "self-discipline," which may be translated into current parlance
as "self-policing." At the same time, customers are asked to "discourage the
few 'outlaw' studios in this country who send out material" that is truly
pornographic. As explicit as these statements may seem, they carry a double-
meaning, simultaneously conveying what the law at the time indicated and
also asserting that self-censorship by studios was preferable to censorship by
conservative legal officials. Moreover, this third issue carried ads for several
photographers whom Mizer must have known dealt in nude photos, such as
Dave Martin, Bob Delmonteque, Frank Giardina, and of course Al Urban.
His series of disclaimers were meant to provide cover for Physique Pictorial;
if some of the advertisers did trade in nudes, Mizer had formally proclaimed
that he did not know about them.

In the next issue, May 1952, Mizer implored readers to buy photos
from the advertised studios so that more space could be devoted to photos
instead of to advertisements. In addition to those ads, Mizer managed to
include four full-page prints from different photographers, each beautifully
reproduced. He also asked a price of fifteen cents for what had previously
been free. The next issue, the following August, doubled the number of
large reproductions, and the next, in November, doubled those. Yet this
expansion came at a cost, for the November issue cost twenty-five cents.
Thus, within a year, Physique Pictorial had gone from being a free booklet
of studio advertisements to a quarterly magazine with large reproductions of
physique photographs. Both for its audience and for what it contained, it
was the first publication of its kind in North America. Mizer accompanied
his photos with information about the models, sometimes describing the
young men in some detail; however, as he had done early on, he frequently
commented on issues related to censorship, appealing to his readers to write
to specific officials and join the American Civil Liberties Union (ACLU).
Such statements became lengthier during the magazine's run. Lest the space
allotted to them take away room from the photos and ads, Mizer printed
them in increasingly smaller print.

Physique Pictorial was not the country's only physique magazine for
very long. By the end of 1952, a digest-sized magazine called Tomorrow's
Man started up in Chicago. The numerous pages of near-naked men were

sandwiched by short articles about exercise, nutrition, posing, and photography. In contrast to the gay audience (or rather the "Mr. Collectors" of nude male photos) actively sought by Mizer, Irvin Johnson, a trainer with several gyms, addressed his magazine to young men and boys interested in bodybuilding. Nevertheless, his magazine carried many of the same photos and ads by the same photographers whose work was currently running in *Physique Pictorial.* In 1954, five new physique magazines debuted: *Adonis,* which along with the beefcake offered brief articles on grooming; *Body Beautiful,* which inserted short articles that gushed over the male body; *Men and Art* and *Star Models,* both of which showcased the photography of Lon Hanagan ("Lon of New York") with few interruptions; and *Vim,* which like *Tomorrow's Man* came out of the Midwest and was digest-sized but had shorter articles and more photos. (*Adonis* and *Body Beautiful* were both published by the Weider Organization, which had been printing physical culture magazines for the U.S. market from their Montreal, Canada headquarters for years; their bodybuilding magazines and equipment were fierce competitors of the by now homophobic *Strength and Health,* published by Bob Hoffman, head of York Barbell.)

Before the 1950s drew to a close, more than a score of new physique magazines would follow, and the 1960s would bring even more. Many of them, like *Tomorrow's Man,* placed some emphasis on physical fitness, whereas others focused on art, and others still, especially those that began in the late 1950s and during the 1960s, simply printed the photos with an occasional caption following some sort of first-page statement or editorial at the front of the magazine. In the beginning, there was always a pretext—a written rationale—to explain the publication and to justify its existence, for physique magazines never openly made clear what their actual function was, which was to circulate images that would in some way pleasure their male readers. True, a number of blurb writers would often imply or rather blatantly insinuate the sexuality of the model and/or the reader, but there was, at least in the early years, an alleged reason—a nonsexual reason—for the publication's existence.

Some magazines never made it past their first or second issues, but virtually all of them would come to an end in the late 1960s as a series of legal decisions made it possible for American publishers to reproduce the image of a completely naked man. *Tomorrow's Man* held on until 1971, and *Physique Pictorial* lasted until 1990, although in 1969 it ceased to function as a physique magazine and printed nothing but nudes. Much of the careful camera work and printing that had marked Mizer's early photographic efforts and virtually all of the muscles that had distinguished his models were gone. By the end of the 1970s, physique magazines would be replaced by soft-core pornography, ranging from *Playgirl* to *Mandate,* and by hard-core pornography.

What made physique magazines different from the physical culture magazines of the first half of the twentieth century was that instead of acting as a conduit through which men who wanted to buy photos of naked men could obtain them, the magazines themselves provided, at a much-reduced cost, the photos themselves. A 1957 issue of *Tomorrow's Man*, for example, cost thirty-five cents. Catalogues offered in the back pages of the same issue might range from one to three dollars while smaller photos began around fifty cents but generally went for more. Physique magazines were available at newsstands in larger cities or could be delivered discreetly and legally in plain brown wrappers through the mail; in smaller cities, they might be sold "under the counter," but nonetheless, they were easily and inexpensively obtainable.

As in theater and film during this period, masculinity was constituted with an emphasis on youth, often ambivalent, ambiguous youth but nine out of ten times, white, Anglo-Saxon, Protestant youth. Young men of "other races," Latinos, Asians, "American Negroes," and Middle Easterners, appeared occasionally as exotics among the Caucasians, just as "white" models of marginalized ancestry, including Italians, Poles, Irish—Catholics— and Jews were presented here and there. Rarely, a disabled model might be offered as a curiosity. Because of their precarious status and their homosexual agendas, physique magazines could challenge the status quo only within an often narrow range. Thus, physique magazines, even as they catered to a persecuted minority, tended to fulfill many of the cultural norms held by America at large.

Nonetheless, these photos were viewed by homosexual men within the context of the sexual "revelations" of the postwar period. In the late 1940s, Alfred Kinsey's *Sexuality in the Human Male* indicated not only that the homosexual population of the United States was much larger than originally estimated but also that the number of males who had, at some time, engaged in homosexual sex was larger still. Although Kinsey's statistics were probably erroneous, his data nevertheless suggested that human sexuality was far more fluid than had previously been thought and that most males, or at least many males, were capable of engaging in homo- as well as heterosexual sex. Even as readers were told that the models were heterosexual, the photographs themselves and sometimes the accompanying notes implied, often quite heavily, that these young men were both approachable and available.

The photographs that appeared in the early 1950s show the influence of the physique photography from the 1930s; in fact, many of the photographers who had worked during the depression continued taking physique pictures long after the war. Gradually, many of the earlier conventions gave way to innovation, and by the early 1960s, images changed. Likewise, the male body, even the most developed male body, of the postwar era had not attained the gargantuan proportions that it reached in the seventies and eighties: With such bodybuilding icons as Arnold Schwarzenegger and Lou Ferrigno, even the ultimate 1950s muscleman, Steve Reeves, seemed "built" but not excessively so; Reeves was able to maintain the slim waist along with massive arms, chest, and legs, that somehow managed to appear in harmonious proportion.

At the same time, the fresh-faced models depict a youthful purity reminiscent of "the boys" who had, a decade before, gone off to war. "Even when they were obviously older—in their 20s or even early 30s—they still retained a boyish manner," notes Bronski, adding, "Youth is also equated with innocence and is therefore not stereotypically gay" (171). The young, muscular innocent, WASP type who was still open to new sexual experiences, became the physique magazines' ideal model.

Making Good

From 1969 through the 1980s, Bob Mizer and his now unexpurgated publications, including *Physique Pictorial*, various AMG catalogues, and cheaply shot 8-mm films, had little problem finding models. There seemed an almost limitless supply of young men willing to take money for being pictured in the nude, many of them dropouts, runaways, criminals, addicts of some kind, or street hustlers. However, in its first eighteen years, the rationale behind the magazine's name was "physique." The presiding idea (at least as the magazine presented it) was that readers bought *Physique Pictorial* to look at the muscles; the firm, bare buttocks and posing-strap bulges were merely incidental—indeed, occasional byproducts of Mizer's attempts to display the models' striking builds.

Thus, to break into the early physique magazines, a young man had at least to show some signs of muscular development. Thomas Waugh indicates that the first models pictured in physique magazines were "butch" and well developed (245); Emmanuel Cooper characterizes them as "young bodybuilders who liked to 'work out,' rather than muscular hulks who took part in competitions" (102). Although a variety of such models might be available in larger metropolitan areas, they might be difficult at times to recruit. A majority of the models were straight, and even those who were not for the most part wished to appear so. As Mizer's and Urban's incarcerations had demonstrated, any association with the circulation of explicit or heavily implicit sexual imagery might result in legalized persecution and in public scorn.

Many models insisted that Mizer, as well as other caption writers, made it clear that they had wives, girlfriends, even children. Others refused to pose in the nude, even when their genitals would not have appeared in the photograph. Others still (including the muscleman of all musclemen, Steve Reeves) refused posing straps and stuck with swim trunks. Some models took on a "nom de photo," altering their names for the sake of disguising their identities. Especially in the early years, others might construe as questionable the sexuality of a man whose photo appeared in a physique magazine.

Richard Harrison, who came to Hollywood around 1953 or 1954 from Utah, is a good example of someone who managed to take advantage of his own looks and physique and at the same time, without much compromise, to use them to launch a movie career. As a poor but handsome teenager, Harrison survived as a physical trainer, working and even living in various Los Angeles gyms, eventually turning to modeling. It was not until 1957 when Harrison was 20 that images of Richard or "Dick" began to appear in physique magazines, both in advertisements, then in featured photos and on magazine covers. The very first shot of him turned up in the April issue of Vim. In an ad for itself, the magazine glibly declared that readers, by subscribing to Vim (rather than buying it at a newsstand), could afford a trip to Hawaii. Of course, Vim admitted, it would take 184 years for the savings to equal the amount needed to purchase such a trip. Next to the text is small photo of Harrison in a swimsuit, on a chair reading a physique magazine under some palm trees. Actually, the editors explain, "the lad above isn't in Hawaii at all. . . . He is Richard Harrison, a native Californian. Athletic Model Guild photo."[7]

Of the three models about whom I am writing, I probably know the most about Richard Harrison. Because he appeared in about one hundred films, many of the particulars of his life have been well documented outside the texts of physique magazines. I also had the privilege of interviewing him twice, first on the patio of his Malibu home in 2001 and again in a Santa Monica restaurant in 2004. He was a tall, good-looking man in his 60s, articulate, with a strong sense of humor (especially about himself), and an apparent lack of self-importance. Some Americans, despite Harrison's extensive screen career, may not recall hearing of or seeing him. Indeed, after playing small roles in a few Hollywood films in the late 1950s, he began a new career in Europe, working primarily in B movies made in Italy.

Like musclemen Steve Reeves (with whom Harrison roomed for a short time in Hollywood) and Gordon Mitchell (or "Chuck," an old friend from various LA gyms), Harrison starred in a variety of sword-and-sandal movies—flesh-revealing, heroic epics in which a strongman conquers a seemingly invincible enemy and ends up with an overly made-up Italian actress whose voice was obviously dubbed into English. He starred as well in a series of spaghetti Westerns—indeed, when he was unable to play the lead in A Fistful of Dollars, he recommended his friend Clint Eastwood for the role that would propel Eastwood into stardom.

Figure 7.4. "Enjoy VIM in Hawaii!" urges the ad in which Harrison (by Mizer) made his first magazine appearance; *Vim*, April 1957. (Don Fuller is the model / actor featured in the ad below for Kris Studio.)

Harrison would end up, decades later, in the Far East, in spy action thrillers and karate ninja films. Along the way, from Europe to Hong Kong, he managed to write and direct several films, in a few of which he also appeared. One of his statements, from an interview with John Nada, modestly and dryly reveals his perception of his place in the history of film: "In my opinion, it is a death wish for an actor to be in too many B or should I say C movies. Maybe my greatest contribution to cinema was not doing *A Fistful of Dollars*, and recommending Clint for the part" ("Les Interviews de Nanarland").

Unlike Reeves or Mitchell or most of the other movie musclemen (such as Mark Forrest, Ed Fury, Mickey Hargitay, and many more), who went back to the old world to star in B films, Harrison had actually studied acting with various teachers on the West Coast. His handsome, chiseled face and well-developed body, as well as his talent and sharply tuned social skills, made it possible for him to aspire to a movie career. Such an aspiration might have seemed, when Harrison first arrived in Hollywood, more like wishful thinking.

Born in Salt Lake City, May 26, 1936, he was the illegitimate son of a prominent judge who, already married, lived apart from Richard and his mother. "Harrison," he told me, was an invention, because the Mormon

jurist was unwilling to risk scandal by giving his actual surname to his son.
Growing up in Utah, Harrison recalled, was dreary: "I couldn't wait to
leave." Once in California, however, he had to find ways to support himself.
Early on, he worked as a trainer in Vic Tanny's and then in Bert Goodrich's
gym, where he also managed to work out and even slept in a locker room
(affectionately referred to as "the dungeon") until he had enough money to
find an apartment. Eventually, he took up modeling, both for fashion and
physique photographers.

After retiring from films in the 1990s, Harrison moved back to the
United States and settled in Los Angeles and in Palm Springs, where he
twice ran, unsuccessfully, for mayor in 1995 and 1999. (He credits his ex-
wife, Loretta Nicholson, daughter of James Nicholson, the late head of
American International Pictures, as having a had a hand in the political
campaign against him.) When I spoke with Harrison, his modeling days were
far behind him, but he recalled most of them quite clearly. They were a part
of his past that he seemed to embrace without any shame or embarrassment.
Posing for physique magazines, whatever its implications, was merely something that a young man in Hollywood might do for survival and publicity.
Just as he viewed his roles in the B movies with evident irony, he seemed
aware of the humor of many of the contradictions that had operated in the
physique photography industry.

Figure 7.5. Dick by Kris: The hint of pubic hair made this a racy photo to run in
Adonis (August 1957).

Yet the major paradox underwriting the whole phenomenon of phy-sique magazines, as they had evolved in the late 1950s, may have escaped him, for in the pre-Stonewall world of homosexuals, one of the prevailing myths was that most if not all men were open to sexual advances from other men. Whether a man identified himself as "straight" or "gay" (which were words largely used within an often "invisible" male homosexual sub-culture), he was almost always presented through the magazines as avail-able and accessible. Belief in such "bisexuality" was encouraged by Kinsey's reported findings that most American males had engaged at some point in homosexual activity and was widely presumed and extended by those who created and published the physique magazines during the years that came before the establishment in the culture at large of gay identity.

Getting to Know Dick

As Harrison's photo spreads make clear, the use of text, which put a par-ticular "spin" on the near-nude images, was one of the ways through which photographs were sold. Readers would be given "information" about a par-ticular model; various details about the life of the young man in the picture would expand the visual object of desire into a more three-dimensional image, with a past and a personality. Although there may have been some correlation between the actual model and what was said about him, Harri-son's very first magazine appearance illustrates that the truth was not always included. Contrary to *Vim's* explanation, Richard was not "a native Cali-fornian." Throughout his modeling career, Harrison was described in ways that would make him more appealing to the readers of physique magazines and potential photo buyers.

Initially, however, the physique magazines merely showed more than they told of Richard Harrison. In 1957 alone, he was pictured more than thirty times in them, most impressively making the front covers of *Tomorrow's Man* (July and November) and *Adonis* (October) and the back covers of *Physique Pictorial* (Summer) and *Adonis* (November). These five cover appearances were unusual for any model, let alone a new one, within a five-month period.

The back cover of *Physique Pictorial* was one of several photos by Mizer of Harrison in blue jeans and boots. These and others from the same set would turn up in magazines over the next eight years. Some of these were studio shots and others were taken on a street, a few next to a sparkling Ford Thunderbird convertible. In these pictures, which are in many ways less revealing than Mizer's other shots, the model appropriates the apparel of rebellious youth already seen in *Rebel Without a Cause* and *The Wild One*. The signs indicating young masculinity are more plentiful and stronger in these photos than in many of Mizer's others.

Figure 7.6. Harrison in boots and jeans: On the back cover of *Physique Pictorial* (summer 1957); with Thunderbird (*PP*, July 1962; photos by Mizer).

One of the reasons for his sudden "popularity" was that Harrison had already been photographed by a large number of studios. *Vim*, in its May 1957 issue, might claim that it was including another photo of him in response to its readers' letters about the thumbnail picture in the April ad, but the caption also revealed that this additional shot had been taken not by Mizer but by Chicago's Kris Studio (run by Chuck Renslow) at AMG's (i.e., Bob Mizer's) pool. The image on the May cover of *Tomorrow's Man* was also by Kris, but another photo included in the magazine is by Apollo, and the same magazine's November cover is attributed to Bob Delmonteque and Rex Warner, as is the back cover of *Adonis* for the same month. (Delmonteque, although not named, is also the photographer of a shot of Dick working out in a gym shown in the November 1957 *Tomorrow's Man* [11].) Harrison had, as the photos and their ads show, made the rounds to a number of photo studios.

What were readers of these magazines told about Dick Harrison? In *Tomorrow's Man*, on whose cover he was featured, the text dispelled the myth that he was a native Californian, specifying that he had come to Hollywood from Utah, was now 20 and "attending 20th Century Fox drama school." A "stage and TV star," he had appeared in the movie *The West Point Story*. The blurb also gives his vital statistics: "a six footer, weighs 185, has 17" arms and a 46" chest" (May 1957, 43). *Tomorrow's Man's* second issue featuring Harrison on the cover (November 1957) adds that Harrison was currently working out at American Health Studios on Hollywood Boulevard, had most recently appeared in the film *Jeanne Eagles*, and "is fond of tennis, likes to read a lot, and studies ardently for his career" (4).

Bob Mizer often spent time interviewing his models, putting them at ease and collecting data for the text that accompanied the photos. For his part, Harrison recalled Mr. Mizer's home and pool, his boyfriend named Joe (possibly Joe Leitel, aka Joe la Grosso), and Mizer's pet caged monkey, which appeared in a few of AMG's shots, including at least one with Harrison himself.

Harrison first appeared in *Physique Pictorial* in the summer 1957 issue. In addition to being featured on the back cover, there was also a photo of Harrison in a posing strap, dripping wet, in an elaborate chair beside Mizer's pool (14). A blurb introduced the newcomer:

> 20 6' 185 lbs. He feels he can thank the Mormon church for his background in both acting and in physical culture training because the church he attended had a gym and the Bishops and Elders encouraged his interest. He, Bill Melby, Mike Sills, and other weight trainers often went to different church branches to encourage physical culture interest.

Mizer would repeatedly come back to Harrison's religion in his early copy; it seemed, at least at first, that he relished the exoticism or perhaps merely enjoyed pointing out how a follower of a devout sect could be induced to exhibit his body for homosexual readers. In addition to "Dick's" early credits, Mizer mentions that AMG had hundreds of photos of Harrison and also laments that the studios had asked Richard to loose some of his muscle, so he could play a wider range of parts; the same advice, he notes, was given to Steve Reeves, whose career did not improve from his having followed it (2). Mizer adds that "Fans may obtain directly from Dick Harrison po box 46723 Los Angeles, 46, Calif, a set of 12 4 × 5 photos, autographed on request. Dick will include a little note and will be glad to answer any reasonable question he can (but please don't ask more than 3 with one order)" (2). As indicated previously, Mizer did promote the work of other photographers, but it was unusual for him to talk up pictures for sale by the models themselves.

Mizer offered even more information about the model in a blurb on a photo depicting a hairy (unshaven) Harrison in his underwear—Y-front briefs—published in *Physique Pictorial's* winter, 1957 issue:

[H]e is one of [Hollywood's] handsomest young bachelors. Bodybuilding has always fascinated him, [he] has been room-mates at various times with some of the most brilliant stars in the bodybuilding galaxy, including Steve Reeves and Keith Stephan. . . . If you run into Dick, get him to tell you of the time that Keith nearly threw him out of a second story win-dow—it's a spell-binding exciting story.

A clean, wholesome boy, he neither drinks nor smokes, and has very high moral precepts which he finds must sometimes be severely strained in trying to "make a go of it" in Hollywood, but Richard is very honorable. His father, a lawyer, caused Dick to begin law studies at the University of Utah, but Dick felt much happier on the stage. . . . Recently, he lost a great deal of weight because the studios told him to do so, but in Richard's case, the weight really looked good, and we feel the pictures he has taken recently since the weight loss aren't nearly as pleasing as the earlier ones.

Mizer next describes the extensive catalogues available from AMG on Harrison, noting a set of color shots:

The stereo-color set on Dick is one of the most beautiful we have ever offered. . . . Dick has a beautiful warm skin tone, smooth like velvet, and in color his smile would melt steel. (29)

Understanding Mizer's blurb requires a certain amount of decoding. In 1950s terminology, *bachelor* is an ambiguous term. Although it was generally used to denote a man who had never married, it also connoted, as evidenced in the phrase "confirmed bachelor" (already in use for several decades), a man who was not attracted to women, a homosexual. Additionally, it suggested a man's accessibility: Without any marital commitment, a bachelor might be construed to be sexually available and even promiscuous. Hence, refer-ences to his "roommates" Steve Reeves (with whom Harrison did for a short time share an apartment) and Keith Stephan (with whom Harrison was a friend but never lived) might imply relationships that were, in keeping with Dick's supposed fascination with bodybuilding, more than platonic. (Small photos of Reeves, Stephan, and, for an unexplained reason, Dick DuBois, are inserted into stars surrounding Harrison's torso; Harrison may have worked as a muscleman with DuBois in Mae West's Las Vegas review.)

The "spell-binding, exciting story" about Stephan nearly tossing him out a window is not quite as amusing as Mizer would have had it. Stephan, whose photo appears a few pages earlier than Harrison's, was an impressively large man: At 26 he stood 6 feet, 3 inches tall and weighed 221 pounds; sporting a 51-inch chest and 32 ½-inch waist, his cold 18 ¼-inch biceps pumped to 19 inches. "Keith is so strong," commented Mizer, "he hardly knows his own strength . . ." (25–26). Decades later, Harrison would recall Stephan as a kind man whose mind seemed to work differently from everyone else's. He was constantly getting into fights, not because he sought them out but because whenever he walked into a bar, men would want to take him on. On the whole, however, he was gentle but "different." The incident to which Mizer refers occurred not in an apartment but on the roof of Harrison's apartment building. At some point, Stephan became convinced that Harrison "was too good for this world"; that his innocence would be spoiled by life and Hollywood. He hoisted Harrison above his head, determined to throw him off the roof to preserve his "goodness" forever, but Harrison talked him into letting him down, asserting that he was not too good to live and that he had only lived a small part of his life, of which much more was to come. (Stephan went on to marry, unhappily as it turned out, and after his divorce ultimately committed suicide in 1974.)

The "clean wholesome boy" with "very high moral precepts" that were "severely strained" by Hollywood, probably refers to what, at least in Mizer's mind, amounted to a conflict between Harrison's morals and the demands of the casting couch. Perhaps his being "very honorable" reflects Harrison's own recollections of being "hit on" by influential men in the movie world. As a young man drifting around Hollywood and the studios, he came into contact with a great number of people, some of them, like himself, struggling to get into films, others comfortably established in the industry. When a sleazy agent telephoned to invite him to swim in Cole Porter's pool, Harrison declined politely, aware that the invitation was sexual. Veteran director George Cukor once made a pass at him, but Harrison responded with a deferential rebuff, admitting that he very much respected Cukor's work and admired his brilliance; after that, Harrison told me, Cukor spoke only well of him. More likely, however, as evident from a much later blurb in *Physique Pictorial*, "very honorable" probably alludes to Mizer's belief that Harrison, although a heterosexual, would perform sexually, and very discreetly, to get ahead.

As for Mizer's pronouncements about Harrison's body, the fervor of the photographer promotes and enables the reader's attraction to the model. Regardless of the actual sexuality of the photo's subject, the head of AMG (to whom Harrison even in 2002 still referred as "Mr. Mizer") was in the business of producing images of male sex objects. His sensuous appreciation of Harrison's skin, for example, and his note about a "smile that would melt steel" obviously transcend the supposed objectivity of the lens.

In January 1958, *Adonis* would feature a spread of the model at home, entitled "A Day with Dick," featuring photos by Jacque (of Hollywood), showing him "*à sa toilette*, boning up on Stanislavsky" (a not-so-subtle play on words), "absorbing culture via hi-fi, decorating his new apartment, and viewing critically a reshowing of one of his kinescopes" (12, 44). In the pictures, Harrison in trunks examines his LPs and in posing straps shaves, reads, hangs a poster, and stares at something off camera. Toward the end of the short article, the writer adds,

> These are just a few of the shots of this extraordinarily hand-some actor who, for the first time in this issue, offers his own photographs for sale. Elsewhere in these pages you will find his advertisement.
>
> Dick makes a point of answering each letter personally, which is refreshing considering he's a very busy boy in the studios just now. (44)

Indeed, a small back-page ad announces "A DAY WITH DICK" in "Series No. 2, which shows me at home in my apartment in Hollywood. 12 4 × 5 photos with personal letter from me . . . . $3.00," and gives a Los Angeles post office box number (65). Such "at-home" sets were not uncommon and were often promoted and sold by the models themselves.

Harrison had gone from being the subject of photos to being the subject and purveyor of photos. He was not the first to cut out the studios so that the price of the pictures (rather than a one-time modeling fee) would go directly to him: Three years earlier, model Glenn Bishop (who is the subject of the next chapter) had begun selling shots of himself, sometimes together with friend and posing partner Richard Alan. In the fifteen years

Figure 7.7. Chez Dick: From the *Apollo* spread (January 1958).

in which physique magazines thrived, a number of models advertised their own pictures, but none did it so early in his career as Harrison. Bishop and Alan would sign their photos, personalizing them for each customer. Harrison went the extra step of writing a letter. What was for sale now was not just the model's image but—in a somewhat distant fashion—the model's acquaintance. Throughout his modeling career, Harrison (unlike Bishop) would pose for other photographers, but at the same time he, either on his own or in collaboration with others (such as model Bob Hover and model/photographer Bob Delmonteque), would sell his own images and add a personal touch.

During 1958, similar ads appeared in the back pages of *Body Beautiful* (where he again promised to answer each letter personally) and *Trim* (where he offers "Mystery Set 5," "a very special set of new pictures taken of me" [40]), even as AMG and Bob Delmonteque advertised Harrison's photos elsewhere; indeed, the pictures from "A Day with Dick," originally credited to Jacque were now being offered by Delmonteque (*Tomorrow's Man*, July 1958, 36). When he was named by *Grecian Guild Pictorial* as "Grecian of the Month," in April, honored not for his acting skills but for his "perfect physique and high ideals" (54), the accompanying text rehashed much of what had already written about him, including his acting credits and his intellectual side:

> Muscular Dick is no muscle-head. This young bachelor is fond of reading and is a young man of intelligence and mentality, for he realizes the complete man must have a sound mind in a sound body if he is to achieve the greatness of which he is capable. (55–57)

The "article" even stated when and where Dick worked out, giving the reader information on how to encounter him in person (55). In this spread, Harrison was pictured alone and with Bob Hover; a photo of the pair (by Delmonteque) graces the cover of *Grecian Guild*.

In 1959, Harrison again offered his own photos, some of which appeared (credited to him) in several physique magazines, and also teamed up with fellow model and aspiring actor Bob Hover, to whom he bore a certain resemblance. They ran joint ads in *Trim* (April) and *Muscle Sculpture* (August), in addition to ads that Harrison ran on his own in *Grecian Guild* (August) and *Tomorrow's Man* (December). Perhaps the most interesting piece on Harrison came in August when *Grecian Guild Pictorial* gave him a four-page spread entitled, "A Guy Named Dick" (4–7). Although most of the pictures were reprinted or at least from the same series as those in the 1958 *Adonis* piece, "A Day with Dick," the two pages of text were new and written in the first person. With Harrison himself as the ostensible narrator, recounting his first job in Los Angeles in a filling station and his subsequent self-doubts and loneliness in a strange city, the already-established story of Harrison-the-struggling-actor once more reemerges. His self-confidence wins out, his acting credits are restated, and his hopes for the future are very positive.

The one piece of the rise-to-fame story that seems in keeping with Mizer's earlier blurb is the addition of an unnamed agent, whom Dick describes meeting through one of the new friends whom he made while working in a gym. After seeing Harrison in a local theater production of *Green Grow the Lilacs* (on which the musical *Oklahoma!* was based), the agent advised him to take acting lessons, after which more parts began to come his way, both in film and in television shows and commercials. "I *have* been taken on by the agent who first encouraged me, and he's now my best friend" (5), he supposedly writes. Once more the innuendo of male-to-male bonding is raised in the aspiring actor's career; although perhaps understated, the notion that young men in Hollywood would do what they needed to get ahead lingers in this narrative.

In 1960, Harrison was a contract player at Twentieth Century Fox (or as one magazine would have it, Warner Brothers [*Young Physique*, February 1962, 15]), was about to be offered a contract at American International Pictures (AIP), and would go overseas to make his first gladiator epic. Although he would appear on the cover of *Tomorrow's Man* for November 1960, the photos published this year and those published up until 1966 are significantly fewer than the years preceding. Moreover, none of them is attributed to Harrison himself; there are featured pictures of Harrison by others and ads for Apollo, Bob Delmonteque, AMG, Kris, Rex Warner, and R.A. Enterprises, but all of these appear to be shots taken before Harrison left for Europe, many of them published previously. The implication, of course, is that once Harrison began working in Italy, he ceased to deal in his photographs; he had neither the need nor, perhaps, the inclination. Yet numerous photographers had snapped him throughout the late 1950s and still had sets and collections of him that they were trying to sell. In the 1960s, older photographs circulated along with new ones. Pictures of models that were just emerging were pictured side by side with those of models that had already retired.

By 1962, Harrison certainly seemed to have retired from modeling. Mizer's 1957 shot of him, bare-chested in blue jeans next to a Ford Thunderbird, received a full page in the July 1962 *Physique Pictorial*, but the blurbs are brief. One repeats the family story of Harrison dropping out of law school at the University of Utah and rehashes a few of his acting credits from the 1950s; another vaguely refers to his recent movie career and his marriage to AIP executive producer, James Nicholson's daughter, and yet another succinctly mentions AMG's catalogues of him (3). It appeared that Mizer, like the other photographers with Harrison catalogues, was interested merely in selling off the stock he had.

Leaving Los Angeles

In 1963 there were no Harrison pictures in any of the posing strap magazines that I have been able to examine. By this time, the model had become a familiar face to moviegoers in Western Europe and elsewhere. He was one of the most recognizable stars in Italy. Frequently mobbed on the streets, his enormous popularity caused one actress, who was making her career in teenage beach sagas, extremely jealous; she had been sent by the studio to the Continent, and Richard had been asked to guide her through Rome, but once she realized that virtually no one knew who she was, she became very angry. (One of the major MGM male stars of the 1940s and 1950s [who had been snubbed as a teenager by stage star Monty Clift] was also shown around by Harrison; after becoming extremely drunk, he crudely propositioned the younger actor, who courteously turned him down.)

Although a number of Harrison photos were published in 1964, these were, as previously indicated, all taken seven to four years earlier by various studios that were still selling them. By far the most interesting came in February in *Physique Pictorial*. By this point in its publication, Mizer had developed a code with which he marked many of the pictures carried in the magazine—indicating through specific signs something about the model's "personal life." In addition to the code, however, Mizer added a longer blurb. Here, he reiterated much of what he had said about Harrison since 1957 (his supposed time in law school, his bodybuilder friends, his early credits, etc); however, this time, he again brought up the model's faith:

> Raised in a strong religious (Mormon) home he followed the tenants of the church very closely—used no alcohol, tobacco, or stimulants. With Bill Melby [a Mormon bodybuilder and model, later a pro-wrestler] and other Salt Lake friends he would visit various church groups "spreading the gospel" of healthful living and bodybuilding. (4)

The reason for this "disclosure" is initially unclear. Why would Mizer again exaggerate Harrison's affiliation with the Mormon Church, which he had been happy to leave far behind him? And why mention it now, long after the photo of Harrison lounging in a bikini had been taken (probably in

1957 or 1958)? Was it to offset the attractive image with a gesture toward religion? Was it to "purify" the homoeroticism that he expected his readers would experience in the image or to heighten it?

The answer is perhaps most apparent in Mizer's coded notation at the bottom of the photo. The code was first used in the issue of *Physique Pictorial* from which the photo of Harrison in Fig. 7.9 appeared (and lasted, with some hiatuses, into the late 1980s). Like the catalogues of von Gloeden, AMG issued two sets of decoders, one sent out by Mizer to the general readership and another that was given out more selectively. In the first "Subjective Character Analysis," the symbols appear to have rather bland meanings.

Mizer's notation, according to this sheet, signifies that Harrison is a "self-controlled" young man with "an agreeable personality" and that he is exceptionally "ambitious and enterprising" and strongly wanted "to get ahead." Mizer admits that his "knowledge of [this] subject's personal traits is very limited." However, according to the second version of Mizer's code, these innocent remarks take on a more sexualized meaning. Indeed, the second version suggests that the code is all about the subject's sexuality.

However, translated by the more explicit decoder, Mizer's statement is no longer innocuous: Harrison is said to be a "self-controlled" young man who is "open to fooling around with guys" and "[c]an be sucked." He is also characterized as someone who "[h]ustles." Perhaps in this context, the admission of limited knowledge has something to do with Mizer's own experience with (rather than knowledge of) the subject. In conjunction with Mizer's blurb about Harrison's devout Mormonism, the coded message seems to imply what Mizer had been suggesting since 1957: Dick, like any young man in Hollywood, was available for sex.

Harrison made clear to me that he was aware early on, when he first began appearing in physique magazines, that his picture would be viewed by men in Utah whom he knew were homosexual. He told me that that had not mattered to him; indeed, around 1961, when one of the "confidential magazines" threatened to place a posing-strap photo of him on its cover, thus questioning the sexual orientation of the soon-to-be son-in-law of AIP's Nicholson, he and his in-laws thought this supposedly negative publicity was ridiculous and ignored it. In 1961, some actors would have tried to squelch such insinuations—for men who actually were homosexual, a tell-all in *Confidential* could end a career in film. Harrison was sufficiently secure not to worry about it.

In addition to his feelings of security, Harrison had also come through Hollywood at a time when homosexuality was increasingly accepted in private. His reactions to actor James Dean's apparent preferences were totally nonchalant: "Jimmy would bring male friends to various parties, so we all figured he must be gay." Harrison's only *faux pas*, he revealed, was when

Figure 7.8. Mizer's decoder (above) and the alleged actual meaning of the symbols (below).

Figure 7.9. Harrison in a floral bikini notated with Mizer's code in *Physique Pictorial* (February 1964).

he had recently used the terms *active* and *passive* while with a group of gay friends. "Gore Vidal corrected me," he confided. "Now it's 'pitcher' and 'catcher.'"

Only four photos attributed to Harrison himself appeared after 1960. These were considerably older shots in *Manual*, July 1966 (18–19) and two others in *The Big Boys*, September 1966 (26–27). Both magazines acknowledge him as the source of the pictures, but in the latter, the blurb indicates that the photos "are not for sale currently" (26). Harrison's final appearances in the now-disappearing physique magazines come in 1970, with three shots in some of the surviving publications.

Conclusion

One of the first photos of Harrison that Mizer took was of young Dick dressed in a sailor suit. Although the picture never appeared in any of the physique magazines, the portrait readily marks the subject with the signs of a serviceman: In addition to the uniform itself, there is his youth, his

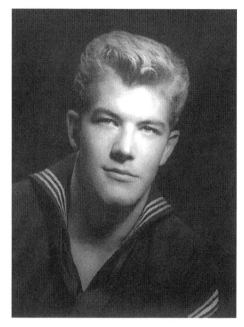

Figure 7.10. An early AMG portrait of Harrison.

open yet innocent gaze, and his handsome smile. These qualities were all emphasized in AMG's photographs in general and in Harrison's pictures in particular, whether he was in military dress or in underpants, posing straps, swimsuit, or the boots and jeans associated with the postwar teenager.

In his copy, Mizer kept returning to Harrison's religious background, in part because some of the customs associated with Mormonism reflected the purity his readers wanted to see in his models: no drinking and smoking, no premarital sex, and healthy, clean living with an emphasis on exercise. That Harrison exuded all these is supported by Mizer's attempt to repeat the anecdote involving Keith Stephan. Aware of the pressure and corruption his friend faced in Hollywood, the well-meaning giant believed Harrison was better off dying before he succumbed to the inevitable sleaze. Yet Mizer also wanted readers to believe that a young man like Harrison could retain his innocence while accepting sexual advances from other men. *Physique Pictorial's* message was that a young man could remain pure and still engage in sex with members of his own sex.

Harrison's blond hair and blue eyes, his chiseled features and handsome physique, even when Mizer complained he preferred him with more muscle, made him an all-American object of homosexual desire. He shared glimpses of his private life and even corresponded with his gay male fans. His success in landing film roles in Europe marked the end of his physique model career.

In Italy, Harrison, like many of the other American musclemen who came to play lead roles in the "sword-and-sandal" films, had to appear pumped up and beefy. Likewise, his body was shaven, and he now sported a beard. No longer to be viewed as a handsome young male, his image became that of a demigod or hero, a manly superman capable of enormous feats. Unlike major roles played by Clift, Brando, and Dean, his roles did not involve him playing characters with whom the audience could identify. He became a larger-than-life protagonist whom the audience could admire from afar.

The dynamics of the ancient hero films, as opposed to some of the films coming out of Hollywood, were supposedly traditional. For example, Tennessee Williams's A *Streetcar Named Desire* deliberately draws Stanley and Blanche as two extreme examples of gender construction; through this

Figure 7.11. Harrison in peplum as he appeared in *Gladiators Seven* (1962).

depiction, Williams is able to critique the contradictory qualities that make a male a man and a female a woman. However, in all of the Italian gladiator epics, including Harrison's, the enormous contrast between masculinity and femininity is invoked as natural and authentic. In the ancient world, these garish films seem to proclaim to spectators, men were men and women were women, and it was easy to see the differences between the two. Without the sense of irony that Harrison brings to his own discussions of his early roles, the gladiator films seem to take themselves terribly seriously; they are, then, reactionary statements about gender and sexuality that couch themselves in the classics. Ironically, if it weren't for this very obliviousness to just how ridiculous they are, they would be unwatchable today.

CHAPTER 8

As Beauty Does

The Retreating Dr. Bishop

Overture

Sometime, as the 1950s wore on, the tone of the physique magazines relaxed and the various alibis for the display of homoerotic imagery—some publications defended themselves by indicating they were intended for artists and collectors, others as physical fitness champions—became less imperative. By 1960, the models too had changed. As Thomas Waugh explains it,

> As the gay market began to be catered to with increasing directness, a shift in iconography was the inevitable by-product. . . . One index was the noticeable evolution away from the traditionally favored "butch" body; by the end of the fifties, slim sensitive types in moody introspective poses had made inroads into the galleries of impassive jocks. . . . Grace challenged power as an aesthetic ideal, and the boy-next-door look became as common as the superhuman. (245)

Part of what Waugh fails to explain, however, was the uneasy presence from the very beginning of physique magazine publication of literal "boys" with physiques that were just starting to develop.

Although the majority of male models who appeared in the physique magazines were 18 years old or older, in the first years of publication there were a few teenagers who posed as well. The August 1952 issue of *Physique Pictorial* featured a shot of one of Bob Mizer's earliest subjects, Forrester Millard (aka Forrest D'Orlac), who had started posing for AMG when he was 16 years old. The spring 1953 issue of *PP* displayed a shot of 16-year-old Peter Ramm, whom Mizer had met in London. In the fall 1954 issue, he showed a series of photos documenting Gene Meyers's development at ages

12, 14, 16, and 18. In the same issue, he introduced Frank Veitenheimer, who was 14, and the spring 1955 *PP* featured a two-page spread of Arnie Payne, also 14 years old. Jim Richardson, just 16, had received a two-page spread in the previous issue (winter 1954–1955). The cover man for summer 1955 was 16-year-old Joe Survilas. These underage images were relatively rare, both in Mizer's magazine and in others, but they did show up.

Most readers preferred models who were no longer boys but rather young men who might have boyish looks but who had clearly gone through puberty. The notion of adult males looking for young teenagers played directly into the stereotype of mature men who were looking to corrupt children, an idea unwelcome to both the physique magazines themselves and the more serious homophile journals that were beginning to appear. Most physique publications generally applauded men who showed clear muscular development. However, there was a notable exception.

As indicated in the previous chapter, a year after *Physique Pictorial* was first printed, another magazine that claimed not only to carry the kinds of beefcake that had made Mizer successful but also to offer serious and detailed articles about bodybuilding, diet, and other related topics. *Tomorrow's Man* was founded by a rather odd Chicago gym owner named Irv Johnson, who had particular, if not peculiar, ideas about exercise and the use of supplements. His model of choice, the one whom he believed best exemplified the ideal male body, was a 15-year-old boy from Michigan, who appeared on the magazine's very first table of contents page and, as months went on, throughout his magazine. Although Johnson incorrectly revealed that the boy's name was Glen (rather than Glenn) Bishop, the young model soon became something of a celebrity among gay readers of *Tomorrow's Man*.

Glenn Elwood (it was a family name) Bishop was born in 1937 and grew up along the shores of Lake Michigan in Grand Haven, not far from Bangor. He reportedly began lifting weights at the age of 13. Very little is known about him before 1952 when he was first pictured (but remained unidentified) on the contents page in the premiere issue of *Tomorrow's Man* (December 1952, 7). In the next issue, the same image was reprinted on the same page but was now clearly identified as "Glen [sic] Bishop" (February 1953, 5), and in the issue following, the image returned but was enlarged and more prominently identified (March 1953, 5). By April, not only was the table of contents again adorned with his photo (credited to editor Irv Johnson), but he appeared on the back of the front cover, as Shakespeare's Puck, above the quotation, "What fools these mortals be" (20), and he and a friend, cover model Richard Alan, were shown in briefs arm wrestling; beneath the picture came the promise that the next issue would contain a "complete picture story on Glen and [we] know you won't want to miss it" (24).

For nearly two years, from December 1952 until the end of 1954, Bishop seemed to be the exclusive property of *Tomorrow's Man* and its enigmatic editor. Finally, in December 1954, Bishop, now called "Glenn," made his debut in *Tomorrow's Man's* imitator and rival, *Vim*. From this point on, Bishop became a widely known model, posing for several photographers and eventually launching his own studio (sometimes in collaboration with his friend, Richard Alan) and a swimsuit line, and on occasion speaking out to set the record straight. Always a favorite with physique fans, he retired from modeling in 1967, just as the physique magazines were losing readers to publications that showed full nudity, notably *Drum*, which beginning in 1965 offered naked images to a gay male audience.

Bishop put himself through college, then chiropractic school, and into a chiropractic practice, supposedly (at least in part) through funds from his photo and swimsuit sales. Although he appeared, like Richard Harrison, to have negotiated his way successfully through the "physique business" and into adulthood and a career, Bishop seemed to walk and later run from his fifteen years of posing. The past clearly became something he wanted to leave behind, both literally and figuratively.

After some searching, I found Glenn Bishop, DC, out west. He was relatively easy to locate, obscure though his circumstances were. When I first contacted him, by phone, he denied he was the same Glenn Bishop whom I was trying to find, but after corresponding with some of his relatives and his former wife in Michigan, I wrote to him, indicating that I knew he must be the person I sought, briefly describing my project to him and requesting an interview. I received in reply a letter from him (late in winter 2003) indicating with certain indignation that he was indeed the person I sought and if I would stop annoying his ex-wife, he would allow me to phone him and ask him what I wished to know. Because of the way his letter was worded and because of his obviously indignant and homophobic tone, I found myself unable to avail myself of this opportunity; I wrote back saying that I had not intended to cause anyone any discomfort and that I was not trying to apply pressure to someone who preferred not to discuss his past, offering that if he ever wanted to discuss his modeling career, I would be honored if he would share it with me.

In writing this chapter, then, I have had to consider what I might learn from sources other than Bishop himself. Why would someone who had been so active in the physique photo trade and who had done so well in it, now be so incensed about talking about it? With the advent of the Internet and a plethora of websites, online clubs, forums, and blogs, various rumors about Bishop have circulated for the past decade. Among these have been assertions that he had become a rightwing fanatic and that he was an extreme homophobe. For both, there was at least some substantiation. Yet as a researcher, even a snubbed and scorned researcher, I decided to begin without prejudice. What I discovered more than explained Bishop's anger and aversion to the topic. Although outwardly his resembled an American success story, Bishop's life—even the little I was able to glimpse of it— offered evidence of adolescent disillusion, betrayal, and even abuse.

Figure 8.1. Top: Bishop's first appearances in *Tomorrow's Man* were adjacent to the contents page. Bottom left: in April 1953, he was shown with Richard Alan. Bottom right: as Shakespeare's Puck (photos by Irvin Johnson).

Glen(n) Bishop: Johnson's Trademark

In its fifth issue, published in June 1953, *Tomorrow's Man* replaced its usual table of contents photo of Bishop in a swimsuit with a naked rear-view studio shot of him in subdued light, taken by editor and magazine founder,

PICTURE CREDITS
Cover, 2, 4, 8, 9, 13, 14, 15, 16, 17, 18, 19, 32, 33, 36, 41, 43; Irv Johnson 10; Al Urban
24, Back Cover: Athletic Model Guild
28: Frank Giordina
45: Warner Bros. Studios
6, 7: Cliff Ottinger
Production-Layout: Bill Bunton
Printed by Cari Gorr Co., Chicago
Persons submitting photographs for publication should enclose a stamped, self addressed envelope for return of same.
LEFT: Glen Bishop

Irvin Johnson ....Editor and Publisher
William Bunton ....Managing Editor
Joseph Voorhees ....Business Manager
Cleo Dawson, Ph.D. ....Consulting Psychologist
George MacGregor, M.D. ..Consulting Physician

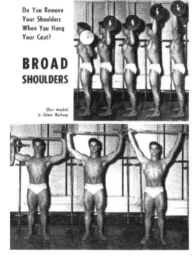

Do You Remove Your Shoulders When You Hang Your Coat?

BROAD
SHOULDERS

Our model is Glen Bishop

Glen Bishop: Matinee Idol in the Making

Figure 8.2. Bishop was featured prominently in *TM* for June 1953 (photos by Johnson).

Irv Johnson, who had opened a gym in Chicago in 1947 or 1948. In following issues, the swim trunks photo returned and became larger until it took up an entire page in November 1953, and then entirely disappeared from the publication. (Later, for a few months *TM*'s physique mascot became Forrester Millard [aka Forrest D'Orlac], a model photographed by Bob Mizer since the mid-1940s.) Yet Bishop's image was truly launched in the June 1953 issue, which, in addition to showing the nude picture just mentioned, also depicted him demonstrating shoulder lifts and introduced him to *TM*'s readers through a four-page photo spread with text.

Johnson had claimed, in the text that accompanied the picture of Bishop arm wrestling with Richard Alan, that the forthcoming photo feature would "answer a good many inquiries about the man whose picture we have been using on our contents page." Glen, he attested, "has developed one of America's most symmetrical, streamlined physiques, mainly because he has trained for shape rather than 'hulk and bulk'" (April 1953, 24). These seemingly innocuous words would pave the way for Johnson to link Bishop with the training methods and supplements that he and *TM* were promoting.

The nude photo emphasizes Bishop's "symmetrical, streamlined physique," a marked contrast to the more developed physiques photographed by others during this time, while the exercise shots illustrate how, despite his lack of "hulk and bulk," he was obviously strong. And the opening for the spread, a page-sized picture of Glen, "Matinee Idol in the Making" (14), shows a civilized-looking young man, in a sport coat and tie, smiling into the camera.

The text attempts to summarize him:

> He's not so tall (5'9") but he's certainly dark and handsome. His name is Glen Bishop and don't be too surprised if you see his name in lights over the door of your neighborhood theater a few years from now.
>
> Glen is only 16 years old, but already he has developed one of the nation's most ideal physiques. We first began using Glen's picture on our contents page when we first began publishing *TM*. The pictures on these pages are in answer to a flood of inquiries about him.
>
> Bishop has been in weight training for the past three years and has added 30 pounds of solid muscle to his frame in that time. He weighs 168 pounds. A major factor in the success of this Johnson pupil is good food and the use of supplements. (15)

Not only is Bishop praised as a future Hollywood star, he is linked to the publication from its inception and more important, to Johnson himself.

Without much explanation, we are told that the young man follows the Johnson method of bodybuilding.

Yet on the following page, we may wonder how Bishop, due to his numerous activities, had time for Johnson and his tutelage:

> Clothes didn't make this man, and whether he's dressed, or undressed, Glen Bishop's classic physique is evident. A popular lad at Grand Haven (Mich.) High School, Glen edits the school newspaper.
>
> A man of many talents, Glen has many artistic inclinations. He is an excellent singer, and also enjoys freehand drawing. Glen is also an avid sports fan, likes hockey, tumbling, swimming, and skiing (water and snow). Of course, his favorite sport is body building. (16)

How could this dynamic 16-year-old, involved in high school and a full-range of extracurricular activities, have managed to travel from Grand Haven, Michigan to Johnson's gym, in Chicago, Illinois, a nearly two-hundred mile journey that now takes three hours by car or (via Bangor) two-and-a-half hours by train? Obviously, he could not have made this trip three times a week; possibly on weekends he might have undertaken this journey. So in what sense was he in fact a "pupil" of Johnson's?

If the article's text fails to explain why this adolescent had been so idolized, the photos certainly indicate Johnson's adulation. In this spread, Bishop is pictured either in his coat-and-tie ensemble, as on the lead page, or almost completely naked. The first page with text shows a nude Glen using an electric razor at the bathroom mirror; the article's title ("We'd Like You To Meet GLEN BISHOP") cuts across the model's crotch as if to hide his privates. "CLOSE SHAVE," reads the ironic caption, crediting Bishop's hygiene with "his unflecked skin, glistening hair, and polished teeth" and attesting that he is a hearty eater who also takes "concentrates" (15).

On the two pages that follow we see a dressed-up Glen lounging near a window, at the keyboard, and, surrounded by enlarged physique photos, reading a copy of (what else?) *Tomorrow's Man*, juxtaposed with shots of a naked Glen toweling dry after a shower and in a posing strap holding two dumbbells. As with the photo spreads of Richard Harrison at home, this one of Bishop strives through picture and word to familiarize him, to present him as an entity to which readers will want to relate. The image constructed is not so much of the "all-American boy," as of a modern version of the classical kouros, the idealized youth depicted naked in Greek statuary of the Archaic period.

In subsequent months, *TM* kept alive this image by running at least one picture of Bishop in every issue. For example, *TM* for July 1953 shows

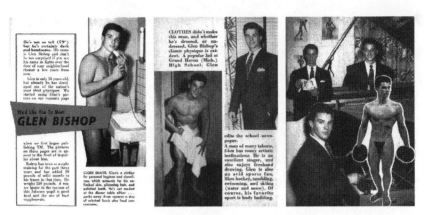

Figure 8.3. "Glen" Bishop is introduced to an inquiring public, TM June 1953 (photos by Johnson).

him winning second-place in a national "Mr. High School" competition, beside the first- and third-place winners (10).[1] This photo was taken by Cliff Oettinger, a Chicago-based photographer whose work was starting to appear in physique magazines around the country. Oettinger's pictures of Bishop, beginning in 1953 and taken over the next few years, would make the covers of other physique magazines and be featured and sold widely. The August 1953 issue introduced a nude photo of Bishop kneeling (11), one that Johnson would reprint in a later spread. In October, the usual photo opposite the contents page was captioned, "Glen Bishop, TM's 'trademark'" (5). In November, Glen appeared in a sport shirt to demonstrate that body-builders looked good in clothes (20), and in December, in a swimsuit at the gym (presumably Johnson's); the larger, featured photos all offer captions linking Bishop and his physique to the Johnson system.

These appearances led to another spread, entitled "A Gallery of Glen Bishop," in the January 1954 issue. By this time, the model had turned seventeen. Johnson reiterates that much of Bishop's success came from his use of food supplements and that he could often be seen training in Johnson's Chicago gym (10–13). As before, there are shots of Glen in a coat and tie and also in posing straps, as well as another picture of him in trunks in a gym (presumably Johnson's) and the reprint of the August 1953 nude kneeling shot.

Curiously, TM's "trademark" disappears from the magazine until April 1954 when a photo of Bishop in what would later be marketed by him as the "Bishop Bikini" is included. Glen, the April 1954 caption reveals, "was a lifeguard last summer" (5). The photographer of this picture is not identified. After two months out of the magazine, Bishop appears again as Puck (in the same shot of him printed in 1953) on *TM*'s cover. In the issue itself is a silhouetted seated nude shot, similar in style to the June 1953 contents page photo and the nude picture of him kneeling, as well as a beach shot, presumably taken in the summer of 1953.

Bishop's pictures continued to appear in *TM*, in one form or another, until December 1954, mostly to promote Johnson's photo albums of him. The advertisements, which began in July, suggest that the photos contained were taken much earlier, probably in late 1952 or early 1953; the subject is noticeably younger in these pictures than in the more recent shots.

The October and December 1954 issues carried smaller ads for these albums, but there were no further photos of Glenn in *TM* for a year. Recently, photos from these albums have been offered for sale via eBay; they show Bishop wearing a posing strap that had no straps, but was in some other way attached to the model's crotch. These photos closely resemble pictures of Bishop taken by Doug Julef, known as Douglas of Detroit, who may in fact have taken some of these photos on behalf of Johnson. The December 1955 issue shows him and Richard Alan posing in swimsuits on a railway bridge, a photo taken by Cliff Oettinger and later sold by Bishop and Alan themselves. What had happened between the end of 1954 and the end of 1955 to account for *TM*'s omission of its own "trademark"? During Bishop's "absence," Richard Alan's photo had continued to run in the magazine, along with ads for Alan's studio, which operated out of Ann Arbor in conjunction with Bishop. Yet Bishop's name was never mentioned, only Alan's. Why had Bishop suddenly become persona non grata at *Tomorrow's Man?*

Figure 8.4. Glen for sale: Johnson's Bishop albums, the first offering of Bishop's photos (*TM*, July 1954).

One explanation perhaps lies in the fact that during this same period, Bishop's pictures began appearing in other magazines, some of them strong competitors with TM. Simultaneously, Johnson was selling the magazine to a group on the East Coast. Johnson himself disappeared from TM in August 1955, when the editorial page that had always shown his own face unexpectedly showed someone else's. Johnson's departing words are interesting. In previous issues, he had offered anecdotes and made claims for the success of his bodybuilding program and nutrition system. His editorials had become increasingly transparent sales promotions. This last editorial is clearly written toward that same end, but Johnson has added something more, a surprising discussion of physique and gender identifications that reveals his unusual beliefs on these subjects:

LOOKING INTO THE FUTURE

There will be a great change in the physiques that will win Mr. America and other types of contests in the future. Before too long the prize winning physiques will exhibit more masculinity and will have less feminine characteristics. The physique of the future will have broader shoulders and a trimmer waist. There will be less development on pectoral and thigh development and more stress on the shoulders and deltoids and calves. The future bodybuilder will put less emphasis on size and bulk and will build his physique from an aesthetic point of view.

The future bodybuilder will be completely male and he will be healthy because his body will be built without any force or strain, using scientific methods which feature balancing the body chemistry.

The Mr. America physique of today has to be posed in order to look good. So does a woman have to pose to look good. A male physique should look good at any angle without any posing whatsoever. . . .

When a balanced and male-type physique becomes a reality in the future, then bodybuilding will become one of the most popular of sports and will be practiced and followed by millions of people compared to the minor few now engaged in the field. . . . (3)

Here, Johnson reiterates his preference for physiques that do not depend on what he earlier called "hulk and bulk." Contemporary professional bodybuilding competitors sported such massive physiques. Instead, the body of the kouros is the prototype for his remarks—a boyishly athletic body that does not appear excessively developed. "Hulk-and-bulk" winners of the Mr. America title during this period included Bill Pearl in 1953, Dick DuBois in 1954, and Steve Klisanin in 1955. By later steroid-era standards, these men do not seem muscle bound or inflated. Even so, in contrast, Bishop's physique appears sparer, more lean than large. Perhaps the ultimate comparison, however, could be drawn between Bishop and 1947 Mr. America winner, Steve Reeves.

In later years, some would recall Bishop as a trimmed-down version of Reeves; Bishop himself would even reveal in an interview that he had looked up to Reeves and strived to develop a body like his (*Vim*, June 1956, 33). Yet the two men had physiques that differed noticeably. Reeves's was huge by 1950s standards.

In lauding Bishop's body to the detriment of more traditional strongman physiques, Johnson was obviously advancing his own concepts of what looked "good." Yet by effeminizing the more developed bodybuilders' physiques, Johnson was insinuating views that were counterintuitive to some of the readership's understanding of masculinity at this time: Big muscles had constituted masculinity for decades, if not centuries; indeed, overly developed, muscular women would have been regarded at the time as inappropriately masculine. Here, however, Johnson seems to be saying that the construct of femininity was so blatantly a construct that it could be depicted as "natural" only through photographic trickery and that the majority of

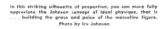

In this striking silhouette of proportion, you can more fully appreciate the Johnson concept of ideal physique, that is . . . building the grace and poise of the masculine figure.
Photo by Irv Johnson

Figure 8.5. From left: Bishop in silhouette (*TM*, June 1954); Steve Reeves by Spartan of Hollywood.

male bodybuilders reflected a machismo, based on their massiveness and gross enlargement, that was also an all-too-obvious construct.[2]

One might argue that Johnson was anticipating the health boom that began in the 1980s, when millions of Americans would join gyms, take supplements, and strive for lean rather than immense bodies. Nonetheless, these remarks reveal his underlying notions of gender. Despite his assertions that someday "bodybuilding . . . will be practiced and followed by millions of people compared to the minor few now engaged in the field," he is clearly not including women in "people," for the proper gender for the bodybuilder is masculine: "Only when a balanced and male-type physique becomes a reality in the future, then bodybuilding . . . will be practiced and followed by millions of people." In other words, the female body and the basis for femininity are artificial—as artificial as altering the body through grueling exercise and the resultant ostentatious development of muscularity; the only authentic body is that of the young male.

The editorial that appeared the following month, August 1955, was an evident repudiation of Johnson's tenure at TM:

> TOMORROW'S MAN has grown up—yes, it is now a magazine mature enough to recognize that Bodybuilding and Good Health are not secrets confined to any one person or any one publication.
>
> . . . .
>
> Because we recognize the tremendous scope of bodybuilding, TOMORROW'S MAN will henceforth no longer devote itself exclusively to any one method or system, even though the IRVIN JOHNSON System, which has been thoroughly described in this magazine heretofore, has well proven its value and importance to the cause of the bodybuilder.
>
> . . . .

Signed by the new editor-in-chief, Paul Lange, this editorial (the only one Lange seems to have contributed) hints at some of the conflicts that may have arisen during the publication's transition from Chicago to New York. Perhaps the most informative aspect of the change comes in the first paragraph with the use of "grown up" and "mature." Not only had TM become a magazine devoted to selling Johnson's "System," it had followed Johnson's aesthetics and peculiar values. No longer, Lange implies, would "tomorrow's man" exclude the vast majority of American bodybuilders, who were trying to gain mass. No longer would these muscle-bound young men, as opposed

to growing boys, be regarded as phony males whose claims to masculinity would be questioned. The kouros might receive some attention in the
magazine, but the real heroes were the more developed adult males, such as
Seymour Koenig, whose photo by Lon graces the cover, and Keith Stephan,
Bob McCune, Tom Sansone, and Gene Meyer, just to name a few of those
big musclemen who appeared in Lange's first issue.

And to remind readers of what real masculinity was all about, *TM*
included a picture of busty English film star, Diana Dors. Oddly enough, the
bikini-clad, blonde bombshell, with an extremely curvaceous figure, appears
on the first page of an article about vitamin E—"The VirilE Vitamin." "The
United Press," the photo's blurb announces, "certainly captioned this photo
well when they titled it 'Blonde Shocker,' She is Diana Dors, lovely—and
may we add, virile—British actress" (7). Real, zaftig women, this caption
implies, are as masculine as massive bodybuilders.

Johnson may have been in part responsible for connecting Bishop with
photographers Cliff Oettinger and Douglas Julef (aka Douglas of Detroit),
both of whom presented the model as an object of desire. Although their
pictures of Bishop, which were published in the magazines, were considerably less erotic, the shots both photographers sold privately (which I discuss
later in this chapter) amply demonstrate how they perceived him. Johnson
too, with his obsession for Bishop's body, seemed to present and describe
his subject as an appropriate object of attraction.

Johnson would sell his gym in 1958 to photographer Chuck Renslow,
who would make it a health club well known to gay Chicagoans. By 1960,
Johnson had moved to the West Coast, settling in Los Angeles under a
different name. He began again selling vitamins and supplements, this time
to Hollywood stars and California bodybuilders,[3] whom he began to train
privately. By this point, Bishop too had moved on. No longer the property
of any single editor or photographer, he had become, beginning in December 1954, a top model who, like Richard Harrison, would pose for different
photographers and at the same time sell his own photos directly to his fans.

Glenn Bishop: Free Agent and Entrepreneur

Between December 1954 and October 1959, Glenn Bishop reigned as the
most popular physique model. His departure from *Tomorrow's Man* heralded
a plethora of appearances in a variety of magazines, not only physique publications but also some of the more accepted physical culture monthlies
marketed to aspiring bodybuilders.

His first appearance in *Vim* (December 1954) not only captured the
cover but offered many beach shots of Bishop, all credited to "Michael of

Detroit." Who exactly Michael of Detroit was remains unclear. He is not listed among the photographers who contributed to the issue (38). Because the only photos attributed to "Michael of Detroit" are of Bishop and because these were all published soon after his apparent separation from Johnson and only in *Vim*, some have speculated that these photos are actually by Johnson; indeed, they may be related to his beach shot of Bishop printed in *TM* in June 1954 (33). Although it is also possible that Oettinger took these pictures, there seems no reason why *Vim* would change his name; however, *Vim* had a very good reason to change Johnson's name. Having been scorned by the magazine he had founded and ridiculed for his odd views and hard sell, Irv Johnson would not have been a welcome name in this former rival publication. *Vim* implied as much by declaring, in one of its captions of Bishop's photos, "Glenn is not the product of any particular school of weight training or any program of food supplementation" (29). This contradiction of Johnson's frequent assertions is clearly intentional.

In January 1955 *Vim* carried another photo of Bishop, also attributed to "Michael." Once again, no mention of this photographer appeared in its credits list. The same month, *Body Beautiful* printed a spread of pictures of Bishop taken (probably in summer 1954) by physique model and photographer Bob Delmonteque (who would later photograph and appear in photos with Richard Harrison).[4] According to rumor, Delmonteque had paid Bishop the unheard of fee of five hundred dollars for a day of modeling; Bishop appeared in the nude, although of course none of the shots in *Body Beautiful* displayed his private parts. The pictures were captioned with quotes from Walt Whitman's poetry and followed by an ad by Delmonteque for additional Bishop photos. At this time, Delmonteque had settled in Detroit and in the same ad requested, "Any bodybuilders in the vicinity of Detroit who wish to be exploited in picture stories in the Weider Publications [of which *Body Beautiful* was one], call the Delmonteque Studios" (48). The choice of words is interesting.

In spite of *Vim*'s claims earlier about Bishop not being the "product of any particular school of weight training or any program of food supplementation," Bishop (along with Alan) appeared on the cover of the Weiders's physical culture magazine *Muscle Builder* in February 1955, and allegedly contributed an article ("I Gained 54 Pounds of Muscle") in the first person:

> My Dad signed the freight bill and the truck man dumped the big cardboard boxes and the long wrapped bar onto our back yard. I watched him impatiently, my fingers itching to get the packages open. "Well . . . it's here at last," I told myself, thinking over the ten days I'd had to wait, days that had appeared

endless after I'd finally persuaded Dad to buy me a Weider 225 pound gym set and he'd sent away for it. (10)

Although "Bishop" denies that at 13 he was a classic 95-pound weakling (weighing in instead at 127 pounds), he does claim a certain ineptness and lack of athletic skill:

> Put me in a ball game and I'd strike out if I was batting. . . . Put me on the football field and I'd fumble every pass. . . . But I'd watch the other lads with envy . . . watch them score touchdowns and home runs . . . have them out-speed and out-distance me in swimming meets just because I was all fingers and thumbs, and had two left feet as the saying goes. (43)

The cure for all this, the narrative predictably explains, was the purchase of Weider weights and the use of the Weider Bodybuilding System, including Weider Food Concentrates and Supplements (44). Like most of the articles in *Muscle Builder*, the one ascribed to Bishop ends up as an endorsement of the publisher's methods and products.

This article was accompanied by beach and exercise photos of Bishop, which were credited to Delmonteque. It also included one of him with a young woman about his age; "Glenn and the girlfriend," the caption disclosed, "enjoy a sunbathing session on the beach. Popularity and appeal come to all fellows who exercise with weights" (11). The appearance of females in male bodybuilder photos not only demonstrated the caption's moral but also reminded readers that real males, whether they were attractive to other males or not, were heterosexual.

In the same month, another physical culture magazine, Bob Hoffman's *Strength and Health*, published by the makers of York Barbells, a major competitor of Weider's business, featured Bishop on the cover and offered two Oettinger beach photos and a one-column article. Although the article refrains from mentioning York Barbells and other products, it does indicate that Bishop played on his high school football team and was captain of the gymnastics team for two years. It further lists the competitions in which Bishop had participated: the 1952 Mr. West Michigan contest, in which he placed third; the 1953 National Mr. High School competition, in which (as noted earlier) he placed second; and the 1953 Most Ideal High School Physique competition, in which he placed second. (In August 1953, one of Oettinger's photos of the 1953 Mr. High School contest [another of which had appeared in *Tomorrow's Man*] appeared in *Strength and Health* [7].) One key bit of information missing from the *Muscle Builder* article about why

Glenn started working out was revealed here: "Glenn . . . began exercise to strengthen his abdominal muscles after an operation for hernia" (February 1955, 31).[5]

In addition to *Vim*, *Muscle Builder*, and *Strength and Health*, Bishop's photo also appeared on the covers of *Adonis* (February 1955) and again on *Muscle Builder* (April 1955), while his photos appeared again in *Vim* in April 1955 (with another photo by "Michael" and a doctored nude photo in the pose of the discus thrower on the back cover photo by Douglas of Detroit,[6] as noted, an actual photographer); in *Adonis* in June (photographed by Delmonteque); and in *Physique Pictorial*'s summer issue, in which Bishop is pictured with Alan; Mizer lists them both (at the same address) as contacts for additional photos. This appears to be the first time that the Bishop–Alan collaboration is mentioned (although Alan had already advertised his own photos in *TM* under his own name).

Bishop continued to be featured throughout 1955, with additional photos in *Adonis* (June, August, and October), *Muscle Builder* (June and July), *Man's World* (August and then front cover for November), *Vim* (November), and finally, as noted earlier, with Alan in *Tomorrow's Man*. The February 1956 issue of *Vim* ran an Oettinger photo of Glenn in a swimsuit with a caption that mentioned in passing that Bishop had married:

> Unfortunately, the Bishop name and fame are sometimes "borrowed" by one barbell promoter or another and used without Bishop's consent or knowledge. The most flagrant case in point is the recent of a publication of a story titled "I Was Ashamed Of My Skinny Sweetheart" purportedly written by "Glenn's wife, Marlene." (26–27)

Although I have been unable to locate the story mentioned, its title suggests that it had been published in one of the Weider organization's magazines; *Muscle Builder* had at the time a regular feature called "They Were All Weaklings," which consisted of letters supposedly sent in by Weider pupils who had made enormous gains. Moreover, the reference to some "barbell promoter" seems to point to Weider and the company's self-promotions, rather than to York. (By this time, Johnson was no longer a major player in the physique world.)

In March 1956, *Body Beautiful* handled the matrimonial news far less casually, printing a photo of Glenn and Marlene and reprinting the sunbathing beach duo that had originally appeared in *Muscle Builder*, although now the photo (along with the spread itself) was attributed to Oettinger, not Delmonteque. Jokingly the article, entitled "Bridal Path," referred to Marlene as "Glenn's squaw" and coyly added,

And so, gentle reader, love, as it does to all men, came to Glenn Bishop, and we at BODY BEAUTIFUL and ADONIS extend to the Bishops our warmest good wishes for a lifetime of connubial bliss. May all their pains be champagnes and may all their ails be bottled.

The Broken Hearts chapter of the GLENN BISHOP FAN CLUB will sponsor a mass drowning at Fire Island on New Year's Eve. All interested parties are invited to attend. (54, 58)

This last reference, understandable to virtually every male homosexual on the East Coast, seems a clear indication of who the magazine's readers were and how they may have felt about Bishop's nuptials. "Fire Island," by the mid-1950s, was a name that virtually screamed "homosexual" to people who identified themselves as homosexual. Its use is a telling sign that *Adonis* and *Body Beautiful* (which often reprinted each other's photos) were more blatantly gay than *Physique Pictorial*.[7] The text of this photo spread reiterates the idea that Bishop had been a sex object for the magazine's gay male readers; if his marriage signaled his heterosexuality, it only made him more attractive to gay readers who wanted real (non-gay) men.

In June 1956, *Vim* printed an interview with Bishop, along (of course) with photos (that were not credited). "The True Glenn Bishop Story," by Glenn Bishop followed a question–answer format, and the headlines on the second page proclaimed, "So much hooey has been written about this popular American bodybuilder that we decided to get the real story from the man who knows . . . Glenn himself" (7). As it had done earlier, *Vim* debunked certain allegations made about Bishop:

The claims made by the publisher of a certain body building system about you being one of his "pupils" are untrue. Is this correct, Glenn?

Yes, that is correct. Until now I have never written anything for any of the bodybuilding magazines. . . . Also an article which appeared in a winter issue of a bodybuilding magazine was NOT written by my wife, Marlene. This story turned out to be a "pipe dream" of the editor which turned out to be a ridiculous story about me. I'm sure it must have been meant for advertising purposes because things like that don't happen in reality. (8)

In his response, Bishop not only reiterates the falsity of the "Marlene" letter, but also contradicts his own supposed authorship of the earlier *Muscle Builder* article. He later indicates that he and Marlene have recently had a daughter, which would suggest that the marriage announcements in *Vim* and *Body Beautiful* had been extremely belated.

The interview also mentions the distinctive swimsuits worn by Glenn in a number of his photos, which Bishop reveals were created by his mother

Glenn and Marlene at one of Michigan's lovely lakes

Figure 8.6. *Vim*'s tell-all interview: Top, Glenn and Marlene, from *Body Beautiful*, March 1955 (originally printed in *Muscle Builder*). Bottom left: Glenn with Marlene in bikini. Bottom right: the "Glenn Bishop Bikini" first advertised in this issue of *Vim* (June 1956).

and were now on sale to the public (44); in fact there is an ad for these bikinis in the back pages of the same issue (46).

Two months earlier, *Vim* had carried an ad for pictures of Bishop and Alan together as well as separately, directing customers to send for catalogs at Michigan Models (in Grand Haven, Michigan) which became the new name for the Bishop, Alan, and Alan-Bishop studios (April 1956, 42). The interview in the June issue does not identify the photographer of the accompanying photos. They may have been taken and submitted by Oettinger or they may have been Oettinger photos now sold by Michigan Models or photos taken by Alan—or they may have been a mix of all three. There is an Alan-Bishop ad for photos, in addition to the one for the bikinis, and both carry the name and address of Michigan Models. During its last two years, the Alan-Bishop partnership advertised in *Muscle Builder* and *Muscle Power*.

Sometime during 1956, Bob Delmonteque published a one-time magazine called *Artistry in Physique Photography* (although his name was misspelled as "Delmontique"). He featured several photos of Bishop, one of them taken by Douglas of Detroit and previously featured on the back cover of *Vim* for April 1955. Unlike Mizer, Douglas specialized in nudes although the photos he submitted to the physique magazines were always adjusted for publication; indeed, the photo of Bishop as the discus thrower had been doctored so *Vim* readers would not view the young man's privates.

From this point on until October 1959, various photographs of Bishop that were carried in physique magazines and others were credited to Delmonteque, Oettinger, or Michigan Models (sometimes with Alan listed as the photographer). However, the last advertisement for Michigan Models came in July 1957 (*Muscle Builder* 56). Following this, Bishop and Alan continued to share the same post office box, but Bishop's ads were subsequently addressed to Bishop himself, who by September of that year posted a new box number in Grand Haven (*Muscle Sculpture* 33). Michigan Models (or perhaps Alan) continued to sell photos of Bishop, as well as swimsuits, up until November, when Alan launched his own swimsuit, the "Denak" (34).

Whatever had occurred, Alan seems to have dropped entirely from the business—both from Bishop's and his own—by 1958, by which time Bishop was always pictured alone and interested readers were directed to his own post office box in Grand Haven. Their final duo photo appearance (the one on the railway bridge taken years before) appeared in *Popular Man* in January 1958 (12). Alan's photos (all from years earlier) are featured in an article attributed to Joe Weider in *Muscle Builder* for June 1961 (18–19), an issue that also carried photos of Bishop, including a recent one from a series Bishop was about to launch, taken in Saugatuck, "Michigan's Fire Island" (25). (Alan's photo from 1961, with a blender, was reprinted in *Muscle Builder*, April 1962, 29.) Alan's last appearance appears to come nearly eight years later, in 1970, when the German homophile journal, *Der Weg*, reprinted an old arm wrestling photo (c. 1953 and presumably by Johnson) in which Bishop seems on the verge of kissing Alan's clasped hand (16).

Michigan Models, whose last credited photo appeared in *Popular Man* in October 1959 (21), had also for a time introduced other bodybuilders, notably Grand Haven native Rudy Edwards; a Latvian friend, Helmuts Mednis; Junior Mr. Michigan Doug Pedon; 14-year-old Dave Wright; and the formerly "pigeon-breasted" teenaged cousin of Richard Alan, Bob Alan. There is a shot of Bishop doing "donkey calf raises" with Mednis on his back, in *Muscle Builder*, July 1961 (16); this was probably taken five years earlier. These pictures were all that remained of Michigan Models.

Otherwise, Bishop would be portrayed singly. His last family appearance would be in *Vim*, in December 1957, when he is pictured with Marlene on his shoulders while their daughter is seated on Marlene's shoulders (3). The following July, when *Grecian Guild Pictorial* named Bishop their "Grecian of the Month," the article would identify the child as Christine Marie (9). Yet if Marlene was now literally out of the pictures, she was not figuratively "out of the picture." She apparently took many of the photos Bishop subsequently sold and handled the mail orders for photos and swimwear. Glenn had graduated from the University of Michigan, and by fall 1957, the family had moved to Chicago, where he was attending chiropractic school.

Glenn Goes Solo

In January 1958 Bishop announced in an ad in *Vim* two new catalogs, "57-A and 57-B," with "[e]ach picture superbly posed against the beautiful Michigan outdoors." Each catalog went for one dollar each, the same price as the "8 × 10 silk photos" (44). As in the past, the ad referred to a catalog from which a print could be ordered. Here, however, there was no nudity either suggested or provided. The photo arrived neatly inscribed with a personal message from the model.

The following spring, *Physique Pictorial* included one of the 57-B shots, along with a blurb that indicated that Glenn's "silk photos" were now going for $1.50 "autographed to your specifications, $2." (5). A number of other magazines followed suit over the next year, instructing readers interested in Bishop photos to write directly to Glenn (and clearly not to Michigan Models). Incidentally, "57-A" and "57-B" are so numbered to correspond to the year the photos were taken, a numbering convention Bishop would maintain until he stopped issuing catalogs. He also offered catalogs numbered "1" and "2," which appear to be compilations of photos taken by others (pos-

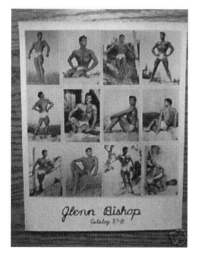

Figure 8.7. Top: An ad in *Vim*. Bottom left: a catalog sheet. Bottom right: an autographed photo of Glenn Bishop.

sibly Oettinger, Alan, and even Delmonteque, who would continue selling Bishop's photos into the 1960s), which later ads indicate are from 1955.

Despite Bishop's denials (in *Vim*) that he followed any established methods, equipment, or food supplements, he appeared in a new Weider publication, *Young Physique* (which incorporated Weider's now-defunct *Adonis* and *Body Beautiful*), several times between summer 1958 and the end of 1959. Another first-person narrative featuring Weider products and to a great extent repeating (verbatim) the February 1955 *Muscle Builder* story, appeared in Volume 1, Number 1 (August 1958, 22–26, 38, 40, 43). He was interviewed (again, making several Weider endorsements) in June 1959, and in December 1959, *YP* presented a spread of (nude but discreet) Bishop photos that were taken in summer 1958 (10–13, 40, 42), for which there is a back-page ad announcing the newest catalog (40).

Figure 8.8. Nude photos and ad, *YP*, December 1959 from the 1958 catalog.

A 1959 catalog, entitled "Down on the Farm," featuring Bishop in blue jeans, performing various agrarian tasks, was first announced in *YP* in April 1960, and photos from it were reprinted in *YP* in June of that year. (The blurb in this spread also noted that Dr. Bishop had recently been graduated from chiropractic school.) In October 1960, Glenn was featured on the back cover with a number of other popular bodybuilders, color posters of whom were now available from *Young Physique*.

About a year later, Weider launched *Demi-Gods*, another large-sized, glossy photo magazine like *YP*, and Bishop appeared on the front cover of the second issue. The back pages sported an ad for Bishop's newest (1960)

Figure 8.9. Top: "Down on the Farm," ad in *YP* April 1960. Bottom left: from a spread in *YP*, June 1960. Bottom right: from *Muscles à Go-go*, November–December 1966.

catalog, which as mentioned earlier, was shot on "Michigan's Fire Island" (*Demi-Gods*, May 1961, 44). The very same issue sports an ad for two short Bishop color films produced by *YP*, one entitled "Pose Please," and another (presumably based on the 1959 catalog) "Down on the Farm" (48). I have had no luck in tracing the latter, but the former has appeared on the Internet. It is a nearly six-minute silent that looks as though it was shot in 8-mm color and depicts Bishop posing on the Grand Haven or perhaps Saugatuck beach, lifting weights, tumbling, and running in an out of the water, all the

Figure 8.10. Top: Initial ad for Saugatuck "Fire Island" catalog 60, *Demi-Gods*, May 1961. Bottom: photos from catalog 60 in *Muscle Builder*, June 1961; *Demi-Gods*, July 1961, and *YP* annual 1962.

while clad in one of his "Glenn Bishop Bikinis." The same month, *Muscle Builder* featured a photo of Bishop from his Saugatuck "Fire Island" catalog, as well as a time-lapse tumbling spread; a month later, *YP* published three from the same set (June 1961 8–10).

Bishop's pictures went on appearing in Weider and also other publications through the early 1960s. In 1962, *Young Physique*'s 1962 annual issue showed Glenn in a white tennis sweater behind the wheel of an early 1950s Jaguar roadster drop-head convertible and included as well a full-color centerfold and also a picture from the "Fire Island" set. In March 1962, *Demi-Gods* compared a now-bearded Bishop with film strongman Steve Reeves, who wore a beard in many of his European films; like Harrison, Reeves had been encouraged to lose his clean-shaven, boyish looks in favor of a more mature, manly face. The following October, *YP* featured older beach photos of Bishop, lamenting that the editors had commissioned a new set of color sunbathing pictures but that Glenn had been unable to deliver because he had accidentally shot himself—in the behind—while cleaning his gun (49). The last photo shown was of Bishop in a long sweatshirt on the beach, again with a beard. In the December 1962 issue of *Demi-Gods*, which showed on its cover a painting of Glenn by George Quaintance, whose work had appeared in the early issues of Mizer's *Physique Pictorial*, there was printed an ad for a new catalog, "The Bearded Bishop" (78). The comparison made in the *Demi-Gods* spread is between Bishop and Steve Reeves, who had also grown a beard (like Richard Harrison) to reemphasize his masculinity in Italian gladiator epics. Although the older man is invoked to compare the two models, the contrast remains significant: Bishop is clearly the smaller, more compact version of Reeves's substantial display of muscle. He is moreover pictured as the more approachable and hence the more available of the two. In one of the *Demi-Gods* photos, he has a hand on his hip; in another, published in *Young Physique*, he has both hands on hips. Yet in neither of these pictures does Bishop appear "effeminate." Again, his relative youth and his less-than-bulky build combine to make him the more appropriate object of desire for a gay male audience,

In June 1962, *YP* included an advertisement for new Bishop swimsuits, just in time for the summer season, all in "boxer style" (71). They ranged from four to six dollars, but the response probably was not very strong, for there was only one more ad published for this series, in *YP* for the following August (71). Subsequently, ads for his bikinis returned, and then were discontinued, so that only ads for his photos remained.

Bishop's final advertisement, featuring one of the Saugatuck pictures, appeared in another Weider magazine, *Muscleboy*, in its April–May 1966 issue, and the May–June issue of *Young Physique*, with which Bishop had, in part, become identified, printed a letter in the letters-to-the editors column,

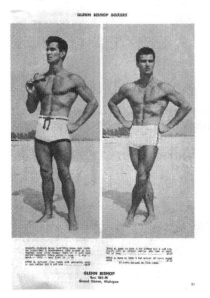

Figure 8.11. Bishop boxers versus bikinis: Ad for new swimsuit line and *YP* cover, March–April 1964.

which was called "Loved This . . . Hated That," asking about why Glenn had not appeared in the *YP* for so long:

A BISHOP ADIEU

Dear Editors: Why is it that you no longer show any pictures of my favorite of favorites, Glenn Bishop? After an appearance on the July [1965] *Muscleboy* cover that's the last I've seen of this unqualified muscleman [*sic*]. How about more Bishop . . . and why have you taken his advertisement out of your magazines? Seems a shame you can't even give us an ad picture of Glenn.

Doris Potts
Pittsburgh, Pennsylvania

We're sorry too, Doris, but a recent letter from Glenn tells us and you why. Says Glenn, "I'd like to thank you all for your splendid coverage of the Bishop 'bod' through the years . . . but I have decided to abdicate in favor of my handsome son, Jonathan Glenn (now four) and to discontinue the sale of my pictures. I still keep in the very same shape I have always had and I wouldn't let a single day go by without vigorous exercise . . . but I don't have time for posing any longer, and your library should tingle with new photos of new young bodybuilders . . . and so at thirty I'll sign off and wish you and all my fans the best of good luck." And so ends a fabulous era . . . will we ever see another to take his place? (6)

The YP editors reprinted two earlier photos of Glenn as an appeasement to Doris and others. So ended Bishop's affiliation with the Weider organization.

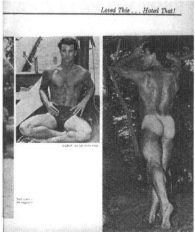

Figure 8.12. From left: Glenn's last Weider cover, last Weider ad, and last Weider appearance.

Yet with so many catalogs and photographs in circulation, Bishop's image continued to appear in physique and other magazines. In 1966, a magazine and catalog for "gay products" called *Vagabond* showed on its cover a well-known Delmonteque shot that had been reprinted for years; however, in this version, the print was not cropped as usual, and the model's pubic hair was exposed, a practice that had been outlawed during the early years of the posing strap era. In issue 9 of the nude magazine, *Butch* in 1967, the same photo with no cropping was featured, with Bishop completely exposed.

There were, it turned out, a great many naked, full-frontal shots of Bishop from early on. Delmonteque and others had sold them, just as photographers had sold nudes in the 1930s, through catalogs and in person. Perhaps the reason Bishop had been able to sell photos by other photographers was that the real money had come from the more revealing pictures, which the original photographers retained and sold. Yet by the time his privates had been revealed, Bishop was out of the business. He was working as a chiropractor, raising two children with his wife, and living what he may have thought of as a private life, back in Grand Haven, Michigan.

Nonetheless, his photos and his past were not so easily erased.

Looking Backward

A little less than a year after *Young Physique* had announced Glenn Bishop's retirement from modeling, a curious letter appeared in the gay magazine, *Drum*, which had begun printing nude shots in 1965 but continued to shift

Figure 8.13. Delmonteque's shot in *Body Beautiful*, January 1955; as seen in *Vagabond*, 1966 and *Butch*, 1967.

between nudes and posing-strap photos for several years. Unlike *Young Physique*, which was backed by the Weider organization, *Drum* was a small-time Philadelphia operation that used a typewriter typeface, showed photos in black and white only, and focused on gay history and culture rather than bodybuilding exercises. "Drum," read the blurb at the top of its table of contents page, "is published monthly by male homosexuals for the entertainment and information of other male homosexuals" (March 1967, 5). Despite this particular issue's avoidance of full-frontal photography, *Drum* was blatant about its editors' and readers' sexual orientation. The letter to *Drum* read as follows:

> Your purpose and magazine is [sic] of the lowest class and should be taken out of circulation. This country has enough trouble without crack-pots like yourself [sic] trying to promote abnormal sex ideas. Can't you find something more worthwhile to do in your life than cater to queers?
>
> Copies of your magazine are being sent to our Senator in Washington with my request that he does something about your publication.
>
> —Glenn Bishop, Grand Haven, Michigan.

The editors pointed out the irony in this missive:

> *The above letter is remarkable only in that the writer is well known to physique magazine fanciers. For those who—not unlike the now Dr. (of chiropractic) Bishop—have short memories, here is the all-time-great physique star on a The Young Physique cover.—Ed.* (40)

They added a tiny black-and-white reproduction of the YP March–April 1964 cover, with Glenn in a Bishop Bikini and a caption reading, "The 'More Worthwhile' Bishop" (40). In the following issue, *Drum*'s editors admitted that "*Glenn Bishop's letter prompted the heaviest volume of mail* Drum *has received on anyone* [sic] *subject.*" They even reprinted several letters from gay readers who found his remarks amazingly (and comically) hypocritical (August 1967, 37). Although the reaction seemed to die down, the magazine included a larger photo of Bishop (again in a bikini) in the following issue (September 1967, 9).

There is little in the previous issues of *Drum* that are available to me to explain this sudden outburst, no articles about Bishop or photos, nude or otherwise. What could have occasioned this letter? Surely Bishop must have been cognizant early on that many, if not most (if not virtually all)

Figure 8.14. Bishop's letter to *Drum* (March 1967) and *Drum*'s reprint of a kinder, gentler Bishop (September 1967).

of the men who purchased his photos, as well as his swimsuits, must have been homosexual. Bishop's own marketing of his pictures demonstrates some awareness that he was selling to gay males.

For example, the 1960 catalog, which equated Saugatuck with Fire Island (which may well have been a valid comparison at the time), certainly invites gay interest. Bishop, if he read the copy to the articles printed about him, would have come across the Fire Island reference from the 1956 *Adonis* article about his broken-hearted fans committing suicide there after their learning of his marriage. More recently, in May 1963, *YP* had run photos of Bishop on a letters-to-the editors page ("Loved This . . . Hated That") that carried a query about gay resorts, mentioning by name Acapulco and Fire Island (5). It is difficult to believe that Bishop was ignorant about what the phrase signified, not only geographically but also in terms of sexuality.

Indeed, Weider's earlier physique publications, *Adonis* and *Body Beautiful*, which had been subsumed by *Young Physique*, certainly did very little to cover up their homosexual connections. Weider, in addition to *YP*, also published the large-sized glossies *Demi-Gods* and *Muscleboy*, which were obviously intended not for bodybuilders but for men who liked to look at bodybuilders. Why did Bishop allow himself to appear in Weider's magazines, along with his many ads, and yet at around the same time protest *Drum* magazine, which after all actually came out and told its readers it was a gay publication?

Bishop's relationship with the Weider organization was clearly fraught with conflict. Although he advertised, toward the end exclusively, in Weider publications and continued to allow them to print photos of himself and articles about him (some supposedly written by him), all of them sales pitches for Weider products, he simultaneously seemed to deny his affiliation to Weider or to any other bodybuilding and nutrition system. Bishop may have felt that he did not need any external help with his training regimen, but he obviously believed that he needed Weider in some way. He let *Young Physique* sell his posters and movies in the early 1960s and apparently chose Weider's *YP* to announce his farewell to modeling.

A review of Bishop's history as a model suggests that throughout his career before the lens, Glenn had associated himself with others who, to some degree, had taken care of selling his image. After all, before Weider, he had depended on Richard Alan, and before that on Irv Johnson, Bob Delmonteque, and Cliff Oettinger, who had advertised their photos of him and even let him use some of their pictures as his own.[8] There had always been someone (for a while his wife served as his photographer and mail-order manager) to assist Bishop in his self-promoting enterprise. In the late 1950s and well into the 1960s, the Weider brothers became the top-selling publishers of physique and physical culture magazines, so was it any wonder that Bishop would choose, despite any personal differences, to work with them?

By the early 1970s, censorship laws and cultural attitudes had changed substantially. Only now were the more explicit nude photos taken during the early 1950s available for publication. Although Delmonteque's and Oettinger's had been sold privately for years, their circulation had been limited. Once they emerged, however, in printed form, it became clear that the five hundred dollars Bishop had received from Delmonteque for his modeling in 1954 had been well spent; not only were these beach pictures spectacular, but they brought Delmonteque money for more than a decade. (Like Bishop, Delmonteque left the modeling and photography business in the 1960s.) Moreover, it was eventually clear that Delmonteque's were not the only nudes of Bishop taken between 1952 and 1955.

In fact, Oettinger too had taken at least two series of naked photos of Bishop at least a year (or possibly two years) before Delmonteque. True, a number of outdoor photos were taken in 1954 at Saugatuck—some of them were difficult if not impossible to distinguish from Delmonteque's—but there were also others that evidently came from the previous summer when Glenn had been a lifeguard. And in addition to these beach shots, there were others still that seemed to be taken indoors and at the same period during which Johnson had taken the photos of Bishop that had appeared in the first spread in *Tomorrow's Man*, back in June 1953. These early Oettinger pictures may have been taken in the winter or the beginning of spring 1953 or perhaps even late in 1952. Although many believe that Oettinger first snapped Bishop at the 1953 Mr. High School competition (his photos of this contest appeared in *TM* in July 1953 and in *Strength and Health* in August 1953), it is possible that these "indoor" Oettinger shots were taken earlier.

The reason I suggest this is that in the past ten years, a large number of Oettinger's nudes of Bishop have been advertised on eBay. The seller, who is named Lloyd Curry but calls himself (in the style of 1950s physique photographers), "Lloyds of Hollywood" or "L.A. Curry," has given all sorts of dates to some of Bishop's nudes by Oettinger, including at one point 1948 and 1949 (at which time Glenn would have been 11 and 12), but more recently, has settled on 1952 for some of the naked color photos he has been selling. I did attempt to communicate with this seller regarding Oettinger's work, but he remained elusive, and after I actually telephoned Oettinger, who was living in Los Angeles and listed in the L.A. directory, Mr. Curry emailed me a threat, indicating that he owned all the rights to Oettinger's photos and that if I tried to contact Oettinger again, Mr. Curry would go to his local police station and file a restraining order against me. This reaction, which I found oddly inappropriate, suggested to me that Curry, whom Oettinger told me was writing a book about him, was guarding his subject a little too carefully.

Whether these particular pictures were taken in 1952 or 1953, Bishop would have been 16 years old. Even if Mr. Curry (who subsequently launched a website called "The Oettinger Collection" in addition to his online ads) did not own these negatives and images, I would not have printed the ones to which I am about to refer because they depict pornographic poses of someone who is still alive and who would have been considered a minor when the photos were taken. True, the latter consideration would not have prevented me from including some of the racier pictures by von Gloeden, but these were nearly a century old and, at least in modern terms, do not necessarily seem extremely pornographic.

The indoor nudes of Glenn Bishop by Oettinger clearly do: They depict him in a small bedroom or perhaps a motel room, at first in coat and tie, and then undressing; he is posed shirtless on a couch, looking seductively into the camera, and then in bed, first in his underwear, removing his sox, and then completely naked, exposing his privates and his anus. In all these pictures, the model's eyes are closed, as if he were asleep; in one case, his leg is raised at a ninety-degree angle, which makes the pretext of a sleeping model absurd. In one of the shots of Bishop still dressed, he is smiling before a darkened window, through which the naked limbs of trees can be seen. These are not summer photos.

Some of the shots taken by Douglas Julef (aka Douglas of Detroit), seem to present Bishop as a sexual object who, like Ingres's *Odalisque*, is pictured in exotic, Middle Eastern subjugation. In others Bishop is subordinated before two turbaned and robed adult males. Unlike Oettinger's photos, the model's private parts are hidden in Douglas's shots, but nonetheless their sexual implications at the time must have been quite clear.[9]

Such photographs demonstrate that the kind of pedophilic interest associated with the much earlier Sicilian images was obviously still alive. Oettinger's pictures implicate the subject in an unsettling way. If these images show what was caught on film, is it unimaginable what might have occurred when the camera was not clicking? It would seem that Delmonteque's peculiar word choice in an earlier ad, that "[a]ny bodybuilders in the vicinity of Detroit who wish to be exploited in picture stories in the Weider Publications, call the Delmonteque Studios" may not have been as strange as it first appeared.

Such speculation, although not definitive, must also bring us back to Irv Johnson, Bishop's supposed first mentor. After selling his gym in 1958 to Renslow, Johnson migrated to California. A devotee of bodybuilding and nutrition, he was also interested in the occult. According to one website, he changed his name to Rheo H. Blair because his numerologist advised him that his actual name contained the wrong number of letters and needed more Rs in order for his new business in Los Angeles to succeed (Forums on Bodybuilding.com). Apparently, although articles about "Blair" in the 1950s and 1960s occasionally referred to a girlfriend, he was gay, and as he grew older he became increasingly open about his sexuality. As a result his family became estranged, and after his death, in October 1983, they destroyed many of his private papers (Palmieri).

When I wrote to Blair's/Johnson's biographer, Charles Welling, about how it was possible for Bishop, who lived in Grand Haven, to have trained with Johnson in Chicago, he replied that some of the young men pictured in *Tomorrow's Man* actually moved in and lived with him for a time. He also noted,

> You may be interested to know that Rheo thought Glenn had the ultimate male physique. In fact, in Los Angeles, Rheo kept a large, oh about 18 by 24 inch foam mounted blow up of Glenn in the trunk of his Cadillac; a photo of him on the beach. He always marveled at the beauty of that picture when he opened the trunk. He had the same photo, blown up larger, in his living room. (January 2009)

As to whether or not Bishop had "lived with" Blair, I rather tend to doubt he did, for as I noted earlier, Bishop was supposedly a full-time high school student who was engaged in numerous other activities. Moreover, his summers, beginning in 1953, appear to have been spent as a lifeguard. But was it possible that he visited Johnson's gym and stayed with him in Chicago? Such visits were, given the photographic evidence, probable, even likely. Johnson's adulation of Bishop, so evident in the early issues of TM, obviously did not end with Johnson's departure from the magazine, the gym, and Chicago. One might construe that Johnson or rather Blair was infatuated with Glenn, as were so many men (and possibly someone named Doris Potts of Pittsburgh) who looked at his published pictures, sent for his catalogs, and ordered the large-sized photos especially signed by him.

Perhaps the most pointed piece of evidence about Bishop's career has emerged more recently, when the estate of a photograph collector was offered over the Internet. Over a period of months, complete nudes that had originally been attributed to Oettinger were offered as the work of Michigan Models. Moreover, another web source of vintage bodybuilding photos (BigKugels.com on eBay) displayed nudes that were not only said to have been shot by Richard Alan but actually to have come from Alan's private collection. In other words, Bishop had apparently posed for and sold frontal nudes of himself for several years. Bishop, then, had for years been ready and able to "cater to queers," as he put it in his letter to *Drum*. The only difference was that now, the queers did not have to pay Bishop for his naked photos but were free to view them in cheap and widely available homosexual publications.

There is no doubt that Glenn Bishop was a beautiful looking young man who had been an attractive teenage boy. Where this beauty led him is not exactly clear. In 1978, Bishop left Grand Haven and his marriage, and from what I can discern, went to Texas. Ultimately he drifted farther west and farther north, where, according to him, he could find the freedom (now vanishing in this country) that he was seeking and where people like me have continued to bother him. Whatever was done to Glenn Bishop, he does not seem to have managed to undo; whatever he did, he has preferred to behave as if it had never occurred.[10]

Like most of the young men featured in the postwar physique magazines, Bishop became the object of sexual interest for the largely (if not exclusively) gay male readership. What made him different was that he began with and retained for a very long time a boyishness that many other models gave up. Even with facial hair, he looked like a very young man trying to grow a beard, whereas others (such as Reeves and Harrison) looked older, more mature and manly. Bishop remained trimmer and smaller than many of his contemporaries, and to some extent this made him popular over a prolonged period. Yet by the time he was pushing 30, being a kouros was suddenly both not profitable and somehow rather shameful.

The masculine gender construct, as it was shaped by the war, underwent major revisions, most significantly lowering the age when a male could be viewed as masculine. Thus, a certain amount of boyishness and adolescent sexual ambiguity became important in performances and portrayals of a postwar masculinity. Glenn Bishop's images seemed to incorporate the same kind of anxiety about masculinity that other young men of the 1950s (like Brando and Dean) also reflected. His uneasiness at being portrayed as a sexual object clashed with his project of supporting himself by selling photos that relied on him being regarded as a sexual object. Given his history, it was probably a very difficult balance to maintain.

CHAPTER 9

Johnny, We Hardly Knew Ye

Male Sex, Sexuality, and Gender

In a previous chapter, I referred to one of Michael Bronski's comments in *Culture Clash* about how the male body was portrayed in the postwar physique magazines; however, I quoted only that part of his discussion that applied to Richard Harrison and to so many of the other models in these publications. Nonetheless, some of what he suggests is worth examining in light of the extremely popular model, John Tristram:

> In the 50s, the predominant stereotype of a gay man was the limp wristed swish. . . . Homosexual attraction to muscle magazines [i.e. physical culture magazines] like *Iron Man* and *Strength and Health* was partially the simple appeal of uncovered male bodies. But these publications were also appropriate sexual objects for gay men because they were clearly *unlike* the standard gay stereotype. When gay-oriented muscle [i.e., physique] magazines first appeared—*Vim* and *Physique Pictorial*—the images were slightly different. The men were muscular but they were also slightly effeminate; they had the slim waists and shoulders which were generally associated with the image of the queen, but they also sported huge arm, pectoral, and thigh muscles. (170–171)

This idea of the non-queeny queen, a muscular young man with a "slight" effeminacy that Bronski ascribes to some of the images of physique models, sounds contradictory. A search through the physique magazines from the early 1950s onward yields very few examples of such a subject.

Clearly Richard Harrison, Steve Reeves, Dick DuBois, and Keith Stephen, all familiar names in *Physique Pictorial*, *Vim*, and other physique magazines, did not in themselves appear "effeminate." Although their physiques may seem less massive and more chiseled than those of the models who began to appear in gay pornography a decade or more later, they all succeeded in performing masculinity even when posed in a way that may have compromised their machismo. At such moments they, or at least their images, look "camp," excessive, overdone, almost silly. But were they slightly effeminate?

Perhaps Bronski is referring to the muscular teenagers, like Glenn Bishop, who from time to time turned up in various physique publications. Yet, while these adolescents certainly embodied youth, they rarely if ever seemed effeminate. Perhaps a viewer could read into their photos the sexual ambiguity of the juvenile or the transitional, experimental nature of adolescent masculinity. Yet Bishop's physique was consistently described as masculine, especially by Irv Johnson (whom we now know was gay), who identified him as the personification of "Tomorrow's Man."

In actuality, the effeminacy Bronski mentions resides more with the photographers, with their strategies of composition, their direction of the subjects' poses, use of props, and more, than with the models themselves. This is evident through a progression of physique images of John Tristram, who made the transition from 1950s physique model to 1970s gay muscleman. Of the models whom I have researched, I know the least about Tristram, the British-born bodybuilder who began his modeling career as John Trenton in posing-strap magazines and ended up as a Mr. America contestant and one of the muscular, naked men of that major post-Stonewall pornography outlet, Colt Studio. In many ways, what remains of Tristram is typical of what remains of most physique models: a history comprised of unsubstantiated rumors and anecdotes with very few facts to support them.

Nonetheless, Tristram himself was hardly a typical physique model. In addition to being a leading contestant in a variety of big-name professional competitions, he was one of the few bodybuilders of his time who was apparently "out," that is, who admitted his homosexuality. Although a muscle-bound "hunk" in his own right, Tristram made his living in the uncharacteristically cerebral world of academia, as a professor of French, in which he had a master's degree. Yet the verifiable particulars of his life seem to be few. With Richard Harrison, I found extensive documentation and a few rumors. In spite of a mountain of gossip regarding Glenn Bishop, this sometimes-elusive star model seemed to have left a concrete trail. Yet Tristram's life appears to have faded into a past that cannot (or perhaps will not) recall him clearly.

One aspect of Harrison's career that I have been unable to verify, and therefore left out of my discussion of him, is the claim that he won the Mr. Apollo title. I have checked who came in first, second, and third during the period when he might have competed for this title in the United States and in Europe and have repeatedly tried to contact the Amateur

Athletic Union (AAU), which at the time sponsored the competition, but there is no evidence that he ever even entered these contests. In the case of Bishop, the claims are far more sensational, mostly concerning his sexuality. Chuck Renslow, for example, in an unpublished 1991 interview with *Outcome* magazine, asserts that Bishop "had a male lover, a sugar daddy, who sent him through chiropractic school." (The interview appears at http://models.badpuppy.com/archive/kris/krisof.htm.) Similarly, Hugh McCurley, in an online comment that appears on the "Tim in Vermont" website, writes that Bishop and Alan worked together as Michigan Models but that "Alan soon bailed out. Rumor has it he had a huge crush on Bishop." McCurley also claims that sometime after the end of their partnership, Bishop had ranted against homosexuals in a published interview:

> Bishop went on to form his own studio with another photographer with wife again always in tow. THEN . . . just when things were starting to go well for them, Bishop opened his big mouth, ripping into gays who were (in his words) destroying the picture business for fine, young, upstanding men like himself. Bernard McFadden [sic] of *Strength And* [sic] *Health* agreed with him and published the interview while ripping into "fags" himself. S&H's sales plummeted. Bishop's studio quickly went out of business.
>
> (What kind of "inspiration" did Bishop think his buyers were getting from pix of his cock? End of that career! Idiot!)

Again, I could find no substantiations of these claims. Moreover, I reckoned that MacFadden died in 1955, which meant that Bishop could have been no older than 18, which would have predated his marriage. For these reasons, I excluded such comments from my review of Bishop's career.

However, in the case of Tristram, in addition to relatively few facts, there are too many stories in circulation that cannot be proven and much incorrect information. For instance, the now-defunct Yahoo! Group, "John Tristram Fans," offered on its home page a short biography of the bodybuilder, claiming (among other things) that Tristram was born in 1935 in Gloucester, England, taught French at UCLA, and died in 1985 of a misuse of steroids; he is also credited with directing a documentary film, *The Quest of Jimmy Pike*. The same writer elsewhere on the site indicated that Tristram was the longtime lover of actor James Mason, and another writer declared that he was told by bodybuilding writer Gene Mozee that Tristram died in 1995 of AIDS at the age of 67 or 68.

Yet there are even more lurid claims: Hugh McCurley emailed me that Tristram was photographed in the nude by a photographer named George Price, and that even though these photos were never published, they somehow circulated, leading to Tristram's dismissal from his UCLA teaching job, which in turn made him "very bitter." Wayne Stanley, at AMG, emailed me the following:

> I knew a fellow who "claimed" that Tristam [*sic*] and he had a long-term sex scene, with [Tristram] as the Gladiator top and my friend as the Slave. This gladiator fantasy was a real turn-on for [Tristram]. [Tristram], who posed for many photographers in Britain and the United States, including Colt Studio, died of AIDS a few years ago after a long and arduous illness.

A far more disturbing entry on a Yahoo! Club website devoted to merchant seamen, alleged that Tristram was a pedophile:

> Now there's a name out of the past. John Tristram was a chicken hawk who worked the Santa Monica Pier (AKA Muscle Beach, which relocated to Venice Beach in 1959) area daily. Many a time he showed me the shortcut under the pier . . . until I was 14. Too much hair turnned [*sic*] him off. I am now 65. You do the math.

Having tried in various ways to authenticate some of the allegations made above, I find that there is not much that I can actually verify. Some of the rumors derive from 1950s sources, such as Bob Mizer's commentaries in *Physique Pictorial*, and thus have been in circulation since the beginning of Tristram's West Coast career; others have emerged since Tristram's death.

Here are some of the facts: California state coroner's records indicate that John Heber Tristram (mother's maiden name: Shu) was born January 23, 1933 and died in Los Angeles on July 10, 1986, at the age of 53. Mizer repeatedly tells us that Tristram came from Ripon, England, but sometimes this is Ripon in Gloucestershire, and at other times Ripon in North Yorkshire, two very different places. (*Man's World* in October 1957 maintains that he was born in Yorkshire but raised in Gloucestershire [38].) Mizer also specifies that, after leaving school at an early age (probably 13), he apprenticed and worked as a member of the British Merchant Marine. Tristram turned up in New York around 1956, was photographed in the nude by Lon Hanagan (Lon of New York), and was said to have trained at Abe Goldberg's gym.

He reportedly worked in New York, and later in Los Angeles, where he relocated around 1958, as a travel agent. He received a bachelor's degree in French in September 1965 and a master's degree in the same in June 1966 from UCLA; the university personnel office had no record of him ever having taught there. He did, however, teach French in the foreign languages department of Los Angeles City College (LACC), probably—if the LACC yearbooks are to be trusted—between 1968 and 1985 or 1986, eventually attaining the rank of associate professor.

The contests in which he competed and his status in each, include the following:

1957 AAU Mr. Eastern America, Medium Division, sixth place

1962 IFBB Mr. America, Short Division, first place

1962 Mr. Venice Beach, first place[1]

1963 NABBA Mr. Universe (Amateur), Medium Division, second place

1964 IFBB Mr. Universe (Amateur), Short Division, second place

1974 WBBG Mr. International, Short Division, second place.

This sequence would suggest that he abandoned competitions during his undergraduate senior year at UCLA, only to return about the time he received tenure from LACC.

This assemblage of data also confirms that Tristram continued posing for photographs and was selling some of his own while an undergraduate and a master's candidate. During the first years he worked at LACC, photos of him appeared in various physique and physical culture magazines, although in diminished numbers. As noted earlier, Tristram ultimately posed for Colt Studio, nude, and these photos were published before he received tenure. Although stories of him losing his professorship due to his pictures may sound appealing, he appears to have held onto his job up until his death.

Finally, the confusion between John Tristram the bodybuilder and John Tristram the Australian filmmaker is rather puzzling. *The Quest of Jimmy Pike*, the latter's best-known movie, came out in 1989. How someone, even someone as intelligent and resourceful as John Tristram of physique fame and LACC, could continue producing films after his own death, defies explanation.

Part of my goal in this chapter is to record what may be known and to comment on some of the mythology surrounding John Tristram. Although the rumors are in themselves interesting, even when baseless, they nevertheless represent how many of the physique models of the 1950s and 1960s, not unlike the film icons discussed earlier, have become, at least for some nearly four decades later, the stuff of legend. Just as many more have hung larger-than-life identities on the scaffolding of Monty, Marlon, and Jimmy Dean, a select few have allowed their image of Tristram (and others) to replace the actual person he was. As I suggested previously, John Tristram truly was an interesting man, but one must question whether or not he was interesting in the way that others have made him.

He was in fact a man who posed for a large number of photographers, many of whom published their photos of him in physique and physical culture magazines. As with Harrison and Bishop, the photos continued to circulate for years; hence, Tristram's earliest photos continued to be sold and published more than a decade after they were taken. To a certain degree, one can tell approximately when a photo was taken by the development of the model's body as well as by the lines on his face. Over the years, physique fans got to watch Tristram go from a well-built, boyish young man into a giant of a bodybuilder with a certain boyish quality.

Of the models whom I have discussed, Richard Harrison, who came out of the same Hollywood as Clift, Brando, and Dean, appears to have been the most fortunate in that he was never completely overwhelmed by the response to his achievements—indeed, he became one of the most skeptical critics of his own career, sometimes mocking his B-movie image. Glenn Bishop eventually fled the world in which he had lived and from the life he had created. Way out west, men may still enjoy the last vestiges of "freedom," but are men there free not to be men? Bishop's flight may be construed, at least in part, as an escape from a culture in which homosexuality might be regarded as normal; inevitably he abandoned the sexually ambiguous 1950s and 1960s to which he belonged for a value system from the years preceding World War I.

Figure 9.1. John Tristram stands at left, beside kneeling Dave Draper, with Hugo La Bra next to Draper and at far right, Larry Bondura. (Man between La Bra and Bondura is unknown.) The 1963 photo was taken on what was, until 1959, Muscle Beach, Santa Monica, possibly by Wolfgang Schramm.[2]

If Harrison was a man of his times and Bishop, a man who sought an earlier reality, John Tristram was a man ahead of his time, which perhaps is another way of saying that he was a man with whom his own times eventually caught up. This young Englishman appears on the modeling scene four years after Bishop and a little less than a year before Harrison. He begins in cosmopolitan New York City but then is drawn, like so many other British émigrés, to southern California. His modeling career continues through pictures taken by a variety of photographers across the United States, from the West Coast to Chicago and New York, and to Britain and France.

One observation I should like to add is that when Tristram entered UCLA in 1962, he was probably aware of the 1960 scandal created by the arrest, trial, and firing of Newton Arvin, a professor of literature at Smith College, in part for his possession of physique magazines (including *Grecian Guild Pictorial*, which for several of its 1960s issues featured Tristram on the cover and in its pages). Arvin's exposure led to additional charges against and dismissals of other gay male Smith faculty and panicked many other homosexuals across academia, some of whom, out of fear, destroyed their own collections of such publications. Yet Tristram continued to pose, even as his studies led to his first and second degrees and he secured a tenure-track teaching position; such defiance of the morality of American higher education was uniquely brave at the time.

Early Images

John Tristram first appears in photos by Lon Hanagan in two publications put out by his alter ego, Lon of New York, *Men and Art* and *Star Models*. In the former, the pictures are nudes, one from behind, another with painted-on posing straps. Another similarly censored shot is featured in an ad for Lon's catalogues. In the latter, yet another censored shot is shown and the same ad is repeated. Photos released publicly long after show these same pictures were indeed taken of Tristram in the nude.

Alonzo James Hanagan was born on December 20, 1911, in Lexington, Massachusetts. In his introduction to *The Male Ideal*, Reed Massengill describes Lon's journey to New York and his photographic career. Gifted musically, Hanagan studied keyboard and played on the radio. When his family moved to Lockport in western New York, he continued his recitals and played music in local cinemas, eventually landing a place at Julliard. While in New York City, Hanagan got to meet some of the physique photographers and models whom he had admired in physical culture magazines. He was befriended by Tony Sansone and included in a crowd of regulars, straight and gay, who hung out on the beaches at Coney Island and later at

Riis Park. In the late 1930s, physique photographer Robert Gebhart (who signed his work, Gebbé), taught Hanagan the rudiments of the art, and in 1942, Lon published a series of photos of the quintessential bodybuilder of the late 1930s and early 1940s, John Grimek, which were published in *Strength and Health,* and he also brought out his first catalogue. After the war, Hanagan abandoned music and devoted himself to photography (11–24).

In an interview with Hanagan published in *Torso* in December 1996, Matthew Rettenmund writes,

> Beefcake photography sold like hotcakes because it also appealed to the aesthetic ideal of super masculinity—even if it was exhibited in a way traditionally reserved for female beauty. Gay men who had to feign heterosexuality could revel in unadulterated maleness in their stash of nudes. Lon was disinterested in prospective models who camped it up or looked effeminate—it was extreme masculinity that he sought to portray in his work, and his motto had always been, "You can love a man, and you can still be a man."
>
> It's interesting then that he also photographed many drag queens in studio portraits so glamorous they look like they could have given Lana Turner a run for her money. (81)

Unlike many New York physique photographers, such as Edwin Townsend and Al Urban, who also shot fashion and other commercial pictures, Lon specialized exclusively in male nudes. His photos rarely seem ironic. Unlike Urban's, for example, the masculinity of Lon's models is never so exaggerated that it at times appears "over the top." His credo ("You can love a man, and you can still be a man") stands in stark opposition to the postwar definitions of masculinity featured so prominently in *Tea and Sympathy* and relates to some of the ideas that George Chauncey assigns to prewar New York, namely that homosexuals who did not act effeminately were not regarded as different from heterosexual men (13) and that gay or bisexual men who played "the man's part" in the sexual act were seen as "normal" (119).

Lon's photography often contained classical allusions: a tall or short fluted column, an antique bust, a centurion's helmet, a sword, spear, or saber. As *The Village Voice*'s Vince Aletti mentions, in an article preceding Lon's 1999 gallery show in New York,[3]

> Though many of Lon's models in the later '50s and '60s weren't the competition bodybuilders he began his career with, he always managed to turn the working-class Italian, Puerto Rican, and black men before his camera into embodiments, however imperfect, of the Greek ideal. Even if some of these lugs look out of their

element perched on a fluted column in a posing strap, their vulnerability is as touching as Lon's aspirations. For all their glamorous stylization and formalist chill, Lon's best photos have the warmth of portraits and a feeling for the soul under all that sculpted flesh. They're about yearning and desire.

. . . .

[His models] came to him to be photographed in the heroic style, their bodies shining like burnished bronze under the studio lights. He played Sibelius and Stravinsky to set the mood. "I used to call it photographic sculpture, like the Greeks," he says. "Instead of in marble, I sculpted with the camera."

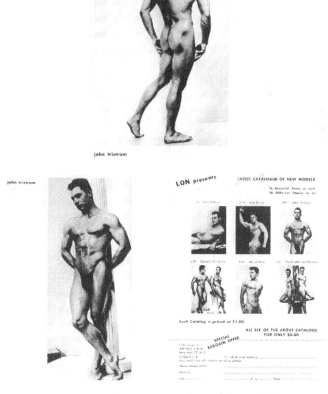

Figure 9.2. J.T. in Lon's *Men and Art*, 1956.

The photos themselves are often stunning though sometimes a little too monumental. Whereas Urban shot photos of incandescent gods, Lon dressed up the common man without dwarfing his humanity—as his pictures of John Tristram illustrate.[4]

Tristram appears as a well-developed young man, not so much a typical man on the street as the worked-out boy next door. In Lon's lens, Tristram seems posed but nonchalant, contemplative rather than active. The fluted column against which he leans is not as big a focus of attention as the post-production posing straps. Although naked, his eyes are for the most part averted. He is aware that he is an object of admiration, even of desire, and at the same time, he is not engaged in outright seduction.

The next photographer to snap "John Trenton," as he was now called, was Anthony (aka Tony) Guyther, who would work over the years under various studio names, including Vulcan Studio (in New York), Capital Studio (in New York and Washington), and Discus Studio (in New York). According to Thomas Waugh, Guyther was also a fashion photographer (250) although his output of physique photos seems extensive. For more than a decade, he was linked to one of the more curious figures connected with physique magazines, Dr. Herman Lynn Womack, an albino former college professor based in Washington, D.C. who published a number of magazines, including *101 Boys, Big Boys, Fizeek, Grecian Guild Pictorial, Grecian Guild Studio Quarterly, Manorama, Manual, Trim, Trim Studio Quarterly*, and between 1963 and 1966, *Vim*. Womack was repeatedly prosecuted from 1960 to 1979, when his last appeal was denied by a Norfolk, Virginia court. In one case, Guyther and Capital Studio were named in a suit led by the federal government and the U.S. Post Office for distributing his photos. According to the official court report, among those testifying was Dr. Albert Ellis:

> Dr. Albert Ellis was called by the Respondent. He has been a Doctor of Psychology since 1943, and has written hundreds of papers and several books. Much of his work has been in the field of sex. He . . . has testified before in Post Office cases and in courts. He has treated about 100 homosexuals. (Tr. 168)
>
> Dr. Ellis said: "There may have been two or three cases of all the homosexuals I have seen who specifically reported that they were aroused when having this kind of material which they may or may not have obtained."
>
> Dr. Ellis believes photos such as those in this case operate as an escape valve on most homosexuals—some of their pent-up emotions are let out. He thinks there would be less [sic] overt acts if a male homosexual looked at these photographs. . . . Dr. Ellis believes there is no prurient interest by homosexuals in

the exhibits. . . . Dr. Caprio [another expert witness] believes a
nude or nearly nude photo of a young boy would stimulate the
sex appeal in a homosexual but Dr. Ellis says the interest is one
of love—not necessarily sex. (Tr. 179)
    (In the Matter of the Complaint Against . . .)

This last question posed to Dr. Ellis was particularly relevant because by the
early 1960s, many of the subjects of Guyther's photos for Womack (credited
to Capital Studio) were boys in their teens (and possibly younger). Indeed,
Discus Studio seemed to have specialized in this sort of subject matter. (The
court also complained that the posing straps used to hide the genitals of
Guyther's models were too revealing in showing off the outlines of their
privates.)

    However, in the 1950s, Vulcan was associated with young adult body-
builders, including Steve Wengryn, Ed Fury, Mark Nixon, Kip Behr, Billy
Connors, Bob Delmonteque, Bob Bishop, and John Sweeny, as well as many
more hopefuls. The first Vulcan photo of Tristram to appear, in *Grecian Guild
Pictorial* for spring 1956, shows "Trenton" as a lithe, gracefully proportioned
young man kneeling on the floor, his arms and head upraised (31). Another
shot of him appeared in the summer 1956 issue. In this shot he is seated on
a stool, his body turned sideways and his legs crossed, but his eyes are looking
squarely into the camera. The seductive look on his face, which is void of
any humor or even a trace of a smile, is provocative (14). The following fall
(October 1956), *Body Beautiful* devoted several pages to the model (29–33).
The first photo, which was previously published in *Grecian Guild,* is included
but there are additional shots, all of which reemphasize Trenton's toned but
not yet massive body. He appears totally naked; the poses themselves (except
for one) make the usual straps unnecessary, and in the final centerfold, his
crotch is draped with a towel. One may see that the model's waist is small
and that his shoulders do not appear pronouncedly large.

    The centerfold shot would be reprinted in *Young Physique* in April
1961, but there seem to be no other publications of Guyther's photos of
Trenton (although the uncredited shot of Tristram at his lightest weight
in *Young Physique* in December 1962 [26] at Abe Goldberg's Gym in New
York may have been taken by Vulcan). In these pictures, the viewer may
observe the deadly seriousness of the model's poses and facial expressions.
There is also a striking contrast between his narrow waist and large chest,
triceps, and thighs.

    Although Vulcan's images of "Trenton" would not circulate widely
after their initial appearances, the work of another photographer would
show up a little more frequently; Togof Studio, also in New York, was run
by Melvin Sokolsky, who had at the early age of 21 been made a member

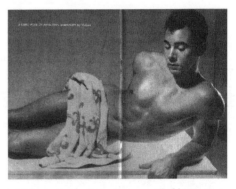

Figure 9.3. Vulcan's Trenton: Top: two Vulcan nudes from *Grecian Guild*. Bottom: the first and last pages of Trenton's spread in *Body Beautiful*, all published in 1956.

of the photography staff at *Harper's Bazaar*. "Togof" (which is an anagram of "fotog")[5] was the name he used to shoot physique pictures. Widely known for his fashion photos, Sokolsky went on to make films and commercials, but much of his work was done in advertising; even in this realm he endeavored to make his photos (which were, after all, printed anonymously) pointed expressions of his own sensibility and view of the world (Melvyn Sokolsky Facebook).

Sokolsky became interested in making a career in photography in 1954 when a friend at the Eastside Barbell Club confided that his boss, a commercial photographer, had been paid four thousand dollars to photograph a box of Jell-O for an advertisement (Melvyn Sokolsky Facebook). His interest in the male physique, which perhaps led him to this venue, soon resulted in the founding of Togof Studio, initially located at 125 East 39th Street and then at 118 East 28th Street, between Park and Lexington Avenues (and three blocks east of the notorious Everard Baths at 28 West 28th and Broadway).[6]

Sokolsky's models were youthful and handsome. Many of them, such as Buddy Basil, Bob Hover, and others, posed for him repeatedly. Most of his pictures are well composed without looking too grandiose; he usually avoided reusing the same props that other photographers relied on, such as Lon's classical accessories, and although much of his work took place in his studio, he also ventured into other rooms and outdoors. He tried in his physique studies, as in all his other work, to be inventive and offer a fresh look at his subjects.

One series of pictures of John Trenton depicted him in a swimsuit that laced up the sides (a brief fashion craze in the late 1950s) on a rocky beach. In all of them, he seems muscular and masculine, well but not overly developed.

The photos in Fig. 9.4 and others from the same shoot reappeared for several years. They were featured in Body Beautiful for February 1957 (41), Mr. America for September 1960 (11, where it was wrongly credited to Russ Warner), and in Manual for June 1960 (36–37), where the photographer claiming credit is Bob Anthony.[7] Anthony was notorious for ordering prints from other photographers and then copying them and reoffering them as his own work.[8] Another pair of photos, supposedly by Anthony, appeared in Manual for May 1961 (25–26), and around the same time, the British physique magazine, Model Man placed one of the "Anthony" shots on its cover.[9]

Pictures from another series of photos—these taken in the studio—had appeared a few months earlier, in an advertisement at the back of Muscle Power, in November 1956 (61) and for the same month, on the cover of Adonis. The advertisement was one of several photos in which the model wore an eye patch and reclined in front of some driftwood. Photos from this set also appeared in Hercules, The Body Beautiful's July/August 1957 issue (19) and in Manorama, February 1961 (14). The Adonis cover shows Tristram kneeling in the nude, but instead of a graceful pose as in Guyther's photo, he is gazing directly into the camera as he puffs out his enormous chest. The photo inside the magazine (11) features Trenton in briefs standing behind the driftwood. The accompanying text within the magazine mentions "the classic elegance of the Tristram physique" (57).

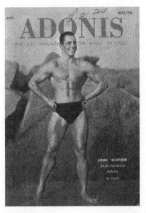

Figure 9.4. Trenton on the beach by Togof. Top: Front cover of *Adonis* May 1957. Bottom left: back cover of *Tomorrow's Man*, March 1957. Bottom right: *Manual*, June 1960 (credited to Bob Anthony).

     Three months later, in February 1957, *Body Beautiful* printed a spread on Trenton, beginning with a cropped version of Togof's beach shot that would run on the back cover of *Tomorrow's Man* the following month (as previously mentioned). It also included a discreetly and elaborately composed study by Togof: Trenton is shown, posed as an antique sculpture with a swathe of fabric draped from an upraised hand to a lowered hand, tastefully hiding his crotch (42). The pose seems graceful but slightly forced. There are also in this same spread two additional pictures taken by someone named Vic Richards. I have been unable to find any other pictures by this

JOHN TRISTRAM

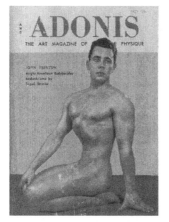

Figure 9.5. Top: Trenton in eye patch. Bottom left: a photo from the set first advertised by Togof in November 1956 (reprinted with Tristram's real name), in *Manorama*, February 1961. Bottom right: on the cover and within *Adonis*, November 1956.

photographer, but these are clearly studio shots. The text in the spread calls Richards "an excellent, new physique photographer" (41). One shot is a rear view of the model ("note the unusual beauty of the legs," urges the caption, 43), and the other shows him in posing straps on a ladder (44). Togof or even possibly Vulcan may have taken these photos.

Yet another shot of Trenton in briefs with driftwood would appear in *Adonis*, for October 1957 (14). I believe that this photo is the last of Togof's studio pictures of him to be published before the model left for California.

In these and most of the New York studio photos, Tristram's trim waist contrasts with his large pectorals and upper arms. Is this the image to which

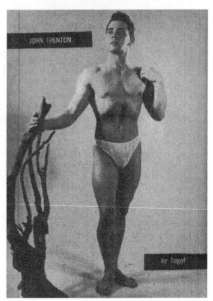

Figure 9.6. Last of the New York photos: Top left, Togof's classical pose. Top right and bottom left: two shots by Vic Richards (all from *Body Beautiful*, February 1957). Bottom right: Togof photo of Trenton with driftwood (*Adonis*, October 1957).

Michael Bronski refers in *Culture Clash*—of the model who is muscular but "queeny"? Is Tristram, in these photos, one of "[t]he men [who] were muscular but . . . were also slightly effeminate; . . . [with] waists and shoulders which were generally associated with the image of the queen, but . . . also [with] huge arm, pectoral, and thigh muscles"? Again, as in the early pictures of Glenn Bishop, the presentation of the male body is complicated by the poses designed by the photographers. There is certainly less possibility of ambiguity here, perhaps because the model is older than Bishop was, but at the same time he appears submissive, more of a sex object to be admired than an independent agent.

Although the contrivances of the New York pictures lend a certain air of camp to some of them, the gender issue remains unsettled and even unsettling. Is Tristram's gender ambiguous or is he, as a developing male, transitionally masculine? Or is he rather trapped in a frame that requires that viewers interpret the photos according to their own understandings of sexual and gender constructs? These pictures make it difficult to ascertain definitively the model's gender; ironically, the poised, posed Tristram here appears to be a good-looking gay man, which of course was exactly what he was. Yet the decisions made by the photographers have much more influence upon how Tristram is perceived than the model himself, as subsequent photos would show.

Go West, Young Man

The pseudonym "Trenton" did not originate with Lon, whose photos are all of John Tristram. In Vulcan's photos, he became John Trenton, a name that he retained, at least initially, with Togof. Yet by the time *Tomorrow's Man* showed the Togof beach shot of him, in his side-laced swimsuit, on its back cover (March 1957), he was being called Tristram. He continued to be known as Trenton in *Adonis,* but at the same time, in *Muscle Power, Man's World,* and *Popular Man,* he was Tristram. From this point onward, "Trenton" stopped being used with one exception: The fourth issue of *Young Physique* (August 1959) printed a spread of Tristram photos by various photographers but referred to him throughout as John Trenton (5, 16–19, 45); Bob Mizer advertised one of this model's photo sets in the back pages, and although he had always referred to him as Tristram, Trenton was used instead (48). This mistake was corrected by the December issue (39). The error was never made again, even with the photos by Vulcan and Togof that had originally carried the Trenton name.

The first indication that Tristram had relocated to the West Coast came in *Tomorrow's Man* in May 1958, which published a photo of him, in

front of the American Health Studio's gym in California (28). This photo
and others, illustrating various neck exercises (29), were credited to Bob
Delmonteque, who worked with both Harrison and Bishop. Although first
based in Detroit, Delmonteque had relocated his studio, first to Miami and
then to Hollywood, California; he often traveled the country because much
of his business was in selling naked photos (such as the ones mentioned
previously of Bishop). A Texan by birth, Delmonteque began weight training as a teenager. According to him, he was first featured on the cover of
Physical Culture Magazine in 1939 (Miller). In the 1940s, he posed in the
nude for Douglas Julef, eventually selling some of these photos himself and
photographing other bodybuilders. Along the way, he made a physique film
with Artie Zeller and Jimmy Apollo, "Days of Greek Gods," produced and
directed by Richard Fontaine in 1954. In this four-minute short, he and the
other two models strike poses of classical statuary. The short begins with
the arrival of Zeller and Apollo at Delmonteque's home, where he has been
reading up on Greek mythology. As he narrates each myth, Zeller turns into
Hercules, Apollo poses as Narcissus, and Delmonteque becomes the Apollo
Belvedere. This was the first posing strap movie to be filmed with sound, but
as Waugh points out, most physique film collectors at the time did not own
sound projectors and thus were spared the pretentious narration (266–267).[10]

The photos in *Tomorrow's Man* showing the neck exercises, along with
another set (*TM*, December 1958, 3–4) illustrating four barbell exercises,
are the only pictures of Tristram attributed to Delmonteque. Perhaps he did
not "hit it off" with Tristram as he had with other models; perhaps Tristram's acknowledged homosexuality made their relationship uncomfortable;
or maybe Delmonteque had been assigned by *TM* to take the photos but was
busy shooting other models. In any case, these workman-like pictures are all
that survive. Tristram's body appears consistent with the New York pictures,
but the poses are far less "artistic." His presence, although isolated, seems
more pronouncedly masculine. In the solo shots (without the weights) that
accompany each of the articles, he looks directly into the camera seriously.
He looks young but robust, and not in the least effeminate.

The next two photographers for whom Tristram would pose would
greatly increase his popularity with physique fans. The first was Bob Mizer,
who shot several sets with Tristram; in at least two, he was featured with
another model. As he had done with Harrison, Mizer also featured Tristram
in an AMG film. The photo sets and movie circulated for years. The second
photographer was Russ Warner, who had himself been a bodybuilder and
who had begun taking pictures of other musclemen after World War II, first
in Oakland, then in the Los Angeles area. Warner's models were notable
muscle contenders, including major title holders and fitness experts, many of

Figure 9.7. Delmonteque's Tristram in *TM*. Top: two pages from May 1958. Bottom: two pages from December 1958 (uncredited).

them in the nude, including the famed duo consisting of Mr. America, Jack Thomas, and the future television exercise guru, Jack LaLanne, who years later vainly tried to buy up and destroy prints of his naked poses. Whereas Mizer's pictures typically depicted a model's more private side, such as his personality and sexuality, Warner's were studies in physique development: In Mizer's photos, Tristram appears likeable, attractive, even available; in Warner's, Tristram seems increasingly muscular and jovial.

In *Physique Pictorial*'s summer 1958 issue, Mizer included a full-page swimming pool picture of Tristram with Forrester Millard (Forest D'Orlac) (12), who (as noted previously) was one of AMG's earliest models (possibly the very first). AMG's early photos of Millard date from the mid-1940s, before Mizer's arrest, and although authorities did not confiscate them, they were suppressed by Mizer himself because they revealed the model's genitals. Millard possessed a physique that was spare and defined, as opposed to overdeveloped and bulky, which had led Irv Johnson to use him (for a brief time) to replace Glenn Bishop as the mascot on *Tomorrow's Man's* table of contents page beginning in February 1954. There had been numerous sets published by many physique photographers that included a pair of models, but most of them (such as Oettinger's and Delmonteque's photos of Bishop and Richard Alan) seemed formal and posed and others (such as Delmonteque's of Harrison and Hover) were less studied but relatively few in number. Mizer's catalogues of the Tristram–Millard duo are numerous and include playful moments, in and out of the AMG pool. There is also a set of dress-up pictures, with Tristram as cowboy and Millard as Indian, which suggest role-play games. These photos, which would eventually appear in other physique magazines, were first published in *PP* for fall 1958 (17). With regard to all the Tristram–Millard photos, the concept of two good-looking, nearly naked men enjoying each others' company was incredibly appealing, not to mention suggestive, to gay male readers. Mizer is especially successful in linking the homosocial to the homoerotic in these photos.[11]

In the same issue in which the twosome first appeared, there was in addition to the Tristram–Millard photo a solo shot of Tristram at Mizer's pool (*PP*, summer 1958, 13). The winter 1959 issue featured the model on the cover, posed in the desert, holding a bamboo rod. On the inside of the front cover, Mizer also included solo catalogue photos from several different sets, one set showing Tristram in the desert, another of Tristram in the AMG yard, yet another of Tristram in sailor's pants, and also one of Tristram in blue jeans next to a railway train (2). (There was also a page including catalogue photos of the twosome with Millard [3].) Mizer would reprint these pictures for a decade or longer. Although they were all shot in 1958, they would appear as well in a variety of other physique magazines well into the 1960s.

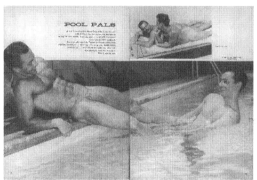

Figure 9.8. Tristram and Millard. Top left: in pool, *PP*, summer 1958. Top right: cowboy and Indian, *PP*, fall 1958. Bottom: in and out of the pool, *Young Physique*, August 1959.

Throughout the vast majority of his AMG photos, Tristram is shown smiling, happy to show himself and just as pleased at being observed. The poses look far less artificial than the ones in the pictures taken in New York. The model looks naturally good-humored and at the same time, available.

Mizer's blurbs on Tristram would become the major source of information about the model. Not only does Mizer reveal his measurements, but he tells us in the model's first solo appearance in *PP* that Tristram was born in Ripon, Yorkshire, where he was raised on a farm and "rode a bike a great deal." He adds that John had no faith in protein supplements but ate a "normal healthy diet," that he worked out four to five times a week,

Figure 9.9. Solo Tristram by AMG: from left, Tristram in Mizer's compound; Tristram in the desert and on the cover; Tristram (aka Trenton) in denim (*YP*, August 1959); Tristram the sailor (*PP*, February 1968).

and that despite currently working as a travel agent (a position he had held in New York), he hoped to become a writer (13). In the issue of *PP* in which Tristram was featured on the cover, Mizer announced that Tristram would soon be featured in a new AMG film release (2) and that the film footage Mizer had taken of Tristram and D'Orlac together had been lost by Eastman-Kodak's lab, which had also lost another movie (3). In a blurb accompanying a photo in the June 1960 issue of *PP*, Mizer reveals that Tristram is featured in the AMG short, *Pose Please* (11).[12]

I have viewed *Pose Please* via an Internet site. The plot concerns an artist (Larry Marinan) who has brought his model (Tristram) out to the desert. The conditions are so terrible and the artist so tries the patience of the model that the latter ends up leaving but not before bashing the painter with his own canvas.[13] True to Mizer's main objective, both artist and model stripped down to posing straps in the film.

Of course, by the middle 1960s, many of *PP*'s readers wanted to know much more about the models, and as indicated in Chapter 7, Mizer had created a code to communicate his evaluations of his models' personal proclivities. He encoded Tristram's photos twice, first in 1963 and again in 1967. The earliest version of his understanding of Tristram can be decoded to mean that Tristram was a typical man (i.e., heterosexual) who would engage as an active party in both anal and oral sex with other men. Mizer added that he believed him to be "aesthetic (mother oriented)" and very much a hustler (October 1963, 8). The later version, however, leaves out the possibility of heterosexuality, noting instead that Tristram would engage in either role in both anal and oral sex, that he was extremely "horny," and that he remained strongly interested in hustling (April 1967, 30). Whether or not Mizer had seen much of Tristram after 1958 is questionable, but as a physique photographer, he would have known a great many people connected with the bodybuilding community, some of whom would have

Figure 9.10. Two stills from *Pose Please*.

known Tristram very well. As Mizer himself admitted, his judgments about
his models were always highly personal—each was a "Subjective Character
Analysis."

Probably because Tristram continued to be a well-known bodybuilder
until the end of the 1960s, Mizer continued to advertise the various Tristram
catalogues and *Pose Please* through winter 1968, at a time when he had
stopped selling many of his earlier catalogues and films.

Throughout the AMG catalogues of Tristram and Millard, the two
men are presented in posing straps and also in Western-themed gear. Their
playfulness remains boyish, innocent, and yet enticing. A few of the pictures
from this shoot remained popular in physique magazines until the late 1960s
because they portrayed an intimacy between two masculine-looking males.
Mizer's catalogue of solo Tristram shots shows the model, a little more massive than in the Delmonteque photos, in posing straps and in tight blue
jeans (in which he had dressed Harrison) and tight sailor trousers. The effort
to "butch-up" the model seems to pay off because the resulting photos take
on an iconographic performance of masculinity.

Figure 9.11. Tristram encoded: Mizer's "Subjective Character Analysis," from left,
in 1963 and 1967.

Unlike Lon of New York and Bob Mizer and many physique photographers, Russ Warner was heterosexual; at the same time, he was keenly aware that many of the audience for his photographs were homosexual. Hence, the gleaming muscular men whom he photographed had to appeal to the viewer not only in terms of their size and physiques but also through what they revealed. As noted previously, his pictures of Jack Thomas and Jack LaLanne together in the late 1940s were, by the 1950s, considered sufficiently inflammatory by the homophobic LaLanne that he sought to get rid of them entirely. Compared with Mizer's more casual pairing of Tristram and Millard, the 1947 Thomas–LaLanne shots seem rather formal, almost silly in the way that the models have been posed. Nonetheless, the way the models themselves actually looked, without body hair and covered in oil, and also completely naked, and the way that Warner captured them, made them difficult for a gay male audience to ignore. Warner's work, recalled Dave Draper, who would often model for him, "exuded drama, inspirational might." Although several physique photographers, among them Lon, Mizer, Urban, and more, suffered the loss of many of their prints and negatives as a result of police raids, Warner's more than 25,000 photos have remained. Perhaps because he was "straight," a number of serious bodybuilders, who were cautious about revealing themselves, trusted him not to expose them. Hence, models such as Steve Reeves and Larry Scott, who both strictly avoided showing their genitals to the camera, allowed Warner to photograph them.[14]

In Warner's lens, Tristram's greased-up body seems to take on a massiveness that is not completely there. This is especially apparent from the Warner photos that appeared in the physique magazines. On *Tomorrow's Man's* cover (for February 1959), the model's glossy muscles stand out through the use of light and reflection. On closer examination, however, his expanded chest and deltoids seem to dwarf his arms and waist, which (as in the New York photos) appear to be developed but not overly so. A centerfold from *Gym* (March 1959), presents a three-quarter view of Tristram from head to toe. Again there is a sense of muscular development but the physique seems not entirely well proportioned. Only in Warner's photo of Tristram in posing shorts, a leg raised onto a table, his hands at his hips, is there a clear sense of the physique's potential for mass. The torso is poised and expanded, the thighs are large, and the model's grin gives him the appearance of a confident man.

Additionally, Warner had the means to place his models' photos in major bodybuilding publications. For some time during the early 1960s, Warner worked for Joe Weider. Another Weider organization employee, Dave Draper, remembered how he and Warner struggled to keep the organization's office at Venice Beach going, and that when Weider needed photos in a rush

Figure 9.12. Tristram by Warner. Top: Cover of *TM* (February 1959). Bottom left: centerfold in *Gym* (March 1959). Bottom right: in *YP* (August 1959).

for one of his magazines, Warner would take out his camera and ask Draper to pose for him. Warner's association with Weider, as well as Tristram's developing body, made Tristram a good candidate for the supposedly more serious physique culture magazines published by the organization. "Serious," of course, is a relative term: Certainly, *Mr. America* and *Muscle Builder* were less interested in delivering titillating pictures to a gay readership than

Tomorrow's Man and *Vim*, but their objectives were no less transparent. As implied in the previous chapter, most of the articles in these Weider publications, such as the ones purportedly written by Glenn Bishop, were not very subtle testimonies to the organization's various products, including supplements, weight sets, and training manuals.

Nonetheless, unlike many of the posing-strap magazines, the physique culture publications actually did include texts and often illustrated a variety of exercises; they were actually read by bodybuilders. Thus, Tristram's

Figure 9.13. A spread from *Mr. America*, September 1960 with images by Warner (and a miscredited Togof photo) and text by Leroy Colbert.

ongoing appearances in them indicate a shift in his career. He was on his way into competitive bodybuilding and had begun to look like a possible contender. For example, in one of his earliest appearances in Mr. America, bodybuilder Leroy Colbert, who worked for Weider, wrote an article about how Tristram trained (September, 1960, 9–11, 44, 46, 48).

Thanks in part to Warner's photographs, Tristram had gained entry to one of Weider's most prestigious (and non-gay) bodybuilding publications. Suddenly recognized as a serious contender, Tristram had crossed over; however, unlike some other models, he continued to appear in both physique and physical culture magazines. Still, his appearance in Mr. America signaled an ongoing relationship with the Weider organization and a career in major bodybuilding contests.

Broadening Horizons

By 1963, Warner's photos of Tristram were rarely seen.[15] Perhaps one of the reasons for this was that by 1962, Tristram looked noticeably different than he had in 1959. He had become an important player in what would be a succession of competitions. He would find many more photographers for whom to pose.

In 1960, British photographer, Tom Nicholl (aka Scott of London), who was visiting southern California, took photos of a posing strap-clad Tristram on an overcast beach. The beach was littered with pieces of some wrecked ship, and the interaction of the now more-developed model and the odd-looking pieces of machinery in the dull light took on an almost surreal look. Tristram appears bulkier and blank. Robbed of Tristram's usual smile, the viewer can focus only on his enormous build, the mechanical debris, and the murky surf and shadowless strand.

These photos circulated for about a year and later turned up in 1967 in Beach Adonis, a new magazine published by Bob Mizer (22). They illustrate the growth of his musculature but subordinate any subtlety to broadening Tristram's body. (Tristram would later pose again at Nicholl's London studio with very different results.)

Sometime before 1963, Tristram had been photographed by Chuck Renslow, who ran Chicago's Kris Studio (founded in 1950), and who had taken over Irv Johnson's gym in 1958. Like George Platt Lynes, Renslow had been a noted ballet photographer. He and his partner, Dom Orejudos, an artist who signed his drawings and paintings, "Etienne," contributed their work to two physique magazines that they themselves published, Mars, a posing-strap monthly, and later Rawhide Male, which featured nude photos and sketches. (According to the Chicago Gay History website, Renslow

Figure 9.14. Tristram on the beach again. Top: Scott of London's initial offering in *Man Alive*, August–September 1960 (14–15). Bottom left: another shot published in *Manual*, September 1960 (29). Bottom right: a pair of photos from the same set, in *TM*, February 1961 (47).

opened the first leather bar in the United States, The Gold Coast, in Chicago in 1958, had gone on to open a number of clubs during the 1960s, and was a founding member of several gay organizations.)

The first Kris photos to appear in magazines showed up in *Young Physique* in March 1963. The cover photo in color, of a kneeling Tristram in swim trunks, his arms locked around his head, depicts the model gazing into the camera and offering a strong, direct smile. However, the shots inside the issue (which had been taken in color but here appeared in black and white), showed a rather vacant-eyed Tristram who, as in the Scott pictures, loomed large. Even the shot of Tristram emerging through curtains and looking into the camera reveals little if any facial expression (42–46). A blurb preceding the spread (41) indicates that Renslow took these pictures two days before the Mr. America contest; because Tristram did not compete for this title in 1963, the photos must have been taken in 1962, when Tristram placed first in the short category. In these he appears substantial: His shoulders are noticeably larger and his pectorals and triceps look pumped-up.

An advertisement for Kris Studios in *Muscleboy* in April 1963 (68) featured a pose that was far more striking and provocative than the ones seen in *YP*, as were two photos that appeared in *Manual* in June 1963 (18–19). These were obviously taken in black and white because the lighting is better, the use of shade is far more pronounced, and the pictures seem to hold more drama and focus than the *YP* color set. Predictably, two more shots from this set were printed in Renslow's own publication, *Mars*.

In these photos, more typical of Renslow at his best, the play of light and dark highlights the model's muscles, making him an object of mystery and desire. The shadows in the folds of the posing strap are especially noticeable, recalling how Tony Guyther had been fined for using the hiding device as a membrane for exposure. As in the shots in *Young Physique*, Tristram's body appears bigger and bulkier. A comparison of the Warner cover photo for *Tomorrow's Man* and Kris's shot of a similar pose indicates just how much heftier Tristram had become. These and other pictures from this set (and also the color set) would reappear in magazines three and four years later.

Around the same time, Tristram was photographed by Jimmy Caruso, who made his home in Montreal, where the Weiders had their headquarters. Although Caruso had worked independently (and had been prosecuted several times by Quebecois authorities), by the early 1960s he was one of the photographers on whom the Weider organization had come to rely. Compared with Kris's black-and-white photos, Caruso's are far more straightforward and far less alive with sensuality. Tristram is shown standing next to a trophy, his left hand at his hip, his right arm up to display his prominent bicep, and his entire body flexed, as he smiles into the camera. This picture appeared on the cover of *Mr. America* in March 1962. A variant

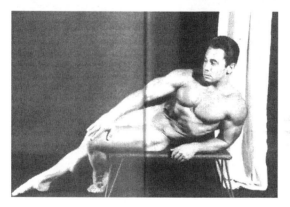

Figure 9.15. Tristram by Kris. Top left: Tristram on the cover of *YP*, March 1963. Top right: a studio shot with curtains. Bottom: reclining blankly on a bench.

of this photo, in which Tristram has both hands at his hips, appeared in *Mr. America* for April 1963 and came with a blurb that extolled Tristram's "excellent symmetry" but added that he "has gained 20 pounds since this photo was made and he just looks all the more impressive without sacrificing one iota of shape or definition!" (33) True to the Weider body ideal, John bigger was John better. Additional Caruso pictures of Tristram appeared in various Weider publications, including *Muscle Builder* for April 1963 (23),

Figure 9.16. Black-and-white photos from Kris: from above, two from *Manual*, June 1963; below two from *Mars*, July 1963.

Mr. America for May 1963 (69), *Mr. America* for October 1964 (28), and *Muscleboy* for November/December 1966, 40–46).[16]

As court photographer to the Weider publishing empire, Caruso's pictures indicated the organization's interest in Tristram. Indeed, between 1960 and 1970, Tristram made numerous appearances in a number of physical

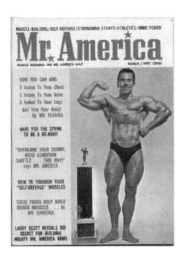

Figure 9.17. Caruso's Tristram. Top: Award winner on cover of *Mr. America* (March 1963). Bottom left: in *Muscle Builder* (April 1963). Bottom right: *Muscleboy* (November/December 1966)

culture magazines. These included Mr. America (for which he appeared on one cover), Young Mr. America (one cover), Muscle Builder (one cover), Muscle Training Illustrated (one cover), Health and Strength (at least seven covers), and in the French muscle magazine, Entrainements et Méthodes.

Interestingly, on the covers of Weider's Young Mr. America and Muscle Builder, Tristram was pictured with a bikini-clad female.[17] Such pairings were not uncommon: A blurb about the male–female duo on the cover of a different issue of the Young Mr. America (October 1964), attests, "OUR COVER PROVES THAT IT'S THE WEIDER MAN WHO ATTRACTS THE PRETTIEST GIRLS" (3). This need to reassure heterosexual male readers that the only reason for a man to build his body was to attract women, was perhaps prompted by the enormous success of the physique magazines, which by this time were clearly targeted toward a homosexual audience. Thus Tristram, despite his more masculine presentation in physique magazines, had to be "straightened out"; indeed, by this time, most physique models, whether gay or straight, needed to identify themselves as "manly" men engaged in the "manly" enterprise of bodybuilding. The heterosexualization of Tristram's image, realized by Caruso, stood in clear contrast to how other photographers (such as Renslow) were now portraying him.[18]

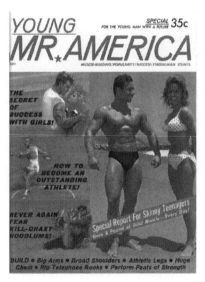 

Figure 9.18. Tristram and "Friend": Sharing cover with girl in bikini, Young Mr. America (July 1964) and Muscle Builder (August 1966).

Almost simultaneously, Mizer ran a Tristram photo in *Physique Pictorial* supposedly taken by someone named Roy ___, "a professional photographer . . . whose work is rarely seen in physique magazines (simply because he can make more money in other phases of photography) but as a special favor to John he did this group" (October 1963, 8). A month later, another photo from this set turned up in *Young Physique* without any attribution (November 1963, 8). An advertisement, the previous spring, in the back pages of *Muscleboy* had shown a photo from this series (June 1963, 67) and the same ad rain in *Young Physique* a few months later (September 1963, 72); both indicated the pictures came out of van Loon Studio and were available from a post office box that, as it would turn out, belonged to Tristram himself. Indeed, Mizer would admit in *PP*'s October issue that John was the distributor of this set. I have been unable to find anything on an American commercial photographer named Roy van Loon or just van Loon. Whoever took these pictures of "this superbly built young athlete . . . amid the rugged beauty of the Santa Monica Mountains," as the ad described them, has remained anonymous.

Three photos, at least one of which clearly comes from the van Loon set, later appeared in *Young Physique*'s January/February 1964 issue, sent by Tristram "just before John flew to London" (for the September 21, 1963 NABBA Mr. Universe competition at the Victoria Palace, in which he took

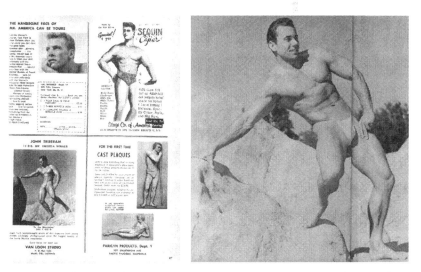

Figure 9.19. The so-called van Loon photos: from left, as first advertised in *Muscleboy* and shown in *YP*.

second in the medium height category, 11). All three of the pictures were reproduced on double pages, amounting to three "centerfolds" (8–13). This marked the model's first foray into selling pictures of himself.

In January 1964, Renslow's *Mars* announced that Tristram had come out with his own photos. Whereas Richard Harrison and Glenn Bishop had clearly worn posing straps or trunks in the pictures they sold of themselves, Tristram appeared for the most part naked, although of course his privates were carefully obscured, either by an object in the scene or by the frame itself. In this initial offering of the "Tristram by Tristram" photos, the model is seen first kneeling in the outdoors, toweling himself off (22) and then reclining on what appears to be a leopard skin, a corner of which has tastefully been drawn up to hide his crotch (23). These pictures appear to be related to the ones shown with the van Loon photo in the January/ February issue of *Young Physique*, mentioned earlier. An advertisement, in the back pages of this issue, sounds as if it had been composed by the same writer who had described the van Loon set: "Superbly built athlete excitingly photographed against rugged mountain backgrounds. Two 8-photo sets available . . ." (40); I suspect Tristram wrote both these descriptions. I also suspect that either "van Loon" or Renslow took the photos.

The next issue of *Mars*, for March 1964, included a far more personal photo of Tristram facing a window and looking out, perhaps at a private garden or yard. As with Harrison's "Dick at Home" set, these were clearly taken by someone other than the model, who is noticeably posed in each of them, and offered informal glimpses of the bodybuilder naked around the house (29). Again, in the back pages there was an ad, this one describing "two 8-photo AT-HOME sets" (42). Later in September of that year, *Mars* offered a spread of Tristram's at-home pictures. The reader gets to see Tristram, in posing strap, reclining on a sofa (24–25), and also asleep in bed (26) and choosing a record for his hi-fi (27), completely in the nude. An ad in *Man Alive* for the same month offered all four sets (26); the outdoor sets are represented by a shot that matches the van Loon photos while the more intimate shot shows Tristram potting a plant. Some of the already-published pictures from the at-home and outdoor sets reappeared in the Canadian physique magazine, *Face and Physique* in its 1965 Annual issue: For the first time he is shown looking up from the leopard skin (47), and he is posed emerging from the bathtub (48) and seated on a barstool. The barstool shot also included a coupon to be used to obtain all four photo sets (49).

The at-home photos of Tristram are far more intimate and inviting than Harrison's. Moreover, instead of the run-down apartment furnishings in "A Day with Dick," Tristram is seen in comparatively luxurious bachelor digs. Free to roam about the flat, naked and welcoming, Tristram has gradu-

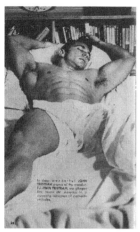

Figure 9.20. Chez Tristram: Upper row, two at left from *Mars*, September 1964; at right from *Face and Physique Annual*, 1965; lower row, also from *Face and Physique*.

ated from being the tight-waisted, graceful young man with large muscles to the "built," adult male homosexual.

Of course, for the most part the images of Tristram published in physique magazines were not reproduced in the physical culture publications; there were still two separate audiences. For the straight bodybuilder, Tristram represented the possibilities of weight training, careful dieting, and using supplements. For the gay observer, he became a muscular but approachable man who was sometimes eager to please and at other times in need of being pleased. Over the next few years, even before the Stonewall uprising, Tristram's photos would anticipate the look of the male models of the 1970s and 1980s.

Tomorrow's Man

In 1964, Tristram was busy competing, finishing his undergraduate degree, and then beginning his master's at UCLA. His competing temporarily stopped, but he continued to train and started taking supplements—ironically supplied by Rheo Blair, who despite his preference for the Glenn Bishop physique now advised some of the hulkiest and bulkiest bodybuilders on the West Coast. As Harrison and others had anticipated, the look of masculinity for the later 1960s and the decades that followed would be large, even oversized, as the physique contest portrayed in the film *Pumping Iron* would show. Tristram began to look truly massive, even as the Weider magazines insisted that he remained symmetrical and defined. Two additional photographers, both well known in France, document his growing size. Gregor Arax, whose studio in Paris had been producing high-quality male nudes since the 1930s, was a Greek who had kept his studio at 31 Boulevard Raspail for more than three decades. Primarily known for his meticulous studio pictures, his photo of Tristram, among other competitors at the 1963 Mr. Universe contest in London, appeared in *Tomorrow's Man* for April 1964 (39). Jean Ferrero, who had studios in Nice and in Paris (in the same building as Arax), captured Tristram in 1964, when he competed in the IFBB Mr. Universe contest (and came in second in the short category), with another bodybuilder, flexing along a beach on the Cote d'Azur (*Male Classics Annual*, 1964, 29). Both photographers, who had produced some extraordinary studio and outdoor shots, also took less-studied photos of various bodybuilding events.

In both of these photos, Tristram stands out not so much for his build as for his height, which usually qualified him to compete in the "short" category, With taller people within the frame, his body takes on a compactness that is not perceptible in his solo shots.

Figure 9.21. En français: Left, Tristram (third from left on floor) by Arax at Mr. Universe ceremony; right, on the Riviera with another bodybuilder by Ferrero.

Sometime, probably in 1963, Tristram posed again for Tom Nicholl, whose Scott of London studio was perhaps appropriately located in Leather Lane. The pictures from this shoot were published in London, in three undated magazines, *Beau*, *Sir Gee*, and the British version of *Body Beautiful*. Scott's use of props and costumes seems somewhat akin to Renslow's, even though Renslow had never dressed Tristram in any kind of gear (aside from the inevitable posing strap); Nicholl, however, places Tristram, not just in a posing strap, but in sunglasses, shiny high boots, and a leather cap, atop a motorcycle. The facial expression is rather stern, and there is something threatening if not dangerous in the image (*Beau*, No. 4, 9–10).

A similar image graced the cover of *Sir Gee* (no. 14), only this time Tristram wore black leather trousers and reclined across the front and back seats of the cycle. It is difficult to know if he is again wearing sunglasses because the motorcycle cap shades the upper half of his face; what can be seen of the facial expression is once more humorless, strict. In the same issue is another photo of Tristram, in posing strap, cap, sunglasses, and leather gloves, staring into the camera without even a hint of a smile. This photo is at once arresting and disturbing. Another photo from this set comes at the end of a spread of several photos from another set, described later. This final photo, which is in effect an advertisement for Scott of London, shows Tristram in leather trousers and cap, apparently lying across the cycle seats but without sunglasses and with a broad, good-natured smile across his face (*Body Beautiful UK*, No. 33, 24). Here the motorcycle regalia seems far more benign, as if part of a dress-up game rather than an expression of the

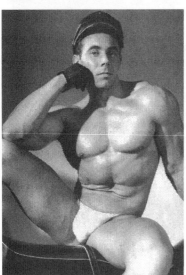 

Figure 9.22. The Wild One. Top left: photo in *Beau*. Top right: a cover and interior shot in *Sir Gee*. Bottom: an advertisement for the cycle and white-shorts sets, *Body Beautiful UK*.

model's potential violence and cruelty. The ad mentions four sets of "leather photos" for sale, as well as two sets of classical poses and one set of "white shorts" pictures.[19]

Fans of Scott would have recognized the reference to "white shorts" pictures. Scott often dressed his models in tight stretch briefs or shorts that accentuated what the garment was supposed to hide. In these photos, the hard, muscular leather man becomes the object of desire, flaunting his physique as well as those particular parts of his body that are supposed to remain unseen. His gaze never crosses the camera—rather, he is turned away from the lens so that he may be admired by the viewer. We see him from the front, with the outline of his private parts quite evident, his face turned to the left (23); from behind, with the tight knit material clinging to the cleavage between his buttocks (24); and again from the front, this time before a net, his face turned to the right (25). Suddenly, the predator has become the prey; the object of fearful respect and obedience is turned into the hunted.

Although Kris had refrained from dressing up Tristram, two of his photos released later suggest that Renslow's fascination with bodies emerging from the dark led him to view Tristram as a subject of great power as well as an object of desire. The first one appeared in *Mars* in March 1967, probably a shot that had not been published before in a magazine but had been sold as part of an earlier set (17). In it, Tristram is kneeling, turned away before a mirror, looking forward but not into the lens. The viewer gets to look at his front and back simultaneously. The twist in his body—his legs are turned one way and his torso another—complicates the image, making his reflected back and buttocks appear unnaturally contorted, even vulnerable.

Seventeen years later, this photograph appeared in a book, *Photo Flexion*, edited by William Doan and Craig Dietz. The former was head of the

Figure 9.23. Three of the "white shorts" set by Scott in *Body Beautiful UK*.

Doan Foundation, which, according to the publication's endpaper, was "dedicated to the collection and preservation of photographic art"; more recently, the Doan Foundation, which received what was left from Al Urban's studio, published a volume on Urban's work. Dietz, whose endpaper blurb indicates that he was a photographer who had worked for Joe Weider, later contributed pictures to the gay *In Touch* magazine in the 1970s. The book looks back on the role of photography in bodybuilding, and reprints, among many others, the mirror photo published in *Mars* along with another similar to it. Here again Tristram is kneeling before a mirror, but this time, his face is turned away from the camera and his eyes are visible only through the mirror, even as they focus on the lens. The viewer glimpses the model's powerful back, and by way of the glass, a profile of his torso. Significantly, although Tristram appears to be wearing posing straps in both photos, the viewer never glimpses the pouch; the body itself appears engorged, erect. Rather than narcissism, these photos suggest self-reflection, self-acceptance, and affirmation. In a sense, these pictures present a revised, more positive statement about sexuality and manhood. Tristram becomes an emblem of what was up until the late 1960s unthinkable in Cold War America, that an adult male could be both beautiful and masculine.

Figure 9.24. Through a Glass Darkly: Two photos from *Photo Flexion* by Kris of Tristram with a mirror. (The one at right had appeared previously in *Mars*.)

Things to Come

Sometime around 1969, Tristram posed for Jim French (aka Kurt Luger and Rip Colt), who had begun publishing his sketches and then his photographs of muscular men. French, who would name his operation Colt Studio, had to some degree appropriated the already-appropriated iconography of Tom of Finland (as mentioned in chapter 5) and of Kris Studios's Etienne, the very same kind of costuming that had been deployed three or four years earlier by Scott of London.

Colt Studio did not sell photos of boys; those pictured in French's work were clearly men, mature, well-developed, often hairy, and always at least partially naked. They were frequently marked with signs supposedly linked with virile masculinity: tattoos, unshaven faces, facial hair, caps or undershirts, or boots. The butch, masculine male now became an iconic image of gay pornography. Such men were usually depicted as manly and presumably straight, although in the shifting subculture, the models were obviously posing for photos for other men. Suddenly, the apparent contradiction of how

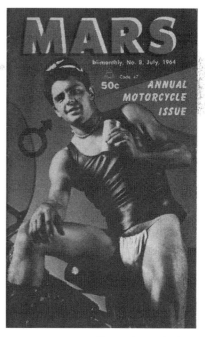

Figure 9.25. "The Leather Look": Drawing by Etienne (aka Dom Orejudos) in *Mars*, July 1964 (12); Renslow's cover for the same issue.

masculine a homosexual male could be was open to question. If effeminacy had been the earlier marker for homosexuality, what was it being replaced by? The answer, visible in French's drawings and photos, was a "hyper" masculinity in which well-developed males flaunted their secondary sexual characteristics.

In 1969, Tristram would have been a perfect candidate for this up-and-coming studio. He had already posed in the total nude for Lon in 1956, had retired from competing and posing and thus had stopped shaving his body, and he had lost most of the boyish looks he had previously boasted. Complete with hirsute chest and pubic hair, mutton-chop sideburns that characterized the era, Tristram, massive and mature (he would have been 36 at the time), was, as with Renslow, posed beside a mirror while he stood naked against a background that today looks like psychedelic decoration.

One could argue that Tristram had reached a point when the culture at large had caught up with him: He was in many ways the ideal Colt man—offering a performance of a masculinity, contrary to the physical culture magazine covers that had secured his gender and sexuality beside a woman, that was unapologetically male. With the rise of the women's movement, gay depictions of manhood came to rely not on what females wanted to see but on what males desired to be and/or to possess. The ambiguity visible from the late 1940s to the early 1960s had finally given way to a masculinity that was in many ways traditional in its reliance on secondary sexual characteristics but also transgressive in its focus on alternative sexualities and radical in its ability to see beauty as a genuine characteristic of "authentic"

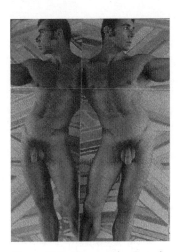

Figure 9.26. Tristram by French.

masculine performance. In an email to me dated August 31, 2009, French, now retired from Colt, wrote as follows:

MY ART DIRECTOR DELIVERED YOUR E-MAIL REQUEST-ING INFORMATION ABOUT AN EARLY MODEL OF MINE, JOHN TRISTRAM. I AM CURIOUS AS TO WHAT KIND OF BOOK YOU ARE WORKING ON WHICH WOULD INCLUDE JOHN TRISTRAM. YES, I WAS THE LAST PHOTOGRAPHER TO HAVE PUT HIS IMAGE ON FILM AND IT, ALONG WITH THE FIRST IMAGE, WAS A VERY SPECIAL OCCA-SION. JOHN WAS ONE OF A HANDFUL OF MODELS OVER THE YEARS WHO HAD THAT RARE COMBINATION OF STUNNING GOOD LOOKS AND HIGH I Q. I MISS HIM AND I CONSIDER THAT PERIOD OF MY LIFE OF WHICH HE WAS A PART AS PRIVILEGED.

SINCERELY,
JIM FRENCH

In reality, Bronski's image of the straight-looking queen applies to relatively few of the photos seen in the physique magazines; certainly, there was a tendency among some of the New York photographers to effeminize their pictures, not only to lend credence to their claims that their work was artistic but also to appeal to an audience that wanted to see homosexual men. With "queeniness" as a sure indicator of queerness, as much in photos as in the protocols determining who would serve in the military, gay read-ers occasionally wanted to see males like themselves in the pages of the physique magazines. Of course, as Mizer repeatedly tried to demonstrate, any good-looking young man was an appropriate object of desire who might be induced to engage in sex with other males.

Perhaps it is unnecessary to point out that the onslaught of macho men who followed Tristram into the images of Colt and the other creators of post-Stonewall pornography were neither more nor less "genuinely" masculine than the posing-strap models who had preceded them. With the artifice of youthful innocence and cultural normality replaced by mature experience and subcultural marginality, the images of males transmitted through maga-zine publications relied on the signs developed and preserved within the gay community. The staggering number of pictures that proliferated following the demise of the physique magazines erased for many viewers the earlier images. It is difficult perhaps to see past the coyness of physique photogra-phy and into the construct(s) of masculinity from which they were derived.

In a variety of ways, the legacy of late twentieth-century gay pornography has helped to hide the earlier notions that a male could be vulnerable, sexually ambivalent, and emotional and still remain a "man." What is recognized now as "masculine" seems so much less in touch with the imminent contradictions inherent in this culture's sense of what it may mean to be a man. Oddly enough, men continue to be considered beautiful but too often in the service of stabilizing manhood rather than in the service of deconstructing it. Our culture is so much the poorer for that.

Conclusion

Even before the war broke out in Europe, the United States had created at least two broadly popular figures, one from motion pictures, the other from popular music, who personified the young male on the brink of what had been traditionally thought of as manhood: Both seemed devoid of the toughness of what was then thought of as conventional masculinity and were of middling height and physique. Unlike Rudolf Valentino a generation before, Mickey Rooney and Frank Sinatra excited the romantic adoration not of grown women but of adolescent girls; yet these two celebrities never threatened the masculinity of male audience members as Valentino had, perhaps because of their youth. Thus, their popularity was not confined to the girls who pined for them but extended to movie fans and music lovers in general, who embraced them as well.

One might argue, then, that a younger alternative to the he-man solidity embodied and enacted by older, more mature film stars and musical crooners had already taken hold in the United States and that even if the country had not entered the war, this new construct of masculinity would have become a serious competitor for the more established masculinities. Of course, America did enter the war, and its affect on masculinity remains indisputable: Even as those on the home front wept for and extolled the virtues of the "boys" overseas, the nation as a whole was obliged to refer to them as "fighting men."

The pervasive imagery of these young but adult combatants, of their strength, courage, and competence, may have been repeated ad nauseum simply to dispel the reality that America was once again sending children into battle. Only after the war did the popular medium of film offer a variety of narratives that showed the physical and emotional casualties, who were sometimes still in their teens. Perhaps the combination of the wartime remaking of manhood and the postwar revelation of that manhood's vulnerabilities, was most influential in constructing a masculinity that was neither physically nor emotionally threatening to other males. Rooney and Sinatra may have been popular and likeable, but the young vets were not only both but they were also ennobled by their experience.

Possibly the fact that Marlon Brando, in his first film appearance, had, in addition to his muscular body, handsome face, and compelling personality, a major disability, allowed male spectators to accept his almost inescapable beauty. Similarly, Montgomery Clift, who presented a haunted presence before the camera, and James Dean, who performed as if driven by some terrible inner need, transcended the usual boundaries that men in cinema audiences had set for their responses to what they observed on the screen. Clift and Dean, along with Brando, inspired the problematic homosocial/homosexual response of identification: Male spectators frequently wanted to be like the male characters portrayed by these actors.

The distance between the caustic, elusive wartime homosexual poet of *The Glass Menagerie* and the gay bodybuilder and college professor who posed nude in the year of the Stonewall riot for Jim French's Colt Studios, seems at first far greater than the twenty-five years that separated them. Yet the line leading from one to the other is discernable, even direct, enough. If Tom Wingfield is not in himself beautiful, then his father clearly was, at least physically. This is verified by the photograph Amanda has hung on the wall, which serves as a shrine to the beauty and also the treacherousness of masculinity. (Tennessee Williams's insistence that the household icon bear the image of the actor playing Tom is perhaps a cruel comment on how what passes for male beauty is not as appealing when viewed up close.) Although Laura's fondness of Jim seems to make him appear beautiful in her eyes, her less sentimental brother notes his supposed comrade's flaws, even as Tom's appraisal of how Jim perceives him—as an oddly fashioned dog—would suggest that Tom himself has little patience with the possibility of male beauty, in spite of his implied attraction to men.

Tom Lee, however, is a far more ambiguous figure, for he is created to represent a masculine male who pretty much lacks masculine characteristics. Although Robert Anderson makes it plain that such characteristics are arbitrary and even false markers of gender, he fails to address the homosexual panic, fueled apparently by the attractive nudity of a good-looking teacher displayed during a homosocial interaction, which at first appears to be the problem in what would seem, at least at first glance, to be a problem play. In some of the other scripts written or revived in response to the rumor-mongering of the HUAC, there is a similar dynamic: The problem is not witchcraft (in the case of *The Crucible*) nor lesbianism (in the case of *The Children's Hour*) nor pollution (in Miller's version of Ibsen's *An Enemy of the People*)—the problem is the human capacity to vilify others. Similarly in *Tea and Sympathy*, there is little exploration of the connection between the homosocial and the homosexual; the script treats suspected homosexuals (such as the handsome teacher or the brawny housemaster Bill) with deserved intolerance. In the end, Tom Lee is given the choice of proving the rumors about his sexuality false or true, and by implication, due no doubt largely to issues of censorship in force when the play was written and first produced, Tom supposedly makes good on Laura's contention that he is straight. Nonetheless, the conclusion leaves open the question of whether Tom "performs" a heterosexual role because he is genuinely attracted to Laura or because he needs to be seen by others—Laura included—and himself as a heterosexual male.

The Zoo Story, which functions on a seemingly more simple dramatic level, pitting one character against the other, approaches sexuality in a far more complicated way. Instead of giving the audience characters that represent such binary oppositions as masculine–effeminate and gay–straight, Edward Albee offers them two figures who at first appear to be drawn from two different environments—one from the culture at large, the other from a counterculture. Yet as the play progresses, the peculiarities of the two individuals' circumstances seem to have shaped their masculinity as much as their cultural backgrounds. Neither the middle-class masculinity of Peter (which one may associate with the "organizational man" of the 1950s) nor the offbeat masculinity of Jerry (which one may associate with what David Savran calls the disaffected, white "hipster") is presented as authentic; clearly the two versions of manhood embodied in each are in competition, but just as there can be no masculinity without the supplement of femininity, there can be no "decent" masculinity, such as Peter's, without the aberrant masculinity of Jerry. The beauty of Jerry is present by its near absence—he shows traces of having once been a handsome man. In their fatal encounter, the foundational manhood of Peter (a suitably named rock of a man) survives an onslaught by the ghost of what was once male beauty.

If the hipster willingly gives way to the husband and father, the provider in contemporary society, the film stars who in many ways embodied the disaffected white boy, whom the British called "the angry young man," did not go so easily. True, Dean was gone at the age of 24 after three films; by 1960, Clift had become difficult, if not impossible, to work with; and Brando grew older and heavier and increasingly odd; however, the images created by each in his prime remained potent, even in the 1970s when most past icons of American masculinity were being rejected. The New Left and other Vietnam era movements remained respectful of George Eastman, whose struggle to rise to the middle class ended in a death sentence, of the sullen Johnny Strabler in his leather jacket and cap, and of Jim Stark, the rebel whose cause it was to rebel. Despite the misogyny and homophobia of this period, even sexist hippies could espouse love for such figures.

By the time of the Stonewall riot and the beginnings of gay liberation, the images portrayed in the physique magazines—many of which had either disappeared or transformed into nude magazines—were already dated. The demise of the posing strap in many cases led to the end of the physique parade: Naked photos of ordinary young men would flood the market and appear in the pages of the one-time leader in the depiction of fine physiques, Bob Mizer's *Physique Pictorial*. Just as many in the new gay movement rejected the politics of the past, including the ideals and methodology of Mattachine and the frequently doctrinaire policies of *One*, they laughed at the artificiality and the absurdity of the posing strap. Eventually, studios like Colt and Target would bring back the overly developed musculature of some of the 1950s models, but in the first few years following Stonewall, a wide variety of physical types would appear in gay periodicals.

As a veteran of physique modeling, Richard Harrison was able to climb into bit parts in Hollywood films and then up to a successful career in what even he recognized were B movies, almost all of which were shot overseas. His modeling career no doubt got him through some hard times. Although posing never brought in much, selling his own photos was probably a little more lucrative. They also brought him to the attention of a number of readers or at least consumers of what were then deemed homosexual publications, among whom were probably men connected in some way with the entertainment industry. The anecdote about "Dick" getting an agent through a friend at the gym may be true, or it may be, as some of Mizer's stories are, just a somewhat accurate description of something that happened. In any case, it suggests that there were some intersections between the Muscle Beach crowd and the world of show business. Harrison's own anecdotes about his attracting the interest of Cole Porter and George Cukor imply as much. And even if *Confidential* sought to sully his reputation (and the reputation of his producer father-in-law) through the publication of photos taken to appeal to a homosexual audience, at least for Harrison, there was (as is often still said in Hollywood) no bad publicity.

The same probably cannot be said for Glenn Bishop. Of all the models who appeared in the pages of the physique publications, he gained more from the sale of photos of himself than any other, largely because he sold so many of them himself. This was true from the beginning of his career, when shots similar to the ones being sold by Irv Johnson, which were taken either by Johnson or Douglas Julef ("of Detroit") or both. Cliff Oettinger took a number of photos of Bishop, many of which made their way into the inventory of Michigan Models, run by Bishop with Richard Alan. Later still, Bishop's wife apparently took pictures that ended up in the catalogues Bishop marketed through ads in Weider magazines.

In the early years, the money these photos brought in was evidently sufficient to make Bishop continue to produce and sell them and also create new ones for sale. If various blurbs that accompanied Bishop's pictures in physique magazines were true, the funds from sales were instrumental in putting Bishop through college, at the University of Michigan in Ann Arbor, and then chiropractic school in Chicago. By 1966, however, after Bishop had graduated from the latter and presumably had begun a practice, at a time when he was a husband and the father of two children, he formally ended his posing career, leaving, he believed, this part of his past behind him.

Of course, what he did not and never could control was the influence of his pictures and of the persona to which they had contributed. Evidently, a number of gay men recalled his image with too much enthusiasm: His angry and rather obtuse letter to *Drum*, printed in 1967, was recognized even back then as exhibiting an obvious contradiction, for Bishop had been marketing his image, and quite successfully at that, to gay males since 1954. Even if the images Bishop himself sold were not "explicitly queer," the images for which Bishop posed, taken by Oettinger in the first few years of Bishop's career, clearly were. They can be put into a sequence that offers the narrative of the boy stripping and displaying his nude body for the pleasure of the observer. They appear to be and probably are what is today spoken of as "kiddie porn."

Bishop's reactions to this exploitation may have been responsible for his irrational letter to *Drum* and may possibly explain his later refusal to discuss his posing career; John Tristram, however, who had little control over the sale of his own images except for the brief period between 1963 and 1965, was far less vexed by his modeling past. Tristram, as much as (if not more than) Harrison, seems to have risen from very little: One of millions of British youths who left school at 13, he served aboard ship and ultimately landed himself in New York, where he began weight training and posing while working as a travel agent. His move to southern California gave him greater access to the center of bodybuilding culture; here there were a large number of gyms and a wide range of photographers eager to snap the pictures of men who came out of them, but there was also the possibility of easy reinvention. For Tristram, being a viable contender in major bodybuilding competitions was not enough: He did what he could never have done in Britain at the time, by going through university for a first and then an advanced degree and becoming a professor in an institution of higher education. Although the stories about Tristram being "outed" and fired from his teaching position are attention grabbing, they are not as interesting as the reality in which Tristram pursued his separate career paths in the muscle world and in academia without encountering any conflicts in either.

At the same time, if Tristram himself was comfortable with his own sexuality, those around him were no doubt less so. The mid-1960s magazine covers that paired him with a buxom, bikini-clad brunette are only the most blatant reminders that at least for the fans of physical culture magazines, being a homosexual male was being something less than a man. Likewise, those with whom I have communicated from the physical culture scene, including Gene Mozee, Larry Draper, and the late Gordon Scott, recalled Tristram well and even thought of him as a friend but never alluded to (or perhaps even knew about) his sexuality. Nonetheless, *Physique Pictorial* devotees, who had decoded Bob Mizer's cryptic hieroglyphics, as well readers of other magazines, who would have noted how much more sexually intimate Tristram's "at-home" shots were than those of other models, such as Harrison's, no doubt received the message regarding which way Tristram "went."

Ironically, the second wave of physique photography, led by French's Colt Studio and others, not only depicted men whose muscles were clearly developed, but whose secondary sexual characteristics, such as the presence of facial and body hair, size, height, ability to sweat, approaching baldness, and enlarged penises, were prominently displayed. The shaved-down bodies and smooth faces of the earlier bodybuilders had given way to more traditionally manly images. Indeed, the muscular and boyish young men, such as Harrison, Bishop, and Tristram all had been at the start of their posing careers, eventually became sex objects of the past. If Tristram caught the admiration of French, it was not as John Trenton, the youth, but as John Tristram, the man.

Thus male beauty moved from males who somehow embodied a certain boyishness to males who in many ways conformed to previously held notions of what constituted manliness. Media personalities reflected this change as much as the gay photo industry, making men such as Burt Reynolds and Tom Selleck the pin-ups of heterosexual women. In spite of their resemblance to contemporary gay porn stars, such men never threatened male spectators.

The decades following Stonewall have seen major changes in the way society has treated its gay minority. *The New York Times*, long an arbiter of what could and could not be said in legitimate discourse, began to use the adjective "gay" to denote homosexual individuals. Raids on gay bars, which were notoriously frequent during the "posing-strap" era, ceased, as did the newspaper publication of names of suspected deviants, and the American Psychiatric Association stopped listing homosexuality as an abnormal mental condition. For a time, the love that dared not speak its name began screaming it in the most boisterous ways possible: It was the disco era, a period whose excesses would later appear so grotesque at times that they became the subject of laughter of later generations.

What was originally called "the gay plague" of the mid-1980s and early 1990s altered the zeitgeist from constant carnival to serious determination. AIDS suddenly became the single significant issue around which gay men organized, and although the vanguard of the anti-AIDS movement would fracture and split, the very presence of the unchecked disease seemed to unify rather than separate what was left of gay society. During the many years that followed, as various improvements were made to the lives of

AIDS patients and the disease itself was found to be vulnerable to medical treatment and even prevention, many Americans gradually began to think of gay men and women as men and women who were different but were nevertheless men and women. The lifting of the well-intended but terribly abused "Don't Ask, Don't Tell" rule governing the participation of homosexual men and women in the armed forces and the institution in some states of same-sex marriage laws demonstrate a growing tolerance. Of course, tolerance is not necessarily the same as whole-hearted acceptance, but it is a definite improvement over the outright oppression that reigned previously.

Yet for some, homosexuality in any form will never be tolerable. I recall E. M. Forster's profound doubts, which he noted at the beginning of the posthumously published novel *Maurice*, that despite the evidence offered by the Wolfenden Report, the British would never accept homosexuality; although time has proven Forster's belief overly pessimistic, it is not entirely false. Even as the divide between "straight" and "gay" has somewhat narrowed because of the acceptance of homosexuals into more and more parts of Western culture, the divide has deepened: The closer gay and straight come together, the more the culture seems to insist on emphasizing their differences. Of course, the same has been just as true between men and women: No matter how much women have been able to gain access to society at large, the anger and resentment of men—and not only heterosexual men—has increasingly hardened, and the list of what is properly masculine and feminine has grown.

The public at large has long accepted the possibility of masculinity and femininity existing without an immediate association with males and females. Furniture, jewelry, dishware, even automobiles have been described using the adjectival forms of what is proper to one or other of the sexes. What makes a chair, a watch, a place setting, or a motor car masculine or feminine, however, seems to be more a reflection of current associations with gender. Hence, the color pink, once assigned to the swaddling of male babies, has over the years come to suggest femininity. Such associations may be so strong that they seem intrinsically connected to what they represent rather than arbitrarily. I remember a dental technician who was about to offer me a complimentary toothbrush but withdrew the offer quite suddenly. "Oh," she explained, "you wouldn't want one this color." The color was pink. I was about to answer that it didn't matter to me what color my toothbrush was, but as my eyes scanned the photos on a nearby shelf, I noticed one of her infant daughter all in pink and also a family portrait in which she herself had a pink ribbon in her hair. Obviously, if I had told her I preferred a pink toothbrush, I would have been telling her much more.

If Western culture has come to allow for the assignment of gender to inanimate objects, it has also permitted using gender-specific adjectives to members of the opposite sex. Calling a male "feminine" is traditionally a massive insult; similarly, although not equally, referring to a woman as "masculine" may contain a highly pejorative slur. Yet because "masculine" also carries positive meanings valorized by an almost unrelentingly sexist culture, its use may not necessarily be negative. Indeed, the appropriation of masculine behavior, either in earnest or as parody, has become for many females a liberating mode of critique of gender and culture.

If one subscribes to a progressive view of history, one is required to insist on how much better things are now than they were in the years following World War II. Yet the combination of my memories and research suggests to me that in some ways gender matters were perhaps better during and after the war than in the present. There is, as Sartre observed, something to be said for being part of an underground minority and working in an assortment of ways toward one's own and one's group's liberation. If gay liberation brought many new rights to gay Americans, it brought as well a more open forum for the discussion of sexuality and a good deal of hate speech. Society remains largely heterosexist, grouping its gay members together through the binary of straight–gay. Although scholars may argue that gay is supplemental to straight and that sexuality is far more complicated than an either/or dichotomy, most Americans accept the reductions of hate speech, whether or not they are in favor of the hate.

Rather than view the years between the war and the 1960s as a quaint transitional period leading to our own supposedly enlightened age, I propose that we have much to learn from that earlier time about the way people saw and presented themselves to each other. Jungian psychoanalyst Warren Steinberg two decades ago postulated a transformative masculinity that in many ways transcends the usual view:

> A man who develops into a male human being does more than add traditionally feminine attributes to his masculine repertoire. He understands that they are not feminine to begin with. He realizes that the categorization of human qualities into masculine and feminine creates a false dichotomy that can only be resolved by means of an internal synthesis. All of the characteristics normally considered masculine and feminine . . . are really part of his potential as a human being. (5)

Twenty years later, one may question whether such an enlightened possibility is more likely today than it was previously. One may consider the number of women who have entered the workforce and climbed above managerial positions and the number of men who stay home to raise children as signs that certain behaviors once deemed "masculine: and "feminine" have lost much if not all of their gender-oriented significance. Simultaneously, however, with the increase of transgendered and trans-sexual individuals, many of whose goals seem to be to reassign such gender-oriented behaviors rather than to strip them of their gender significance, one may wonder if it is possible for our culture, as it is presently constituted, to escape the masculine–feminine binary.

Perhaps the recognition of males as beautiful takes us a step closer to recognizing that part of being human is to possess some kind of discernable beauty; or perhaps it simply places males in the same position that women have occupied for many centuries. I prefer to hope it is the former.

Notes

Chapter 1

1. *The Glass Menagerie* opened in Chicago on Christmas Eve, 1944, and played two weeks. It did not open in New York City at The Playhouse until the end of the March 1945; it played 563 performances.

2. The Performance text is published by Samuel French, which licensed subsequent productions of the play.

3. Performance text, 10; Reading text, 144.

4. In the version of the play that was written as a "Provisional Film Story Treatment," in 1943 for MGM, Williams calls Mr. Wingfield "extraordinarily handsome" (2).

5. Ironically, when the original production toured in 1946 and the actors were replaced, the set pieces and props from the premiere run were retained, including the photograph of Dowling as the father. Thus, Richard Jones, who played Tom, looked nothing like Mr. Wingfield's picture.

6. Significantly, Amanda offers no aspersions for the supposed antithesis of the "old maid"; instead, she rhapsodizes about the wealthy old bachelor she might have had (Williams, *The Glass Menagerie* 14; 149).

7. In the Performance version, the photo is illuminated; in the Reading version, Amanda turns to the picture.

8. Readers now familiar with some of Williams's short stories, such as "Hard Candy" and "The Mysteries of the Joy Rio," written, respectively, in 1949–1953 and 1941 but not published until 1954, easily answer the questions posed above; yet the original audience would not have been able to "know" this, and although it is tempting to use these accounts of what homosexuals did in cinemas as definitive, they must remain, at least in a discussion of the first production of *The Glass Menagerie*, extra-textual.

9. In the mythology of American popular culture of the time, pimps were often characterized as homosexuals.

10. Lilly goes on to interpret Laura's infirmity as a metaphor for homosexuality (155), an idea that strikes Paller (38–39) and myself as a misreading.

11. In the Performance version, Tom's short moments of sleep mark the end of one scene and the beginning of the next (Act I, Scene 5). In the reading version, the scene that began with Tom's arrival home continues on, remaining Scene 4.

12. Gilbert Debusscher proposes, perhaps wisely, "So let's respect each other's—"secrets of the heart" (64).

13. I concur with Granger Babcock that the D.H. Lawrence book m question is undoubtedly *Lady Chatterley's Lover* (22).

14. In the Performance text, the scene (I, 6) opens with the monologue. In the Reading text (in which it is Scene 5), a short passage of dialogue between Amanda and Tom precedes the monologue.

15. According to Williams's biographer, Lyle Leverich, Williams was reading Isherwood's Berlin stories in 1943, about the time he began working on *The Gentleman Caller* (488).

16. The Chicago and New York programs show a variety of reminders for the audience to buy and hold on to War Bonds.

17. All reviews of the original New York production have been taken from The New York Public Library's Theatre Research Collection's compilation of theater reviews.

18. Myles Weber identifies this quote in his essay on "Catching the Streetcar" (482).

Chapter 2

1. All reviews of the original New York production have been taken from The New York Public Library's Theatre Research Collection's compilation of theater reviews.

2. The manuscript of this unpublished story is in a special collection at Harvard University Library.

3. Decades earlier, a clubfoot had served as a metaphor for homosexuality in Somerset Maugham's *Of Human Bondage*.

4. These particular words come from Samuel French's description of the play, in the Samuel French edition of *Tea and Sympathy* but are representative of how reviewers of the first production summarized the storyline (4).

5. In the 1948 version, the girl actually comes over. What happens between her and Tom is disastrous.

6. Nor is Al able or perhaps willing to imitate Tom.

7. A fascinating series of clippings scrapbooks, kept by the Playwright's Company, into which Anderson was welcomed as a fresh, new member, hold the specific materials to which I refer here. These are included in a special collection of The New York Public Library's Theatre Research Collection (MWEZ+NC, 18,469A).

8. Anderson's association with The Playwright's Company was frequently followed by a list of its members, including Maxwell Anderson, to whom (readers were told) he was not related. Similarly, writers pointed out that Miss Kerr and Mr. Kerr were not related either.

9. Alan Sinfield's synopsis of *Young Woodley* reads like a synopsis of *Tea and Sympathy*: "a sensitive boy [is] harassed by hearty boys and masters but [is] rescued for heterosexuality by the love of his housemaster's wife" (15). The play, which fared well on Broadway, was banned in London.

10. The film version leaves out Harris altogether, along with all explicit references to homosexuals and homosexuality. Anderson's screenplay has the boys call Tom, "sister boy," throughout. Although Laura never clearly implies that Bill's homophobia is an unmistakable sign of his own attraction to other males, Vincente Minnelli's depiction of Bill hanging onto and touching the boys who are shown in swim suits in a beach scene implies the homoeroticism in prep school sports. The addition of a scene in which new boys are stripped of their pajamas around a bonfire also adds to the charged atmosphere.

Chapter 3

1. In part due to its placement on the bill with Beckett and the recent publication of Martin Esslin's *Theatre of the Absurd* (which connected Beckett with the French "absurdists" and with Harold Pinter), Alan Sinfield notes how some came to see *The Zoo Story* as "a Pinteresque flirtation with the mysterious menace of queerness" (226).

2. Because the Dramatists Play Service edition of *The Zoo Story* was revised in 1999, I refer to the mass-market paperback edition, first published by Signet in 1963 and reprinted without changes.

3. In her 1962 article on *The Zoo Story*, Rose A. Zimbardo discusses the biblical implications of the play; Peter Spielberg responded to her in an article of his own four years later.

4. All reviews of the original New York production have been taken from The New York Public Library's Theatre Research Collection's compilation of theater reviews.

5. Michael Bronski, who lent me a copy of *The Season* back in 1971, refers to Goldman's homophobic comments in *Culture Clash* (128).

6. In "The Efficacy/Effeminacy Braid: Unpacking the Performance Studies/Theatre Studies Dichotomy," Bottoms links the 1960s bashing of homosexuals in the theater to the inception of Performance Studies, offering numerous examples by Richard Schechner and other critics of homophobic rhetoric.

Chapter 4

1. Bosworth (191) reveals that Clift had a very small sexual member. Although this probably contributed to his feelings about his identity, I am neither qualified nor particularly interested in exploring this factor.

2. If Williams seemed too gay for Clift, Tom Wingfield apparently did not: Clift played Tom at least twice, first in 1951, opposite Helen Hayes's Amanda in a Theatre Guild radio broadcast of *The Glass Menagerie*, and again in a 1964 spoken-word recording directed by Howard Sackler, with Jessica Tandy as Amanda, Julie Harris as Laura, and David Wayne as Jim. The Theatre Guild broadcast, which was performed before a live audience at the Belasco Theatre, used a script revised (extensively) by Robert Anderson.

3. The review is included in The New York Public Library's Theatre Research Collection clipping file on *The Road to Paradise*. The reviewer is abbreviated as *Brat*.

4. All subsequent references to play reviews come from The New York Public Library's Theatre Research Collection review files for each specific production mentioned.

5. Coleman seems to be somewhat confused here, for Clift's appearance in *Yr. Obedient Husband* was not in what anyone had thought of as a "good play."

6. The reviewer is abbreviated as *Ibee*.

7. The reviewer is abbreviated as *Hobe*.

8. However, the four-page booklet that accompanies the 1998 DVD version of the film indicates that Hawks had seen him in *The Searching Wind* (3).

9. The reviewer is abbreviated as *Ibee*.

10. There were numerous casting changes. John Wayne's role was originally offered to Gary Cooper, who passed on it (indicated in the above-mentioned booklet that accompanies the CD [3]). Cherry Valance, Matt's friend and competitor, was originally written for Cary Grant, who turned it down. The part, which was cut down, was given to John Ireland. Hawks explained the cuts in the role as due to Ireland himself, whose drunken conduct on the set made it difficult for Hawks to direct him. Gossip on the set had it that Ireland was making out better with Joanne Dru than the director was, and so Hawks retaliated with cuts. Maggie Sheridan, who was first cast as Tess, became pregnant and was replaced by Dru, who later married Ireland. In the first version of the screenplay, her character had more scenes with Valance, but since casting Ireland, Hawks cut them (O'Brien 183–184).

11. Many critics have noted that the scene in which Garth and Cherry show each other their guns is obviously phallic.

12. In a peculiar moment of liberation, the Jewish boy who took Carel's name and his comrades leave the displaced children's facility to journey to Palestine; they exit singing "The Battle Hymn of the Republic" in Hebrew.

13. The only way I know how to describe it is that it is the same honking horn that used to accompany the jingle for Fifth Avenue Candy Bars in television commercials.

14. On the same DVD commentary track with George Stevens Jr., associate producer Ian Moffit discloses that before they shot the film, he had a dream in which Kaiser Wilhelm's statement, that Germany deserved its place in the sun, came back to him. He suggested the title to Stevens who liked it.

15. I am grateful to Steven Cohan for reminding me of Pauline Kael's remark that Shelley Winters's Alice is "so horrifyingly, naggingly pathetic that when Clift thinks of killing her he hardly seems to be contemplating a crime: it's more like euthanasia" (qtd. Cohan 235; Kael's *5001 Nights at the Movies*, 462). The late Ms. Winters had previously played the actress whom Ronald Coleman (convinced he is Othello) strangles in *A Double Life* (1947). She would go on to make many other films in which her characters were murdered, although perhaps none so deservedly as *A Place in the Sun*.

16. Dreiser had previously allowed a film to be made by Josef von Sternberg (*An American Tragedy*, 1931), in which a very sympathetic Sylvia Sidney played Alice Tripp; the author disowned any connection with this earlier production.

17. The production notes offered by Patricia Bosworth refer to the character as "Rev. Morrison," which would suggest he was a Protestant clergyman and not a Roman Catholic father, but Paul Frees, who played the role, is attired as a priest.

18. "George Stevens and His Place in the Sun," is included on the DVD version noted previously.

Chapter 5

1. All subsequent references to play reviews come from The New York Public Library's Theatre Research Collection review files for each specific production mentioned.

2. The screen test is included on the DVD of A *Streetcar Named Desire*, on the second disc of *The Two-Disc Special Edition*.

3. My original discussion on this trend can be found in *The Drama of Fallen France: Reading La Comedie sans Tickets*, 184–187.

4. This documentary is included on the DVD of A *Streetcar Named Desire*, on the second disc of *The Two-Disc Special Edition*.

5. As noted in the previous chapter, Kazan was known to have been homophobic; his use of "girlish" to describe Brando betrays his discomfort with a male whose performance of gender was not conventionally masculine.

6. Thus he joined a few other partially clothed Hollywood players in the pages of physique magazines, including Guy Madison and Tab Hunter. James Dean was pictured with the latter in a photo that appeared in *Trim* in November 1958 and in a solo head shot in *Body Beautiful* in August 1957, but in both he was clothed; Clift never made it into the physique magazines.

Chapter 6

1. Susan Bordo links Dean to Brando because he "took Brando's legacy in the direction of the more sensitive, vulnerable, and extremely sexually ambiguous masculinity" (133). Bordo never mentions Clift, for whom Dean left lengthy telephone messages (that Clift left unanswered) in New York, but perhaps Dean's real achievement was in integrating the performance styles of both actors, combining Clift's thoughtful silences and Brando's more dynamic, sometimes violent, histrionics.

2. This and all subsequent references to play reviews come from The New York Public Library's Theatre Research Collection review files for each specific production mentioned.

3. After Dean's death, Newman would be cast in two roles that were originally to go to Dean.

4. In actuality, the lawyers at Warners had discovered a clause in their contract with Cinemascope that the wide lens could be used only with color film (*Rebel Without a Cause: Defiant Innocents*).

5. These black-and-white scenes (without sound) are included on the two-disc Special Edition DVD version of *Rebel Without a Cause*.

6. Ironically, Backus played opposite Joan Davis—the mother of the girl Dean had once dated—on the comedy show, *I Married Joan*.

7. Hudson had frequented some of the same pick-up places where Dean and John Gilmore hustled.

Chapter 7

1. In "Crippling Masculinity: Queerness and Disability in U.S. Military Culture, 1800–1945," David Serlin examines the "Amputettes," a cross-dressing dance group comprised of members of a ward at Walter Reed Hospital who had an artificial leg. The group performed for the public as well as other members of the hospital. The medical staff and others believed their performances were excellent therapy and "revealed 'just what rehabilitation can do'" (149).

2. Naoko Wake presents a thorough review of how psychiatrists participated in the induction process well before Pearl Harbor. Although Sullivan ultimately resigned, his fear of being exposed as a homosexual probably kept him from arguing too vigorously against the military's hatred of homosexuals (484).

3. For a detailed account of the Mattachine-*ONE* war on "swish," see Craig M. Loftin's "Unacceptable Mannerisms: Gender Anxieties, Homosexual Activism, and Swish in the United States, 1945–1965."

4. Bronski estimates the circulation of the two homosexual journals in 1960 as follows: *One*: 5000; *Mattachine Review*: 2500. He also speculates that issues of these publications were passed around and thus read by more than one reader (146).

5. Hence, David K. Johnson's "Physique Pioneers: The Politics of 1960s Gay Consumer Culture," provides an historical perspective of the role of queer consumerism even before the Stonewall Riot and the gay liberation movement.

6. Den Bell, currently the president of AMG and a member of the Bob Mizer Foundation, verified the length of Mizer's sentence.

7. Other photos from this early AMG shoot appeared in the August/September 1958 issue of *Muscles Magazine*, published in France.

Chapter 8

1. Another photo by Oettinger of the same event appeared in the August issue of *Strength and Health* (7).

2. In a way, Johnson was, no doubt unwittingly, echoing the implications of Tennessee Williams's *A Streetcar Named Desire*, in which masculinity was presented as a construct as unnatural as femininity. Johnson's preference was obviously the more ambiguous gender of a youthful male.

3. Among the West Coast bodybuilders whom Johnson/Blair trained was John Tristram, who is discussed in chapter 9.

4. An advertisement for these photos first appeared in *Muscle Power* in December 1954 (48).

5. In *Muscletown USA: Bob Hoffman and the Manly Culture of York Barbell*, John D. Fair suggests that Bishop was later critical of Hoffman (231–232).

6. Douglas Julef had been the first to photograph Bob Delmonteque in the nude; Delmonteque went on to sell some of Douglas of Detroit's picture of him as his own, a practice that Bishop followed. There is also some evidence that Delmonteque may have promoted some of Julef's pictures of Bishop as his.

7. According to Thomas Waugh, both *Adonis* and *Body Beautiful*, which were put out by Weider in alternating months (both in the United States and Britain), had as their editor Hal Warner (aka Wally McMannis), who was permitted to make careful references to the gay audience (230).

8. Photos from Johnson's albums that were recently sold on eBay are stamped on the back with Bishop's home address.

9. As previously noted, Douglas had taken a photo of a totally nude Bishop as the discus thrower; he had also taken less-revealing nudes, similar to Johnson's, using silhouettes and discreet poses. Comparisons between Douglas's earliest photos of Bishop and those sold by Johnson in *TM* suggest that the latter may have been taken by Douglas and merely marketed by Johnson; there is even some evidence that before Delmonteque actually photographed Bishop, he was selling doctored versions of Douglas's pictures of him.

10. For a short time in 2009, Bishop's son sold digitally improved prints from his father's later catalogues, including "Down on the Farm," on eBay.

Chapter 9

1. A photo of Tristram competing in the 1962 Mr. Los Angeles Contest appeared in *Male Figure* (Number 23, 18). This was possibly an additional competition to the one listed or was the contest in which he won the title of Mr. Venice Beach.

2. This photo appears at http://www.davedraper.com/draper-workouts-60s.html.

3. This was the first gallery show Lon received during his lifetime. He died a few months later.

4. Lon apparently also took a number of shots of Tristram exercising. These did not emerge until they appeared as illustrations in *Tomorrow's Man* for October 1964 (30–32) and for March 1965 (30–32), where they are credited to Lon-Olympia (a name Hanagan had begun using in the 1960s) and also in *Jr.* in March 1967, a full decade after they had been taken, without credit.

5. In some of his early advertisements for Togof, Sokolsky actually used the headline, "Artistry in Fotografy."

6. He later moved his studio to 110 Ridge Street and then to 144 Rivington Street, both on Manhattan's Lower Eastside.

7. Although it is not credited, a picture shown in *Muscle Power*, October 1957, featuring Tristram with three other bodybuilders flexing on a rocky beach (19), was probably taken by Togof.

8. Waugh recounts how at the final censorship trial regarding photos in physique magazines, held in Minneapolis in 1967, the prosecution introduced a bevy of witnesses including Anthony Dumbrowski, whose physique photography name was Bob Anthony (282).

9. The cover states the month (September), but I am able to find any reference to the year.

10. As of this writing, Delmonteque remains in fine physical shape, plugging fitness products through late night television infomercials and appearing, tanned and pumped, in posing briefs.

11. Recently, Big Kugels offered on eBay an AMG catalogue sheet of Tristram with Robert Rex, which appears to have been taken around the same time (1958). The catalogue is numbered XZ-2.

12. *Pose Please* happens also to be the name of the Glenn Bishop film (distributed by *Young Physique*) mentioned in the previous chapter. The two are completely unrelated.

13. There is some evidence from some of the stills that the desert shots that appeared in *PP* in 1958 may have been taken at the same time when this film was shot.

14. I have not found any totally nude shots of Scott; the only one to show Reeves naked was an amateur snapshot taken in the South of France of him sunbathing.

15. An ad for Warner's set of Tristram and of others, including Richard Harrison, appeared in the back pages of the July/August, 1964 issue of *Muscleboy*, but the photo shown (like the one of Harrison) does not seem like a recent one.

16. Among the photos featured in this spread is a color shot which appears to be exactly the same as the one attributed to Kris that had appeared in 1963 on the cover of *YP*. The picture was probably taken by Caruso and incorrectly identified as one of Renslow's.

17. Both cover photos seem to have from the same Caruso shoot and featured the same female model in the same bikini.

18. Both photos ran on Weider's European French-language magazine, *Santè et Force*; under one was the title, "CATCH FEMININ."

19. The very first page of the spread in *Body Beautiful UK* is probably from one of the "classical" sets; Tristram is posed almost like a statue in a posing strap (22).

Bibliography

Written Works Cited and/or Referenced

Albee, Edward. *The Zoo Story. The American Dream and The Zoo Story*. New York: New American Library, 1963. 10–49.

Aletti, Vince. "Physique Pictorial" *The Village Voice*. Feb. 23, 1999. http://www.villagevoice.com/authors/vince-aletti/1999/.

Als, Hilton. Review of NY revival of *Tea and Sympathy*. *The New Yorker* (83:5), Mar. 26, 2007, 90–91.

Anderson, Robert. Draft of *Tea and Sympathy*. New York: NYC Public Library Theatre Research Collection, call number NCOF+ [1948].

Anderson, Robert. *Tea and Sympathy*. New York: Samuel French, 1953.

Artaud, Antonin. "The Marx Brothers." *The Theater and Its Double*. New York: Grove, 1958. 142–144.

Bamberger, Theron. "The Children's Corner: Notes on the Young Players Appearing in "Fly Away Home." *The New York Times*, Jan. 27, 1935, X2.

Bast, William. *Surviving James Dean*. Fort Lee, NJ: Barricade Books, 2006.

Bellafante, Gina. Review of NY revival of *Tea and Sympathy*. *The New York Times*, March 17, 2007, B7.

BigKugels.com on eBay: http://www.ebay.com/sch/bigkugels/m.html?_nkw=&_armrs=1&_from=&_ipg=50

Blankenship, Mark. Review of NY revival of *Tea and Sympathy*. *Variety*, Mar. 26–April 1, 2007, 34.

Bordo, Susan. *The Male Body: A New Look at Men in Public and in Private*. New York: Farrar, Straus & Giroux, 1999.

Bosworth, Patricia. *Marlon Brando*. London: Phoenix, 2001.

Bosworth, Patricia. *Montgomery Clift: A Biography*. New York: Harcourt, 1978.

Bottoms, Stephen. *Albee: Who's Afraid of Virginia Woolf?*. Cambridge: Cambridge UP, 2000.

———. "The Efficacy/Effeminacy Braid: Unpacking the Performance Studies/Theatre Studies Dichotomy." *Theatre Topics* 13:2 (September 2003), 173–187.

Brandes Uta. "From Here to There: Maleness as a Fluctuating Gender." *Material Man: Masculinity, Sexuality, Style*. Ed. Giannino Malossi. New York: Abrams, 2000, 138–143.

Brando, Marlon with Robert Lindsey. *Songs My Mother Taught Me*. New York: Random House, 1994.

Brecht, Bertolt. *Galileo*. Trans. Charles Laughton. New York: Grove, 1991.

Bronski, Michael. *Culture Clash: The Making of Gay Sensibility*. Boston: South End, 1984.

Butler, Judith. *Gender Trouble: Feminism and the Subversion of Identity*. New York: Routledge, 1999.

Capozzola, Christopher. "Fifty Years of Tea and Sympathy." *The Gay and Lesbian Review* 13:7 (Jan.–Feb. 2007), 34–35.

Chauncey, George. *Gay New York: The Making of the Gay Male World, 1890–1940*. London: Flamingo, 1994.

Chicago Gay History website: Chuck Renslow. http://chicagogayhistory.com/biography.html?id=772.

Cluck, Nancy Anne. "Showing or Telling: Narrators in the Drama of Tennessee Williams." *American Literature* 51:1 (Mar. 1979), 84–93.

Clum, Joh M. *Still Acting Gay: Male Homosexuality in Modern Drama*. New York, St. Martin's, 2000. [Originally published in 1991 by Columbia UP]

Cohan, Steven. *Masked Men: Masculinity and the Movies in the Fifties*. Bloomington: Indiana UP, 1997.

Cooper, Emmanuel. *Fully Exposed: The Male Nude in Photography*. New York: Routleledge, 1990.

Crandell, George W. "The Cinematic Eye in Tennessee Williams's *The Glass Menagerie*." *The Tennessee Williams Annual Review* (1998), 1–11.

Draper, Dave. "Russ Warner—A Most Unforgettable Character." http://www.dave-draper.com/article-304-russ-warner.html.

Dziemianowicz, Joe. Review of NY revival of *Tea and Sympathy*. *The New York Daily News*, Mar. 16, 2007, 52.

Ehrenreich, Barbara. *The Hearts of Men: American Dreams and the Flight from Commitment*. Garden City, NY: Anchor/Doubleday, 1983.

Esslin, Martin. *The Theatre of the Absurd*, 3rd ed. New York: Vintage, 2004.

Fair, John D. *Muscletown USA: Bob Hoffman and the Manly Culture of York Barbell*, State College, PA: Pennsylvania State UP, 1999.

Feingold, Michael. Review of NY Revival of *Tea and Sympathy*. *The Village Voice*, March 21, 2007. http://www.villagevoice.com/2007-03-13/theater/comforter-zone/.

Fisher, James. " 'The Angels of Fructification': Tennessee Williams, Tony Kushner, and Images of Homosexuality on the American Stage." *The Mississippi Quarterly* (Winter 1995–96): 49:1, 13–33.

forum.bodybuilding.com/archive/index.php/t-3296421.html

Forums on Bodybuilding.com RE Rheo Blair's name.

Gerstner, David. "The Production and Display of the Closet: Making Minelli's 'Tea and Sympathy.' " *Film Quarterly* 50:3 (Spring, 1997), 13–26.

Gilmore, John. *Live Fast, Die Young: My Life with James Dean*. New York: Thunder's Mouth Press, 1997.

Goldman, Jason. " 'The Golden Age of Gay Porn': Nostalgia and the Photography of Wilhelm von Gloeden." *GLQ: A Journal of Lesbian and Gay Studies* 12:2, 237–258.

Goldman, William. *The Season: A Candid Look at Broadway*. New York: Limelight Editions, 1969.

Hart, Kylo-Patrick R. "Gay Male Spectatorship and the Films of Montgomery Clift." *Popular Culture Review* 10:1 (Feb. 1999), 69–82

Hellman, Lillian. *The Children's Hour. Six Plays by Lillian Hellman*. New York: Vintage, 19789. 1–77.

Hine, Thomas. "Mickey Rooney and the Downsizing of Man: Male Discontent in the Society of the Spectacle." *Material Man: Masculinity, Sexuality, Style*. Ed. Giannino Malossi. New York: Abrams, 2000, 100–105.

Hoskyns, Barney. *Montgomery Clift: Beautiful Loser*. New York: Grove, 1991.

In the Matter of the Complaint Against Capital Studio Anthony M. Guyther. http://www.usps.com/judicial/1962deci/2-47.htm. [also http://www.timinvermont.com/vintage2/z7001.html].

Isherwood, Christopher. "Goodbye to Berlin." *The Berlin Stories*. New York: New Directions, 1945, 1–207.

Jensen, Robert. *Getting Off: Pornography and the End of Masculinity*. Cambridge, MA: South End, 2007.

Johnson, David K. "Physique Pioneers: The Politics of 1960s Gay Consumer Culture." *Journal of Social History* 43:4 (Summer, 2010), 867–892.

Krauss, Kenneth. *The Drama of Fallen France: Reading La Comedie sans Tickets*. Albany: SUNY UP, 2004.

LaGuardia, Robert. *Monty: A Biography of Montgomery Clift*. New York: Arbor House, 1977.

Leverich, Lyle. *Tom: The Unknown Tennessee Williams*. New York: Crown, 1995.

Lilly, Mark. "Tennessee Williams: *The Glass Menagerie* and *A Streetcar Named Desire*." *Lesbian and Gay Writing*. Mark Lilly ed. London: Macmillan, 1990, 153–163.

Lindner, Robert Mitchell. *Rebel Without a Cause: The Hypnoanalysis of a Criminal Psychopath*. New York: Grune & Stratton, 1944.

Loftin, Craig M. Loftin. "Unacceptable Mannerisms: Gender Anxieties, Homosexual Activism, and Swish in the United States, 1945–1965." *Journal of Social History*, 40: 30, 578–596.

Malossi, Giannino. "Material Man: Decoding Fashion, Redefining Masculinity." *Material Man: Masculinity, Sexuality, Style*. Ed. Giannino Malossi. New York: Abrams, 2000, 24–33.

Manso, Peter. *Brando: The Biography*. New York: Hyperion, 1994.

Massengill, Reed. *The Male Ideal: Lon of New York and the Masculine Ideal*. New York: Universe, 2003.

McCann, Graham. *Rebel Males: Clift, Brando and Dean*. New Brunswick, NJ: Rutgers UP, 1993.

McCurley, Hugh. Tim in Vermont Website. (http://www.timinvermont.com/vintage2/3421index.html)

McIntire, Dal. "Tangents." *ONE* 3.12 (Dec. 1955), 10.

Mellen, Joan. *Big Bad Wolves: Masculinity in the American Film*. New York: Pantheon, 1977.

Miller, Martin. "Buff—and 84." *The Los Angeles Times*, May 31, 2004. http://articles.latimes.com/2004/may/31/health/he-bodybuilder31.

Morella, Joe and Edward Z. Epstein. *Rebels: The Rebel Hero in Films*. New York: Citadel, 1971.

Nada, John. "Interview with Richard Harrison." Les Interviews de Nanarland. Nov. 2003. http://www.nanarland.com/interview/interview.php?id_interview=richar dharrisonvo&vo=1.

O'Brien, Sheila Ruzycki. "Leaving Behind 'The Chisolm Trail' for *Red River*—Or Refiguring the Female in the Western Film Epic." *Literature Film Quarterly* 24:2 (1996), 183–192.

Paller, Michael. *Gentlemen Callers: Tennessee Willaims, Homosexuality, and Mid-Twentieth Century Broadway*. New York: Palgrave, 2005.

Palmieri, Alan. "Rheo H Blair and Blair Protein." http://www.palmieribodybuilding. com/Rheo%20H%20Blair%20and%20Blair%20Protein.pdf.

Peru, Minnie. Review of *Tea and Sympathy*. ONE 1:11 (November, 1953), 16.

Porter, Darwin. *Brando Unzipped*. New York: Blood Moon Productions, 2005.

Reeser, Todd W. *Masculinities in Theory: An Introduction*. Chichester: Wiley-Blackwell, 2010.

Renslow, Chuck. "Interview with *Outcome Magazine*." 1991. http://models.badpuppy. com/archive/kris/krisof.htm.

Rettenmund, Helmut. "Striking Poses: Photographer Lon of New York and the Rebirth of Beefcake." *Torso* 14.5 (December, 1996), 78–82.

Richardson, Brian. "Voice and Narration in Postmodern Drama." *New Literary History*, 32:3 (Summer, 2001), 681–694.

Sanderson, Jim. "*Red River* and the Loss of Feminity in the John Wayne Persona." *Literature Film Quarterly* 32:1 (Winter, 2004), 39–45.

Savran, David. *Communists, Cowboys, and Queers: The Politics of Masculinity in the Work of Arthur Miller and Tennessee Williams*. Minneapolis: Minnesota UP, 1992.

———. *Taking It Like a Man: White Masculinity, Masochism, and Contemporary American Culture*. Princeton: Princeton UP, 1998.

Schmundt-Thomas, Georg. "Hollywood's Romance of Foreign Policy." *Journal of Popular Film and Television* 19:4 (Winter, 1992), 187–197.

Serlin, David. "Crippling Masculinity: Queerness and Disability in U.S. Military Culture, 1800–1945." *GLQ: A Journal of Lesbian and Gay Studies*. 9.1–2 (2003), 149–179.

Sheridan, Liz. *Dizzy & Jimmy: My Life with James Dean, a love story*. New York: Regan Books, 2000.

Sinfield, Alan. *Out on Stage: Lesbian and Gay Theatre in the Twentieth Century*. New Haven: Yale UP, 1999.

Sokolsky, Melvyn. Melvyn Sokolsky Facebook page. http://www.facebook.com/pages/ Melvin-Sokolsky/108554399169826.

Spielberg, Peter. "The Albatross in Albee's Zoo." *College English* 27:7 (Apr. 1966), 562–565.

Spoto, Donald. *Rebel: The Life and Legend of James Dean*. New York: Cooper Square Press, 1996.

Steinberg, Warren. *Masculinity: Identity, Conflict, and Transformation*. Boston: Shambbala, 1993.

Stern, Ralph. "*The Big Lift* (1950): Image and Identity in Blockaded Berlin." *Cinema Journal* 46:2 (Winter, 2007), 66–90.

Wake, Naoko. "The Military, Psychiatry, and 'Unfit' Soldiers, 1939–1942." *Journal of the History of Medicine and Allied Sciences* 62:4 (Oct. 2007), 461–494.

Waugh, Thomas. *Hard to Imagine: Gay Male Eroticism in Photography and Film from their Beginnings to Stonewall.* New York: Columbia UP, 1996.

Whitehead, Stephen M. *Men and Masculinities: Key Themes and New Directions.* Malden, MA: Blackwell, 2002.

Whyte, William H. *The Organization Man.* Garden City, N.Y.: Doubleday, 1957.

Williams, Tennessee. "The Catastrophe of Success." *The Glass Menagerie. The Theatre of Tennessee Williams, Vol. I.* New York: New Directions, 1971 [Original copyright, 1947].

———. *Provisional Film Story Treatment of "The Gentleman Caller" (first title).* The Historic New Orleans Collection, New Orleans: Williams Research Collection, mss 562, Item 574 (2001-10-L) [June, 1943].

———. *The Glass Menagerie.* New York: Dramatists Play Service, 1945. [Performance Version]

———. *The Glass Menagerie. The Theatre of Tennessee Williams, Vol. I.* New York: New Directions, 1971, 123–237. [Reading Version; original copyright, 1945]

———. *Promptbook for The Glass Menagerie.* New York: NYC Public Library Theatre Research Collection, NCOF+ 99-3499 [1945; annotated by stage manager].

Zimbardo, Rose A. "Symbolism and Naturalism in Edward Albee's *The Zoo Story*." *Twentieth Century Literature* 8:1 (Apr. 1962), 10–17.

Films Discussed

The Big Lift. Twentieth Century-Fox, 1950. DVD: Double DVD Features, 2006.

"Days of Greek Gods," Apollo Films, 1954.

East of Eden: Two Disc Special Edition. Warner Brothers, 1954. DVD: Warner Brothers Entertainment, 2005, disc 1.

"Elia Kazan: A Director's Journey." 1994. *A Streetcar Named Desire: Two Disc Special Edition:.* DVD: Warner Brothers Home Entertainment, 2006, disc 2.

"George Stevens' Place in the Sun." *A Place in the Sun.* Paramount Pictures, 1951. DVD: Paramount Pictures, 2001.

Giant. Two Disc Special Edition. Warner Brothers, 1956. DVD: Warner Home Video, 2005, disc 1.

The Heiress. Universal Studios, 1949. DVD: Universal Pictures, 2007.

Julius Caesar. MGM, 1953. DVD: Turner Entertainment—Warner Home Video, [2006].

The Men. Republic Pictures, 1950. DVD: Republic Entertainment, 2003.

On the Waterfront. Columbia Pictures, 1954. DVD: Columbia Pictures Industries, 2001.

A Place in the Sun. Paramount Pictures, 1951. DVD: Paramount Pictures, 2001.

"Pose Please." AMG Studio [1958?].

"Pose Please." The Young Physique [1960?].

Rebel Without A Cause: Two Disc Special Edition. Warner Brothers, 1955. DVD: Warner Brothers Entertainment, 2005 disc 1.

"Rebel Without a Cause: Defiant Innocents" *Rebel Without A Cause: Two Disc Special Edition.* DVD: Warner Brothers Entertainment, 2005, disc 2.

Red River. United Artists, 1948. DVD: MGM/UA Home Video, 1997.

Rothgeb, Douglas L. Commentary. *Rebel Without A Cause: Two Disc Special Edition.* DVD: Warner Brothers Entertainment, 2005, disc1.

The Search. MGM, 1948. DVD: Buddha Video, undated.

Viva Zapata! Twentieth Century Fox, 1952. DVD: NTSC [undated].

The Wild One. Columbia Pictures, 1953. DVD: Columbia Tristar Home Video, 1998.

Index